FROM THE GROUNDS UP

From the Grounds Up

BUILDING AN EXPORT ECONOMY
IN SOUTHERN MEXICO

Casey Marina Lurtz

STANFORD UNIVERSITY PRESS
STANFORD, CALIFORNIA

STANFORD UNIVERSITY PRESS
Stanford, California

© 2019 by the Board of Trustees of the Leland Stanford Junior University. All rights reserved.

No part of this book may be reproduced or transmitted in any form or by any means, electronic or mechanical, including photocopying and recording, or in any information storage or retrieval system without the prior written permission of Stanford University Press.

Printed in the United States of America on acid-free, archival-quality paper.

ISBN 9781503632615
First paperback printing, 2022

The Library of Congress has cataloged the hardcover edition as follows:

Names: Lurtz, Casey Marina, author.

Title: From the grounds up : building an export economy in southern Mexico / Casey Marina Lurtz.

Description: Stanford, California : Stanford University Press, 2019. | Includes bibliographical references and index.

Identifiers: LCCN 2018033670 | ISBN 9781503603899 (cloth : alk. paper) | ISBN 9781503608474 (electronic)

Subjects: LCSH: Coffee industry—Mexico—Soconusco (Region)—History—20th century. | Agricultural industries—Mexico—Soconusco (Region)—History—20th century. | Soconusco (Mexico : Region)—Commerce—History—20th century. | Soconusco (Mexico : Region)—Economic conditions—20th century.

Classification: LCC HD9199.M63 .L87 2019 | DDC 382/.6097275—dc23

LC record available at *https://lccn.loc.gov/2018033670*

Typeset by Kevin Barrett Kane in 10/12.5 Sabon

Cover design: Rob Ehle

Cover photo: Cuilco River, Finca La Chiripa, Soconusco, Mexico, 1930. Courtesy Jose Toriello, Finca Hamburgo.

Contents

Illustrations	vii
Acknowledgments	ix
A Note on Currency, Units of Measure, and Terms	xiii
Introduction	1
1 An Uncultivated Eden	17
2 Fixing the Border	45
3 From Bullets to Bureaucracy	63
4 The Landscape of Production	87
5 Scarce Labor and Unrealized Reform	117
6 The Circulation of Codes and Commerce	141
Conclusion	167
Appendixes	175
Notes	179
Bibliography	241
Index	267

Illustrations

Maps

Map 1: The Soconusco District of Chiapas, Mexico — 2

Map 2: Map of the Soconusco, 1872 — 20

Map 3: Selection from Map Prepared to Study the Different Dividing Lines Proposed between Mexico and Guatemala, 1882 — 53

Map 4: Map of the English Company's Division of the Soconusco's Coffee Plantation Zone — 89

Map 5: Croquis of the Division of Terrenos Baldíos, 2nd Fraction, Soconusco, Chiapas, 1889 — 103

Map 6: General Plan of the Department of Soconusco by the Mexican Land and Colonization Company, 1913 (Selection) — 109

For expanded versions of maps, please visit https://caseylurtz.com/groundsup/maps.

Figures

Figure 1: Coffee Exports from the Soconusco, 1880–1919 — 4

Figure 2: Number of Property Sales Registered in the Soconusco, 1893–1913 — 92

Figure 3: Price per Hectare of Large and Small Sales as Compared to Global Coffee Prices 1893–1913 — 93

Figure 4: Median and High Values for Advance Contracts in MX$, 1894–1910 — 155

Figure 5: Median and High Values for Mortgage-Backed Loans in MX$, 1890–1913 — 158

Tables

Table 1: Distribution of Small Property Sales by Origin of Purchaser — 108

Table 2: Distribution of Large Property Sales by Origin of Purchaser — 111

Appendix 1: Coffee Exports from the Soconusco
and Mexico, 1867–1920   175

Appendix 2: Population of the Soconusco
and Its Municipalities, 1778–1930   177

Acknowledgments

I grew up in a small town in coastal northern California, six hours from anywhere. Distance defined the place as much as the towering trees that drew timbermen to the area in the late nineteenth century. Yet distance never meant isolation. While the railroad that transported massive logs south was in shambles by my childhood, our ties to the rest of the world were never in doubt. It was a few years into this project before I began to see the similarities between the Soconusco and Humboldt County. Yet I know that my experiences of rural interconnectedness shaped this book from the start.

My childhood also gave me an understanding of the communities that form in places where so many are from elsewhere. This has indelibly marked my understanding of both the Soconusco and the academic world. Given the itinerant life of a young academic, I owe thanks to a number of universities that have provided communities for this book over the past years. Whether in offhand or in-depth ways, innumerable people have given something to this book. I hope its final form does their insights and aid justice.

This project found its feet at the University of Chicago. Emilio Kourí's rigor, pragmatism, and empathy for the often grimy work of paging through municipal archives have indelibly shaped who I am as a historian. Mauricio Tenorio, Dain Borges, Paul Cheney, Brodwyn Fischer, Leora Auslander, David Nirenberg, Emily Lynn Osborn, and others shaped its early stages and demonstrated the multitude of ways one can be a historian. The Center for Latin American Studies and Katz Center for Mexican Studies provided funds for exploratory trips, and the Fulbright-Hays Fellowship supported the first extended period of archival research for this book. Much gratitude also goes to the members of the Latin American History Workshop. They prodded the project into a more readable, cohesive whole and provided insights and models in their own work. Amanda Hartzmark, Aiala Levy, Matt Barton, Nicole Mottier, José Luis Razo, Patrick Iber, María Balandran Castillo, C. J. Álvarez, Patrick Kelly, Julia Young, Antonio Sotomayor, Carlos Bravo Regidor, Mikael Wolfe, Ananya Chakravarti, Luis Fernando Granados, Romina Robles Ruvalcaba, Ben Johnson, Marcel Anduiza Pimentel, Chris Dunlap, Chris Gatto, José Juan Pérez Meléndez, Marco Torres, and Emilio de Antuñano all had a part to play in this work, and I thank them for it. Sarah Osten, Jaclyn Sumner, and Diana Schwartz deserve particular gratitude for repeated readings and now years-long conversations. Along with Kathryn Schumaker, Natalie Belsky, and Tessa Murphy, their friendships remain among the best things I found in Chicago.

The Center for U.S.-Mexican Studies at the University of California, San Diego, gave the project its next home. Particularly, I would like to thank my carpool of historians—Michael Lettieri, Vanessa Freije, and Froylán Enciso—for their camaraderie and advice. Thanks, too, to Eric Van Young for his mentorship during that year. Geoffrey Jones and Walter Friedman at the Harvard Business School provided the subsequent round of support with the Harvard-Newcomen Fellowship. Along with Laura Phillips Sawyer, Elizabeth Koll, and Jessica Burch, they introduced me to a literature and set of questions about entrepreneurship and global capitalism that helped move the work beyond Mexico.

The Harvard Academy for International and Area Studies and its staff and scholars saw the book through the fruitful and frustrating work of revision. Thanks to my fellow fellows, particularly Malgorzata Kurjanska, Rishad Choudhury, Timothy Nunan, Xenia Cherkaev, Cristina Florea, Lina Britto, Zachary Howlett, Adam Leeds, and Chris Gratien for good spirits, lunchtime debates, and commiseration. My gratitude to Kathleen Hoover and Bruce Jackan for running such a supportive and tight ship knows no bounds.

Thanks to the Academy, too, for the opportunity to reconnect with John Womack. Professor Womack merits pages of appreciation for introducing me to Latin American history as an undergraduate and greeting me again years later with generosity and the same nuanced consideration that initially drew me in. He also served as chair for a book conference sponsored by the Academy, where a group of scholars I have long admired proved to be as giving as they are astute. Thanks to Margaret Chowning, José Moya, Allen Wells, Graciela Márquez Colín, and Aurora Gómez Galvarriato for taking the time to read a manuscript still in process and guiding it toward completion.

Finally, the history department at Johns Hopkins University has proved as accommodating and intellectually stimulating a home as I could hope for. My new colleagues began shaping the manuscript even before I joined the department. During my first semesters, they have provided advice on all fronts that has eased my transition and made it possible to finish this book. Thanks especially to Gabriel Paquette, John Marshall, Katie Hindmarch-Watson, Jessica Marie Johnson, Yumi Kim, Tobie Meyer-Fong, Elizabeth Thornberry, and Michael Kwass. The incoming Latin Americanist cohort I joined also merits thanks for their camaraderie and hard work—Christy Thornton, Alessandro Angelini, and Bécquer Seguín. Truly, so many people at Hopkins have helped bring this book to fruition.

Along the way, conferences and coffees have reassured me of the kindness and giving nature of our profession. Karen Caplan, Teresa Cribelli, Leida Fernández Prieto, John Soluri, Jennifer Eaglin, Carlos Dimas, Sandra Kuntz

Ficker, Anne Hanley, Bill Summerhill, Aldo Lauria Santiago, Renata Keller, Rob Karl, Ben Siegel, Kirsten Weld, Arunabh Ghosh, Rachel Nolan, Derek Burdette, Emily Remus, and Mónica Salas-Landa have all provided key insights and suggestions regarding both this project and the history profession as a whole. Juliette Levy and Ted Beatty were generous enough to come out from behind the anonymity of reader reports and spend considerably more time with this book than anyone could expect. Their critiques, questions, and willingness to talk through matters large and small have made my work here and elsewhere vastly better.

Throughout all of these moves, the community of scholars and archivists who work in and on Chiapas has provided a stable center for my research. Justus Fenner, as all lucky enough to pass through archives in the state know, is an invaluable champion of the history of his adopted home. This book would not exist without his knowledge of all the state's hidden piles of paper and his compulsion to offer that knowledge up to all who ask. With hot chocolate, lists of citations, and tours through the highlands, Jan and Diane Rus have made research trips into so much more. Scholars including Janine Gasco, Stephen Lewis, Catherine Nolan-Ferrell, Aaron Margolis, Marc Antone, Oscar Barrera, Lean Sweeney, and Juan Pedro Viqueira Albán are all owed my gratitude for the comments and information they have shared. By allowing me to stay in their home and on their finca, the Bracamontes Gris family have provided insights into the day-to-day life of coffee growing otherwise inaccessible. At the Archivo Histórico de Chiapas at UNICACH, I owe a great deal to Armando Martín Sánchez García and his team. The multitude of women who oversee municipal and departmental offices in Tapachula gave me space, popsicles, and constant reminders that it is individuals who make bureaucracy function.

Innumerable archivists in Mexico City also deserve my appreciation for their ongoing efforts to preserve and protect the nation's heritage. The staff of the Archivo General de la Nación, the Colección Porfirio Díaz at the Universidad Iberoamericano, the Mapoteca Manuel Orozco y Berra, and the Biblioteca Miguel Lerdo de Tejada all provided support across years of research. Regina Tapia Chávez at the Archivo General Agrario helped find the material that gave Chapter Four narrative heart. Anyone who has heard me talk about Matías Romero knows how much I enjoy his archive. It is thanks to Luis Eduardo Cristiani Sierra, Claudia Rangel León, Mireya Quintos Martínez, Eunice Ruiz, and Miguel Ángel Solis that I have had such pleasure working in Romero's papers.

I also owe thanks to all those at Stanford University Press who have shepherded this project from proposal to page. Margo Irvin, Gigi Mark, Nora Spiegel, Catherine Mallon, and Harvey Gable have made this book a reality, and I am grateful for their patience and expertise.

Books, of course, do not happen solely in academic settings. Friends and family have also lived with this work for the past many years. Whether providing a spare room, a supportive shoulder, or a much needed distraction, there are far too many people who deserve my gratitude. Thanks, first, to the community that raised me in and around Arcata, California. Beyond, thanks to Andrea Tsurumi, Rachel Stern, Rowan Dorin, Ellen Quigley, Currun Singh, Xin Wei Ngiam, Leah Pillsbury, Melissa Goldman, Emma Katz, Fran Moore, Anna Hendricks, Lisa Crossman, Caroline Chidley, Annemarie Munn, Karen Taylor, Anicia Timberlake, Elanor Taylor, and Tom Ozden-Schilling. Katherine Bickford is my oldest, dearest friend and I would not be who I am without her.

My family are remarkable people and I thank them for their unending support. My aunts, uncles, cousins, and in-laws have listened, questioned, applauded, and provoked as needed throughout this long process. My mother, Linda, and father, Tom, encouraged me to read and imagine as a child and continue to make sure I know I am part of a much larger community. My brother, Noah, inspires with his perseverance and his good humor. My husband, James, joined this adventure as I moved from research to writing. He knows the rhythms of my work and has talked me through more knotty challenges than I can count. I could not have done this without his love and confidence.

A number of people who inspired and guided me have left this world since the start of this project. This book is for them. Jody, Peter, Shelley, Tim, and Jan, thank you for all you gave.

A Note on Currency, Units of Measure, and Terms

The economic and political processes explored in this book involved a multitude of currencies, units of measure, and terms of art, many of which were in flux because of those very processes. A brief explicatory note will, I hope, provide some clarity.

Transactions recorded in the Soconusco between 1870 and 1920 were carried out in currencies from across the Americas and Europe. Most were registered in pesos *Centro y Sud Americanos* (CYSA$), that is, Guatemalan pesos also known as *cachucas,* until around 1890, when Mexican pesos (MX$) slowly began to dominate the record. When I am not sure of the currency in use, I have simply marked value with $. When comparison is called for, I have converted all values to MX$. Conversion rates are based on the going rate in the Soconusco, drawn from the many legal documents that included values in both the currency being used and MX$. Generally, one Mexican peso was worth 1.5 CYSA pesos. Rates for other currencies varied across time.

A *quintal* was equal to about 43 kilograms of first-grade coffee and was the customary measure across much of Latin America. A quintal of second-grade coffee weighed slightly more.

A *caballería* of land was equal to 42.8 hectares. A *cuerda* was 1/1000 of a caballeria, or about one twentieth of a hectare.

A *finca* is a coffee plantation. A *finquero* is the person who owns that plantation.

The Soconusco is a *Departamento* of the state of Chiapas, but I have translated this as "district" throughout the text.

Many historians have translated *jefe político* as "political boss" or "political chief." I have left the original term in place to emphasize the official rather than informal nature of the position.

I have translated *ayuntamiento* as "municipal council" throughout the text and *alcalde* as "municipal councilor."

What I call the "public records office" in the text was the *registro público de la propiedad y del comercio*, which opened sometime around 1894.

There were at least three separate court systems in the Soconusco across the period in question. The municipal court of each municipality, the Soconusco's district-level court, and the federal district court (opened in 1875) each had a particular realm of oversight with regard to civil and criminal activity in the region. Both the municipal and district-level courts could serve as a court of first instance depending on the issue at hand, often decided by the value of the matter under consideration. Cases only occasionally moved from the municipal court to the district-level court and from there, on very rare occasions, to the state-level courts. Unfortunately, the criminal justice records for the region have not survived, and I have not gained access to records for the federal district court, if they still exist. The archives for most of the municipal courts outside of Tapachula, including the court that opened in the coffee zone sometime after 1900, are also missing.

FROM THE GROUNDS UP

Introduction

There had been many attempts to build a pier. A railroad too. But when Helen Humphreys and her family arrived at Mexico's southernmost port of San Benito in 1888, their ship had to moor far offshore. The *City of Panama*, a Pacific Mail steamship, dropped anchor, and the few passengers looked shoreward with trepidation. "Steamers do not care to call," the British consul in the Soconusco wrote, because currents were temperamental enough to make the journey to land a consistently dicey affair.[1] Helen saw an unbroken swath of beach backed by green jungle, with no visible sign of habitation or welcome. To a young American girl, it appeared the perfect tropical frontier, an expected manifestation of the expansionist imaginary in which she had been raised. Slowly, a small lighter barge came into view, its Spanish captain in the stern with a little flag in hand. Six Mexican men were seated in front of him, hauling on their oars. Helen, her siblings, her cousin, her parents, their dog Juno, and her father's violin were tucked into the small boat between the sailors. Hands wrapped in old coffee sacks, they rowed shoreward. On reaching the beach, the men threw the children over their shoulders like the heavy quintals of coffee to which they were accustomed.[2]

Having already journeyed thousands of miles from San Francisco, the Humphreys were not pleased to learn that they would spend the night sleeping on a warehouse floor. The port had no other facilities, just the one building that served as customs office and storage depot. The lack of creature comforts was disappointing, but it fit easily within the Americans' pioneer narrative of their voyage, as retold years later by Helen in her memoir. She and her family were here to strike it rich on virgin lands. Never mind the cohort of warehouse workers who handed out tortillas and helped them bed down among the other off-loaded goods. Never mind the scheduled caravan of oxcarts that carried them inland the next morning. Never mind the deep

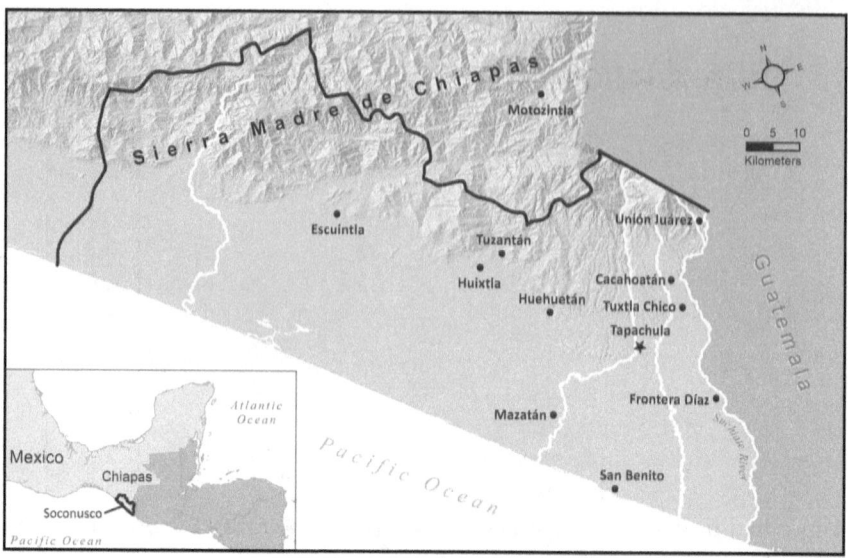

MAP 1. The Soconusco District of Chiapas, Mexico. Map prepared by the Harvard University Center for Geographic Analysis.

grooves in the path they followed, carved by the regular to and fro of traffic from town to port. None of these fit the narrative of individual trial and triumph that structured Helen's reminiscences. Instead, she emphasized the isolation, the warnings about snakes, the tropical heat broken by a siesta in the shade of the cart. Only a boisterous reception in Tapachula's town center interrupted her narrative of wilderness and solitude. Greeted by cheerful Chinese lanterns, unfamiliar marimba music, and a joyous welcome from the port agent's family, an exhausted Helen fell asleep chewing on a French roll.

After a brief reprieve, Helen's father and cousin began the trek into the foothills of the Sierra Madre de Chiapas to stake a claim for their new *finca*, or coffee plantation. As with the journey from port to town, their destination proved further afield than they had been led to believe. An American company's advertisement for cheap, easy to obtain property had drawn the family south.[3] Unfortunately, the advertisements proved false. Just prior to the Humphreys' arrival, the Mexican government refused to extend the company's concession, leaving its clients in limbo with regard to their rights as settlers and their land titles. Nonetheless, the Humphreys men set out on the two-day journey from Tapachula to find the land the company had promised. On the way, they passed well-established smallholdings planted with subsistence and market crops. Alongside corn, beans, and squash, local villagers grew cash crops like bananas, sugar, and, as the elevation slowly rose, an increasing number of coffee bushes.⁴ With their own property rights so uncertain, the Humphreys had no desire to challenge the villagers' land claims. Instead, Matthew Humphreys chose to squat on a plot of land deep in the foothills and returned to town to collect his family. Ten-year-old Helen, whose memoir reads like a Mexican *Little House on the Prairie*, took scarce note of the Mexican and Guatemalan farmers they passed on their hike back into the hills. Instead, she focused on the poor state of the roads and happy meetings with the region's few other foreign settlers. Having absorbed an idea of an unpeopled frontier ripe for settlement, Helen refused to see anyone unlike herself. Finally, the family arrived at San Antonio Nexapa, the land Matthew had chosen as their new home. The Humphreys set up camp beneath a copse of banana trees that sheltered a vegetable garden abandoned by previous colonists. Beyond loomed the tropical forest, its dense greenery a vibrant reminder of the work ahead.

That forest had to be hacked down, the land ploughed before the Humphreys could make the fortune promised by the land company's advertisements and Mexico's seemingly untapped landscape. Even once cleared and planted with slow-growing coffee shrubs, it would be at least four years before the family could harvest and export any product.⁵ In the meantime, the Humphreys women learned to make tortillas and fed their family on the same corn, beans, and squash that local villagers ate. Like those villagers, the Humphreys also cultivated sugar and bananas alongside their staples. These they brought to town and sold or traded for tools, coffee seed, and other necessities. For the first years, the Humphreys worked the land themselves. As soon as they could afford it, they hired a few laborers to speed the toil of clearing, planting, tending, and harvesting. Matthew Humphreys had to travel far into the Sierra Madre and offer good wages and additional incentives to find anyone willing to join them at San Antonio Nexapa. The villagers whose farms they passed on the trek from Tapachula were not interested. Smallholders had no need for supplementary wage work as they grew the same cash crops the Humphreys produced. While Helen wrote with affection of the family who came to live and work alongside them as laborers, her memoir ignores the neighboring villagers. Despite the similarity of their endeavors, language and topography kept the smallholders of the Soconusco far from Helen's circle of acquaintances.

Yet villagers and the Humphreys alike were caught up in and integral to the whirlwind that was Latin America's late nineteenth-century export boom. Both contributed to the Soconusco's rapid ascension from backwater to Mexico's predominant exporter of coffee in the decades between 1870 and 1920 (see Figure 1). While coffee was never Mexico's principal agricultural export, it ascended the ranks across the same era, settling firmly at second or third most valuable export by the 1890s and remaining in that position

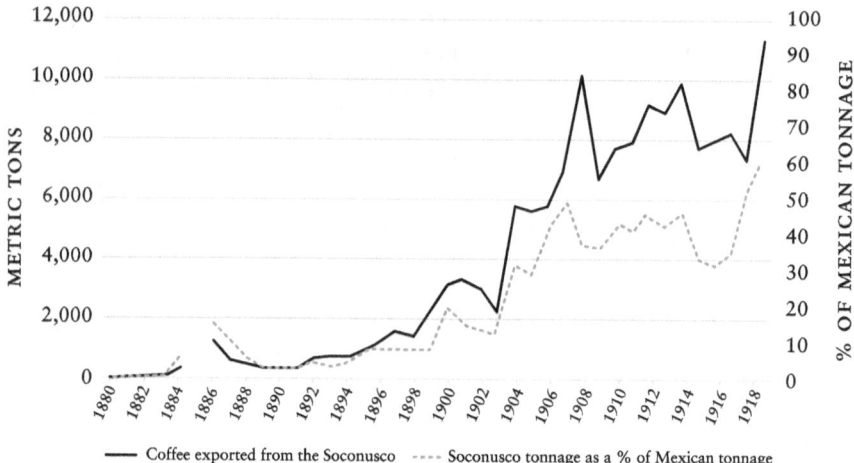

FIGURE 1. Coffee Exports from the Soconusco, 1880–1919. Data for 1885 is not available. 1902 was the year of a volcanic eruption in Guatemala that blanketed the region in ash not long before the harvest. 1906–1907 was the year exports transitioned from steamship to rail, leading to a lost year of export data. It was also the year Brazil, the world's leading coffee exporter, implemented a valorization program. See Appendix 1 for detailed data and sources.

for the coming century.[6] By 1900, approximately half of the Soconusco's coffee was produced on plantations like the one owned by the Humphreys, and half on the village holdings that Helen ignored.[7] As this local economy globalized, producers at all scales determined its new shape. While Helen's account of her young adulthood rarely touched on the experiences of her Mexican neighbors, their aspirations, traditions, and decisions defined the parameters of her family's life and livelihood in the Soconusco.

Focusing solely on Helen's story and those of other North Americans, Europeans, and Mexican government officials who cast their endeavors as pioneering would lead us to an understanding of the Soconusco that hews closely to traditional narratives of the export boom. In her telling and that of later chroniclers, this was an empty and uncontested commercial frontier.[8] It was a place where an English land company held title to large swaths of territory and where the foreign presence was so notable that the heart of the coffee zone is now known as Nueva Alemania, or New Germany. From here, Mexican and migrant letter writers registered complaints regarding usurious loans from foreign creditors, abusive labor bosses, and finca owners encroaching on village land. This is a place where all of the traditional narratives of Latin America's export boom come together.[9] And this is a place where none of those narratives hold.

These narratives do not hold because they ignore the more than half of the economy that Helen did not see. Historians, too, have long failed to register the welter of ways small-time local producers integrated Latin America into global trade. Yet we cannot understand the export boom without understanding all those who produced for market. Neither the liberal policies of Latin American elites nor the capital and connections of migrant investors could absolutely disenfranchise and disentail regional participants in the shifting political and economic landscape of the era. From the first years of production, numerous factors constrained commercial investors as they attempted to turn places like the Soconusco into model plantation economies serving global markets. Chief among these was the active participation of local villagers in the selfsame global market.

Historians have done much to recuperate popular participation in Latin America's political transformation across the nineteenth century. This book seeks to do the same for popular contributions to the region's economic restructuring. While the people rallied and proclaimed, they also privatized and contracted. An ever-growing literature has examined how popular embrace of the liberal tenets of individual rights, equality before the law, and local rule spread across rural Latin America in the mid-nineteenth century. Elections were taken seriously, constitutions debated, patriotic hymns sung with fervor. Liberalism as a political ideology had staying power because the people embraced and embodied it, even if its practices rarely proved durable.[10]

I argue that the spread and endurance of liberalism's economic and institutional aspects should be viewed through a similar lens as popular politics.[11] By the 1870s, national governments across Latin America had embraced the provisioning of global markets as a key feature of their future prosperity. To achieve this promised growth, administrations passed legislation to adopt and standardize liberal commercial and legal institutions in the service of national and international trade. They worked to promote contract law, privatize land, uphold wage labor, ease access to credit, and promote economic development.[12] Yet these programs had little life off the page. Only when those who lived and produced in the countryside embraced the utility of liberal institutions did they come to have real meaning beyond capital cities. Even as engagement with the political aspects of liberalism ebbed, its institutional framework came to form the bedrock of Latin America's economic life.

The Soconusco's engagement with globalizing markets was governed by bargains and compromises, not just laws and legal institutions. People, not abstract markets, provided avenues for multiple modes of production and participation. What became one of the most successful and durable agricultural economies of the era was the result of producers, both natives and newcomers, reaching outward for reforms and implementing them as circumstances dictated. Some participants had greater sway than others, but all had a role to play in determining the shape and speed of engagement with international markets. In taking on those roles, producers on all scales also facilitated the consolidation of state institutions, though not always the consolidation of state power. By including villagers, laborers, small-time merchants, and local politicians alongside the traditional cast of foreign and state actors, I use the experiences of one peripheral region to better understand the penetration of globalization and new state institutions during the late nineteenth century. Reading outward from the Soconusco, this book demonstrates how producers on all scales played a role in the significant reorientation of both economic and institutional life during the late nineteenth century.

The Winding Path to Market Integration

The late nineteenth century was an era of environmental and institutional expansionism. Whether growing coffee or rubber, excavating guano, or extracting oil, producers of new commodities pushed production into spaces where land was not yet private property, markets were not yet integrated, institutions of capitalism and the state were not yet cemented. These were not empty spaces, but rather sparsely populated areas where the scale of governance and cultivation was minimal. In the parlance of the day, they were deserts ripe for exploitation.[13]

Such deserts were far removed from the markets their products might serve. That remove was not just spatial but also ideological and institutional. The great thrust of the nineteenth century was to integrate the spaces of production and consumption through the transformation of exchange as well as landscape. To achieve this end, a multitude of actors sought to facilitate flows of capital and goods across institutional frameworks and broad geographies. Progress toward this end meant deploying new technologies to drill through mountains, tame rivers, and clear jungles. It also meant homogenizing the institutions of global commerce. The liberal tenets of private property, contract law, and free trade emerged as paramount markers of the globalizing world.[14]

By the turn of the century, Latin America's producers were sending raw materials and foodstuffs of all sorts to consumers in Europe, the United States, and urban and industrial areas within their own countries. The iconic crops of the era—coffee, rubber, henequen, guano, bananas, oil—were only one part of the export boom. Latin American countries also shipped tons of cotton, beans, dyes, spices, grains, meat and leather, fibers, and myriad other goods to market.[15] This activity led to remarkable economic growth.

By the 1920s, the region as a whole had a higher GDP than any part of the world excepting the United States and Western Europe. Though unevenly distributed—Cuba and Argentina saw much higher growth than Central America or Paraguay—and still meager compared to economic expansion in the United States, this growth represented a significant shift in Latin America's commercial outlook.[16]

Those responsible for enacting this transformation were far from unified in their approaches, their outlooks, or their circumstances. There is no easy way to carve out stable categories of actors involved in the process. While some of the commodities that contributed to the export boom were plantation crops, most could also be grown alongside subsistence goods. There was considerable consolidation of landholding during the period, driven in large part by the same liberal policies that supported commercial integration. Yet smallholding villagers also held onto their lands and carved out new spaces for cultivation.[17] When it came to enacting the policies that enabled global trade, anyone producing for market had a role to play. Their approaches were not necessarily consistent. Individuals changed their minds, companies renegotiated their terms, communities shifted their strategies, governments reevaluated their priorities. Alliances formed across social groups and conflicts festered within them. People pursued the same ends for different reasons and by different means. This book demonstrates that we cannot simply divide the world into those advocating for globalization and those fighting against it. Rather, the end result of globalization on a large scale was driven by many often contradictory aims.

All that said, those involved in the move toward an integrated global economy can be sorted into more or less stable social strata based on the scale of their engagement with that economy. For the purposes of this book, there were elites and there were popular groups. The meaning of *elite* depended on circumstance. At the grandest scale of Latin America as a whole, the usual coterie of economic and political magnates had a clear role to play in the export boom. Both Latin American and foreign, these politicians, bureaucrats, merchants, and planters expressly advocated the standardization and integration of the global economy. They reformed civil codes along French lines, copied the language of English commercial contracts, imported dollars from the United States, uprooted their families from Spain, and counted out coffee beans on wharves from San Benito to Hamburg. They did so in the name of order and progress, a positivist-influenced liberal ideal that envisioned a virtuous circle of economic growth and political stability.[18] After the decades of civil war that followed independence, such a promise held much appeal.

Elite investment in order and progress paid dividends. The export boom's first decades brought the relative stabilization of political systems across

Latin America. While the success of their state-building can be questioned, the export-oriented economic success such actors achieved was, at least temporarily, quite remarkable.[19] Not all were made rich through extraction and exploitation, but those who achieved success cemented their place as the icons of the export era.[20] The palatial homes of the Yucatán's henequen hacendados, the wheat- and beef-funded boulevards of Buenos Aires, the factories and theaters built with São Paulo's coffee incomes, Mexico City's centennial celebrations: all expressed triumph in the increasingly universal language of wealth and modernity.[21]

The Soconusco's elite demonstrated their wealth on a smaller scale but in similar terms. They built a theater, installed electricity, and celebrated national holidays at the newly installed bandstand. By 1910 they together owned about 100 fincas averaging 180 hectares of land apiece. A very few encompassed over 1,000 hectares.[22] These planters, known locally as *finqueros*, sold their crops directly to foreign merchants based in Tapachula and commercial houses based abroad. In turn, these commercial agents infused millions of pesos into the local economy as mortgages, futures contracts, and other types of loans. What most clearly defined this group was their focus on market-driven production and trade, rather than subsistence.

As in many export-oriented regions, the region's elite was a mix of locals and newcomers. Ranchers turned coffee planters from the Soconusco could trace their ancestry back to the miniscule *ladino* and Spanish elite who supervised the end of the region's cacao economy in the colonial era.[23] Some, as we will see, resisted the turn to coffee while others embraced it. Alongside this entrenched local elite worked migrants from elsewhere in Mexico. These men—almost all were men—came from across the country to try their hand at the next big thing.[24] Some settled and stayed in the region for generations. Others soon gave up and headed elsewhere to try again with another promising crop.

Many foreigners who landed on the Pacific coast were similarly in search of their fortunes. Americans, Spaniards, Germans, English, and others shared the entrepreneurial spirit of the Humphreys family that opened this introduction. Unlike the Humphreys, a good number of these emigrants failed and quickly. Those who succeeded and stayed were small in number, but their impact was outsized.[25] By 1910, eighty-six Germans had followed family ties and commercial apprenticeships to the Soconusco. Their economic strength was such that that would eventually endow the heart of the coffee region with the appellation of New Germany. Yet they were far from singular. Some 350 Chinese migrants ran small businesses in Tapachula. A government sponsored Japanese colony farmed in the northern reaches of the district.[26] More than seventy Spaniards played a vital role in the region's commercial houses and other aspects of trade. American dairymen, British engineers, Turkish and

Danish and French and Italian and Central American planters all carved out spaces for themselves in the Sierra Madre.[27] While the Germans came to constitute a somewhat insular community, they and everyone else partnered, transacted, and quarreled across bounds of national origin.

No single nationality formed a community large enough to maintain itself apart from the others or be called an enclave. Instead, these regional elites formed a mutually recognized sphere of commercial actors engaged in globally directed enterprises. While few were prosperous in a way that would have allowed them entrée to elite circles in Mexico City, their activities and aspirations would have been intelligible and admirable in that sphere. Mutual recognition and intelligibility, though, need not imply cooperation or peaceful collaboration. The Soconusco's elites grappled with each other and with their national and international counterparts over everything from the interpretation of mortgage regulations to the location of Mexico's southern bounds. They took each other to court on a regular basis, cheated on their contracts, and skimmed off the top. They bankrupted their neighbors and threatened their employers with whiskey bottles and shotguns. Sometimes they changed their minds about the potential benefits of moving toward export production and manifested that shift with armed marches in the streets. Yet through their conflicts and cooperation, this cohort shared the goal of transforming the untapped ecological riches of the Soconusco into a source of personal and public prosperity.

Elite actors were not the only ones interested in the potential offered by new markets for Latin America's products. The deserts that political and economic elites found so enticing were in no way empty. Their populations may have been sparse, but people who lived in these areas before the booms were knowledgeable about the very terrain that all found so promising. From Brazilian rubber to Mexican vanilla, they already produced cash crops for market alongside their staple goods.[28] As demand expanded, villagers also sought to benefit by expanding cultivation and finding a way into global commodity flows. This new directionality of production, though, generally supplemented rather than supplanted their primary focus on subsistence. The export boom was a new development for elites but often represented an intensification of existing patterns for others.

Non-elite actors both contributed to and constrained elites' efforts to integrate frontiers of production into global markets. The heterogeneous approach to governance and commerce that marked these spaces was a major hurdle to elite and non-elite interest in commercial expansion. Decades if not centuries of conflict and relative isolation from central governments shaped institutional norms that did not always smoothly interface with those of foreign markets.[29] As elites forcefully worked to overcome these dissonances, small-time producers also appropriated the new economic and legal tools meant to incorporate them into a global economy. Villagers, laborers, and petty politicians reworked codes, regulations, and norms to both facilitate their participation in commerce and to shore up their autonomy.[30]

Local communities, themselves internally stratified by occupation and social standing, were more and less successful in their endeavors to capitalize on global demand for what they could produce. Many saw their lands seized or finagled away by wily and powerful elites. This is the history that has long dominated our understanding of the export boom and its fallout for the have-nots of Latin America.[31] Yet many others established their own means of engaging elites and the market-oriented reforms they promoted. Whether growing coffee in El Salvador, vanilla in Veracruz, or bananas in the Caribbean, smallholders entered into commodity trade on a global scale. The durability of their relatively autonomous engagement was not uniform. Nor did they avoid the conflicts over contracts, land usage, and labor exploitation that plagued their elite counterparts. Nevertheless, producers who mixed subsistence with market agriculture were a key element of Latin America's export expansion.[32]

In the Soconusco, this less commercially oriented cohort included a mix of locals and newcomers to the Sierra Madre, just as with their elite counterparts. Differences of origin were smaller in scale but no less meaningful. At the beginning of the period explored in this book, the population of the Soconusco was 17,000 people, just about three per square kilometer of territory.[33] Villagers lived in or around the district seat of Tapachula or in the coastal plains. Because of a demographic history that will be explored in Chapter One, the foothills of the Sierra Madre were mostly unclaimed. In much the same way that coffee's ascendance drew commercially driven actors from across Mexico and the world to the Soconusco, so too did it draw new smallholders into the fertile foothills. The next decades saw an influx of Guatemalan villagers who settled in the disputed land along the frontier without clear legal claim to the land they began to work. Villagers from Tapachula also moved further into the Sierra to establish new towns through the legal processes established by Mexican law. As the coffee economy expanded, the labor demands of finqueros like the Humphreys facilitated the movement of workers from other parts of Chiapas and Guatemala into the region. They, too, swelled the ranks of small-time subsistence and market producers. By 1910, almost 55,000 lived in the district, giving the Soconusco one of the nation's highest growth rates in an era marked by a notable population expansion (see Appendix 2).[34]

What did these residents do? For the most part, they worked the land for subsistence and export. By doing so, small-time producers and laborers also engaged with the spread of the institutions of global trade. The largest number toiled as finca laborers. By 1910, some 2,000 or so families—men, women, and children—lived on coffee plantations as resident laborers. Their numbers doubled or trebled with migrant workers during the harvest.[35] At least another 2,000 families, individuals I refer to alternately as villagers or smallholders, worked small plots of land they claimed as their own.[36] There, alongside corn, chilies, and squash, they grew cash crops like coffee. Not all villagers grew the bean, but those municipalities with terrain appropriate for the export crop saw higher growth rates than the municipalities that hugged the coast.

For those looking to capitalize on demand, cultivating and selling coffee facilitated and sometimes required the use of new commercial and legal forms. Villagers signed contracts, privatized their land, argued before the municipal and district courts, and bought small luxuries on credit. Unlike finqueros, they rarely sold their harvests directly to commercial houses abroad. Instead, neighboring planters and merchants in Tapachula took smallholders' beans in payment for outstanding debts or purchased their harvests outright, consolidating the crops into lots large enough to export. Yet while villagers' transactions remained local, small-time producers, harvesting a few quintals of coffee from a few hectares of land, also shaped the emerging institutions of global capital. Their use of the Sierra delimited the spaces available for plantations. Their disinterest in wage labor dictated the shape of labor contracts. Their engagement with local politics defined who could lay claim to administrative and political positions. Their understanding of the terrain determined the bounds of Mexico itself.

The eventual consolidation of an export economy in the Soconusco was the result of elites and non-elites deciding to direct the productivity of their lands toward global markets. The solidification of the institutions through which they did so was the result of all engaging with and shaping those institutions to their own needs. Neither state actors nor international elites swept in and dictated the terms of the export boom to the people of the Soconusco. Rather, villagers and planters gradually sued, fought, and collaborated their way toward market integration.

This approach helps us understand the growth that occurred during the export boom in its own terms. Histories of this period in Mexico have long been burdened with what John Womack has termed *precursorism*, that is, the weight of explaining the revolutionary violence that broke out across Mexico in 1910.[37] Recently, historians have instead sought to explore the economic and political transformation of the years between 1870 and 1910 without simply characterizing them as the preface to later histories.[38] Rather than examining the Porfiriato, the thirty-year reign of Porfirio Díaz (1876–1910) that overlaps with much of this book, for the causes of the Mexican Revolution, historians are looking at the ways institutional norms were stabilized and homogenized.[39] Similarly, rather than approaching the export boom to understand "why Latin

America fell behind" in the twentieth century, researchers are investigating how market production expanded on all scales during the years in question.[40] Beyond the realm of policy and institutions, scholarship on rural production has slowly moved to include the non-elites described above. A rich literature on coffee cultivation across Latin America illustrates how varied modes of production, from massive plantations to minuscule polycrop plots, coexisted within the region's tropical zone.[41] In Mexico particularly, new work on land usage has resulted in considerable renovation of our understanding of the actors responsible for implementing new liberal norms.[42] Across Latin America, scholars are diversifying the body of players involved in remaking Latin America's countryside in the late nineteenth century.

This book embraces this approach by examining how an economy was built by all those invested in it. In conflicting interpretations of market involvement, we find an explanation for why the commercial plantation complex that epitomized capitalist agricultural production did not come to dominate everywhere.[43] In local producers' flexibility and openness to innovation, we come to understand the spread of new cultivars, new institutions, and new linkages. The integration of the modern global economy and the consolidation of the modern state were thus multidirectional processes that relied on local, national, and international embrace of exchange.

Organization and Overview

The book is organized around a series of hurdles to economic integration as laid out by elites seeking to overcome them. The organization should in no way imply that their success was inevitable. Rather, the book addresses each of these challenges in turn as a means of demonstrating the fragility, sluggishness, and contingency of the changes that resulted. It also illustrates how new bureaucratic and practical institutions emerged from the intersection of local practices and national and international projects. Through a local lens, we see in heightened miniature the sweeping changes occurring across Latin America's rural spaces. The Soconusco comes to represent export frontiers across the region. Chapters overlap chronologically, but each one builds on the material in the chapters that precede it. Because each chapter delves into a particular component of the economy, it is useful to have a broad portrait of the whole here at the start.

In the first chapter, we see all that stood in the way of Latin America's reincorporation into the global flow of commodities. The chapter delves into the Soconusco as a site that magnifies the challenges facing rural regions as demand for their products increased. From the rugged landscape to the lack of legal fixity, from political violence to recalcitrant workers, the district presented many obstacles to entrepreneurial locals and migrant investors. Yet many saw promise in the fertile hillsides and valleys. Using the correspondence of Matías Romero, Mexico's Minister of Finance, the chapter explores why so many would devote themselves to overcoming the Soconusco's geographic and institutional failings. Borrowing the words of its primary interlocutors, I present the untapped but enormous ecological potential of the Soconusco as an exemplar of the riches rural Latin America was imagined to hold.

Romero's dream of exploiting Eden was not to be for another two decades. Coffee took root as the region's leading cash crop during the 1870s, but its hold on the landscape was tenuous. The first recorded exports from the region amounted to only a few thousand kilograms, much of which was likely reexports from Guatemala.[44] Romero did not stay long in the Soconusco, and the dozen or so migrant entrepreneurs and local ranchers who took up his cause found their project challenged on all fronts. First among these challenges was the region's undefined border with Guatemala. As it stood, two nations claimed to govern the physical territory of the Soconusco under two bodies of law. This confusion of legal mandate provided none of the security that real investment in the land required. It also invited rampant violence as government-sponsored raids, counterraids, and local rivalries disguised as raids tore apart the lives of villagers and planters alike. Chapter Two looks at the diplomatic and everyday resolution of the border dispute. It illustrates how local demands for legal clarity dovetailed with a national mandate for territorial integrity. While a treaty had to be wrought by those at the highest levels of power, its implementation was left to those on the ground. Only with the territory's nationality settled could planters and villagers commit to new endeavors that relied on fixed legal regimes.

While Guatemala and Mexico battled over national sovereignty, political sovereignty within the nation was also in question. Fights over central versus federal governance plagued much of the Americas during this era. Local authorities fought with national leaders over where sovereignty resided. In the Soconusco as elsewhere, this meant great confusion over whether or not national law had any local meaning. In Chapter Three, we see how the desire for reliable institutions to facilitate export agriculture helped overcome battles between political elites. While a local political boss refused national mandates for integration into the nation, planters and villagers worked to put into practice reforms that they desired. The insecurity of the situation meant that export producers' numbers remained small. Yet those engaged in growing for export did essential work in building the scaffolding for administrative reliability. They turned the courts into sites for hashing out the nuances of the commercial and civil codes. They filed for land titles with local and national officials. They built infrastructure to ease coffee's way out of the region. Despite the political boss's active opposition to new economic endeavors, coffee producers exported almost ten times more coffee in 1890 than they did in 1880.[45]

This growth was nothing compared to the explosion of coffee cultivation that occurred between 1890 and 1920. During those years, an ever-growing body of producers capitalized on the calming of inter- and intranational violence and the attendant emergence of relative institutional reliability. Together, smallholders, laborers, and planters built the export economy. To do so, they further engaged liberal reforms directed toward land, labor, and capital as they became useful for local conditions. The rest of the book describes these engagements in detail. The reforms producers drew on to facilitate commercial expansion predated their enactment in the Soconusco by decades. In these chapters, I illuminate how and why local actors put them into practice when they did.

With Mexico's territorial bounds defined and its legal institutions gradually becoming reliable, planters and villagers alike carved up the Sierra Madre into defined properties. Chapter Four follows the intersecting processes by which these two sets of actors drew on new bodies of property law to secure spaces for market production. While a foreign land company enacted national plans for public lands, its scope was curtailed by villagers' use of the landscape. Smallholders maintained and even expanded their property holdings through engagement with laws requiring privatization of communally held land. They did so on a timeline dictated by local politics and need rather than by state mandate. Only in the spaces villagers did not claim for their own cultivation were planters able to begin the work of transforming virgin forests into productive plantations.

Once they had land, planters and villagers both needed labor to clear and tend it. Villagers for the most part worked their own lots. In doing so, they withdrew themselves from the pool of potential workers available to finqueros. Chapter Five explores how this labor scarcity shaped the type of production possible in the Soconusco. Constant labor shortages provided those who did work on fincas with the ability to negotiate for better wages and better conditions. Traveling seasonally from inland Chiapas and across the still permeable border with Guatemala, migrant workers set the terms for their own employment by refusing to stay when employers proved stingy, violent, or dishonest. Elites both economic and political attempted to mold the region's labor market into a recognizable iteration of the desired plantation form through legislation, coercion, and innovation. Yet the stickiness of older forms of incentivized labor and the continual availability of both village lands and flight as alternatives to wage work gave laborers space to negotiate. Legal reform had little meaning until taken up by local actors. Even by the 1910s, the scarcity of labor meant most planters cultivated only a quarter to a third of their land with coffee bushes.

That level of production was enough, though, to connect the region ever more securely to global markets. Through the lens of credit and commerce, Chapter Six explores how international capital made its way into the Soconusco and coffee made its way out. The commercial reforms passed by national governments beginning in the 1850s only slowly blossomed into new types of enterprises in the provinces. The Soconusco, like many rural regions, lacked the formalized and normalized institutions entrepreneurs might have hoped for. Instead, merchants and coffee producers large and small created an informal credit network that melded foreign commercial customs with localized understandings of liberal reform. Enthusiasm for the export crop's potential led to an overabundance of credit in the 1890s. When global coffee prices collapsed late in the decade, the local economy was hit with a wave of foreclosures and defaults. Instead of restricting credit, lenders and borrowers tempered their activities by combining greater reliance on the new codes with an embrace of flexibility. These commercial flows demonstrate how local actors created a useful and durable economic vernacular from the era's liberalized financial regulations.

Together, these chapters reveal how many players were involved in the massive expansion of export production that occurred between 1870 and 1920. The economy that villagers, planters, merchants, and migrant laborers built did not look precisely like what any of them might have desired or imagined. Villagers complained about planters encroaching on their lands and acquaintances not repaying their debts. Laborers complained about employers not paying their wages on time or providing the incentives they promised. Planters complained about neighbors invading their fincas and workers running away without fulfilling their contracts and merchants charging exorbitant interest. Merchants complained about the volatility of the local market and the insufficiency of transportation infrastructure. Yet as much as these players' activities constrained those of the other participants in coffee's expansion, each also relied on the others' contributions to the growing economy. The economy they built together was the result of all involved taking up the drive toward global commercial integration and molding it to their circumstances.

The book concludes by analyzing more recent history to show how the locally driven engagement with the global market explored here represents an important alternative to our usual stories of the export boom. The Soconusco essentially did not take part in the Mexican Revolution. This was not the result of overt oppression and dependency keeping villagers and workers from rising up, as some scholars have contended.[46] Instead, it was because most players saw little appeal in the promises of revolutionary leaders. Mexico's economy continued to grow across the revolutionary decade, and so too did the Soconusco's.[47] The Soconusco is still the largest exporter of coffee from Mexico, with production based primarily on *ejidos*, or communally held village lands, and smallholdings. Many of those participating in ejidos or growing on small private properties are descendants of individuals and families who migrated to the Soconusco as seasonal workers or resident peons a century ago. Fincas are still owned by the great-grandchildren of those who settled in the nineteenth century. The institutions built around land, labor, and capital preserved space for many to participate in the new economy. Returning to Helen Humphreys, we are reminded that appearances can be deceiving and that the weight given to certain sources has distorted our understanding of the export boom. The dominant narrative does not by its visibility preclude the presence of parallel means to the same end.

I   An Uncultivated Eden

In 1872, Matías Romero, the Mexican Minister of Finance, quit his job and moved as far from Mexico City as he could manage. Claiming ill health and a need to fill his days with rejuvenating exercise and new activities, he relocated to the Soconusco.[1] He had never seen the place before, only read of its potential and its challenges in a steady stream of letters from men he had never met but who nevertheless found in the minister a fruitful avenue for their economic ambitions. These local promoters and Romero schemed and dreamed grand plans for the region. Together they posited the Soconusco as a leader in Mexico's integration into global markets for agricultural goods. Romero's journey to the Soconusco took weeks as he traveled through the rich agricultural lands of Mexico's southern states. By railroad, carriage, steamship, oxcart, and horse, Romero scouted other possible sites for investment and development.[2] The Soconusco, though, was always the destination. His arrival was greeted with cheering crowds and a lively band, all drummed up by local luminaries happy to welcome the man they had already made an honorary citizen.[3]

His welcome did not last long. Within three years Romero had retreated back to Mexico City. His coffee plantations were in flames, his finances in arrears, his allies in the region either turned enemy or themselves under threat. Recalcitrant local politicians, villagers, and the terrain itself undermined efforts to harness Mexico's modernizing schemes to the world's growing demand for tropical goods. Romero did not enter the Soconusco unwarned. The endless letters sent his way included innumerable cautions about the hurdles that stood between the Soconusco and economic development. The finance minister had believed in the power of public and private intervention to overcome these hurdles. The local landscape—natural, social, and political—shook that belief.

This chapter uses Romero's adventure in the Soconusco and its prehistory to enumerate the myriad challenges that stood in the way of export development.[4] These are the challenges that the rest of the book will address, one chapter at a time. They are also the challenges that make it impossible to understand Mexico's economic and institutional expansion from only a top-down, outside-in perspective. Romero's mix of public and private interventions in the Soconusco mimics in miniature the usual extractive story of the export boom. The responses he received to those interventions, both in letters and in actions, illustrate the impediments that stood in the way of his imagined easy entrance into the global economy.[5]

The chapter begins with a foray into the region's deep historical engagement with export agriculture and an exploration of its landscape. Prior to and for the century following the arrival of the Spanish, the Soconusco was a key site of cacao production for regional and global consumption. By the time locals began writing to Romero, that export history had been largely forgotten and its landscapes mostly abandoned, though the earlier economy continued to indelibly shape the region's makeup. The Soconusco was neither empty nor completely isolated, but its small population and geographic situation in no way set it up for growth. There was no assurance of personal or property security from either neighboring planters or the neighboring country. There was no easy way to survey, title, or purchase public lands. There were few willing workers and no contractors to secure labor from further afield. There were no merchants to provide credit, export coffee, or supply staple goods. There were no transportation companies to carry coffee from finca to port or from the shore to distant markets. There were no reliable legal institutions to register the contracts or mediate the disputes each of these prior needs would entail.

The men who wrote to Romero—ranchers, surveyors, small-town politicians—identified these problems and proposed that the minister help them find solutions. In turn, Romero sought to fill these gaping holes with a patchwork of policies from the Mexican liberal arsenal.[6] That arsenal of contract law, relatively free trade, and private property was not always to the liking of those seeking answers. The federal development program Romero was helping to write removed the reins of economic and political governance from local hands. It inserted state actors into interactions locals saw as outside state purview. And so they, both petty elites and villagers, became a further impediment to the enactment of Romero's grand plan for the Mexican countryside.

Looking at a modernizing, globalizing project for integration and progress from the periphery, this chapter slows down the narrative to match the pace of those who found themselves resisting the economic change they had initially championed. By taking up both their early enthusiasm as well as their about-face, the chapter demonstrates that there was no inevitable motion toward global market integration even when many involved seemed eager to take part. The complaints, requests, petitions, and negotiations of those experimenting with new crops in the Soconusco embody local intractability while at the same time hinting at how a new economy might eventually grow. Even the positing of plans for progress involved negotiation over what progress might mean and who would take part. This chapter sits and contemplates the unstable status quo. It identifies the barriers standing in the way of a new economic orientation, leaving the rest of book to illustrate how those invested in this shift eventually worked around—but rarely displaced or eliminated—these seeming impediments to growth.

A Geography of Plenty

The Soconusco sits at the southernmost tip of Mexico. It comprises a 240-kilometer long, 35-kilometer wide strip of coastal plains and foothills where the Isthmus of Tehuantepec broadens out again into Central America. There, mangrove swamps give way to flat beachfront and volcanic soil. With the Sierra Madre de Chiapas mountains protecting its eastern approach and a marshy estuary demarcating its southern reaches, the terrain naturally provides a stratified differentiation of productive zones. Humans have taken advantage of the sheer abundance of that landscape since at least 5500 B.C. where, as one archaeologist quips, "The countryside is so productive that one would have to be a fool to go hungry."[7] With soils fertilized by eons of volcanic activity, the foothills of the Sierra Madre and the fluvial plain at their base are some of the richest agricultural lands in Mexico.

The chain of small dormant and extinct volcanoes that march upward toward the peaks of modern-day Guatemala splits as it moves southward, defining the Soconusco within a shallow semicircle of mountainous terrain. The region is hot and humid, one of the rainiest in the world. While its rapid ascent from sea level to mountain peak results in great variability in temperature, the mountain range that forms its eastern front serves as a break, trapping warm, wet Pacific air over the entire region. Average rainfall across the region ranges from 2,500 to 6,000 mm, or about 98 to 236 inches, of water a year, spread across an exaggerated rainy season that stretches for up to two hundred days from spring through late fall. Even in the dry season, the 4,062-meter Tacaná volcano and its sisters lead to the formation of generous morning and evening cloud cover.[8] Rushing out of the mountain range flow streams and rivers, none navigable, but all carrying with them the mineral-rich detritus of their volcanic headwaters (see the multitude of rivers in Map 2). Pushing toward the ocean, these streams gather into estuaries and natural canals, irrigating the plains with water further enriched by the florid biome

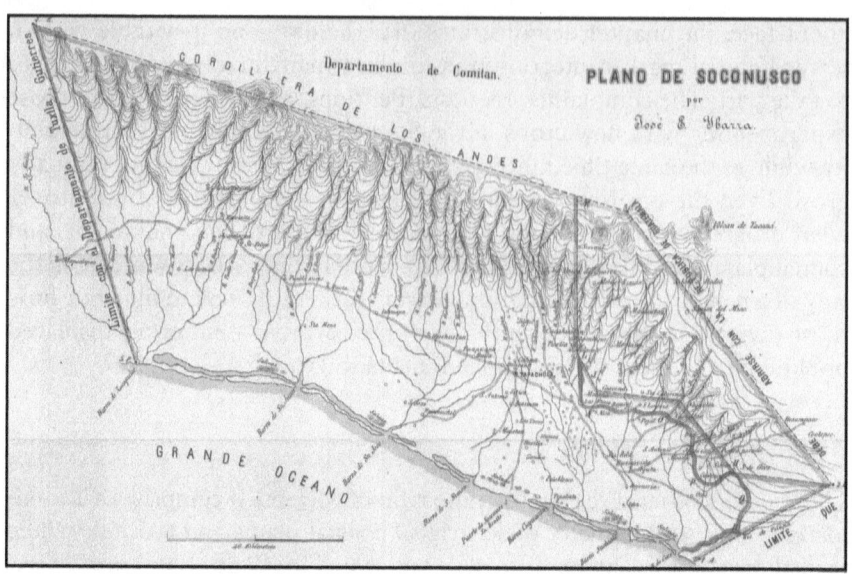

MAP 2. Map of the Soconusco, 1872. Source: Plano del Soconusco, by José E. Ibarra, 1872. Mapoteca Manuel Orozco y Berra, Colección General, Estado de Chiapas, No. 399A-CGE-7274-P. Reprinted with permission.

of the subtropics. As much as the Sierra Madre defines the Soconusco, so too does this generous, astonishingly wet climate, particularly in contrast with the drier territory that surrounds it on all sides.[9]

Across the millennia this abundance fostered first localized plenty and later imperial intent. Romero was in no way the first man to speculate on the riches the Soconusco might contain. Though the ancient inhabitants took their time in embracing sedentarism and agriculture, their eventual turn to domesticated cultivars mediated the region's entrance into ever-widening spheres of exchange.[10] Cacao was the most important of these cultivars prior to the introduction of coffee. A traveler or merchant brought it to the Soconusco sometime before 1850 B.C, and it was enshrined in the region's farm basket by 400 B.C.[11] The commerce driven by this sumptuary good, used in rituals and eventually as currency, drove the formation of new polities and new elites. Yet its cultivation in forest plots rather than plantations also facilitated the maintenance of dispersed and diversified production. As historical archaeologist Janine Gasco has demonstrated, local families managed small numbers of cacao trees alongside their subsistence crops. This kept population density low even as production boomed in the new millennium.[12] Because subsistence continued to rely on a mixture of agriculture, hunting, gathering, and fishing, primary forest was left intact. Families cultivated groves and farm plots interspersed among the trees, and much land remained unclaimed and uncultivated.

Even as merchants and conquerors from first the K'iche' and Mexica empires and then the Spanish Crown followed cacao into the Soconusco, local producers maintained this dispersed mode of production. Claimed for the Mexica Emperor Ahuitzotl in 1486 A.D. and then for the Spanish Crown in 1524, the Soconusco was a plum possession. Merchants turned administrators, first the Pochteca and then a series of well-connected Spanish governors—Cervantes once solicited the posting—sent feathers, animal pelts, gourds, amber, gold, and cacao to Tenochtitlán and across the Atlantic. Yet they never took on the cultivation or ownership of the land itself. Instead, they left production of the finicky tropical goods to locals who best knew how to coax them out of the earth.[13]

The loose imperialism of the Mexica was accompanied by population growth, but the Spanish Conquest decimated the region. By 1526, the 30,000 tributaries represented in the pre-conquest Codex Mendoza had been halved to only 15,000. Forty years later the Spanish Crown recorded only 1,600 tributaries. By 1684 the population had bottomed out at about 3,000 individuals, a demographic collapse that mirrored the catastrophic losses that struck so much of Latin America.[14] Official attempts to bolster the population with the importation of highland workers for the cacao orchards failed. The same diseases that had slain local villagers also killed new migrants. Spaniards also tried to import enslaved Africans and mulatto laborers from central Mexico. The new labor force lacked the experience necessary to successfully cultivate cacao and quickly proved too expensive.[15] The Soconusco had once been one of the most expensive and profitable postings for crown officials in Central America. Wracked by disease, violence, famine, and overwork, it faded from prestige by the end of the seventeenth century.[16]

As was the case across the Americas, indigenous peoples adapted to and adopted new practices, new goods, and new languages to deal with this catastrophic transformation.[17] Forced migration meant that the local community was small but diverse. The descendants of Spanish merchants and administrators continued to live in town, while the few remaining local and emigrant villagers continued cultivation of cacao in the foothills. As the population began to slowly recover from its nadir, Spanish became the lingua franca. *Ladino*, a Central American term used to describe Spanish speakers, replaced indigenous as the primary category of identification.[18]

The Bourbon Reforms of the mid-eighteenth century further cemented this transformation and left the Sierra Madre even more sparsely populated. Previously, villagers without official title to their lands had nonetheless held onto them by paying tribute in cacao. Implemented by the Spanish Crown to modernize and streamline the imperial bureaucracy, the reforms mandated tribute payment in cash and the clear demonstration of land ownership.[19] Nearly half of the communities that had existed in 1735 disappeared as a result. Their former residents moved to the district seat of Tapachula to work on new cattle ranches or establish residency in town and hopefully gain access to the village commons.[20] Those that remained produced small amounts of cacao, vanilla, achiote, and other forest products for local consumption and trade with neighboring areas in Chiapas and Guatemala. By 1811, at least a few villagers had also begun to plant coffee, another market crop that might shore up their fortunes against a poor harvest.[21]

The people of the Soconusco never fully abandoned the rich soils of the Sierra Madre. Yet by the end of the colonial regime, most economic activity in the Soconusco was focused in the plains. The tiny economic elite of the district likely purchased tropical goods like vanilla and cacao from foothill residents who made the trek to market, but they concentrated their own efforts on a small but steady trade in fattened cattle for export south. Aside from these mobile assets, few commodities traveled in or out of the Soconusco. Precolonial trade routes along the coast and to the interior fell into disuse. The region was neither isolated nor untouched, but its commercial connections were quite curtailed in comparison to earlier periods. Importantly for later developments, only non-elites made any claims to the Sierra Madre and its agricultural potential.

New Opportunities in a New Nation

Newly independent Latin America was full of places like the Soconusco, economic backwaters neglected because of sparse population, distance, and lack of capital. Those fighting for independence promised, among other things, new opportunities for trade and development as self-governing countries threw off the yoke of mercantilism. Yet it would take another half century for that promise to become manifest. In the meantime, political turmoil and the inherited baggage of colonial institutions curtailed the integration of national political and economic spheres. Local actors experimented and extrapolated from their own experiences to slowly establish the stability necessary for further development.

In the Soconusco, lowland haciendas and ranches continued to supply the petty elite who managed the region's integration into the new constellation of postcolonial governance. The district's entrance into that constellation was rockier than most due to an accident of political geography. As Spain relinquished its claims in the Americas, those who lived between Central America and Mexico found themselves pulled in both directions. Both new republics desired to claim the regions of Chiapas and the Soconusco, but neither outright asserted territorial dominance. Within the region, few wanted to maintain their default independence. Elites, defined by their accumulated social and economic capital or their ability to muster some military might, called congresses and plebiscites. Those who could, attended, voted, shouted, fought, bribed in an effort to sway both sides. Chiapas joined Mexico, claiming the Soconusco along the way.[22]

Yet most in the Soconusco had voted for Guatemala and disputed the order of events that led to their inclusion in the deal that annexed Chiapas to Mexico. The district's commercial ties were divided between cattle breeders in northern coastal Chiapas who supplied young calves, and customers on the emerging export plantations of Guatemala who bought the finished beef.[23] Ties to consumers had won out in local plebiscites, but wealthier, better-connected elites in central Chiapas overrode those votes. With tensions high in both new republics, the governments of Guatemala and Mexico agreed to leave the matter for later. The Soconusco would be autonomous. Even when Santa Anna crusaded south in 1842 to definitively claim the area for Mexico, little was done to shore up that assertion of sovereignty.[24] The lack of real political or institutional incorporation that was everywhere a tacit reality was here made explicit.

This did not mean that the Soconusco lacked politics. Rather, politics remained highly localized, with citizenship more clearly defined by belonging to a particular municipality rather than a nation-state. *Vecindad*, or the status of being a *vecino*, that is, a recognized legal member of a particular municipality, defined one's ability to access shared resources including land and water.[25] That status was, in turn, governed by the ranchers and *hacendados* who dominated municipal councils in Tapachula and the coastal plains. Only in the foothills did villagers maintain much sway over the disposition of resources.[26]

Ranchers' dominance did not mean that their power was absolute. As was the case across Mexico, villagers and smallholders embraced the tenets of popular participation and individual rights that marked mid-century politics.[27] Popular liberalism was alive and well in the Soconusco, even if political power continued to be defined as much by violence as by voting. Campaigns and elections occurred on a regular basis.[28] Those who won monopolized the rifles and munitions and soldiers that higher powers sent south when tensions with Guatemala occasioned a heightened military presence.[29] Violence was a key route to power.

This small well-armed elite, though, also oversaw the more mundane work of governance. Municipal officials recorded and punished runaway workers, organized responses to locusts, and monitored and redistributed the planting and harvesting of staples when the region faced famine.[30] They registered and taxed cattle brands and sales, they negotiated late payment of the capitation tax for villagers, and they facilitated the protection and expansion of Tapachula's communally held *ejido*, or village lands.³¹

This last provided villagers with important new knowledge about Mexico's legal precepts for the formation and expansion of villages. As the hemisphere's population finally began to recover from the devastation of the early colonial period, traditional village bounds no longer provided enough space for their residents.³² In some regions, urbanization was the result, with cities growing through both natural reproduction and migration from the countryside. Elsewhere, villagers established new towns or reestablished old ones. Such was the case in the Soconusco. By the 1860s, with the district's population edging toward 15,000, the Sierra Madre again became an attractive site for settlement. Villagers took their experience with the expansion of Tapachula's ejidos with them as they moved back into the long-neglected foothills to form new municipalities of their own.³³

The real political and economic power of the Soconusco, though, remained outside the Sierra Madre. Members of the four families who constituted the local oligarchy held almost all political positions in the district until the last decades of the nineteenth century.³⁴ They also claimed the majority of land held with private title, almost all of it cattle ranches in the coastal plains.³⁵ The scion of one of these families, Sebastián Escobar, dominated the scene by the early 1860s. Escobar built his reputation during the myriad civil and foreign wars that wracked Mexico across the mid-nineteenth century, switching sides as expediency directed.³⁶ In the process, he made valuable allies in the state and national government while also gaining access to the arms and troops that cemented his local role as regional *cacique*, or strongman.³⁷ Setting aside his flip-flopping, the national government recognized his local monopoly on power by granting him the position of *jefe político*, or district political chief, with charge over the military and political apparatus of the Soconusco.³⁸

Like the rest of his extended family, Escobar was not wealthy by the standards of Mexico City. Yet ranching provided incomes and commercial networks unavailable to villagers cultivating small amounts of cash crops alongside their corn and beans. Even though some of those villagers were already producing potentially profitable crops like coffee, they lacked the connections necessary to market their goods beyond the Soconusco. Escobar and other ranchers, on the other hand, already had well-established if relatively thin pathways along which goods, knowledge, and capital could flow. Guatemalan coffee plantations, which had expanded rapidly from mid-century onward, purchased most of the cattle exported from the Soconusco. The lucrative upward trajectory of these customers provided an example of the potential prosperity of the Sierra Madre for those ranchers, like Escobar, willing to take a risk. As importantly, ranching afforded these families small amounts of capital to begin imitating Guatemalan innovations. In the late 1860s, ranchers like Escobar began to take up coffee as a supplement to the steady but less lucrative work of ranching.

A Liberal Experiment in Eden

This is how Matías Romero found the Soconusco when he began corresponding with Escobar and other local notables in 1868. What had been a prosperous participant in imperial commercial networks four centuries before was now a backwater cow town. Yet it was beginning to aspire to something more. Ranchers and villagers both saw possibilities in the cash crops embraced by their Guatemalan counterparts. All also recognized that, as things stood, the Soconusco lacked much of what could enable and secure new economic possibilities. A ranching-based economy was not set up for export agriculture. It lacked the institutional reliability that would support long-term investments in agriculture. Cattle could be branded as a person's property and walk themselves to market; coffee could not.

The Soconusco's inspired but underresourced ranchers were happy to enumerate all that stood in the way of their new economic endeavors. Matías Romero was the perfect audience. Born in Oaxaca in 1837, Romero had cut his teeth in the diplomatic corps in the United States during the American Civil War, but economic issues were always his bread and butter. When the deposed liberal president Benito Juárez triumphantly retook the government from the conservative-backed Emperor Maximilian in 1867, Romero returned to Mexico City as the new Minister of Finance. Inspired by his observations of American Reconstruction, he hoped to use markets and investment to reintegrate a Mexico itself torn apart by war.[39]

Romero seemed well positioned for success. Mexican elites, like those across the Atlantic, were interested in standardizing economic institutions in order to facilitate international trade. The new Minister of Finance's plans for promoting internal markets and foreign trade and investment were in line with broader projects emerging from across the government. Happily, Maximilian had reinforced rather than repealed the liberal reforms mandating private property and modernizing contract law that Juárez had instituted during his first tenure. While not yet implemented in many places, these reforms at least set the tenor for the construction of liberal institutions.[40] Beyond the legislature, the Department of Fomento, or Development, had ambitious modernization projects of its own. Infrastructure investments, colonization and public land sales, scientific exploration, and information collection all dovetailed with Romero's own ideas about progress based in the exploitation of natural resources.[41] Beyond Mexico, the booming export economy of Brazil and the recent resurgence of Costa Rica and Guatemala based on their own embrace of export production provided examples of what might be. With increased demand for raw materials and tropical goods from rapidly industrializing North Atlantic countries, the time seemed ripe for coordinated investment in new externally oriented rural production.[42]

None of these projects had yet reached far beyond the halls of national government, let alone to the distant Soconusco. Yet the Soconusco seemed the perfect site to experiment with all the potential benefits they promised. If its backwardness could be overcome, anywhere in Mexico might be made prosperous. Or, as Romero stated in a report on the means proposed for improving the region, work in the district would "indicate the best manner of realizing convenient and altogether beneficial improvements for the Republic."[43] While friends and relatives had suggested many other sites for public and personal investment, the southern coastal region seemed to present the best blank slate for intervention.[44] Armed with an arsenal of liberal reforms aimed at global economic integration, Romero took on the Soconusco as a test case in public intervention for the common commercial good.

Romero's interventions in the Soconusco can be divided into three phases. During the first, from 1868 through 1872, Romero worked as Minister of Finance to institute legislative changes that would favor the Soconusco's development. He also began investing personally in the region during this time through the mediation of Escobar and other local elites. From 1873 to 1875, Romero lived in the Soconusco. He left Mexico City in a huff, frustrated by the legislature's failure to take his advice on the federal budget and matters of trade. While in the Soconusco, his relationships with the local elite soured as they realized that Romero's interventions often meant ceding local control to new arrivals and outside authorities. Once again frustrated by his failures to make progress, Romero returned to Mexico City in 1875.[45] This marked the beginning of the third phase of his involvement with the region. This last period began with the destruction of his plantation by violent raiders, likely sponsored by either Guatemalan or local elites who saw their authority undermined by Romero's intercession. In the years that followed, Romero again took up the mantle of Minister of Finance, but also kept up a correspondence with a number of federal employees and migrant investors who had followed him to the Soconusco. In those letters, Romero's utter disappointment with the district is impossible to ignore.

That disappointment is particularly striking given the minister's early optimism and collaborative spirit. Romero wrote to Sebastián Escobar in 1868 to ask for local insight into the region and its needs.[46] The political boss and his friends were happy to oblige. For aspirational ranchers in the Soconusco, Romero represented a conduit for funds, information, and legislative fixes that might provide the means to follow their Guatemalan counterparts into prosperity. As quickly became apparent, the minister had little idea how many hurdles stood in the way. To start, Romero assumed that the national government's market-oriented reforms had already been implemented. He was quickly disabused of this belief. It was not that the ranchers who wrote to Romero expressly opposed these reforms. Rather, they made quite clear that the terrain and the existing state of regional economic and legal norms meant that more than new legislation was needed to truly exploit their home's economic potential.

Local elites also made clear that any reform needed to benefit their interests above all others. Unfortunately for both them and Romero, this was not the minister's intent. Nor was it the intent of the villagers who had long been growing coffee in the Sierra Madre or the migrant investors who followed Romero south to join in his experimental endeavor. Each group had its own interests to serve. While villagers shifted their loyalties or tried to stay out of the line of fire, migrant investors soon clashed with local elites over who controlled access to key resources. Thus, the initial physical and institutional impediments that locals pinpointed for the minister were soon compounded by another set of interpersonal conflicts. Locals led by Escobar pushed back against individuals they saw as interlopers and carpetbaggers, exacerbating violence and institutional instability.

All of this was documented in hundreds of letters sent to Romero before, during, and after his stint in the Soconusco. Over the years, his correspondents transitioned from primarily local elites to primarily recently arrived aspiring planters. Full of information, proposals, suppositions, gossip, pleas, and threats, the letters Romero received capture the potential and the problems that places like the Soconusco faced as their residents attempted to tap into the accelerating global flow of goods and capital. The rest of the chapter will address the hurdles in turn, following the lead of the letter writers as they articulated their hopes and frustrations. First, I will examine two types of insecurity and violence that plagued the region, those of borders and of political bosses. Then, I will turn, as Romero's correspondents did, to the difficulties of securing and maintaining key inputs to the new economy. Each of these hurdles represented a significant challenge to economic development. And each represented a common problem across the Mexican countryside, the site of Romero's imagined future prosperity for Mexico at large. If, as he imagined, the country would flourish on the back of its natural endowments, success in the Soconusco could represent a path to success nationwide.

The Violence of Borders and Bosses

Writing to Romero in 1871, Sebastián Escobar summed up the most essential impediment to economic development in the Soconusco: "All inhabitants who have capital do not let it circulate, frightened that between one day and the next they will find themselves in the greatest misery."[47] Their fear of misery was based on an ever-present threat of violence. Letter writers blamed that looming violence on two things. Firstly, Romero's local and migrant correspondents pointed to the lack of a border treaty with Guatemala as a constant source of insecurity. Second, migrant planters and federal employees singled out the vengeful nature of Escobar himself as a threat to person and property. In both cases, the specter of violence hobbled investment through its physical destructiveness and its destabilization of incipient commercial and legal institutions. It was not just that a planter feared damage to both his body and his plantation. It was that, were he to experience such violence, it was unclear who might help him seek justice. Without a clear border, no one knew whether the Guatemalan or Mexican legal regime governed the territory they inhabited. And with Escobar asserting that local authority trumped any national government, migrant investors and federal employees feared that impartial justice would not be forthcoming no matter which nation ruled. These insecurities presented significant hurdles to the region's incorporation into expanding global markets and the Mexican nation itself.

Violence was a regularized part of rural life in mid-nineteenth century Mexico. Centers of governance were distant, and law was represented by those with the economic or physical might to claim authority. Challenges to that authority came in many forms. Bandits, raiders, Native American tribes, rival aspirants to power, disgruntled workers, land-hungry capitalists, and foreign nations: all represented potential violent encounters.[48] Mexico, like most Latin American nations, was a country divided by mountains and deserts and jungles. Even when a central government was able to hold power for more than a few years, geography impeded its abilities to implement and enforce new political or economic projects in the provinces. Whether in Guatemala, Argentina, or Colombia, military might was still the primary route to political dominance, but the limited means of provisioning that military meant it had to be used strategically. National governments often left places like the Soconusco to protect themselves, creating a feedback loop in which local politics also enshrined the rule of those who could defend a region.[49] Even with Brazil's strong central monarchy, regional revolts were common and efforts to implement modernizing reforms relied on the buy-in of local elites.[50] The Latin American economy was not entirely stagnant through the first half of the nineteenth century. That said, the constant threat of violence certainly impeded economic recovery and expansion.[51]

THE VIOLENCE OF BORDERS

The undefined border with Guatemala only further compounded this regularized violence. It is no wonder that almost all who wrote to Romero mentioned insecurity as their primary concern. Mexico's internal and external borders were still poorly defined at mid-century. While the Mexican-American War had led to the surveying of the northern border, the country's southern bounds remained unmapped. So, too, did many of the borders between states, leading to conflicts over state sovereignty and occasional regional attempts to either annex or secede from their neighbors.[52]

In the Soconusco, the porous border with Guatemala had long presented both risks and opportunities. For the ranchers and townspeople who composed the majority of Romero's initial correspondents, the undefined frontier had eased the transit of cattle and provided opportunities for both outright contraband and more subtle tax avoidance.[53] When neither of two governments could demonstrate their authority to tax property or commerce, why pay at all? For villagers, the unregulated space provided room to establish new farms and continue age-old patterns of diverse forest cultivation and gathering.[54]

At the same time, the unknowable frontier also meant a persistent threat of invasion from the south. On the diplomatic level, the undefined border invited military claims to territorial sovereignty. On a personal level, the illegibility of legal regimes invited violent seizure of land since no one could undeniably demonstrate clear ownership. Municipal and district authorities constantly wrote to officials in Mexico City asking for more rifles, more soldiers, more anything that might help shore up the border against Guatemalan raiders.[55] While what was labeled raiding was sometimes the result of local rivalries, the threat of invasion from Guatemala was a real one.[56]

By the late 1860s, the shifting political climate in Guatemala led residents of the Soconusco to increasingly focus on the risks rather than the rewards of uncertainty. The new president of Guatemala, Justo Rufino Barrios, laid territorial claims on the Soconusco based on personal as well as diplomatic history. Barrios had grown up in the borderlands of northern Guatemala. As he began to seek national prominence, he used the long history of disputed claims over the Soconusco and Chiapas to rally followers to his side. Once president, this localized claim to territory expanded as Barrios sought to reunify the Central American isthmus under one flag.[57] Barrios and Romero initially exchanged friendly letters and advice, as well as engaging in prolonged negotiations over a property Romero was interested in purchasing from the Guatemalan president's family. Yet as Barrios's aspirations grew, the dream of Central American unity soon interfered with any further collaboration.[58]

As Barrios's ambitions waxed, pleas for help preventing Guatemalan invasion piled up on Romero's desk.[59] Those who wrote made clear that Guatemalans, particularly those supported by Barrios, saw Mexico's lack of attention to the region as an invitation. As Escobar put it bluntly, "The Guatemalans know our weakness, not just because we do not have good weapons, but because they know that Mexico is not ready to take up its responsibility."[60] Guatemala was presented as a competitor for both the region's loyalty and the nation's possible wealth.[61] Politicians from the state government also got into the game, calling upon the national government, which had thus far "suffered the insults and shut up," to care for this poor district that had long been a "theater of spectacular horrors."[62]

THE VIOLENCE OF POLITICAL BOSSES

Barrios and Guatemala were not the only violent impediment to the Soconusco's economic development. Local elites bent on maintaining control of wealth and power in the region also presented a major hurdle to the influx of innovation and investment that Romero envisioned. The district was in no way a reliable, pliable participant in the liberal Mexican project. Local struggles for dominance far outweighed any ideological affinities that might move local actors toward the embrace of uniform national, let alone international, institutions. This was true across the country: the idea of Mexico as a unified nation was still unstable and uncertain in the 1870s. Efforts to impose national incorporation, both political and economic, were not always welcome.[63]

Like many, Escobar had supposed that Benito Juárez's 1867 return to the presidency would assure localized control over governance. As these men understood it, regional autonomy under a loose national umbrella was a vital part of the liberal project.[64] Many were soon disappointed. Once president, Juárez attempted to consolidate a strong central government through the extension of bureaucratic and political institutions. This led many regional strongmen in southern Mexico to refuse to vote for his reelection in 1871. Instead, they favored General Porfirio Díaz, a man they saw as one of their own. Regional strongmen's tactics in support of his election were not always clean. Romero received complaints that Escobar had threatened electors with the "sword of Damocles" unless they cast their ballots for Díaz.[65] While Escobar did not join the violent uprising that followed Díaz's loss, the cacique and many like him again began to express their frustrations with increased assertions of political power from Mexico City on Juárez's death in 1872.

Romero's arrival in the Soconusco later that year was a concrete manifestation of the institutional consolidation that local political bosses like Sebastián Escobar most feared. The minister did not come alone. He also facilitated the entry of numerous federal employees—customs officials, engineers and surveyors, a new federal district judge—who represented the first real nonmilitary efforts to bring the Soconusco under the purview of the national government.[66] Mapmaking, tax collection, and the enforcement of federal law by someone located in town rather than a week away undermined the local oligarchy's ability to manage the social and economic order for their own benefit. Romero also facilitated the immigration of a number of investors from other parts of Mexico and abroad. They, too, reinforced the impression that the development of the Soconusco as an export hub would undermine Escobar's monopoly on economic, political, and social power. While Escobar had initially served as Romero's intermediary and advocate, their friendship disintegrated into hostility and outright violence by 1875. Almost as soon as Romero left the Soconusco, men sponsored by either Escobar or Barrios—or both—burned Romero's coffee plantation to the ground.[67]

The violence was not merely personal. It instead represented the most visible means by which Escobar fought against the new institutions and practices that might facilitate both commercial and political integration of the Soconusco into the Mexican nation. As Chapter Three will illustrate, Escobar's push against those representing a centralizing state was part of a much larger political moment. Debates over centralism versus federalism were on going across Latin America. In the early 1870s, those who fought for federalism came together behind General Porfirio Díaz and, in 1876, installed him as president of Mexico. This triumph seemed to reinforce the hold of strongmen like Escobar over the various institutions through which commerce and politics took place. Through means of both force and negotiation, Escobar and his allies controlled the local courts and municipal councils, monitored local commercial routes, dispatched troops to guard against raids, oversaw the disposition of local labor sources, and served as the source for locally recognized land titles. They were the government in the region, and they had the power to ease or impede access to all those resources, both material and transactional, that they controlled. Romero and his allies in Mexico City tried to use legislative reforms to lower transaction costs and standardize the types of interactions that now took place via Escobar or someone like him. If strongmen like Escobar chose not to participate in such reforms, they could become a serious impediment to change. If they chose to respond to such reforms with violence, they could stop change in its tracks.

Instability and unpredictability were the root problems with politics for those seeking to rebuild Mexico's economy. Planters and villagers in the Soconusco had no means of knowing what would come next. The illegibility of the border with Guatemala was an exaggerated manifestation of the general illegibility of the Mexican landscape and the violence that it engendered. Escobar was a particularly nasty manifestation of a usually less vicious problem with ever-changing hierarchies and political institutions. His intractability and outright violence in the face of the proposed implementation of new national policies mirrored more generalized recalcitrance to hand over the management of regional affairs to those in Mexico City. Without the clarification of borders and boundaries, without the cooperation of local elites and regional strongmen, the project of turning the Mexican countryside into a bountiful supplier of global markets would never find its feet.

The Insecurity of Informal and Absent Institutions

Violence and instability caused by internecine and international conflicts were the most frequently voiced complaints of those who wrote to Matías Romero from the Soconusco. Guatemalan raiders killed laborers and villagers who found themselves in the way. Escobar and his followers murdered those who sought to undermine his dominance and drove others into exile. The regular use of violence by so many was not simply an impediment to economic life, but also to life itself.

Yet violence and physical insecurity were by no means the only matters that the ranchers, merchants, and newly made finqueros brought up in their letters to Romero. Violence was highly visible, but less immediately apparent hurdles also stood in the way of new economic activity. Insecure property rights, scarce labor, an absence of credit and commercial agents, and the physical terrain of the place itself stood in the way of these men making good on the new opportunities they saw. Historians and political scientists have long argued over how and to what degree institutional and environmental impediments shaped Latin America's economic activity in the postcolonial era.[68] In their correspondence with Romero, would-be export planters in Mexico's periphery articulated their own versions of arguments about colonial inheritances and factor endowments. They also proposed solutions and attempted work-arounds, illuminating how those on the ground imagined addressing the same problems that distant politicians had been attempting to address for years. With more direct experience with the hurdles that stood between them and prosperity, local producers well understood that despite the breathless excitement of modernizing elites, the process of turning Latin America's natural bounty into real wealth was in no way a foregone conclusion.

In the nation's capital, legislators and bureaucrats had already done copious work to facilitate new economic endeavors. Since the 1850s, politicians both liberal and conservative had revised Mexico's formal commercial and legal apparatus to reduce barriers to trade, open up markets to competition, and enshrine and protect contract law.[69] While there were still improvements to be made, Romero assumed that these legislative fixes had already addressed many of the challenges laid out by his correspondents. He was soon to learn that writing a law and implementing it were two entirely different matters. It was not simply that Escobar or those like him opposed reforms with violence and intransigence. It was that entire landscapes—geographic, institutional, social—had to be overcome, remade, or worked around in order to facilitate economic integration.

The lack of reliable contracts, legal systems, and infrastructure was a problem no matter the type of economic activity at hand. Investment in export agriculture, though, compounded the difficulties institutional insecurity posed. Cultivation for foreign markets required the long-term working of land on a scale large enough to merit inclusion in shipping routes supplying consumers an ocean away. It was inherently different from the old cattle ranches, subsistence farms, and forest foraging that constituted the Soconusco's economic activity in the 1860s. Starting from the ground up, this next section will enumerate those less immediate but just as intractable problems to which Romero bore witness.

AN UNBOUNDED LANDSCAPE

The physical landscape of the Soconusco resisted incorporation into global markets. Topographically isolated, heavily forested, and difficult to traverse, the district's makeup challenged the progress of surveyors and transportation experts alike. To this point local ranchers had gotten around these issues by investing in mobile assets—cattle—rather than the land itself. Villagers who worked forest groves in the foothills relied on the overabundance of land and the disinterest of elites to secure their own investments. As both parties turned to export agriculture, these solutions no longer served. Coffee and other perennial export crops required years to mature. This meant that investors needed to know that their land was, in fact, theirs to invest in and could not be easily seized when cultivars finally started producing.

The Soconusco was distant from everything. Mountains blockaded its eastern approach. Mangrove swamps bogged down its northern frontier. A flat expanse of beach with no natural port to welcome ships bounded it to the west. While the region's sloping volcanic hillsides and prodigious rains meant fertile soils and easy irrigation, they also facilitated natural disasters. One of the first extended correspondences Romero had with anyone in the Soconusco was about aid for towns wiped out by flooding and mudslides.[70] Covered in dense forest, the result of age-old agricultural practices that focused on interplanting rather than clear-cutting, the Sierra Madre would require considerable ecological transformation before it would produce new export crops.

This hilly landscape also resisted easy division into recognizable and defensible properties. The ruling families of the Soconusco could demonstrate ownership of some 72,000 hectares of land by 1880, less than 15 percent of the district's total territory. Most of it lay in the flat coastal plains.[71] That land was perfect for ranching and new experiments with rubber and sugar cane, even bananas, but it would not suit for coffee. Increased interest in this temperamental crop, which required ample shade, water, and suitable elevations to best grow, meant that ranchers turned planters had to shift their focus to the foothills.

Yet there were no properties to buy in the Sierra Madre, no easy way to simply purchase land to turn into a plantation. The few municipalities that existed in the foothills were either tiny remnants of pre-Hispanic villages or recently reestablished communities of migrants from Tapachula and Guatemala. Their residents mostly owned their lands collectively, through the ejido system of municipal management of shared resources and inherited usufruct.[72] They had neither desire nor ability to sell the lands they worked. Those seeking new properties in the Sierra rarely found it worthwhile to bargain with or oust these small communities when the expanses of unclaimed sierra were so vast.

This was the case across the Mexican and much of the Latin American countryside. While some regions had a much higher population density than the Soconusco, most of the territory belonged to the nation as public lands. Labeled as *terrenos baldíos* or *tierras baldías*, these public lands were uncultivated, unclaimed, and often only sparsely populated. Their exact quantity was also unknowable because, in truth, the quantity of private lands was also unknown. As was the case in the Soconusco, it was the rare instance when either communities or private property owners had precise surveys of the lands they claimed as their own. Because of the vagueness of titles granted by the Spanish Crown, property boundaries were usually defined by practice rather than by any scientific or legal process.[73]

Recognizing both this problem and the potential represented by all that empty land, national governments had been working to facilitate the alienation of lands since the 1850s. Epitomized by the Ley Lerdo of 1856, the push to ease privatization of public and communally held lands had proceeded under both liberal and conservative regimes. Yet as with so much policy, these efforts rarely reached the rural areas where they were most needed. When Romero began the process of acquiring property in the Soconusco, he assumed policy had become practice. "I suppose that in the district the law of July 22, 1863 is still in use with regards to the acquisition of terrenos baldíos," the minister wrote to Escobar, his intermediary in the matter.[74] Romero had already lost considerable capital to a previous partner who, despite assurances to the contrary, never secured title to the lands he worked.⁷⁵ The minister was determined that such errors not be repeated with this new investment.

Escobar quickly pointed out that such errors were almost unavoidable. The law to which Romero referred required the mediation of a federal district judge and official engineers to conduct the surveying. When Romero penned his request in 1871, said judge was located in the state capital, a seven-day journey from the Soconusco. So too were the required engineers. The surveying and paperwork required by the 1863 regulations involved multiple trips back and forth between the state capital and the desired property, followed by further bureaucratic wrangling with the Department of Fomento in Mexico City. To drive his point home, Escobar wrote, "The delay suffered in the titling process at the District Court is such that my claim . . . has been in that office for more than a year, to the effect, Mr. Romero, that I have already raised 100 steers on it without being able to substantiate my title."⁷⁶

If Escobar, the most well-connected man in the district, could not acquire title for his lands, no one stood a chance of navigating the convoluted system instituted by the national government. Romero worked to ease the process by pushing for a federal district court for the Soconusco, but the judge would not arrive for another few years.⁷⁷ When he finally did, it was only in time to be run out of town by an anti-government mob who stormed his court room.

In the meantime, locals muddled along with their own unofficial means of defending their land claims. Villagers, for the most part, relied on the continued recognition of their communal claims via the ejido, despite national policies that called for its dissolution. Ranchers, hacendados, and would-be coffee planters fell back on the age-old belief that to work a piece of land was to stake a claim to it. Some, like Escobar and a few of the foreigners who arrived in the 1870s, filed for legal title through the federal government. Few managed to complete the process.⁷⁸ Others, like the planter Romero initially partnered with or the Humphreys who opened this book, simply crossed their fingers. One of Escobar's close allies, capitalizing on the increased desire for defensible claims, drew up more than fifty property maps and attendant titles, all without any legal standing or registration, to provide a semblance of formal ownership to those who would pay him. Many of these almost-properties were later purchased and sold in the local market or eventually resurveyed and sold through officially sanctioned means.⁷⁹

When writing to Romero, most letter writers focused on the Soconusco's fecundity and untapped riches. They described the difficulties of land tenure in less explicit terms than they used to describe the violence that wracked the region. Yet, especially as Romero began to ask for more particulars about the business of planting and harvesting, it became clear that the scarcity of legally titled properties was a major impediment to economic expansion. While fertile unoccupied land was abundant in the district, the irregular, heavily forested landscape was not easily turned into productive property. The delays in purchasing title from the national government and the promulgation of legally questionable local titles only served to compound the investment risks inherent in a zone without a clearly demarcated national border. The mobility of cattle had undercut some of these concerns. Coffee and other export crops were a different matter. New types of agriculture made outright, demonstrable, defensible ownership of land a necessity if a planter was to be sure of his investment.

AN UNINTERESTED LABOR FORCE

The lush forests that spoke to the potential fruitfulness of the territory also impeded the tilling and cultivation of the soil. Before any value could be extracted from the sierra's rich loam, someone had to clear the land. The inter-cropping and forest agriculture practiced by villagers going back to the pre-Hispanic era were unattractive to planters looking to produce on a commercial scale. It also meant that those villagers were mostly uninterested in doing the work new planters needed. Aspiring finqueros wanted regimented rows of crops, modern plantations managed scientifically to maximize production. The Soconusco's villagers had no interest in helping them achieve that dream.

"Prosperity will have no place unless we first protect emigration in order that there are sufficient laborers," wrote one local promoter.[80] It was clear to everyone that the Soconusco lacked the needed workforce for export agriculture. The population hovered around 18,000 in the 1870s. This represented substantial growth since the lows of the colonial era but placed population density at only three people per square kilometer.[81] Given the lax practices around property law, there were few pressures on villagers to turn to wage labor. Why work for someone else when you could instead engage in a bit of market agriculture by expanding your family's holdings or strike out into the sierra on your own? The municipal council of Tapachula had expanded the land held as ejido in the 1840s and again in the coming decades. The villagers who refounded the town of Cacahoatán used knowledge gained in that earlier moment to claim their own communal holdings.[82] When complaining about incursions from Guatemala, planters in the region pointed to the slow creep of new farms and villages infringing on Mexican territory as well as violent raids by military bands.[83] Those who might have formed a labor force were already laboring for themselves.

As with the absence of a reliable property regime, the absence of a system for securing labor was the result of decades of focusing on ranching rather than commercial agriculture. Ranching required few workers. Employers jealously guarded those few individuals who were drawn into wage labor.

While their engagement with state and federal law was selective, local elites did make use of legislative reforms passed over the previous decades that legally bound workers ever more tightly.[84] Extensions of credit enforced through courts and the coercive might of a tight-knit elite kept laborers bound to their employers. When runaway workers were caught, hacendados used the municipal court to add jail time to runaways' punishments, then added the costs of their recapture to their outstanding debts.[85] The scarcity was so severe that local hacendados went so far as to steal, coerce, and trick laborers away from their current employment, facing the municipal judge themselves when the rightful employer discovered the ruse.[86] Mid-century liberal reform had ostensibly done away with this type of debt peonage as it sought to protect individual rights. Yet, in practice, employers across southern Mexico had put contract law to use in formalizing older customary relationships.

This already strained labor system had no capacity to stretch to meet the needs of the plantations Romero and his correspondents imagined. As was the case across Latin America, the expansion of export agriculture brought with it a renegotiation of the terms of employment as laborers found themselves in increasing demand. Debt peonage diversified, with factors including demography and seasonality leading to, as Guatemalan historian Julie Gibbings has put it, "a sliding scale of coercion and consent."[87] While some elites were able to deploy land reform and contract law to alienate villagers from their lands and secure them as indebted laborers, other elites found potential workers well situated to make their own demands on potential employers.[88]

In the Soconusco, newly arrived aspiring planters found the existing labor system both inaccessible and uneconomical. Whether from Guatemala, Guanajuato, or Germany, these men were outside the webs of sociability that facilitated access to what village labor there was. They also disdained its up-front costs and unreliable outcomes. In Romero's 1874 manual for coffee planters in coastal Chiapas, written while resident in Tapachula, he lamented the inevitability of overpaid, underproductive workers. All workers, he wrote, owed their employer a debt. In a region where daily wages ranged from thirty-five to fifty cents, this debt was never less than twenty pesos and often exceeded one hundred. Not only were there not enough hours in the work day to make repayment feasible, but workers were always requesting additional small loans.[89]

Planters tried to work around this system. The promotion of emigration by the letter writer who opened this section was not singular. Before he broke ties with Romero, Escobar insisted that migration was necessary because "I fear, the scarcity of labor will continue to be the largest difficulty that bars our expansion of the multitude of pursuits that might enrich us."[90] An American interested in pursuing investment in the Soconusco suggested the importation of Chinese workers, though he admitted that racial tensions and legal barriers might impede that route.[91] The governor of Chiapas himself admitted the difficulty of securing adequate labor. When Romero suggested that he might make good use of the highland villagers of Chamula who had recently begun a so-called caste war by sending them south to work in the coffee fields, the governor demurred. He thought the plan too expensive and suggested instead the hiring of prisoners from the state. If that did not work, he recommended an extension of the debt system at work in central Chiapas. Planters in the Soconusco might advance substantial sums to highland village leaders to facilitate recruitment. Neither of these methods appealed to Romero as any more reliable or effective than local debt peonage.[92]

In addition, workers rarely found it worth their while to remain on a plantation through the entirety of the season. If planters refused to acquiesce to their demands for additional cash advances, laborers simply left. The porous frontier and the sierra presented plenty of opportunities to disappear if plantation labor no longer appealed. Their work was in demand not only in the Soconusco but also across the border in Guatemala.[93] Finca workers also seemed to recognize they had little to fear from the local justice system. Run by Escobar's family and friends, the local courts had little interest in assisting newly arrived planters with the pursuit or punishment of their runaway workers.[94] The threat of violence also led many workers to leave plantations. Guatemalan raiders kidnapped laborers and burned their subsistence plots and small farms to the ground.[95] The best wages in the state could not overcome either the danger of plantation life or the appeal of autonomy. The local population remained too small and the expanses of land accessible for subsistence and market agriculture too large for even well-paid wage labor to secure a reliable work force for new export plantations.

AN UNDERFINANCED COMMERCIAL NETWORK

In truth, planters also lacked both the currency and the access to credit to pay what laborers demanded. They lacked access to any of the commercial tools that would facilitate the circulation of capital and commodities. The amount of cash in circulation was small, the number of individuals with funds to lend miniscule. There were no banks. Nor were there any commercial houses. What passed for a port was just a stretch of beach, and ships rarely laid anchor as there was little to transport. No matter the fecundity of the landscape, if there was neither money nor transport to get goods to market, there was no point in growing anything. One planter explicitly requested that Romero find a few "capitalists" to settle in Tapachula, advance funds to aspiring planters, and sell their crops abroad.[96] The region needed money, the individuals who made it move, and the legal means to make them reliable. As Minister of Finance, Romero could address some of these issues through legislation. As with other liberal projects that he invoked, political and personal intervention at the national level could only go so far.

The Soconusco's existing economy did not contain the necessary elements to support export agriculture in 1870. The international networks of trade and barter that had facilitated the region's vibrant precolonial and colonial cacao economy were long gone. For the past decades, it had instead functioned on a mix of legitimate commerce and contraband. Neither fattening cattle nor smuggling required the kinds of up-front investments or long-distance trade networks that would facilitate export agriculture. Coffee, rubber, and other perennials required multiple years of tending before they would produce anything worth selling. Even faster growing crops like bananas, sugar, vanilla, and cotton necessitated up-front capital investments in tools, machinery, land, and labor that would not be recouped for at least a year. In either case, the local market was not large enough to absorb expanding harvests. Commerce, as Escobar wrote to Romero, was so limited that villagers and laborers planted sparingly because there was neither a local consumer base nor any commercial house to facilitate export.[97] New producers needed access to foreign markets.

Villagers who grew small amounts of market goods got around these investments by keeping their production limited and diversified. They focused their attention on subsistence goods that would maintain their families through the year. They sold crops like coffee, cacao, and bananas at local markets to serve as supplementary income. Smallholders also had access to traditional borrowing and lending between family and neighbors. These small extensions of credit, whether in cash or in kind, allowed for the purchase of a new mule, the building of a new fence, experimentation with a new cultivar, or the temporary hiring of an extra set of hands. Mostly informal, these agreements were upheld by the social bonds of small towns rather than courts and contracts.[98]

Ranchers who wanted to become planters and outsiders who arrived in the region looking to invest needed more than these informal arrangements. A few local elites like Escobar had enough cash, land, and connections in hand to risk growing a new crop that would take four to five years to provide returns on investment. Across Mexico, ranchers and hacendados like these had kept the economy moving gradually forward in the first half of the nineteenth century. They experimented with crops like silk, sugar, and wine grapes and renovated commercial connections to Europe lost when the new country cut ties with Spain at independence.[99] With their capital mostly tied up in land, this old elite did not represent a ready source of capital for those looking to accelerate growth or initiate new economic endeavors. While they might facilitate the export of some local products, their commercial networks and the transportation systems that supported them were still miniscule.

Unlike many of the other challenges facing the Mexican countryside, transportation was something that Romero could directly address. The Ministry of Finance oversaw commerce and was charged with easing its circulation. In the liberal political parlance of the day, unencumbered trade was seen as a means for improving the lot of the nation and its people. In service of this aim, the Mexican government subsidized railroad building and opened ports across the country to national and international trade. Romero attempted to do the same for the Soconusco. While his project for a railroad and a pier for the port never came to fruition, he did manage to find a way of linking the Soconusco to world markets by ship.[100] After a much delayed process of surveying the shoreline and despite recognition that it left much to be desired, Romero and his engineers determined that the best option was a relatively flat beachfront at San Benito.[101] For once, the national Congress acted quickly to authorize first national and then international trade from the port.[102]

Despite plaudits from local and state-level officials, the authorization of the port did little unless a shipping company could be convinced to stop offshore. In 1871, a year ahead of his move south, Romero again exercised his position as Minister of Finance to secure a regular shipping schedule for San Benito. He also worked to ease the reexport of Guatemalan goods so that the ships that passed would have something to transport while the Soconusco's economy got up and running.[103] Local promoters further connected the two efforts to national security, asserting that trade from San Benito was a means of crushing Guatemalan commerce and securing the Soconusco for Mexico.[104] By 1872, thanks to a little presidential cajoling, the Panama Railroad Company had agreed to stop its ships twice monthly off the coast at San Benito.[105] All predicted that this regular shipping schedule would help fulfill the promise of the Soconusco's, and Mexico's, natural bounty.[106]

Still, though, the local economy was not capable of producing enough goods to make the regularized access to shipping meaningful. The further expansion of production was hobbled by a lack of ready money and commercial agents to move it around. Like the nation itself, most potential entrepreneurs needed additional capital if they were to expand production. Mexico as a whole tried to overcome this hurdle through the renegotiation of its national debt.[107] The sluggishness of this process in turn made individual and institutional investors less inclined to invest in the country. Across Latin America, weak or absent credit institutions, whether formal or informal, hobbled the expansion of new kinds of enterprises. The Catholic Church had long been the primary provisioner of credit, but liberal reformers had seized many of its assets and curtailed its ability to lend. While new commercial codes purported to incentivize private lenders, regulations on banking meant that formal credit institutions remained sparse.[108]

Here, again, Romero tried to step in and facilitate the circulation of both credit and goods. Recognizing that legislation would not act quickly enough to secure the needed funds, the minister leveraged his own connections to access credit and markets abroad. In 1873, he signed an agreement with Nottebohm and Company, a large commercial house in Hamburg well known for its investments in coffee, to advance US$25,000 in funds. He soon signed additional contracts with firms in New York and London. All obliged him to repay much of the loan with bills of lading for coffee shipped out from the Soconusco.[109]

Now living in Tapachula, Romero invested these funds in a number of nascent coffee fincas owned by locals. In doing so, he began to see why his investment ventures remained lonely ones. The district had no import-export merchants to facilitate trade or establish norms around contracts for the future delivery of goods. While both liberal and conservative governments had instituted new civil and commercial codes across the past decades, their proliferation and enforcement remained limited. Because there had been little demand for them, the Soconusco still lacked any regularized means of either registering or enforcing legal contracts. Without a public records office, Romero turned to the court to formalize his agreements.[110]

The efficacy of this local institution would soon prove wanting. In part, this was Romero's own fault. The contracts he drew up were quite optimistic and carried few guarantees. By the spring of 1875, it was clear that the planters he had contracted with could not deliver the coffee they had promised.[111] In turn, Romero also failed to meet his obligations to the foreign commercial houses from which he had borrowed.[112] Where these commercial houses had the backing of formalized contracts drawn up by experienced lawyers, Romero had to rely on shoddily written agreements filed with a local magistrate ever less inclined to assist the interloper.[113] The commercial institutions of the Soconusco were weak and personalistic. Increasingly alienated from a region he had so tried to help, Romero admitted defeat in the face of local planters who earnestly wished to repay him but still lacked the means to do so.

Despite Romero's failures, migrant planters in the Soconusco continued to call for assistance in securing capital for the region. With regard to both the plantations he owned and the region as a whole, letter writers insisted that everything could be put aright with a bit more investment.[114] Adventurous entrepreneurs took up this call by investing their own small amounts of capital in the region. Advertising the possibilities for success in the Soconusco even as his own affairs began to collapse, Romero reported in 1874 that thirty-six finqueros from the Soconusco, Guadalajara, Guatemala, Spain, England, and the United States had almost 9,000 cuerdas—enough for more than 300,000 coffee bushes—of land either planted or prepared for coffee.[115] Included in that number were both eager new arrivals and increasingly disgruntled and hostile locals like Escobar. While the number projected promise, the reality that Romero and his fellow migrants faced was far less sunny. The region as a whole held great promise, as journalists and politicians and planters reiterated again and again. Yet despite legislative efforts to revive borrowing and commercial linkages, both the legal institutions and the commercial actors who might make use of them remained scarce.

"It will not be soon, but there will come an epoch when the whole world will fix its gaze on Chiapas, virgin land . . . where all the plants of Europe and Africa can be grown without great effort . . . where man lives with all manner of guarantees."[116] This was the promise of the Soconusco, of Mexico, of Latin America, here described by one of Matías Romero's partners in an early coffee finca. This overwhelming potential just waiting to be tapped filled entrepreneurs across the region with hope for prosperity and peace. Yet, as this letter writer implied, there was much that stood in the way of growth.

The Soconusco, once the principal source of cacao for the Mexica and Spanish empires, had become a peripheral backwater by the mid-nineteenth century. Like so much of the Latin American countryside, it was wracked by violence and insecurity. The murky border with Guatemala served as an invitation to raiders. Factions of the local oligarchy fought over the meager profits of ranching and contraband. Neither of these economic enterprises required the types of infrastructure or institutions that export agriculture necessitated. The region's rich soils, so long the driver of market engagement and relative prosperity for its pre-Colombian inhabitants, remained alluring. Yet myriad hurdles stood in the way of renewed involvement in global commodity flows.

The desire to overcome those hurdles, though, was growing among those in a position to invest. Cognizant of the swelling fortunes of their neighbors to the south and the increased demand for tropical products abroad, local planters and emigrant entrepreneurs sought to turn this backwater into a hub of global commerce. With Minister of Finance Matías Romero as their interlocutor and advocate, ranchers and planters pushed for interventions that would ease their access to global markets and global capital. They sought solutions to the violence, political and institutional absence and corruption, tenuous land tenure, scarce labor, and scarcer capital that kept them from fulfilling the promise the lush landscape represented. As Romero and other outside investors joined their endeavors, local elites realized that this economic reorientation would undermine their control of the Soconusco. Those who had been early advocates for state assistance and international investment soon themselves became obstacles to change.

Alongside aspiring plantation owners, villagers long engaged in small amounts of market production capitalized on slowly improving commercial flows to send their own products further and further afield. Both asset and impediment to an imagined future of export-led growth, villagers refused to cede their land or their labor capacity. They moved further into the foothills of the Sierra Madre, planting new crops as they went. They took up residence, either full-time or seasonal, on lands nominally claimed by new investors. Some few of these small-time farmers periodically worked for wages as planters cleared the forest and started to plant coffee. Most expressed little interest in laboring for anyone but themselves. With land so plentiful and demand for cash crops, whether staples or specialty export products, growing, small producers and family farmers had little incentive to give up the mixed agriculture that had long provided for them.

This chapter has presented a deep history of the Soconusco and its inhabitants through the early 1870s. In doing so, it has demonstrated both the possibilities and the impediments to export agriculture that so captivated the attention of local, national, and international actors. The Soconusco contained both the potential and the obstacles to development that marked much of rural Latin America at this moment, allowing both those investing in the 1870s and historians today to use it to better understand the contentious and gradual process by which frontiers of production slowly turned toward global markets. With its mix of ambitious and distrustful local elites, entrepreneurial and intractable villagers, interfering representatives of reformist states, and intrigued but hesitant outside investors, the Soconusco shifted warily on the brink of economic transformation. The following chapters will examine how all these actors reinforced, transformed, and sometimes circumvented the barriers that impeded incorporation into global markets. In concert and in conflict, these actors would soon remake the Soconusco.

2 Fixing the Border

October of 1878 saw another group of villagers driven from their homes in fear. Julio and Esteban Pérez were among those who fled as a band of Guatemalan soldiers laid claim to the small parcels of farmland they called home. In search of refuge, they hid on the coffee fincas where they occasionally worked as hired hands. Juan and Tomás Pérez were less lucky. Unable to outrun the raiders, they were kidnapped and kept captive for six days and six nights. When they finally escaped, Juan and Tomás also took refuge on nearby fincas. Julio's unnamed wife was less lucky still. Left behind in care of their home, the nameless pregnant woman was "maltreated" by the soldiers and miscarried not long after.[1]

Rather than the frightened villagers, it was their employers who brought the matter to official attention. All of these men—Pérezes and finqueros—were relative newcomers to the Soconusco. All had established their fincas and farms within the last five years. The Pérezes had come from Guatemala, the finqueros from Spain and the United States. All had begun working the land without substantiated legal claims to the properties they sowed with coffee, corn, and beans. All had further risked their fortunes by planting in land not definitively Mexican. Now all stood together in front of a Mexican court asking for assistance in reclaiming the Pérezes' farms and defending their small and large undertakings against further Guatemalan attack. If Guatemalan soldiers could invade the workers' smallholdings and claim rightful ownership through a Guatemalan land grant, there was little to say that nearby coffee fincas were safe from seizure.

In the coming years, news of this case wound its way from local courts to the halls of the United States Senate. Local tragedies like the Pérezes' shaped diplomatic rhetoric and, eventually, the border treaty between Mexico and Guatemala signed in 1882. This chapter draws on those stories to explore how international debates over sovereignty drew on and helped quell local experiences of violence and instability. In an age when authorities increasingly recognized the importance of knowledge for governance, the absence of clear territorial bounds countered Mexico's narrative of itself as a modern nation. Planters in the Soconusco also wanted territorial fixity. The absence of a definitive national border made aspiring finqueros wary of long-term investments in land they could not definitively claim as their own. Yet, at the same time, the porous border provided planters access to experienced workers from Guatemala. Villagers, too, capitalized on the possibility of free movement across an ill-defined borderland to set up new farms and supplement subsistence with wage work.[2] In its implementation if not its language, the border treaty between Guatemala and Mexico allowed for this combination of fixity and mobility. While international aspirations spurred confrontation between national governments, local experiences and knowledge of the border formed the basis for negotiating its settlement. With national aims satisfied by diplomatic triumph, the actual enactment of the newly defined border was left in the hands of those who lived there.

Détente on the Front Lines of Nation Formation

Violence in the Guatemala-Mexico frontier was nothing new. As the previous chapter established, it was driven by a border that was not simply insecure, but also unknown. This unknowability represented both a real and an ideological threat to the stability of each nation. Yet for the first half century after independence, internal turmoil on either side of the frontier meant that little was done to settle the dividing line. While progress was made toward increasing territorial knowledge elsewhere, the border between Mexico and Guatemala was left mostly alone. Even as those who lived in this region pled for help in defending themselves and their properties, politics made intervention less than urgent for the governments in power.

For most of the nineteenth century, politicians on both sides ignored the southern border. Aside from Mexican general and president Antonio López de Santa Anna's southern campaign in 1842, only a few feeble attempts were made at diplomatic negotiation.[3] Neither local actors nor national ones did much to advance the question beyond the occasional raid or rallying cry.[4] The meager population of the area and the economic focus on cattle rather than the fruits of the soil meant that an amorphous and porous border remained unproblematic. Indigenous villagers claimed neither nationality. They moved throughout the borderlands, tapping into the resources of different ecosystems in different seasons and returning to homes in the highlands of who-cared-what country as the harvest dictated. As often as not, local enmities rather than international disputes drove raiders to wreak destruction on their neighbors.

Questionable territorial integrity was not limited to the southern border. Mexico as a whole was still an amorphous entity in the 1860s. While the Mexican-American War had resulted in the scientific surveying of the northern border in the 1850s, the majority of Mexico's cartography relied on the accumulation of disparate and spotty information from local and historical sources.[5] As one of the country's most famous geographers wrote, the work of the era was that of "compilation and not of creation."[6] Naming practices were inconsistent, coastlines were best guesses, large sections of the country were projections of prior cartographers' hopes and fears.

This was unacceptable in an era when territorial coherence and fixed boundaries were increasingly important to the definition of the modern nation-state.[7] Nations asserted ideas of both national citizenship and territorial integrity that relied on defining lines between "us" and "them." In Europe, emphasis on definite national identities helped countries like France and Spain construct and defend their territorial boundaries. In the Americas, the newness of nations required that solid, stable borders emerge in tandem with or even precede the construction of distinctive national cultures.[8] There was neither a space nor a people that was inherently Mexican at mid-century. Such an entity had to be created, asserted, and enshrined.[9] While what defined the Mexican people as opposed to the Guatemalan was not yet clear, it was hoped that the physical extent of each country could be more easily delineated.

The first step toward this end was the creation of a general map of the Mexican nation. Drawn up in the wake of the Mexican-American War, Antonio García Cubas's 1858 map of Mexico created the first seemingly modern and complete illustration of the country's territory.[10] Yet the scale of the map was too small to be of use when it came to either military defense or future development.[11] While the 1858 map was beautiful and gained great praise, it was still murky around the edges. Both between states and along the southern frontier, the prior cartography on which García Cubas relied lacked the specificity demanded by modern science. The map defined and asserted Mexico as a nation, but there was much work to be done before those cartographic claims could stand up to diplomatic or legal challenges.

The letter writers introduced in the previous chapter effectively tapped into this national insecurity with each exhortation to shore up the southern frontier. The harm caused by raiding parties garnered the most attention, but there was more at stake in Mexico's inability to define its bounds. Locals did not solely fear armed raiders, though the local jefe político, Sebastián Escobar, continually pled for additional guns to fight them off. As worrisome were resourceful villagers like the Pérezes who used the lack of legal clarity at the frontier to carve out spaces for new farms. These new residents, many of Guatemalan descent, in turn facilitated the incursion of Guatemalan officials interested in capitalizing on potential tax incomes.[12] Together, the violence of raiders, the slow encroachment of farmers, and the revenues lost to tax collectors brought home the damage caused by Mexico's failure to define its southern bounds. Ideological uncertainties about the definition of the Mexican nation-state here found everyday expression in the trials of border residents.

That coincidence of interest, though, did not yet lead to action. In the 1860s and 1870s, Mexican President Benito Juárez and his successor Sebastián Lerdo de Tejada were busy enough trying to simply hold the nation together. They supported the rise and early presidency of the liberal Justo Rufino Barrios in Guatemala, seeing him as an ideological ally rather than a competitor for regional dominance. Barrios, who had grown up in the borderlands, used the region as the base for his fight against Guatemala's conservative leadership.[13] His rebellion spurred a spate of letters to Matías Romero concerning increased violence and threats to the region's incipient prosperity.[14] Yet no one in Mexico City or Guatemala City saw need to exacerbate a relatively peaceful détente with the reopening of territorial disputes.[15] These new governments aspired to modernity and embraced the international turn to more state knowledge. For now, though, the border between them would remain an exception to that project.

The work of surveying and knowledge gathering did continue elsewhere. García Cubas and others at the Mexican Society of Geography and Statistics (*Sociedad Mexicana de Geografía y Estadística*) and the rapidly expanding Department of Fomento, or Development, directed their attention toward important cities and nascent infrastructure projects.[16] In some states, including Chiapas, work began on the process of surveying and subdividing communal properties held in usufruct by municipalities.[17] The governments of both Mexico and Guatemala eased the process by which individuals could title public lands, and surveyors there too began plying their trade. In the Soconusco, surveyors sent by Romero searched for the best possible port for the Soconusco and began laying out plans for highways to connect the region to the rest of Chiapas and Mexico.[18] These men also sent Romero reports on local cultivars and potential sites for agricultural investment.[19] For the moment, the gathering of internal knowledge won out over the investigation of contested borders.

Détente Decays

The 1870s saw a shift away from amicable ignorance. Those in the Soconusco who had written to the Mexican government in hope of intervention finally saw returns on their letters. Yet it was not the lost lives, property, or economic potential of which they complained that pushed their leaders to action. Rather, the point of debating the Soconusco's nationality was diplomatic sway and regional predominance. The presidents of both Mexico and Guatemala felt confident enough in their positions within their respective countries to turn their political aspirations outward. While neither was in any way omnipotent and both countries continued to experience internal turmoil, each leader now looked to his country's international standing. The Soconusco became a site to build that reputation.

Initially, Justo Rufino Barrios appeared willing to negotiate. When he first came to power, Mexico's army was larger and better funded than Guatemala's, its diplomatic credentials better burnished, though barely. As yet unwilling to risk everything, the Guatemalan president first sought a friendly diplomatic solution to the border issue. Matías Romero's move to the region provided a ready means to pursue this route. Even before his arrival in the Soconusco, Romero had become interested in purchasing lands owned by the Barrios family. Through the intermediation of jefe político Sebastián Escobar, Romero and Barrios attempted to come to an accord.[20] This deal fell through, but hopeful of an eventual agreement, Romero began the process of purchasing public lands near the Barrios holdings with the idea of one day annexing that plantation.[21] This placed Romero's holding on tenuous legal ground, as the property he claimed was within the zone of contention between the two countries.

For a while, this was unproblematic. Barrios and Romero kept up a correspondence about the mechanics of coffee planting, with Barrios providing much needed advice to the novice finquero. When Romero complained of villagers settling on his newly claimed lands, Barrios explained to the minister that he should in fact encourage them to stay as they might form the basis of his workforce. As Romero later wrote, it seemed likely that so long as no one provoked them to violence, the indigenous villagers occupying his lands were docile and productive.[22]

This seeming agreement as to the potential usefulness of resident villagers soon bore unfortunate diplomatic fruit. Likely on Romero's encouragement, authorities from Chiapas included a number of such villages in a tax census in the early 1870s. Guatemalan borderland residents responded by taking up arms to combat what was seen as a bureaucratic invasion of sovereign territory. While the Mexican census takers fell back, Romero resisted retreat. He blamed Barrios for both the initial settlements and the armed response. Quite riled up, he wrote to the Mexican Minister of War asking for a deployment of troops to defend the nation. Barrios, still not sure of his own military's capabilities, quickly tried to calm the situation. He invited Romero to meet him at his plantation in the borderlands. There the two hashed out an unofficial preliminary agreement regarding the frontier that left Chiapas and the Soconusco in Mexico's hands.[23]

This temporary return to amicable relations did not last long. Romero never quite trusted Barrios again after the census debacle. By 1874, this distrust had become quite public. He and his deputy representative to the legislature both made the case in Congress that Barrios was uncooperative when it came to the amicable negotiation of the border.[24] When Romero returned to Mexico City in 1875, it was to the news that the Guatemalan president had filed an official complaint against him for endangering good relations between the two countries.[25] Adding injury to insult, a group of Guatemalan villagers invaded Romero's fincas immediately upon his departure.[26] They destroyed buildings and coffee bushes and kidnapped workers.[27]

Matters only escalated from there. Barrios issued an arrest warrant for the minister based on false accusations of cross-border raiding.[28] Romero responded with two years of weekly columns detailing the early history of the border, all designed to undermine Barrios's claims to Chiapas. Here he brought to bear all of the stories he had heard and the violence he had witnessed during his years in the Soconusco.[29] Further personalizing the issue, Romero published an almost 400-page-long refutation of Barrios's accusations under the auspices of the Ministry of Foreign Relations in mid-1876. Lauding his own efforts to improve the Soconusco and bludgeoning the Guatemalan president with official documents and private correspondence, Romero made quite clear to the Mexican public that the confusion and lack of security at the southern border represented a real threat to Mexico's honor and territorial integrity.[30]

Romero soon found an ally in the new president of Mexico, Porfirio Díaz. When Romero returned to Mexico City in 1875, Díaz's Tuxtepec Rebellion was quickly gaining steam. The many-time candidate for president now rose to power on the back of local frustrations with an ever more centralized state, frustrations that will be further explored in the following chapter. For the new president, the problems of the Soconusco as described by Romero represented the problems of his early years in power: the cohesion and stability of Mexico itself. Díaz, like his predecessors, was working to build a prosperous country that could play on the international stage. Unlike his predecessors, Díaz had the benefit of a few more years of economic growth and relative national stability to undergird his ambitions. While the apparatus of governance was still spread thin, reforms implemented over the past decades had born some fruit particularly in the center of the country. Juárez and Lerdo de Tejada had managed to build some railroads, start renegotiating the national debt, and begin to professionalize the bureaucracy.[31] Yet even with these increased resources at his disposal, the lack of territorial integrity or even fixity represented an ongoing threat to Mexico's international reputation. In working for the resolution of the southern border, Díaz had an opportunity to demonstrate that Mexico was both a safe place to invest capital and a regional diplomatic power not to be undermined.[32] Even if his reach within Mexico was still limited, Díaz could assert the appearance of state authority by firmly establishing and defending its bounds.

By this time, it was clear that Barrios was also losing interest in quiet neutral illegibility at the border. In Guatemala, the Soconusco and Chiapas had long been used as a rallying cry for national unity. Barrios again took up this call. Having overthrown a conservative government that had overseen the beginnings of the country's burgeoning coffee economy, Barrios also benefited from increased state capacity and state incomes.[33] Harkening back to the once united Federal Republic of Central America, Barrios posited the reclaiming of Chiapas as a means of restoring the isthmus's historical and geographic integrity.[34] Seeking greater political power through expansion, Barrios asserted himself and Guatemala as the leader of the reborn federation. Mexico's historical expansionist exercises, particularly the southward excursions of Santa Anna, represented an existential threat to that project.[35]

By the time they were transformed into a formalized treaty proposal in 1877, the informal accords negotiated by Romero and Barrios in 1874 had no chance. Díaz initially seemed inclined to sign, despite his new Minister of Finance's open enmity with the Guatemalan president. As it stood, the treaty recognized Mexico's sovereignty over Chiapas and the Soconusco without ceding anything to Guatemala in return. This seemed a good deal to Díaz. Barrios, at least publicly, also seemed inclined to pass the accords. Unfortunately, the ratcheting up of political fervor had changed the political calculus in Guatemala. The Guatemalan Minister of Foreign Relations, Lorenzo Montúfar, refused to ratify the preliminary agreement. Instead, he declared it null based on its cession of Chiapas and the Soconusco to Mexico.[36] The two countries were again at an impasse.

Local Tragedies on an International Stage

People in the Soconusco had been complaining about the insecurity of an unknown border for decades. Between the violence of regular raiding and the insecurity of property titles, the lack of a border treaty had made life dangerous and investment unappealing. Now, finally, they found a national audience eager to hear about their woes. Guatemala's threats against the Soconusco represented threats to the territorial integrity of Mexico as defined by the Constitution of 1857, which set its bounds to definitively include that state. Díaz was determined to promote his country as a regional power strong enough to rebuff the foreign incursions that had undermined his predecessors.[37] The Soconusco, where legal arguments conveniently overlapped with true stories of human loss, became a key site for Díaz's assertion of that strength.

After the failure of the 1877 treaty, Barrios and his government again refused to recognize the legitimacy of Mexico's claims to Chiapas and the Soconusco despite having earlier done so. Drawing on a well-established body of international law, the Guatemalans sought to push their case into arbitration.[38] In 1881, Barrios's government officially approached American Secretary of State James Blaine to act as mediator between the embattled nations.[39] This was no spontaneous conversation. Blaine and the American government had spent the past years attempting to find a way to build a canal across the Central American isthmus. With Nicaragua uninterested and France well on its way to beating the Americans to the punch, Barrios had become a key figure in the United States' plans. The newest idea was that peace in the isthmus would be best achieved under a strong leader capable of reuniting Central America under one flag. Barrios seemed to be that leader. In return for Barrios's aid in building the interoceanic canal, Blaine offered North American assistance in reclaiming the Soconusco, perhaps even all of Chiapas.[40]

This arrangement was an affront to Mexico's assertion of itself as a territorially coherent and cohesive nation-state. Border conflicts with both the United States and Guatemala had long undermined this assertion. Now with their two neighbors allied, Mexico had to act. The country's constitutional claims to Chiapas could serve as one vital weapon in the forthcoming diplomatic battle. The military, increasingly professionalized under Díaz's supervision, could also help. More, though, was needed. To build public support for this campaign of national integrity, the government had to incite nationalistic fervor in defense of the still murky territorial expanse called Mexico.

The arsenal of tragedies and loss accumulated in the writings of those who had spent time in the Soconusco suited the task nicely. Romero's newspaper columns and reports on the progress of new economic endeavors in the region had already established the stakes in certain circles. For such a distant and sparsely populated region, the Mexico City press had published a remarkable number of stories about the Soconusco's past and potential future. Images of the confusing overlap of claims like that in Map 3, published at the behest of the Ministry of Foreign Relations, further illustrated the issue at hand. The Pérezes' story, which opened this chapter, and others like it added emotional weight to the legal and historical arguments set forth by politicians. Personal, vivid narratives of kidnapping, rape, and the destruction of property added moral heft to constitutional claims. Diplomats and journalists wove these two strands together in a weighty nationalist language.[41]

Conveniently, the Pérezes' case against the Guatemalan raiders finally made its way to Mexico City authorities in 1881, just as matters between the two countries came to a head. Ignacio Mariscal, the Mexican Minister of Foreign Relations, sent their request for aid on to the Mexican delegation

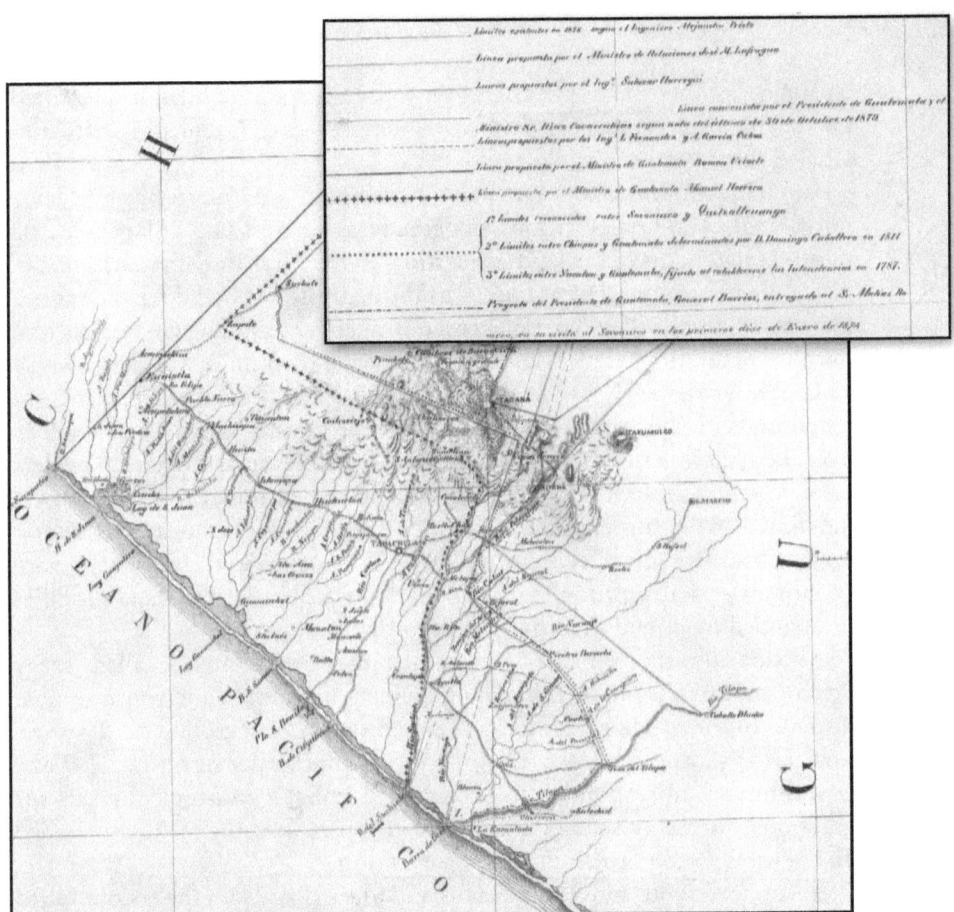

MAP 3. Selection from Map Prepared to Study the Different Dividing Lines Proposed between Mexico and Guatemala, 1882. Source: Carta formada por los ingenieros Don Antonio García y Cubas y Don Leandro Fernández por disposición del Secretario de Relaciones Exteriores para el estudio de las diferentes lineas propuestas como divisorias entre México y Guatemala, by Antonio García Cubas y Leandro Fernández, 1882. Mapoteca Manuel Orozco y Berra, Colección Orozco y Berra, Límites México-Guatemala, No. 1112-OYB-7216-A. Edited by author. Reprinted with permission.

in Guatemala City. What followed was much in the spirit of ongoing diplomatic tensions between the two countries. The Guatemalan government insisted "that it first must be assured that the lands in question belong to Mexico."[42] The Guatemalan foreign minister and the Mexican ambassador wrote bitingly back and forth as the issue escalated, evading the question as they carefully insulted the honor and aptitude of their correspondent. This was by no means the only such invasion that came to first state, then national, then international attention. Journalists and politicians identified the Guatemalan invaders as partisans or employees of President Barrios and labeled them "rapacious filibusters."[43]

Guatemalan politicians and writers presented the case in reverse. They positioned Guatemalan troops as defenders, Guatemalan villagers as the rightful inhabitants of the land in question. In the Pérez case, the Guatemalan government asserted that Mexico was the aggressor. It had done the same a few years before, when Barrios accused Romero of invading Guatemala and burning plantations in the days after Romero's own finca was destroyed.[44] Throughout the early 1880s, Barrios's government used the presence of individuals of Guatemalan birth, like the Pérezes, to assert its dominance over the region. As matters escalated, Guatemala even asserted that raiders were rescuing laborers or avenging violence when they forcibly removed individuals from fincas in the Soconusco.[45] American authorities also took up this strain of rhetoric, accusing Mexico of acquiring the region through "conquest and absorption" and stirring up worries that Díaz and his allies now hoped to extend their borders even further.[46]

Mexico, in turn, responded with what Jürgen Buchenau has called "saber rattling moral suasion."[47] Combining military, moralistic, and constitutional displays of force, Mexican officials refused to give any ground on the question of the southern border. Troops were the first order of business. Díaz's government had responded to Sebastián Escobar's constant requests for additional forces by sending him 5,000 troops. Now, the army dispatched an additional 3,000 to strengthen his position.[48]

In support of this move, politicians and journalists from the Soconusco to Washington, D.C., called up local histories of loyalty to Mexico to demonstrate the region's Mexican-ness. Ignoring the post-independence vote to join Guatemala, Romero and other writers instead focused on the geographical knowledge and institutional affinities of locals and foreigners in the region. It did not matter that the Pérezes had been born in Guatemala or their advocates in Spain; all claimed *vecindad* in Mexico and turned to Mexican courts to seek restitution for their losses.[49] It did not matter that Guatemalan census takers and tax collectors and municipal authorities carried out their requisite tasks in the territory; those who lived in the region agreed that the land they worked was Mexican.[50]

Rallying behind these assertions, the Mexico City press called citizens to action. *El Siglo Diez y Nueve* in Mexico City published an editorial asserting that "40,000 disciplined soldiers and 600,000 happy volunteers will quickly obey the first call."[51] As Guatemalan politicians became more insistent on reclaiming not only the Soconusco, but all of Chiapas as well, Minister of Foreign Relations Mariscal loudly asserted that any attempts to negotiate over the state or any of its constituent parts would violate Mexico's constitution.⁵² The government of Chiapas published its own refutations of Barrios and Blaine's claims of rightful sovereignty, calling Guatemala's actions shameful and cowardly. Hedging their bets, state authorities also threatened secession from Mexico if the national government refused to take up its duties.⁵³

Within the Soconusco, emphasis was still placed on the actual violence experienced, rather than any larger diplomatic aims or the citizenship of those in the region. Diplomats, though, used these very specific stories to argue larger points of statecraft. The strategy was effective. Foreign minister Mariscal's accusations of filibustering soon caused Blaine and his Guatemalan allies to doubt the viability of their position. Mariscal held fast to the Mexican Constitution. He emphasized the repeated petitions to Mexican authorities from those in the Soconusco, whether Mexican citizens or not. He pointed to local assertions that Mexican law governed the land on which they lived.⁵⁴ He outright rejected the U.S. offer of arbitration. Any discussion that required Mexico to admit that Chiapas and the Soconusco were potentially not constituent parts of its territory was out of the question.

The assassination of U.S. President James Garfield in September of 1881 pulled the rug out from under the joint American-Guatemalan position. With the ascension of Chester A. Arthur to the American presidency, Blaine was out of a job and Barrios out of an ally. The new Secretary of State, Frederick T. Frelinghuysen, seemed more determined to "restore harmony and good will between the two governments" than promote any sort of Central American Federation.⁵⁵ At the same moment, a pamphlet was published in English containing key documents related to the conflict. Included were letters between emissaries, numerous proposed accords, assertions that President Barrios was paying filibusters to raid across the border, a detailed account of Romero's time in the Soconusco, and, of course, a multitude of testimony from those directly harmed by raiding.⁵⁶ In its combination of constitutional, diplomatic, and emotional registers, the pamphlet encapsulated the nonmilitary arsenal that Mexico presented to back up its armed forces. Even Guatemalan officials admitted to the impact of the pamphlet, particularly when it came to light that Guatemala had proposed selling the Soconusco to the United States.⁵⁷

Yet though actors in Mexico City now seemed primed for negotiation, Mariscal continued to hold out against arbitration. The longer he waited, the more nervous both Americans and Guatemalans grew about the threat of war. Finally, Lorenzo Montúfar, the Guatemalan representative in Washington, D.C., and the same man who in 1877 had refused to sign a border treaty ceding claims to Chiapas, pushed matters to a head. Montúfar claimed that Romero, now a special emissary to the United States, had promised him an indemnity in return for relinquishing claims to Chiapas and the Soconusco.⁵⁸

Romero called this nonsense. On Marsical's instruction, Romero refused any further attempts at American mediation and demanded direct negotiation with the Guatemalan authorities. Frustrated with his ministers, President Barrios made the journey to Washington himself and sat down to hash out a border agreement with the man whose livelihood he had imperiled just a few years before. Arriving in July 1882, Barrios wasted no time. By August he and Romero had terms that both found amenable.

From Borderlands to Border

The contrasting fixity and fluidity of the resultant treaty captured the overlapping but not entirely shared projects of the local and national actors who took part in the settlement of the border. Mexican authorities emphasized the territorial integrity of their nation through repeated assertions, both rhetorical and material, of the Soconusco's inclusion in Mexico. Those in the Soconusco contributed to and reinforced these assertions by sending their petitions, complaints, and personal narratives to authorities and newspapers in Mexico City. As a result of this mutually reinforcing insistence on the Soconusco's inclusion in Mexico, the borderlands transformed into a border. Planters and villagers in the Soconusco clarified the legal pathways that would help defend their investments. The Mexican government, led by Díaz's temporary successor Manuel González, established itself as a diplomatic power in the region.[59] Yet the economic, demographic, and cultural exchange that also defined the region continued uninterrupted. Territory became fixed, but the lives lived on that territory remained fluid.[60]

The border treaty signed into law in Mexico City on September 27, 1882, handed over some 28,000 square kilometers of land in the Lacandón jungle to Guatemala. In return, Mexico received 3,000 square kilometers of territory and absolute rights over the Soconusco and the rest of Chiapas. In consultation with locals, a joint scientific commission began the task of establishing the actual borderline.[61]

The signing of the treaty, which set the border of the Soconusco at the Suchiate River, essentially ended Mexican interest in the matter. For politicians in Mexico City, the treaty created the desired impression of Mexican diplomatic prowess and territorial integrity. In parallel fashion, the public trouncing of Barrios and his allies led to a rapid abatement in the cross-border violence that had plagued the Soconusco. The Guatemalan president turned his military aspirations southward as he continued to pursue Central American unity. Chastened when it came to the northern frontier, Barrios rarely mentioned Chiapas again. Many of his supporters and detractors lacked the president's reserve. They tried to wring what they could out of the disputed territory, endlessly reattributing blame for perceived losses in the diplomatic battle over the border.[62] Barrios died in battle in 1885 trying to conquer El Salvador, but his successors used the murky language of the treaty to claw their way northward where they could. Miles Rock, the head of the Guatemalan survey team, repeatedly charged his Mexican counterpart with ineptitude and corruption. As they had a few years before, local indigenous voices again rose to the fore as authorities with regard to sovereignty. Between diplomatic delays and the physical hardships of the region in need of surveying, it took sixteen years for the commission to complete its work.[63]

Those in the Soconusco did not have to wait so long. While the Suchiate River occasionally meandered, it was a knowable boundary that provided a fixed sense of what land was governed and protected by what body of law. The federal employees appointed to demarcate the border made quick work of the river and moved on within a short time. From here on out, it was clear which government would govern the titling of land, which courts would hear disputes over boundaries, and which commercial regulations would support mortgages and liens. As Guatemalan raiding waned, local residents made fewer and fewer calls for federal military protection. Most locals had gotten what they needed from the Mexican government with regard to the previously uncertain frontier.

For almost all, this state of affairs was enough. For a very few, including Romero himself, turmoil continued as officials on both sides tried to work through the matter of overlapping claims. According to the treaty, no matter the citizenship of the owner or the nationality of the land in question, property was supposed to remain in the hands of the person currently holding title to it. Going forward, it was to be governed solely by the law of the country in which it now stood. Yet what of lands already claimed by two parties under the two different property regimes? The treaty said nothing of how to settle such matters. In practice, the owner who shared the newly defined nationality of the land in question generally won out. In Romero's case, this meant a reminder of why he had forsworn a place he declared he would rather "leave to the barbarism in which it is currently drowning."[64] Even after raids destroyed his properties in 1875, the minister never sold his properties in the borderlands. When he and President Barrios sat down to negotiate the border treaty, they did so as both representatives of their respective governments and as landowners in the region under dispute. Barrios kept hold of his lands, but half of Romero's property ended up on the Guatemalan side of the line.

Who knows what the two men promised each other during their negotiations, but within a few years it became clear that the Guatemalan government had no intention of respecting Romero's titles.[65] Instead, it backed the villagers who Barrios had encouraged Romero to keep on as laborers. These men and women now asserted that Barrios had granted them title to the lands south of the Suchiate prior to Romero filing claims for the same lands with the Mexican government. Romero pressed for the return of his property for years. Despite a steady stream of letters from the minister and his friends, the Guatemalan government refused to provide any direct response. Barrios himself was dead and could not clarify the matter. Eventually, Romero admitted defeat.[66] At least in this instance, indigenous villagers managed to formalize and defend lands claimed through opportunistic exploitation of institutional absence.

The fear of situations like Romero's had been a key impediment to investment not only in the Soconusco but also across the multitude of unsettled borderlands that riddled the edges of Mexican states. The secession of Texas decades before had provided a critical example of how the confusion of borderlands could invite violence and insecurity.[67] In more recent years, confusion between states over their dividing lines had led to numerous conventions to clarify their bounds and eliminate the jurisdictional muddle embedded in unclear maps.[68] As so many had written, the unknowability of the border had kept the Soconusco mired in uncertainty and unattractive to entrepreneurs. Where villagers like the Pérezes had seen opportunity in the fuzzy legal status of the frontier, planters had seen trouble. Because of this, the number of planters in the Soconusco was still small. Those who had come had mostly avoided the border zone when beginning to work land, and so, in the wake of the treaty, Romero's difficulties were rare. The challenges of gaining title to public lands from the Mexican government had been hurdle enough; most planters had not wanted to add the worry over whether they were claiming land from the proper authorities. With property regimes now fixed, planters and aspiring planters could further extend coffee's reach. The land and the law had become knowable.

Maintaining Mobility

What was not yet knowable was the definitive citizenship of those who lived in the region. This, though, was rarely an impediment to economic expansion. Planters needed the border to remain permeable if they were to have access to the workers they required. Workers and villagers needed to be able to cross into Guatemala at will if they were to maintain their established migratory patterns and escape routes when plantation labor became unappealing. Even the Mexican government seemed to have little interest in closing the borderlands to Guatemalans, as cases like that of the Pérezes demonstrated. In fact, it would be many decades before the border forced any real definition onto the individuals who lived in the Soconusco.

Guatemala had occasionally pointed to the presence of its citizens in the Soconusco as a means of claiming territory, but Mexico had essentially ignored those claims. Locals' own practices around legal and political authority had abetted this rejection of international norms around sovereignty and national identity.[69] In both practice and rhetoric, territory rather than citizenship mandated the body of law in use both before and after the 1882 treaty took effect.

In this vein, the treaty left matters of citizenship up to those in the region. The wording of the agreement allowed individuals to claim whichever nationality they preferred. After a year, they would be assigned the citizenship of the land on which they were living. The enforcement mechanisms for this were never established.[70]

In the coming years, most expatriate finqueros retained their birth citizenship even after decades of living in the Soconusco. Their lack of Mexican citizenship meant they had to receive special permission to purchase land within the border zone or buy properties by way of a Mexican wife, but otherwise had little impact.[71] While a few early settlers naturalized as Mexican citizens, most retained foreign papers. Despite this, they claimed vecindad in the municipalities where they resided, and some even held seats on municipal councils.

Villagers also evaded any enforcement of the border treaty's articles regarding citizenship. Many had been born in either ambiguous or Guatemalan territory. Like finqueros, they engaged with town councils and the district government as vecinos, or officially recognized citizens of the town in which they lived, regardless of place of birth.[72] Some slowly moved to validate their ownership of land through municipal councils, while others continued to tend their small farms without registered claims.[73] Their residence in the Soconusco was rarely challenged. As Barrios had written to Romero a decade before, these villagers were also potential laborers and ought to be embraced by planters and politicians alike.[74]

An approach that saw mobility as necessary to local prosperity continued to guide matters surrounding citizenship well into the twentieth century. By the mid-1890s, the governor of Chiapas and the Department of Fomento had granted two requests from Guatemalan villagers to form colonies on the Mexican side of the border, granting each colonist five to ten hectares of land as an incentive to stay.[75] Political turmoil in Guatemala created another spate of refugees around the same time. The jefe político of the Soconusco welcomed them with open arms and gave them land and permanent residence.[76] In 1900, the census recorded that almost 2,000 of the 34,609 residents of the Soconusco had been born in Guatemala, likely a low estimate given the still porous nature of the border and laxity of documentation around births. Only in the 1930s would government incentives finally cause many residents of the region to fix their own identities by claiming rights as Mexican citizens. This in no way ended movement back and forth across the border, but it did create clearer bounds between those who claimed belonging to each nation.[77]

In its somewhat lax implementation, the 1882 treaty thus settled the question of where the border was situated without transforming it into an impediment to mobility. It provided the Mexican government a chance to flex its diplomatic muscles but did not require any true expansion of government power on the ground. Planters could now rest assured in the knowledge of which nation's offices would oversee petitions for title, which nation's courts would adjudicate disputes, which nation's tax collectors would claim levies. Villagers and potential laborers could continue to move across the border without impediment, seeking land and work where it best suited them. As Chapter Five will illustrate, the permeable border also provided the means to leave employment when it no longer appealed. All benefited from a profound reduction in the violence that the unknowability of the borderlands had invited.

Across the coming decades, Mexican cartographers and surveyors continued to advance the grand project of government knowledge gathering via the fixing of landscapes. Some of this was related specifically to property and the parceling out of public and communally held lands, as Chapter Four will explore. As important, though, was the establishment of clear bounds between the states that made up the Mexican republic and the ongoing negotiation of frontiers between this country and the next. Territorial fixity and integrity were key to elites' arguments that Mexico was a modern nation-state, worthy of international respect and international investment. In beautiful decorative atlases and detailed national and regional strategic schema, the government displayed its acquisition of cartographic knowledge for all to see.[78]

Improved government knowledge about bounds and borders, though, rarely translated into limitations on the people who lived within or moved across them. Most Mexicans continued to die where they were born, but the coming decades saw increased movement of individuals into and around the country. When the Mexican government completed its first national census in 1895, it quantified both internal and international migration by including the state or nation of birth for every resident.[79] Urbanization picked up speed as land reform pushed people from their villages and new industries drew them to centers of manufacturing and processing. Offers of agricultural land for internal colonists drew some northward into the still sparsely populated states of Chihuahua and Sonora.[80] International emigration never reached the numbers that the government hoped for, but a steady trickle of European and East Asian migrants settled in cities and across the countryside and had an outsized impact on local economies.[81] Fixing borders was in no way about fixing populations, and the movement of peoples into and across Mexico served the same economic ends that the newly established bounds promoted.

The negotiation of the 1882 border treaty drew on local knowledge and local narratives to establish and enforce the territorial integrity of the Mexican nation. No matter where they were born, residents of the Soconusco insisted that they resided in Mexico. Yet, while most were pleased with the calming of cross-border violence that had long plagued their homes, not everyone was pleased with the idea of acquiescing to the Mexican national project. Just because they agreed on the bounds did not mean that locals, whether elites or villagers, agreed on the hierarchy of power within those bounds. For those looking for security and reliable legal institutions, it would quickly become clear that intranational disputes over political sovereignty were as problematic as international ones.

3   From Bullets to Bureaucracy

Carlos Gris had such hopes for the Soconusco when he uprooted his family from Zacatecas in 1873.¹ He followed Matías Romero's appeals for investment south and soon befriended the former minister, now finquero, in Tapachula. Yet as Romero returned to Mexico City, Gris found himself under attack. Sebastián Escobar, the district's political chief or jefe político, initially made friendly overtures to the optimistic and progress-minded planter.² Those overtures quickly turned ugly as Gris discovered that Escobar did not take kindly to his continued connections to the national government.³ In early 1881, Escobar's lackeys chased Gris from his home in a hail of bullets.⁴ Gris copied his workers' tactics and fled across the undefined border to Guatemala. From there he began to publish a cascade of editorials in the Mexico City press.⁵ He accused Escobar of destroying his livelihood as well as the Soconusco's burgeoning export economy. The jefe político's violent retribution against those who sought to open the district to commerce meant that no one wanted to invest. Eventually publishing his correspondence regarding Escobar in a small volume, Gris asserted that his control impeded liberty and human rights.⁶ In order to save his family, Gris sold his plantations at a loss and absconded from the Soconusco in the dead of night.⁷ Eventually he ended up in Oaxaca working for the national Department of Fomento, or Development. While he continued to promote coffee as Mexico's future, he rarely returned to the Soconusco.⁸

By the 1910s, Manuel Gris, Carlos Gris's son, was the owner of various properties in the Soconusco's northern municipalities.⁹ He worked as the manager of the largest coffee company in the district and ran his own smaller company with an American partner.¹⁰ Manuel Gris's name appears on endless commercial contracts and land titles and legal filings in the district's judicial archive and public records office.¹¹ He sat on the banquet committee for an ambassador's visit to the region.¹² He grew coffee, cacao, and rubber, as well as staples like corn and beans.¹³ He kept careful accounts and formalized his holdings with proper titles and notarized bills of sale. He was a good businessman who emerged from the collapse of his employer's enterprise in possession of a mature coffee finca and a hefty commercial network.¹⁴ There is little evidence that he had anything to do with local electoral politics.

The Gris family's trajectory from politically driven ruin to bureaucratically documented prosperity captures the transformation of the Mexican landscape across the last decades of the nineteenth century. The thirty-year regime of Porfirio Díaz has long been characterized—and long characterized itself—as one that embraced the notion of "poca política, mucha administración," that is, "little politics, plenty of administration."¹⁵ This, though, was an aim, not a given. Its achievement required the slow winding down of political conflict in favor of consolidated bureaucracy. While national leaders had aspired to an administrative state for decades, it was only in the late 1880s that it was in any degree achieved. Rather than granting Díaz complete credit for quashing political violence and centralizing state bureaucracy, this chapter demonstrates how local actors worked around the first by embracing the second. In doing so, planters, merchants, and villagers shaped administrative institutions into vehicles for overcoming the turmoil of the political sphere.

Large-scale, long-distance economic activity required reliability. While the following chapters will delve into the particular policies and practices that undergirded the emerging export economy, this chapter demonstrates how the formal and informal institutions that enforced those policies and practices became legible and stable. Institutions, in economist Douglass North's definition, are humanly devised constraints that limit political, economic, and social interactions and relationships. Institutions are not necessarily housed in physical buildings or constituted by legislatures. Rather, they are mutually agreed upon norms for activity, both formal and informal. When functioning as intended, they provide predictability.¹⁶ For all those aspiring to make Mexico into a prosperous participant in the world economy, the cementing of administrative and commercial institutions was a necessary first step.

Like much of Mexico, the Soconusco of the 1870s lacked universally accessible and reliable institutions. As much as they agonized over the violence of the frontier, letter writers in the district also complained of the "arbitrariness" of the local government.¹⁷ In particular, they blamed Sebastián Escobar for failing to uphold the legal norms that supposedly governed all as equals before the law.¹⁸ Yet however arbitrary, Escobar and regional political bosses like him were useful to the national government for reasons that necessarily set aside liberal ideals. The central state still lacked the capacity to govern outright. Local strongmen, known throughout Mexico as *caciques*, acted officially and unofficially as its surrogates. In return for keeping the peace, national politicians often granted these men a great degree of autonomy in the management of their local spheres without regard for the legal and procedural norms supposedly governing the nation.[19] State consolidation, then, was built on a careful dance of violence and compromise that gradually brought an end to outright political chaos.

This chapter traces that dance. It demonstrates how locals interested in new types of commercial activity and a president interested in consolidating state power transitioned from violent politics to relatively reliable administration. The chapter begins with Escobar's fight for local autonomy and an exploration of the political negotiations that kept him in power. It then moves to illustrate how, even within the cacique's domain, local actors began to draw on national legislative reforms to create the institutions they needed to secure their interests. Conceding Escobar's dominance of the political stage, those invested in export agriculture turned to bureaucratic mechanisms to achieve their ends. Villagers and planters slowly shaped the physical spaces of state administration—places like local courts and the public records office—into venues for commercial experimentation. This sidestepping of political authority set the stage for local control over the implementation of reform, even after the cacique's death. Administration substituted for electoral politics, but administration itself became a means of asserting local self-governance.

The Ongoing Battle for Local Rule

The political instability and violence that stood in the way of the Soconusco's embrace of coffee was in no way limited to the southern coast. Throughout the nineteenth century, fights between federalists and centralists and conservatives and liberals served as motivation for seemingly endless civil wars. When ousted president Benito Juárez retook Mexico City from the French- and conservative-backed Emperor Maximilian in 1867, he definitively placed federalist liberals in power. Yet this seemingly absolute victory also revealed the many rifts within the winning side. Juárez had never abandoned the title or powers of president during the War of the Reform, as the fight against the French came to be called. In fact, he had used the exigencies of war to extend his executive powers. Both during and after the struggle, many decried the president for abandoning federalist principles, and allies in the provinces regularly challenged his presidency.[20] When Juárez won reelection in 1871, these challenges turned into outright rebellion. General Porfirio Díaz, a hero of the war against the French who had also run for president in 1871, was a vocal advocate for the liberal tenets of no-reelection and regional self-rule. When he lost the election, he took up arms in what became known as the La Noria Rebellion. The rebellion failed and led to Díaz's temporary exile from Mexico City politics, but its failure in no way meant the end of provincial resistance.

While Sebastián Escobar did not join the violent uprising behind Díaz in 1871, he and others like him spent the next years marshaling their resentments and their forces against assertions of authority from Mexico City.[21] To their consternation, those assertions only increased as first Juárez and then Sebastián Lerdo de Tejada, Juárez's successor after his sudden death in 1872, built up the central state's infrastructure. These presidents asserted the central government's authority as a means of pursuing a positivist-influenced project for development and modernization. Positivism, a broadly Latin American interpretation of French political philosopher Auguste Comte's writing, held that order would bring progress, that science and knowledge could be harnessed to improve society through increased state oversight and management.[22] To serve this end, Juárez and Lerdo de Tejada added new administrative departments and mandated tax reforms that provided greater incomes and information for authorities in Mexico City. They deployed bureaucrats and administrators to integrate those incomes and information into new sources of state power, slowly cementing the role of technocrats, known as *científicos*, in the workings of Mexico's central government.[23]

Though appointed jefe político of the Soconusco by the governor in cooperation with the president, Escobar had little interest in bowing to their push toward increased bureaucracy and centralization. His position gave him oversight of the district's military resources, and he used them to cement his role as economic and political chieftain of the Soconusco. For Escobar, Juárez's finance minister Matías Romero's move to the district was a concrete manifestation of the president's push toward consolidation. The customs agents and surveyors and federal district judges who followed Romero south all represented the expanding central state. To aspiring planters, this centralization represented welcome standardization of local economic and political systems that were otherwise hard to navigate. It circumvented the arbitrariness and unpredictability of the informal social, political, and economic institutions that currently governed the Soconusco.

To Escobar, each of these men represented an incursion on his oversight and management of local affairs. Arbitrariness was what kept Escobar in charge. Or, as Carlos Gris put it, "Outsiders, officials or no, who come to the Soconusco bring with them a predictable determination: *make good with Escobar.*"[24] Romero explicitly set out to provide a way around this requirement. Each new official he appointed encroached on Escobar's absolute control over the functioning of local business. Each owed his position to someone in faraway Mexico City rather than to the local cacique. Each took away former sources of economic and social capital, whether through increased crackdowns on contraband or formalized processes of dispute settlement that might once have resulted in bribes or favors. As they worked to implement rules and regulations that would help newcomers function without their own connections to the local regime, new officials undermined the very autonomy that Escobar so valued.

Across the country, this sort of federal incursion into local life prompted a new wave of *pronunciamientos*, or pronouncements of political rebellion, and uprisings.[25] Escobar began to plot his own rebellion in 1875. Joining up with caciques from other parts of Chiapas, he proclaimed against the corruption of the state's governor and called for constitutional proceedings to oust him.[26] Initially defeated despite having momentarily taken the state capital, Escobar took refuge in Guatemala under the protection of his friend President Justo Rufino Barrios.[27]

As he had five years earlier, Díaz ran for president in 1876 on a platform of ending reelection, restoring the constitution, and rebalancing national and local powers. He had spent the years since the La Noria Rebellion in internal exile, dabbling in new economic undertakings and mustering his forces in and around his hometown in Oaxaca.[28] His commitment to local autonomy was an open invitation to Escobar and others with similar frustrations. Across 1876, a growing cadre of military and political bosses advanced Díaz's candidacy through both electoral and armed campaigns, collectively known as the Tuxtepec Rebellion after the *pronunciamiento* that launched the effort. By the time of the election, the rebellion already represented a military alternative to an electoral outcome that favored the incumbent Lerdo de Tejada. Delays in the confirmation of initial vote tallies provided space for the insurgent Díaz to sweep into Mexico City and claim the presidency by force.[29]

In the provinces, this insurgency was in many places accompanied by brutal violence. Escobar and his allies took the opportunity to exact revenge against those who had chipped away at his dominance in the preceding decade. Locals and Mexico City journalists described the cacique's actions and those of his followers as atrocities. Escobar's followers rampaged and pillaged, raped and murdered. Society could never forgive those who had been and continued to be assassins, wrote one editorialist.[30]

Escobar and his men made the new export economy and the federally sanctioned officials who supported it their unequivocal target. By August of 1876, Escobar's followers had destroyed all of the lighters in the port of San Benito, making export of the first harvests of coffee bushes planted through Romero's largesse next to impossible. By fall, they had closed the port and either arrested the customs house officials or sent them into hiding. While local merchants had hoped to shore up the port's business with coffee imported from Guatemala, they now found themselves sending any beans they could save south to be shipped out of Guatemalan ports.[31] Escobar's men occupied Tapachula and from there planned and executed the overthrow of the state's governor, a Lerdo de Tejada loyalist, thus contributing their southern efforts to the national battle while also achieving their own local ends. By November of 1876, local correspondents reported that until the country acknowledged Díaz as president and Escobar as governor of Chiapas, the cacique would prevent the planting of any new coffee for the year.[32] Escobar's participation in the uprising had been clear in its aims: overthrow those who had tried to displace the cacique with their new institutions and their new connections.

Consolidation through Negotiation

The Díaz regime has long been synonymous with a strong centralized state. Contemporaries and scholars, in turn, have credited that centralized state with creating the possibilities for foreign investment and economic growth. Yet this consolidation of governance was a slow process that took place through negotiation and compromise over many years.[33] The term *Porfiriato* lends implicit continuity and prepackaged integrity to a period that was anything but. Díaz's endurance in office was in no way inevitable, and the state he built only ever had limited power to forcibly reach into the provinces. Instead, Díaz had to rely on buy-in from those within and beyond the capital, often at the cost of direct control over the areas in question. Particularly in the early years of his presidency, the president compromised with local leaders and conceded to local demands. In Chiapas, this initially meant wrangling with Escobar and other regional leaders over the distribution of power in the state. After Escobar took up the governorship in early 1877, the rapid realization on all sides that his tactics were poorly suited to statewide rule led to his return to the Soconusco just over a year later. Back on his home turf, Escobar asserted his right to rule through continued violence against outsiders until Díaz ceded oversight of local government operations.

Many of those who backed the new president saw his victory as the latest opportunity to wrest power away from Mexico City and return it to its rightful seat in the states. Having been one himself, Díaz well knew that unhappy regional bosses would make the work of governing impossible. Thus, there was no singular Porfiriato in 1876. Instead, there was a patchwork of relationships between Díaz and local leaders.[34] In some places, popular liberalism and the elevation of the direct vote had a temporary resurgence.[35] In others, the new regime reinforced exclusive local oligarchies that further consolidated their economic and political monopolies.[36] Some states saw the election of savvy governors who would stay in power for decades to come.[37] Others saw rapid turnover in state leaders as the president recalibrated his understanding of local politics.³⁸ To attain and then maintain political peace, Díaz and the caciques who supported his rule had to find a balance between local demands and centralized authority.

As the leader of the southern coalition that backed Díaz and the cacique most familiar with the still problematic southern borderlands, Escobar now seemed the best choice for governor in a state where Díaz had few close ties. The cacique took up the post in early 1877 and was confirmed in the position through elections later that year.³⁹ The selection of Escobar for governor also helped Díaz sidestep the complex web of state politics that enmeshed other possible candidates.⁴⁰ By handing him the governorship, Díaz cemented an alliance at the border and undermined those in the state's center who had never supported him.

Yet instead of helping Díaz consolidate peace and stability, Escobar's governorship led to further chaos. The violence that had marked Escobar's revolutionary tenure in the Soconusco now spread to the rest of Chiapas. Escobar took a challenger's falsified claims to the governorship as an excuse to exercise his control over the military.⁴¹ He used his new might to punish those who had supported the ousted governor, exact revenge on those who advanced the challenger's position, and continue his attack on representatives of the federal government.⁴²

According to some observers, residents of Chiapas, particularly those living in the Soconusco, felt that taxes and import duties were "illegitimate tributes that are paid, not to the Nation, but to whatever employee" was found in the office.⁴³ Escobar's followers called out Díaz's hypocrisy for imposing appointees on those who had expressly fought to oust outside officials.⁴⁴ The Soconusco's new customs officer arrived in a town unwilling to provide the funds necessary for his upkeep or for that of the office he was to run.⁴⁵ The municipal judge in Tapachula, the district's seat and largest municipality, then arrested two of his employees, accused them of murder, and threw them in jail.⁴⁶ Citizens of Tapachula marched in the streets shouting "Death to the Mexicans." The federal district judge charged the new jefe político of the Soconusco, a relative Escobar named to the position on his ascension to the governorship, with corruption. Brought to court, the jefe político took up the crowd's anti-Mexican chants, brandished his pistol, and injured the judge.⁴⁷ The judge fled back to Mexico City in fear for his life, leaving no judicial recourse but the local magistrate, another cousin of Escobar's.

Escobar's reign of terror did not go unnoticed in Mexico City. In the midst of writing his epic history of the Guatemala-Mexico border dispute, Matías Romero made time to publish letters sent to him by beleaguered investors in the Soconusco. Carlos Gris's sorry story was published and republished. Alongside these local accounts, Mexico City editorialists and journalists catalogued Escobar's crimes against the state. They accused the governor of being an official "more addicted to arbitrariness than to the Constitution."[48] While a few tried to defend Escobar as a necessary bulwark against Guatemalan incursions and Escobar himself wrote to complain about the Mexican government's lack of investment in the state, most coverage of state politics painted Escobar as brutal and corrupt.[49]

Directly counter to Escobar's intentions, Mexico City elites now held up the case of Chiapas as justification for increased federal presence in the state. One editorialist wrote that only a reliable federal district judge and a federal military force to uphold that judge's decisions could solve the region's problems.[50] As another writer put it, Chiapas was crying out for good governance. The recent Revolution had vested Díaz's government with the power to oust corrupt and cruel authorities, to wipe away the barbarism that disguised itself as civilized liberalism.[51]

As Díaz attempted to answer these calls for reform, Escobar continued to assert his claims that the Tuxtepec Rebellion had instead been fought in order to return power to regional authorities. Díaz sent new customs officials and refused Escobar's requests for more troops. Escobar retaliated by accusing Díaz's appointees of stealing funds from the customs office and carousing in taverns with "immoral folk." He laid the blame for local unrest at the feet of Romero and his representatives in the region, insisting that the people of the Soconusco were the most loyal and honorable in the nation. He asked for federal troops to help restore order, but he wanted them placed under his leadership, just as he wanted a say in any further appointments made.[52]

Here, finally, was the crux of the issue. Escobar would only ever acquiesce to a central government that placed its authority in his hands.[53] He wanted control over military forces in the state, a say in federal appointments, and respect for local knowledge of what was needed. This was too much autonomy for Díaz to grant to a governor. Yet, given the ongoing border insecurity described in the previous chapter, Díaz needed Escobar to keep the Soconusco Mexican. So the two men compromised. In return for giving up the governorship, Escobar would have a say in the appointment of federal officials, particularly the commander of the national troops based in Tapachula. Díaz defended his appointees to local posts against Escobar's vitriol but agreed to discuss any further personnel decisions.[54]

On the pretense of calming the ongoing turmoil at the border, Escobar departed San Cristóbal in August of 1878. A new customs officer was on his way south, and the president hoped that Escobar would support his work to reopen the port.[55] This did not mean, though, that Escobar was ceding control of the region to Díaz. Escobar became municipal president of Tapachula and orchestrated the installation of his brother as jefe político in 1879. His good friend became the local magistrate.[56] When Díaz appointed a new federal district judge, Escobar had a hand in the selection, leaving those who sought justice in the courts without recourse to anyone outside of the cacique's sway.[57] While Escobar's enemies in Mexico City celebrated Escobar's demotion to municipal president as the triumph of liberalism over corruption, a migrant planter in the Soconusco had a better read on the situation.[58] "Such self-denial, such modesty, such impoverishment!?!?!???" he wrote with sarcasm. "Perhaps in the coming year he'll accept the post of Auxiliary, and finally the position of governor of some jail, only to be able to serve his beloved Patria."[59] The new customs officer also remained wary and sought out assurances of federal protection, particularly given the recent murder of one of Romero's good friends.[60] Romero was able to pass along news of a federal battalion en route to the region. Yet, as he wrote to his friend soon before that man's untimely death, he had "not a single hope in favor of the District, and I almost fear for the luck of the force on its way."[61]

This was what state consolidation looked like in the early years of Díaz's reign. Compromise and negotiation ruled the day. No one, most especially a president who came to power on the back of regional uprisings, could forget the threat posed by regional strongmen. Díaz may have had the loyalty of the army, but the army was unruly, underfunded, and unable to be everywhere at once.[62] The railroads that would later speed its transit around the Mexican countryside were not yet built. The rural police force that Díaz assembled was still in its infancy and, even at its height, would never extend into the south of the country.[63] Díaz did not yet wield the might of any sort of centralized state. Instead he sat at the center of a web of messy, personalistic, but increasingly stable agreements that stood in for any sort of standardized political hierarchy.

Predictable Violence and the Slow Turn to Bureaucracy

Three years after Díaz came to power, the integration of his political regime was still insecure. Political power did not flow smoothly through a stable hierarchy. If Díaz and his growing body of technocratic advisors were to enact the liberal project they believed would bring prosperity to Mexico, they needed more than unreliable subordinates who kept the peace only in return for concessions. They needed allies who would embrace and enforce reliable commercial structures, regularized private property, and liberalized trade. Yet those allies were not always to be found in the political hierarchy Díaz supposedly controlled. In the Soconusco, Escobar's fear that investment in export agriculture would undermine his supremacy seemed a major roadblock on the path to liberal reform. The central government could do little to overcome his obstinacy. Yet in Escobar's stead and without much coordination, planters and villagers in the district quietly took up the tools of liberal policy to secure and defend their interests. Wary of the cacique's violent tendencies, they focused their investment outside Escobar's line of sight. At the same time, they began to slowly reshape the administrative spaces he controlled through experiments with new commercial institutions.

Escobar may not have wielded much formal political power as municipal president of Tapachula, but informally everyone recognized that he was the only one who could maintain the peace in the Soconusco.[64] It was also clear that he had no interest in the types of institutional and commercial innovations promoted by Romero and other Mexico City technocrats. Though he had been one of the earliest hacendados to turn some of his lands to coffee production, he now left the actual growing of the bean to others.[65] Those others like Carlos Gris who sought out the assistance of the central government in easing their progress often found themselves subject to retribution. Escobar's men chased Gris from the Soconusco in 1880 after he sued one of Escobar's local government allies over unfair treatment. Escobar ordered the murder of another of Romero's friend in 1878 after the man lodged protests against the cacique's manipulation of local courts.[66] Another emigrant planter, a Swiss man whose activities will be explored further in the next chapter, worked with Romero to establish a local branch of a national Agricultural Society and a small independent press. He soon found that Escobar had no interest in these local manifestations of national development projects. Both were shuttered within a year.[67]

This retribution, though, was at least predictable. It fit within the pattern of Escobar's negotiations with Díaz over who would control local governance. As Gris put it, "Our screams are lost in the immense distance between Mexico and the Soconusco."[68] Díaz remained committed to the détente he and the cacique had reached, particularly as conflicts with Guatemala came to a head. While Escobar's doubters in Mexico City continued to accuse him of collusion with the Guatemalans, just as many lauded the cacique's bravery and celebrated his determination to pacify and hold the frontier.[69] In this context of national crisis, no one in the capital was interested in rehashing old fights.

That said, predictability was an improvement over the arbitrary violence Escobar had exercised in previous years. Within this context, planters who had invested in coffee in the early 1870s began to slowly reconstruct the informal institutions that had facilitated the early export economy. Where they could, they did so outside of Escobar's direct purview. In 1876, thirty or so finqueros planted coffee in the Soconusco. Most did so outside of Tapachula, the seat of Escobar's power.[70] Instead, they lived and worked a few days' walk away in the small foothill municipalities of Cacahoatán and Unión Juárez.[71] By the early 1880s, a few Mexican-born finqueros gained positions on the municipal councils of both towns.[72] Along with their colleagues, the majority villagers born and raised in the Sierra Madre, these planters managed miniscule municipal funds and dabbled in the liberal land reform projects that make up the subject of the next chapter. They kept their heads down, avoiding Escobar's retaliation by working outside the direct ambit of his domain.

This did not mean that they could avoid Escobar entirely. The informal commercial institutions that Romero had tried to formalize and which planters now tried to resuscitate often involved working with officials in Tapachula. Escobar's judicial appointees controlled the only spaces available for registering contracts or land sales. The only notary in town until the early 1890s was his close ally.[73] The only way coffee could leave the region was through the port of San Benito, where Escobar-approved customs officials oversaw shipments. So finqueros paid bribes and fees and put up with the indignities of trickery where they had to in order to get their crop planted, harvested, and shipped abroad.

This sort of illicit activity is, of course, hard to document. Yet even Escobar's well-known habit of seeking retribution against those who complained did not stop everyone from putting pen to paper. Escobar and his friends tricked the manager hired to take care of Romero's properties into suing the minister for investments made in the plantations. The man, "one of those hard-working Germans, who from their home and school bring with them these principles of honor and good faith that characterize the German people," paid the local magistrate and tax collector $630 for their help in asserting his claims to the land and improvements made. The German lost his claims, but Escobar's cronies kept their cash.[74] Contraband continued to constitute a regular part of Escobar's incomes. Even his sway over appointees did not stop the occasional honorable customs official from writing to the president about local merchants' ongoing smuggling.[75] Well into the 1880s, people wrote to bemoan the corrupt nature of the local courts. The magistrate and other officials did as Escobar told them, and everyone knew that justice could be bought.[76]

Despite the costs, those invested in the recovering export economy slowly began to turn these local official spaces to their own use. While electoral politics and political appointments might be off limits, the everyday needs of business required grappling with the bureaucracy those political officials controlled. Through usage, those engaged with the still small export economy slowly began to reshape these tools to their needs.[77] No matter that the federal district judge was an Escobar appointee, he could still validate their purchases of public lands.[78] Escobar's cousin might run the local court, but planters still used it to file insurance claims for merchandise lost when a lighter barge capsized on the trip from shore to ship.[79] Like Romero had before them, merchants advancing funds to planters filed their contracts at the court.[80] Conceding the inexactitude of property boundaries, finqueros allowed court-appointed surveyors to tromp across their properties and place new boundary markers.[81] Others charged neighbors with falsifying titles and violently invading their lands and sent in their own documentation as support for their claims.[82]

At least initially, the language of these contracts and claims was anything but standardized. People rarely cited the commercial and civil codes that national and state governments had implemented across the past decades to govern such activities. No one was relying on judges to know or make judgment based on formal legal norms. Rather, planters and merchants and villagers were using the formal space of the local court to work out the kinks in the informal commercial institutions that made it possible to grow and export their new crop. As often as not, they were fighting over the inaccuracies and unreliabilities inherent in this way of working. For example, in 1879 Bernardo Mallen sued a local business associate for failure to repay a loan on time, according to the terms set out in a contract filed at the local court. When Mallen sailed north to see family, the debtor countersued asserting he had already paid.[83] Both attempted to make use of the courts to settle their dispute, but neither seemed to entirely trust the magistrate to uphold the documents he had officiated, relying instead on the presentation of new evidence and moral claims.

With or without the formal backing of legal language, the use of the magistrate's offices provided a space for the consolidation of new commercial norms. This, in turn, allowed for the slow expansion of the Soconusco's economic activity. And as the local economy expanded into new physical and institutional realms where Escobar had little experience, his control over the Soconusco's commercial activity became looser. Instead of one merchant who relied on the cacique to protect his interests from bandits and keep him supplied with trade goods from Guatemala, multiple merchants with connections to foreign commercial houses now made use of the monthly Pacific Mail ships. A say in the appointment of the customs officials still provided Escobar with sway over exports and imports, but the quantity and diversity of goods entering the region through these legitimate pathways undermined the value of his contraband operations. With most newcomers settling in the foothills, his knowledge and control over the properties of the coastal plains was less valuable.

Writing in 1883, Romero's nephew was premature in stating that "truthfully, it looks as though [Escobar's] time has already passed."[84] The cacique still commanded the established ranching elites of the coastal municipalities and all those who fell under their patronage. He controlled elections and continued to rail against federal officials who acted outside his authority.[85] He also held onto the leadership of the federal troops stationed in Tapachula, though their numbers decreased in the wake of the 1882 border treaty with Guatemala. Those looking to do business in the Soconusco continued to recognize Escobar's sway. When an American company came to the region to begin surveying public lands in 1887, they offered to put Escobar on their payroll and pay him a percentage of profits to, essentially, stay out of their way.[86] Through the early 1890s, the cacique would continue to inspire diatribes against "the aggressive and disturbed conduct of Señor Escobar."[87] Yet by slowly finding space for administrative reliability within a region governed by a violent political boss, coffee growers slowly expanded their hold. The finqueros and smallholders of the Soconusco exported 600 metric tons of coffee worth about MXP$150,000 in 1887, ten times the value of the region's coffee exports a decade and a half before.[88]

Reforming the Hierarchies of Governance

Escobar and caciques like him represented arbitrariness and lack of predictability for both those living under their sway and for the higher authorities that supposedly oversaw their activities. Even if planters managed to carve out small spaces for new commercial activity, they still lacked the institutions needed to reliably secure their transactions both at home and abroad. In the second decade of Díaz's rule, the president began to push hard against the regional political bosses who had initially been essential to his consolidation of power. Over the second half of the 1880s, Díaz replaced this first generation of regional elites with officials more loyal to the presidency than to the places they governed. He further centralized the power of the central government by substituting appointed officials for elected ones whenever possible. The process was neither smooth nor peaceful.

For Díaz and his government in Mexico City, regional caciques like Escobar had been essential in the early tenuous years of rule. More than a decade into Díaz's leadership, the disjointed assemblage of local powerbrokers who kept the peace in return for relative autonomy no longer appealed. Nor were such local interlocutors any longer absolutely necessary. Increased incomes from a growing economy and the expansion of railroads and other infrastructure built with those incomes gave the central government greater reach on its own terms. The military and new rural federal police were stronger than they ever had been. Constitutional reforms allowing for reelection passed in 1877, consecutive reelection passed in 1887, and indefinite reelection passed in 1890 meant that Díaz could legally hold the presidency for as long as he was able.[89] The further manipulation of electoral laws at the state level and the replacement, rotation, and removal of governors and jefes políticos allowed Díaz to displace the regional strongmen who had helped him come to power.[90] In doing so, he sought to consolidate more than just relative peace in the countryside. He sought political allies who would take an active role in implementing his program for Mexico's future.

Díaz aimed to make the rungs of government hierarchies actually equate to the disposition of political power. Official precedence rather than unofficial power was to be the source of authority. Remember that Escobar asserted his dominance first from the relatively lowly position of municipal president and later from the even less locally meaningful position of substitute senator from the state of Chiapas.[91] Yet despite his official titles, Escobar had been responsible for choosing the succession of jefes políticos who succeeded himself and his brother in the role across the 1880s. This position was one of actual authority, endowing its holder with control over military as well as fiscal resources. Escobar's unofficial hold on power was symptomatic of politics in Chiapas. Díaz had kept the state loyal through acquiescence to a whole archipelago of local caciques who asserted power from outside the official ranks. In this environment, a series of governors had failed to consolidate any sort of real cohesive statewide government.

With the border dispute with Guatemala almost a decade resolved and his hold on authority in Mexico City assured after his first consecutive reelection, Díaz tried something new. Instead of relying on local patronage networks, he turned to outsiders not enmeshed in the webs of regional politics. Díaz first orchestrated the election of Emilio Rabasa, later a key member of his technocratic circle in Mexico City, to the governorship.[92] Then he and Rabasa together took back control of the selection of jefes políticos. In place of locals with established patronage networks, the governor and president appointed outsiders loyal to them.[93]

In 1891, Rabasa installed Lauro Candiani, the leader of the federal battalion stationed at the border, as the new jefe político in the Soconusco.[94] The transfer of power did not go well. A few months after the new jefe político took up his post, Escobar and his armed followers marched on Tapachula's central plaza. Escobar blamed Candiani's ineptitude for the turmoil. As he had with other federal appointees in the past, Escobar accused the man of drunkenness, scandal, and hitting his wife in public.[95] Governor Rabasa, who had taken a personal interest in planting coffee in the Soconusco, saw the danger to the burgeoning local economy that such upset represented. Instead of acquiescing to Escobar, Rabasa held strong behind his new man and threatened to send in federal troops if Escobar continued to disturb the peace.[96]

The violence that marked this period of political transition soon came for its lead instigator. In October of 1893, one of the Escobar's former employees entered his home and shot the cacique multiple times. Though the letters and telegrams that spread the news were decidedly mixed in their sentiments, the "twelve bullets that cut through his heart" were certainly good tidings for the governor and the president.[97] The killer fled across the border to Guatemala but was soon caught. The gun he used had passed through many hands, borrowed and lent among local smallholders for the guarding of their farms. Rumor and accusation flew around the district, as none believed that the man would have acted without the backing of one of Escobar's local enemies.

All feared an outbreak of violence. Governor Rabasa, though, revealed a keen knowledge of the region's politics. Instead of out and out repression, he used the chaos to solidify a new jefe político's authority as well as that of the federal district judge, both appointees chosen in concert with the president.[98] These appointed officials worked with villagers and planters to tamp down any further move toward retribution. In this they were remarkably successful. Instead of Escobar's self-proclaimed heir taking over the cacique's political realm, Rabasa and Díaz seized the moment to essentially empty out politics in the region. As the governor wrote to the president, the jefe político had been instructed to "make sure that Soconusco will never again have caciques."[99]

For the next decade, Díaz and the series of governors who followed Rabasa in office rotated jefes políticos in and out of the Soconusco on a relatively regular schedule.[100] In this way, none were able to consolidate the type of political sway that Escobar had accumulated over years in power. Neither, though, did they accumulate any sort of political clout. Somewhat removed from local society, they rarely provided much information to either the governor or the president regarding the region. Holders of this office elsewhere served as intermediaries for local political disputes or essential actors in the implementation of national programs for modernization. Yet few in the Soconusco seemed to pay their jefe político much mind.

This was not precisely the outcome Díaz had hoped for. It certainly provided him with little means of forcibly implementing the reform-oriented projects passed by his legislature, as we will see in the coming chapters. Yet it at least created a relatively peaceful environment within which those interested in doing so could move forward with projects for economic modernization. The virulent complaints about caciquismo and arbitrary power that had swirled around Escobar never again emerged as a regular genre of writing in the Soconusco.[101] Chiapas as a whole would continue to evade easy management as disputes between entrenched and emerging elites in the state center fought over the future of the state's economic and social institutions. Yet, separated by a mountain range and more interested in the global economy than state affairs, the Soconusco's slowly consolidating cohort of coffee elites rarely engaged with state politics. Nor did they push back against the rotating cast of jefes políticos. Instead, those locals who sought change continued to move forward with the use of administrative spaces and municipal councils as the sites for experimenting with and implementing new kinds of commercial institutions.

The Local Interpretation of National Projects

Escobar's death mattered, but those outside his circle had already begun establishing other means of achieving their ends. Now planters, merchants, and villagers alike took on the work of formalizing those means within the official spaces they had long used to experiment with new commercial institutions. They might, on occasion, petition jefes políticos and elected officials for favors, exemptions, or investments. Yet having learned from Escobar's unreliability and tendency toward vengeance, they mostly ignored these individuals. Instead, judges, notaries, customs officials, scribes at the public records office, and surveyors became the primary vectors of governance. The liberal political promises of the Tuxtepec Rebellion—no reelection, universal suffrage, and a return to local autonomy—were left behind. Instead, those invested in export agriculture took up liberalism's economic project as they enshrined the norms of contract law and institutional reliability in practice.

It was not Escobar's death that ensured the reliability of contract law or property rights. Nor was it the enforcement of commercial and civil legislation from above that made it an integral part of life in rural Mexico. Rather, both were the result of the regular use of bureaucracy by people across the economic spectrum. While governments since Santa Anna had tried to regulate and encourage commerce through the promulgation of civil and commercial codes, they had not been terribly effective. In the Soconusco, it was not until the 1880s that locals interested in securing their livelihoods and their investments finally took up the project. As the following chapters will demonstrate, non-elites and elites alike increasingly employed the language of liberal reforms to defend their property, gain access to credit, and seek retribution against those who had broken contractual agreements. The Soconusco was not a peaceful place, but by 1900 most came to adjudicate their conflicts through legal rather than violent means.

The local embrace of administration can be seen in many forms. The simple quantity of business taking place at the local court is one representative facet. While the archives of Tapachula's courts are barely organized and far from complete, the number of individuals making use of the space increased exponentially across the final decades of the nineteenth century. The increasing standardization of their business is another indication of how locals took up administrative norms. As illustrated earlier, planters and merchants were already using the physical space of the courthouse to experiment with commercial forms that might facilitate the expansion of their businesses and the securing of their interests. Across the 1880s and 1890s, those experiments began to take on regularized forms and employ the language of Mexico's civil and commercial codes with greater frequency.[102]

In many cases, people used the codes' language to give legal structure to arrangements that had previously been more descriptive than definitive. In 1894, Benito Taboada advanced Camilo Robledo CYSA$7,080 to be repaid with coffee and cash in a year's time and filed a record of the agreement at the district-level court. If Robledo did not repay on schedule, the contract stated that he hereby renounced his rights under Article 1093 of the civil code and agreed instead to cover the market price of the coffee in Guatemalan pesos—the law might be Mexican, but the currency in circulation continued to come from abroad. The contractual language the men employed, previously haphazard if used at all, was increasingly rote.[103] In other cases, people used the legal code to explicitly overcome the mushiness of former arrangements. In 1889, Rafael Ortega's lawyer asked the court to oversee the resurveying of his property bounds, "founded on articles 1259 and 1250 of the code of civil procedures," as confusion over previous, unregistered surveys of his neighbors' property had led to many damages and much confusion.[104] Others deployed the civil code to strike back at those who sought to use older means—occupation, violence—to lay claim to property. Genoveva Moya de Ramírez attempted to usurp part of the land Lucio Cárdenas claimed in the ejidos of Tapachula by building a fence around it. He asserted his rights to not only the land but also money to cover costs and damages based on three different articles of the civil code.[105]

This last case is also revealing of the way that those appearing in court were selective in their invocation of national statutes. Cárdenas did not support his claim with title to the land in question, despite the fact that national and state law mandated the privatization of ejidos. Instead, he based his claims on common knowledge and the municipal government's disposition of the community's property. As Chapter Four will further explore, this sort of arrangement was not uncommon. Nor was the usage of the civil code and the local courts to defend it.[106]

The invocation of law within the space of the court could also serve to overcome both the friction and the possibility for deception that existed when business dealings were not carried out in uniform terms. By 1900, at least seventy investors from Europe and the United States were at work in the Soconusco, in addition to the multitude of Mexicans who had migrated to the region.[107] The shared language of the civil code, designed to mesh well with other legal traditions in the Atlantic world, gave them a way to conduct business across cultural divides. Beyond the matter of mutual intelligibility, the multisited nature of commercial transactions—coffee grown in the Sierra Madre was sold in Tapachula, exported from San Benito, imported to Hamburg or San Francisco or London, and then sold again—provided ample opportunities for confusion or outright fraud. By consolidating the contractual business of coffee within one or two physical spaces in Tapachula, all those concerned could at least hope to avoid overlapping claims and contradictory promises.

The case of Louis Brewer, an American entrepreneur who came to the Soconusco sometime around 1880, provides a good example of why so many found the courts and the language of the codes useful. As the general enthusiasm for coffee blossomed in the 1890s, Brewer gained access to massive loans both locally and abroad. He mortgaged his fincas multiple times, backing each contract with promises of coffee to be delivered as well as with the lands on which it was planted. Because his creditors were spread across Mexico and the world, most were ignorant as to his other obligations. By 1899, Brewer had accumulated over MX$630,000 in outstanding loans. Unable to meet his obligations, he sold some lands to neighboring planters who purportedly agreed to take on the mortgages they held. Then he absconded to London and tried to sell the same properties again. As his creditors came to realize the overlapping pile of contracts Brewer had signed, they called on the judge in Tapachula to help untangle the mess. The original loans were in at least four different currencies, the properties divided and subdivided, the terms of the original loans contradictory and impossible to reconcile. In the end, some merchants bought loans off of others, and the land company at work in the region purchased many of the properties. Brewer himself somehow successfully sued another party for damages and returned to the United States.[108]

Embracing the administrative state advanced by the Mexican government clearly did not guarantee against such a mess. But Brewer's mess provides a prime example of why those lending money and purchasing coffee or land increasingly insisted on following legal and procedural mandates that made use of local administrative offices. Brewer's messy transactional history should, by law, have been validated and registered at a local public records office. Yet until 1894, no such office existed in the Soconusco. Only in that year did the quickly expanding coffee economy finally generate enough business to support this particular expansion of the local bureaucracy.[109] At the public records office, people claiming properties from a few hundred square meters to tens of thousands of hectares filed their titles, mortgages, and land sales. Private actors and the district's slowly growing number of notaries mined the civil and commercial codes for the appropriate legal language to secure their contracts and transactions.[110] As the decades passed, the language they used grew ever more standardized, even as the transactions it regulated grew more complex.[111] In the process, they cemented the norms of legal codes and official commercial institutions legislated decades before in the everyday practices of a region far removed from Mexico City.

Keeping Politics Out of Governance

In many ways, the focus on the localized business of administrating exports reinforced and expanded on Escobar's earlier efforts to keep the state at a distance. Planters, merchants, and villagers, out of habit and experience, tended to avoid the political hierarchy beyond the Soconusco. Yet, importantly, they did hold onto control over local government. Elsewhere, the loss of localized autonomy led to rebellions and, eventually, revolution.[112] Here, as local interests and practices generally fit within the broad parameters of the national project, the central government made little attempt to encroach. People in the Soconusco interpreted the liberal program of reform on their own terms and their own timeline, but they paid their taxes and they kept the peace. Asking little of the state and national government, they received little in return. Instead, they did the work of building the commercial and administrative capacity of the state in service of their own interests.

People interested in export agriculture, whether planters, merchants, or villagers, tended to keep their politics local even as their economic interests stretched across the world. Coffee planters were already serving on municipal councils in foothill municipalities by the mid-1880s.[113] With Escobar's fall, the Tapachula municipal council gradually opened up to those invested in exports, first locals and then newcomers from elsewhere in Mexico and abroad. By 1908, Ricardo Bado, a naturalized Mexican citizen from Gibraltar, had become president of the district seat's municipal council. An American finca manager turned owner also served on the council, despite lacking Mexican citizenship.[114] Local committees to organize everything from a reception for a former ambassador to a new theater to a local agricultural chamber came to include a who's who of finqueros and import-export merchants.[115] Yet even at the end of the century, planters did not take up positions outside the district. It took until almost 1900 for someone who owned land in the Sierra Madre rather than the coastal plains to represent the district in the state legislature. From a perusal of the official state newspaper, it is not clear that he did much to advocate for the interests of coffee planters.[116] In one instance, explored in depth in Chapter Five, planters took up the governor's invitation to come to the state capital and participate in attempts to reform the labor system. As the chapter shows, they more or less failed to achieve their ends and thereafter rarely returned to the seat of state government.

Just as they rarely left the Soconusco for the state or national capitals, so too did local elites or villagers rarely invite representatives of government beyond the district to intervene in their affairs. Only occasionally would someone who lost in front of the district magistrate appeal and have their case sent to the state court.[117] Most avoided this, though, and abided by local decisions. Letters to the president and governor from anyone other than the jefe político are scarce, except in cases in which locals were expressly asked for their opinions. Export investors filed the paperwork they had to in order to buy lands in the border zone but otherwise appear infrequently in the state archive.[118] Nor did local elites employ any sort of advocate to advance their interests, aside from a brief moment at the turn of the century when a notable from central Chiapas took up their cause.[119] This was not the crony capitalism, negotiated or otherwise, that elsewhere served to intermingle the private sector and the state.[120] Instead, locals expected little of their governing officials and those officials, in turn, left them mostly alone.

There was one avenue of interaction with government beyond the Soconusco that participants in the local economy somewhat surprisingly embraced. Namely, they paid their taxes. With the expansion of the coffee economy, Tapachula rose to be the most highly taxed municipality in Chiapas. Locals paid MX$4.39 a year per inhabitant in combined federal, state, and municipal taxes, compared to levies elsewhere in the state that amounted to as little as MX$0.23.[121] This was despite the fact that the government exempted many emigrant finqueros from paying taxes during their first decade or so in the district as a means of encouraging emigration and colonization.[122] Even without their contributions, the Soconusco was one of the largest sources of funds for the state's coffers by 1900. In 1896, as coffee cultivation really began to boom, residents of the region paid MX$35,000 in state taxes. Already, this made the district the third most lucrative for the government of Chiapas. By the turn of the century, the incomes from the Soconusco had more than doubled to almost MX$80,000. At the outbreak of the Revolution a decade later, the Soconusco was contributing almost MX$130,000 a year, twice as much as any other district.[123]

In part, this reflected the increased ability of the state to collect fees through institutions like the public records office and more directly oversee taxation.[124] It also reflected growing land values in the region, as property taxes were one of the state's main sources of income. Yet in other parts of the state where property values also increased rapidly, tax incomes failed to attain such heights. Thus, these increased tax contributions signaled the local utility of documents like tax receipts. Proving ownership of a piece of land facilitated the borrowing of capital from abroad as well as the defense of that land against encroachment or theft from neighbors. Tax receipts were a vital means of creating a legible legal trail. Taking part in the administrative state proved useful to those looking to expand the local economy.

Paying into the state, though, did not guarantee a return on investment. Planters and merchants in the Soconusco had to finance much of their own infrastructure, despite the high tax burden they bore. This was not an uncommon situation on economic frontiers.[125] Governments from Mexico to Brazil to the United States had great interest in increasing connectivity in their countries in order to facilitate both economic and political integration. Yet while they made grand promises and set up ministries to oversee such infrastructure investments, they rarely had the capacity to carry through. Concessions to private companies that came with substantial incentives in the form of subsidies and exemptions filled some of the gap. In Mexico, these sorts of partnerships financed large-scale projects like the dredging of the nation's main port at Veracruz, the drainage of Mexico City, and railroad networks that slowly connected the country east to west and north to south.[126]

Yet the types of infrastructure investments that planters and villagers desired—an improved port, better internal roads, bridges to cross the many rivers that flowed out of the Sierra Madre, telephone lines to connect distant fincas to the central mail and telegraph office—were not lucrative enough to attract foreign investment. While Romero had obtained a concession to connect the Soconusco by rail in the 1870s, it was allowed to lapse without a single rail laid as Romero's interests moved elsewhere.[127] No one then took up his advocacy role outside the region. Instead, those within it took on the work of infrastructural bureaucracy themselves, and a railroad was far down on their list of priorities.

The state government had its own Department of Fomento that funded some projects across Chiapas, but the moneys they could provide were neither forthcoming nor sufficient. Even as state incomes grew on the back of export agriculture, financial reforms aimed at promoting commerce cut off key sources of state income, particularly the interstate duties known as *alcabalas*. The federal government monopolized many other avenues of taxation. The local administrative offices and the municipal governments where those invested in coffee maintained their influence had to rely on local taxation of land, alcohol, and sales; mineral production; fees for registering contracts or new enterprises or cattle brands; and whatever other small bits of money they could scrape together.[128] While the budgets published in the state newspaper portrayed a well-financed state able to meet its promises, the actual investments made in infrastructure investments belied this appearance of prosperity.[129] Elsewhere in Chiapas, local governments levied labor for public works projects from villages based on the reimplementation of a head tax. The Soconusco, though, had too few unemployed villagers to make use of this mechanism.[130]

Instead, as was the case in many agricultural frontiers, coffee growers in the Soconusco made do with mule trains out of the foothills and the minimal port facilities built by merchants and those who operated lighters moving goods from shore to ship.[131] What improvements they constructed were built through private investment with minimal state assistance, whether from bureaucrats or political officials. They pooled their resources with what local municipalities could scrape together to build a road to facilitate the movement of labor between the coffee zone and workers' home districts. As the project ran short on funds, its backers complained to the governor about the state's failure to invest in something of such public utility. In return, they got a meager subsidy from the state.[132] The same method was applied to building bridges, highways, a post office, a telephone network, an electrical company, and other needed or desired improvements.[133]

Only the railroad that finally reached Tapachula in 1908 benefited from substantial outside investment.[134] Locals had never expressed much interest in the project, nor did they take part in its financing or management. When the Pan American Railway Company did finally complete the line originally conceived by Romero, it was already at the end of its financial resources.[135] So the railroad that made it to Tapachula was rickety and the locomotive secondhand.[136] Even so, planters and merchants celebrated its inauguration and shifted their business from port to train.[137] Yet, in many ways, the railroad did little to address the planters' most repeated complaints about infrastructure. As with the port, the rails were still distant from fincas, and transit to and fro remained underfunded and difficult. Asked in 1911 about what the government might do to improve conditions in the district, planters once more reiterated their well-practiced diatribe about the poor state of roads in the region.[138]

Both to their benefit and their detriment, the residents of the Soconusco kept their distance from the state in the second half of Díaz's presidency. Where it advanced their interests, they took up the general parameters of the president's modernizing project, as they had with the language of the civil and commercial codes. They paid their taxes because it provided a reliable means of proving ownership. They invested in infrastructure because they needed the means to transport goods in and out of the district, and state funds were not forthcoming. They rarely called on outside authorities to intervene in their affairs because they had learned from years under Escobar's thumb. Abiding by the tenets of order and progress, the region's villagers and elites alike did little to invite state attention.

Overcoming political violence was about more than not getting killed. It was about knowing whom to turn to when someone was killed, or when someone invaded your land, or when your boss did not pay you, or when you could not deliver all the coffee you promised. Overcoming political instability meant moving past Escobar, yes. But it also meant learning to work around him through the employment of bureaucrats and magistrates. It meant building reliable institutions, both within and outside of political hierarchies. It meant becoming part of the shared economic and administrative space of Mexico and, through that, the global market.

Elsewhere in the country, it was caciques themselves who built up these institutions. They capitalized on their connections with the federal government to direct concessions and development money toward their own interests and those of close allies. Serving as intermediaries between the state and the business sector, they lined their pockets and expanded their holdings. Bureaucracy became a means of controlling and exploiting the resources within their domain. Crony capitalism was alive and well in Porfirian Mexico.[139]

Yet in places like the Soconusco, where political might was less concentrated and economic undertakings less favorable for the consolidation of landholding and commercial monopolies, the situation was different. Unless they took active steps to consolidate control of new entrepreneurial endeavors, Escobar and caciques like him found their monopoly on power undermined by those invested in building new routes into and out of regional markets. These routes took the shape of actual communications investments as well as the commercial institutions and legal tools that facilitated economic activity. Díaz and his predecessors facilitated the creation of such new forms through changes in national law and policy, but it was through local activity that they became reality.

For the most part, the rest of the book will refrain from discussing political hierarchies and electoral matters. Instead it will continue to explore the politics of administration that mediated economic growth in the Soconusco. Popular engagement with liberalism here rarely meant engagement with electoral politics. Instead, the physical spaces introduced in this chapter—the district and municipal courts and the public records office—became the key sites for the institutionalization of the liberal project at the local level. Having carved out those spaces through their own experimentation with the language of reform, elites and non-elites alike maintained a hold over that institutionalization as they expanded the bounds of their local economy.

4 The Landscape of Production

The Muñoz brothers had problems with their properties. As with many others taking advantage of the Soconusco's porous border and plentiful lands, they had moved from Guatemala to the foothill municipality of Unión Juárez sometime in the early 1880s. José Maria, Eulogio, and Pedro soon became vecinos, locally recognized citizens of the municipality with access to its shared resources. Instead of petitioning the town council for lots in the municipality's communally held ejidos, they bought the rights to neighbors' lands. Nothing large—by the early 1890s the brothers together held about ten hectares of land planted with coffee, sugar, and subsistence crops. In 1892, the town council decided to take up the task of subdividing and titling the ejido. The Muñozes suddenly found their ownership under attack.

The most serious challenge sought to undermine the community's claim to the ejido as a whole. In response, José Maria Muñoz took up a position as the municipality's legal representative. A finquero used titles going back to the 1840s and surveys done in the 1870s by a good friend of the local cacique to assert that what Unión Juárez claimed as communal property was actually private land. In the community's defense, José Maria pointed to an 1875 decree from the federal government bestowing the new town with its officially mandated land grant. The surveyor quickly admitted that his map was likely mistaken; he had just survived an assassination attempt at the time of its completion and he was quite reasonably distracted. He readily stated that he had likely mislabeled the ejido as public lands. The community kept its holdings.[1]

The Muñozes, though, also faced challenges to their holdings from within Unión Juárez. Other vecinos doubted the brothers' rights to one of the parcels they claimed. The land's original occupant had lost ownership of it when he was declared insane, and his wife had then used the parcel to repay an unfulfilled coffee contract previously signed by her troubled husband. The merchant who took the land in payment sold it to Eulogio Muñoz four years later. Two years after that, Eulogio acquired two additional lots from neighbors. In 1889, he paid taxes on these three parcels, valuing the total at MX$1,000.[2] When it came time to survey and privatize the ejido in 1892, the vecinos of Unión Juárez readily recognized the second two purchases as valid. Yet no one was quite certain that the repayment of debt with a parcel of ejidal land had in fact been legitimate.[3]

The Muñozes' confusion of claims was not uncommon. The volcanic landscape of the Soconusco did not yield to easy surveying and crisp property lines. It undulated and fell into gullies. It meandered along streambeds and raced up mountainsides. Densely vegetated and sparsely populated, it resisted legibility. Yet as export agriculture expanded its appeal to Latin America's rural residents, a growing number of claimants demanded the landscape's rationalization. And as with so many property holders, the Muñozes' muddle was clearly about more than just topography. Centuries of overlapping means of establishing ownership layered on top of eons of volcanic activity made the legal terrain nearly as indecipherable as the physical spaces it purported to govern. Now, those often conflicting property regimes had to be brought into concert. As export crops made the land itself an increasingly valuable investment, producers large and small had a vested interest in defining and defending their claims.

It was not that land was a scarce resource in rural nineteenth century Latin America.[4] It was property that was hard to come by. Yet images like Map 4 make the landscape seem overcrowded with large plantations, leaving little space for other stories of export agriculture. Maps like this reinforce the belief that plantations contain the only export story worth telling. Yet it was the unlabeled rectangles and wandering streams and unresolved bounds that defined the spaces in which those emblematic plantations could come to exist. While maps like this hew closely to the legibility and standardization that governments across the Americas aimed to achieve in this era, they hide as much as they reveal.[5]

This chapter traces the overlapping stories of villager- and finquero-driven privatization efforts and the attendant acceleration in local property markets. In the process, it shows how smallholders like the Muñoz brothers and their neighbors expanded their holdings and defined the spaces within which local and migrant elites could invest. As much as ridges and gullies became natural borders for neighboring plantations, municipalities and their communally held lands were man-made bounds for the spread of fincas as a whole. Counter to a historiography of globalization that has long emphasized the loss of village lands to plantation owners, here villagers maintained and even expanded their reach into the foothills of the Sierra Madre.

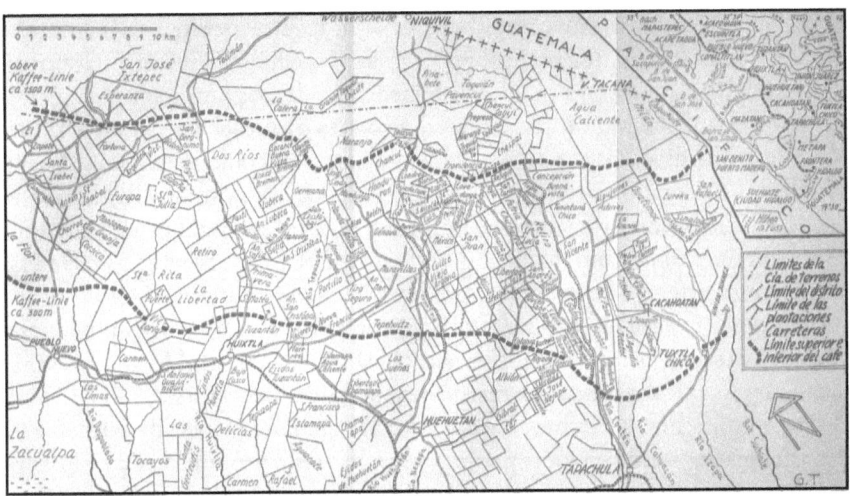

MAP 4. Map of the English Company's Division of the Soconusco's Coffee Plantation Zone. Source: Karl Helbig, *El Soconusco y su zona cafetalera en Chiapas*. Tuxtla Gutiérrez, Chiapas: Instituto de Ciencias y Artes de Chiapas, 1964, appendix.

Drawing on the rich transactional archive of the Soconusco, I use the stories of a village and a land company to counteract the stories told by maps like that above. The Mexican state had attempted to enforce and facilitate the surveying and sale of public and communal lands since the 1850s. Only with the expansion of the export economy did large swaths of Mexico begin to put those policies into practice. In the Soconusco, interest in export agriculture motivated villagers and planters alike to secure or obtain defensible title to that which could provide their livelihood. They did so on timelines that made sense for their circumstances, leading to the endurance of multiple landholding patterns across the region. The state and its surrogates were not able to enact their liberal land reform at will. Rather, individuals and communities slowly formalized the region's property institutions through the selective use of long-standing laws and regulations. By doing so, they turned an emphasis on private property into a means of shoring up their own management of the landscape.

A Brief History of Privatization

For Mexican liberals, the great expanses of untitled land throughout the country represented both an impediment to growth and an untapped source of wealth. In this understanding, lands that remained in public or communal hands encouraged no investment and inspired no exchange. They could not be used as collateral for loans, they could not be sold to underwrite new ventures, they could not be counted on to supply market demands. In seeking to resolve this challenge, reformers quickly realized that demographic patterns and the vastness of the nation necessitated two sets of projects to resolve these concerns. The first was meant to divide the parcels of land held communally by villages, indigenous or otherwise, into pieces of individually held private property. The second was directed at measuring and selling the huge amount of unclaimed public land in the country, known before surveying as *terrenos baldíos* and after as *terrenos nacionales*.[6] In the Soconusco, the two projects emerged in tandem though rarely in competition.[7] As more individuals engaged with export markets, they slowly standardized and formalized the means by which they demonstrated ownership of their lands.

The disentailment of communally held village land, generally termed ejidos though the local legal terminology varied, was a professed aim of liberal Mexican politicians from the early nineteenth century onward. The Ley Lerdo, issued in 1856, set a national procedure for privatization. It was not unprecedented. Rather, it found its basis in elite efforts to divide village lands that began with independence.[8] In Chiapas much of this push was related to a need for labor, rather than for the land itself.[9] While the turmoil of mid-century Mexico paused privatization efforts, Porfirio Díaz's rise brought renewed commitment to the work of *repartimiento*, or repartition. This disamortization was a significant site for negotiation with the state and within communities. In some places it resulted in significant loss of land and autonomy, as in Emiliano Zapata's Anenecuilco. Elsewhere, internally driven processes of division and titling shaped the emergence of new local elites.[10]

The second branch of the national project of privatization was that farmed out to independent surveying companies and strongly interwoven with a drive to attract European and North American emigrants to Latin America.[11] National and state governments had sought the means to monetize public lands since independence. In 1863, Benito Juárez codified the alienation and sale of public lands by instituting legal procedures by which individuals could purchase untitled lands directly from the government.[12] Still missing, though, was any sort of regularized and accessible means for doing so. As potential planters had complained to Matías Romero in the 1870s, the process required a slew of paperwork and the involvement of officials generally located far from the lands in question. Only in the 1880s did the government institute a new policy that acknowledged its own lack of progress thus far. Instead of managing the surveying and sale of lands itself, the Department of Fomento began granting concessions to private companies who would take on the work of surveying, titling, and colonizing the Mexican countryside. The 1883 law dictated that these concessionaires be granted one third of the land they surveyed in payment, leading to the transfer of 21.2 million hectares of public lands to those who took advantage of this law. As Robert Holden demonstrates in one of the few scholarly works to deal directly with these companies, this meant the surveying of some 63.5 million hectares during the decade, or 32 percent of the entire national territory.[13] Yet these companies were not terribly successful at the work they undertook. They failed to sell most of the land they received in payment. They also failed to fulfill colonization clauses and had to fudge the numbers or bargain hard in order to avoid voiding their contracts with the federal government.[14]

The Soconusco presents a place to examine a juncture of the two processes. Through the 1880s, most of the district's 5,475 square kilometers remained empty and untitled. Colonial population collapse and postcolonial focus on coastal cattle ranching had left much of the Sierra Madre public property by default. Verdant and uncontested, this was the ideal landscape for a colonization company to settle. The few foothill villages that existed were of recent establishment, the ink on their constitutive land grants from the federal government fresh. While those grants stated that the new town was supposed to subdivide the lands for its residents, the town councils of Unión Juárez and Cacahoatán had more or less ignored those clauses.[15] Romero and his correspondents attempted to engage villagers with the process in the mid-1870s, hoping to secure their claims to lands they were beginning to plant with coffee.[16] As we will see, villagers did not entirely ignore the reforms these planters introduced. Yet, with village populations and the intensity of cultivation still low, most municipal councils saw privatization as more of a hassle than it was worth.

The beginning of the 1890s brought marked change. The shift toward formalized institutions discussed in Chapter Three became particularly useful in the realm of property. With the population growing and increasingly turning its labor toward export cultivation, demonstrating ownership of one's lands became ever more important. As Romero's correspondents complained and the Muñoz brothers discovered, investing in a plant that would take four years to come into fruit made a producer eager to secure legible and defensible rights to the land that supported the new crop. Also, only properly titled land could be put up as collateral for loans or payment for outstanding debts. Coffee exports from the Soconusco were worth ten times more in 1887 than they had been in 1872. By 1900 they would again increase tenfold to more than two thousand metric tons worth over MX$1 million.[17] The type of investment needed to create such growth could only happen if people felt sure of the land into which they poured their money.[18]

Defending one's land did not mean the same thing for everyone. Most finqueros based their claims on the work of a private land company called the Mexican Land and Colonization Company.[19] This company introduced a regularized means of purchasing titled lands that remained relatively constant across the coming decades. Villages, on the other hand, managed their own intermittent engagement with the process of ejidal repartition. As the rest of the chapter will demonstrate, privatization happened in fits and starts as municipal councils took up the project for a variety of reasons. That said, both the sale of public lands and the privatization of communal ones accelerated across the 1890s and early 1900s, slightly trailing the trends of the global coffee market. So, too, did the resale market for titled lands that developed soon after (see Figure 2). While the growth of each market followed similar timelines, the two remained segregated. Finqueros bought and sold fincas, villagers bought and sold lots in former village holdings.

Slowly, the seemingly boundless foothills of the Sierra Madre began to find their bounds. Large expanses of public lands could be had for less than a peso a hectare if bought from the government or somewhere between 3 and 15 pesos if purchased from the land company. Once someone had planted them with coffee, the value quickly jumped to at least MX$15 a hectare if not double that.[20] The resale price of cultivated properties both small and large

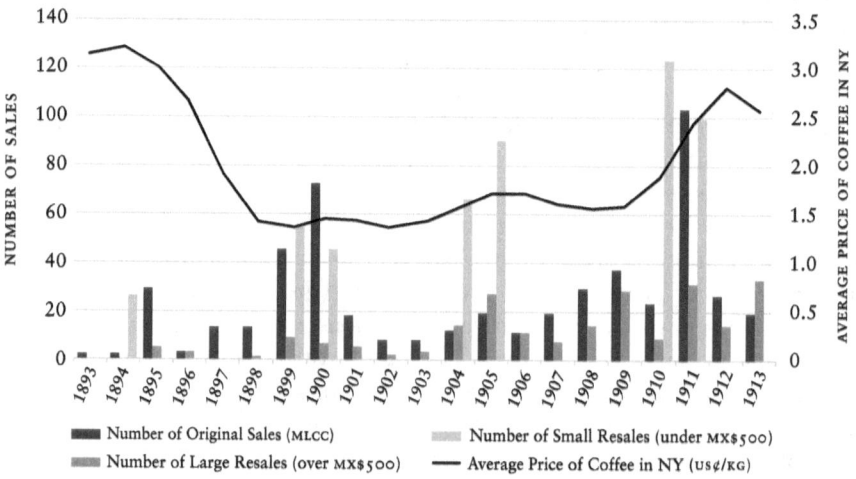

FIGURE 2. Number of Property Sales Registered in the Soconusco, 1893–1913. This figure includes all MLCC transactions as well as resale transactions of properties in those municipalities known to grow coffee. I do not have enough reliably dated information on ejidal repartition to create a timeline for that process. Data on small resales is confined to the nine years for which I have indices of all sales made: 1894, 1899, 1900, 1901, 1904, 1905, 1910, 1911, and 1912. Data on large resales includes all the sales for which I have registrations during these years. Source: Archivo del Registro Público de la Propiedad y el Comercio, Tapachula. Coffee prices from Samper K. et al., "Appendix: Historical Statistics of Coffee Production and Trade from 1700 to 1960."

tended to reflect, if again lag behind, the global price of the commodity (see Figure 3). As recorded in local government offices, the division between the two markets mapped onto the civil code's mandate that transactions valued at more than MX$500 required the presence of a notary, while those under MX$500 did not. As importantly, it reflected a division between elite and nonelite producers that rarely saw any cross-pollination. Large sales averaged 128 hectares and generally took place between local and migrant investors, while small sales usually involved less than five hectares and almost always involved villagers from the Soconusco or, on occasion, Guatemala.[21]

Both villagers and finqueros expanded their holdings across the period in question. In the process, villagers from the Soconusco did not lose ground to local or foreign plantation owners. Surprising in terms of the long historiography of community privatization, but in line with more recent scholarship, private land in the Soconusco was a resource to which locals and outsiders, finqueros and subsistence farmers gained and maintained access through strategic engagement with liberal reforms. The rest of this chapter will detail that engagement through the experiences of those charged with managing privatization—a municipal government and a land company.

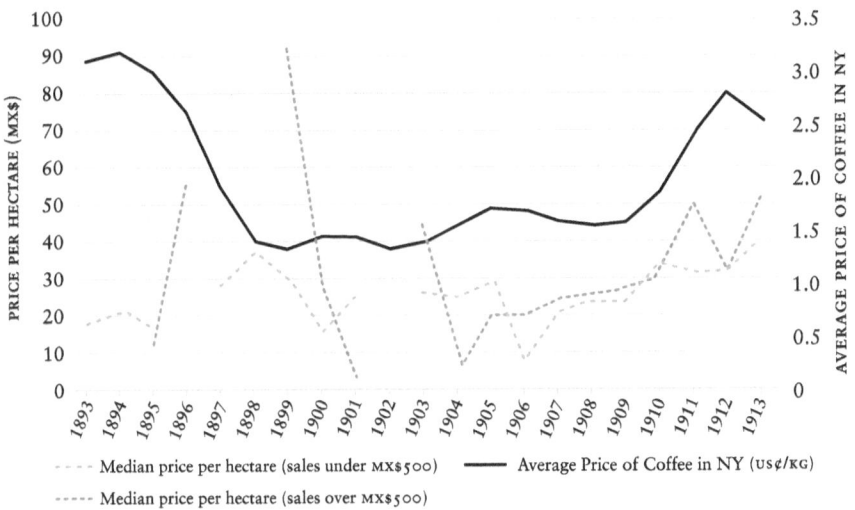

FIGURE 3. Price per Hectare of Large and Small Sales as Compared to Global Coffee Prices, 1893–1913. This figure includes only resale transactions of properties in those municipalities known to grow coffee. No median price is included in years where fewer than three transactions were found in the archive. Source: Archivo del Registro Público de la Propiedad y el Comercio, Tapachula; coffee prices from Samper K. et al., "Appendix: Historical Statistics of Coffee Production and Trade from 1700 to 1960."

Strategic Engagement with Municipal Repartition

In the 1870s, the municipality of Cacahoatán was both an ancient pueblo and a new one. Its strategies for managing landholding were similarly old and new. A narrow north-south strip that stretches from the Suchiate River's northwesterly bend through the foothills of the Sierra toward Volcán Tacaná's peak, the town's past had been built on cacao. Its present was built on recent migrants who sought to reestablish the municipality and secure its lands for export and subsistence cultivation. As they did so, municipal leaders managed the town's communal holdings without regard for the state-mandated timeline for privatization. Individual members of the community sometimes sought private title as a means of better engaging with credit and export markets. Others saw the benefit in title as a means of defending against acquisitive plantation owners. Yet the process was never mandatory or uniform. Cacahoatán's engagement with this process is better documented than most other municipalities, but quantitative analyses combined with descriptive sources make clear that the town's controlled entry into privatization was commonplace in the Soconusco. By strategically taking part in the national project of privatization, town councilors maintained control over the speed and manner of their ejidos' division and kept ownership of lands within their communities.

As its vecinos proudly recalled, Cacahoatán's roots stretched back to the pre-Colombian era. Its founders claimed the survivors of Conquest-era epidemics and colonial exploitation as their ancestors. Village lore held that the town had disappeared only in the early 1800s, destroyed by political turmoil likely related to the contested border. Its current inhabitants had refounded the town in the early 1850s. Within a few years, the state government had granted them the status of a municipality and recognized the municipal government they organized according to constitutional mandates.[22]

By 1870, the federal government had granted the municipality two pieces of land to serve as ejidos for its growing population. Historians are not the only ones who find the land laws of nineteenth-century Mexico confusing. Municipal leaders and state politicians, too, seem to have had trouble reconciling various aspects of the general liberal push toward private land holding. As Chapter Three demonstrated, the central state had little capacity to force the enactment of policy reforms at mid-century. With land policy, the law itself sometimes acquiesced to this contested reality. The 1856 Ley Lerdo demanded the repartition of communally held lands, but federal policy exempted a town's *fundo legal*—the land on which the urban center was constructed—as well as its ejidos from that mandate.[23] Taking advantage of this exemption, towns across the Soconusco either established or extended ejidos for their residents deep into the latter half of the nineteenth century.[24]

While a portion of Cacahoatán's grant mapped onto the land worked by those who had reconstituted the town, the parcels as a whole stretched far beyond. The exact extension of the municipality's holdings is hard to pin down. Whatever the size, it was more than enough land for the municipality's small but growing population, which reached only 900 by 1880.[25]

Some of this growth came from a continual inflow of the same migrants who had traveled relatively short distances from Tapachula and the coastal plains to reestablish the town. As they arrived and established vecindad, these villagers claimed portions of the ejido where they grew subsistence crops and market goods, including coffee, to sell in Tapachula.[26] Emigrant planters also found the fertile and unclaimed lands of the Sierra Madre appealing. Cacahoatán was a key site of investment for those newcomers who followed Romero south and hoped to avoid Escobar's mercurial hold on Tapachula. The two groups, at least in their narration of events, worked side by side in the municipality's ejidos and the surrounding lands. The municipal council called newcomers *impresarios* and seemed to regard them and their investments as welcome additions to the community. By the mid-1870s, at least twenty individuals, both local and newly arrived, had each prepared at least two hectares of land for coffee cultivation.[27]

While newcomers drawn by coffee's potential rarely stepped on toes with regard to land, they did begin to consolidate a position as part of the new municipality's elite. A finquero took up a spot on the municipal council by the end of the 1870s, following the general pattern established in Chapter Three of working around Escobar by staying out of his line of sight.[28] A number established vecindad in the community, though most foreigners maintained their citizenship abroad. Planters' numbers were still small, but their presence slowly began to change the municipal council's approach to land management.

While the council did not act as though its lands or autonomy were under threat from newcomers or the state government, it began to slowly take up the project of repartition in the early 1880s. For one thing, privatization of communal lands represented property tax incomes for the town's coffers. With next to no infrastructure or public facilities, the moneys would be welcome. Also, as newcomers continued to stream into town, repartition presented an opportunity for town leaders to secure the best public lands for themselves. León Saenz, a coffee planter and ally of Matías Romero, was now municipal president. He worked to convince the council that repartition could help resolve slowly emerging tensions between smallholders and finqueros. He never went as far as some other planters might have liked, leading one man to declare that the leadership of Cacahoatán had "small, petty souls" and Unión Juárez was a far better site for investment.[29] Yet he did take up the offer of José Encarnación Ibarra, a local magistrate and friend of Escobar's, to serve as surveyor for the town as need arose.

By the late 1870s, the government of Chiapas had already called for and carried out the repartition of ejidos in other parts of the state numerous times. In 1878, it issued another call for privatization of communal holdings.[30] This was likely what motivated Ibarra's offer, though he had previously traveled to Unión Juárez to carry out similar functions.[31] That Cacahoatán's town council waited until 1880 to begin surveys suggests that the state's mandate came with little in the way of enforcement. So, too, does the municipal council's insistence on supervising Ibarra's activities.

Not everyone was interested in titling their lands at this moment. Out of the town's 900 residents, only 66 individuals took part in the proceedings. On Ibarra's arrival, the council handed him a list of land claims made by those interested in his services. Most claimants were villagers, either locally born or recently migrated. They primarily requested title for the least expensive lands, those the council labeled "third class" and judged to be least valuable. A few lots were as small as half a hectare, but most measured between twenty-one and forty-two hectares, either half or a whole *caballería* in the old system of measures. No matter the size of the lot, claimants named their properties: José María Díaz called his land Bolivar, Manuel Molina named his La Libertad. Those who splurged for second-class land were signing up to pay $18; those who stuck with the lower category would lay out $4 or less. The cost represented about eight days' wages and there is no record of complaint about the price.[32]

A few locals, along with at least five foreigners, paid much more for their lands. In doing so, they took advantage of a newly available formal means to institutionalize their informally held property. For the town council, planters' eagerness to take up this new tool was also a way of extracting something extra from those newly arrived in the area. While the lands these finqueros claimed were usually larger than those paid for by villagers, the correlation between cost and size was in no way exact. Claiming fincas they named Magdalena, San Antonio, La Plata, and La Victoria, planters laid out $40 for lots ranging from 84 hectares to 220 hectares. From the council's descriptions, these lands were on the edges of the community's ejidos and may well have extended onto unclaimed public lands. Many of these properties had been included in Romero's report on coffee in the district seven years before and were already producing beans for those who now sought to title them.[33]

Despite this display of interest in engaging liberal reform, most of this first attempt at repartition went unfulfilled. No one seemed to mind. While all those listed on Ibarra's arrival had agreed to take on the costs of the survey, the process was more expensive than anticipated. Ibarra was elsewhere accused of using his local influence to line his pockets, and the mounting worries about cost expressed in local council meetings likely reflect another instance of graft.[34] Accordingly, the council dismissed him within the year.

Nonetheless, at least a few finqueros completed the titling process, and the council counted that as enough progress for the moment. No one else immediately demanded title. The council decided to send the survey Ibarra had completed to the state as a demonstration of their compliance with the 1878 mandate and to use it as the basis for future titling if interest arose. Any villager who had the funds necessary could come forward and request a proper title. Yet the council did little to incentivize this process. Instead, it stated that villagers would be left in possession if not outright ownership of the lots they currently worked.[35]

With minimal protest, officials in San Cristóbal acquiesced to Cacahoatán's arrangement. This was yet another instance of local leaders managing the processes of reform supposedly governed by the Mexican state. This initial round of privatization had gone smoothly for all involved. Expatriate finqueros gained their titles, and the town council kept control of the process. Yet as forty vecinos, including more than a third of those who had registered a year before, entered into a new round of land divisions in mid-1881, the cooperative atmosphere began to crumble.

The manner in which the town council of Cacahoatán dealt with one particularly aggressive newcomer serves as a clear example of the many tools villagers had at their disposal for managing their lands. Santiago Keller, a Swiss planter, had arrived in the municipality sometime around 1876. Within five years, his ambition and disdain for local practices had turned the townspeople against him. Not trusting political officials in Tapachula to take their side—remember that avoiding Escobar was regular practice at this time—the municipal council wrote to the state government asking for assistance in educating foreigners on Mexico's land tenure system. Particularly, they wanted someone to tell Keller that he had no right to lands in the ejidos of Cacahoatán.

Keller, unlike Saenz and other planters who had claimed lands in the municipality by cooperating with the municipal council, was aggressively interested in dispossessing the community of its lands. His desire to transform the Soconusco into a land of export plantations was based in large part on sweeping aside local ways of doing things. Writing to Romero, he explicitly stated that the best means of developing the region involved promoting European immigration and the displacement of "those who don't produce anything other than beans and tortillas for their own consumption."[36] Pursuant to this interest, he worked to delegitimize the municipality's ownership of ejido lands. He spread rumors among the villagers of Cacahoatán that the money they were contributing to the municipal council for repartition was a complete waste of resources, as the land belonged to the federal government, not the municipality.[37] Suggesting that his interpretation of property law was maliciously self-serving rather than simply ill-informed, he also paid a local woman to claim ejido land in her own name, land he promised to then purchase directly from her.[38]

The rhetoric deployed by the municipal council to counter these accusations was pointed and patriotic. It also betrayed the abnormality of Keller's actions. Forty-three vecinos signed a letter to the state government charging Keller with stealing their land and undermining their republican values. The letter told a tale of a community's determined work for progress, progress that was imperiled when, "like an evil spirit," Keller began to plague them. While the authors portrayed those foreigners who preceded him as respectful of local law and local landholding, Keller acted, "as though we all owe him obedience, forgetting that in this country we have none of the privileges of nobility which kings bestow." The letter's authors underlined their belief in the ejido as an enlightened grant from a government committed to its poor and industrious citizens. Keller's actions thus not only damaged local livelihoods but also damaged the nation's honor. The vecinos of Cacahoatán strategically claimed their rights as members of the Mexican nation and requested protection against an invading force. While they had little interest in allowing the government to take over land reform, they called on it to expel this pernicious foreigner.[39]

In the same manner that it ignored local complaints against Escobar's arbitrary violence, the government ignored the charges placed at Keller's feet. Keller, though, lacked Escobar's clout and connections. Within five months, Keller was dead. Officials in Tapachula arrested a municipal councilor from Cacahoatán and seven other men for murdering the man in his dining room while he read the paper. As far as his widow understood it, Keller had been caught unawares, murdered in cold blood over the ongoing land dispute.[40] Despite vecinos' direct intervention, the finca in question did not return to the municipality. Instead, it passed from creditor to creditor as Keller's widow attempted to pay off the almost MX$60,000 he left in debts.[41]

Carlos Gris, the former planter whose long dispute with Escobar was discussed in the previous chapter, laid blame for the murder at the cacique's doorstep.[42] But the cacique was not the only one in the district to resort to violence when needed. The lack of a criminal justice archive for the Soconusco in this era makes it hard to know how often disputes escalated to this level. The commonality of accusations of invasion and the relatively regular mention of firearms in other parts of the archive suggest that violence should not be ignored as a tactic for defending a community's right to self-regulation. As the previous chapters explored, in the absence of reliable institutions, force served as the primary means of resolving disputes over power.

At least as common in this period, though, were strategies of delay, negotiation, and selective engagement with liberal reform. Rather than the universal and uniform application of privatization laws, repartition in the Soconusco tended to occur sporadically and in an individuated manner. When a villager desired to title part of the ejido, he or she would petition the town council, which would review the claimant's residency and any competing rights to the land in question.[43] Local control over the process meant that vecindad in the community rather than citizenship in the nation continued to dictate access to land. Town councilors knew that the slow and selective pace of privatization helped them maintain control of their community's land. In Cacahoatán, council writings made clear that the villagers knew that their actions countered national policy. "In virtue of there being few vecinos who have a right to hold the land [according to national law]," councilors wrote, they would work to maintain control over future surveys to avoid foreign-born vecinos losing their holdings.[44]

Selective, partial, locally controlled engagement with privatization mandates was the norm across the Soconusco. The slow trickle of sales in titled properties in the neighboring ejidos of Tapachula, Tuxtla Chico, and other towns suggests that these municipalities' initial decades of privatization also countered national and state demands for universal private property regimes. Despite nagging by the state government, only 200 individuals in the whole of the Soconusco were paying property taxes on privatized portions of ejidal land in 1889. At most twenty of these individuals claimed land in Cacahoatán's ejidos, most of them participants in the original survey from 1880.[45] Land was still inexpensive and overabundant, making engagement with private title unnecessary for most people. Local norms regarding community management provided for those who needed to expand their holdings to accommodate new family members or new enterprises.[46] Planters looking to invest substantial sums in new fincas made use of repartition where they could, but they still lacked the sway to universalize the practice. Violent retribution like that turned on Santiago Keller was never far from anyone's mind. Thus, the flexible management of intermittent titling managed by town councils remained the norm for now.

Toward a Standardization of Large-Scale Property

The division of communal lands was only one prong of the nineteenth-century push for privatization. The drive to survey and sell off the huge portion of Mexican territory held by the state was equally as important. Both governments and investors believed that rationalizing titles and simplifying the purchase of public lands were necessary steps toward capitalizing on the expansion of global markets for Latin American goods. Having failed to manage this process itself, the government posited land companies like the Mexican Land and Colonization Company (MLCC) as the best means to turn Mexico's land into property. Yet the company's experience in the Soconusco demonstrates how even government backing and local demand for services were not enough to quickly smooth the way for liberal land policy.

As previous chapters have demonstrated, elites in the Soconusco had little need for regularized, accurate land titles in the first half of the nineteenth century. Most held their wealth as cattle branded with their marks. While elites claimed ownership of the ranches where cattle grazed, the land itself held little value. Because of this, most were satisfied with the vague colonial and independence-era titles that granted their owners expanses of land in the coastal plains without defining much beyond the general size of the property and naming its neighbors.

As the economy began to diversify into export crops in the 1860s and 1870s, elites started to reach for more formal means of demonstrating ownership. Lacking easy access to the federally supervised processes governing public lands, they turned to the same Ibarra who offered his services to the villagers of Cacahoatán. Ibarra, in turn, drew up a slew of property descriptions, accompanied by geographic markers and rough sketches of the lands in question. Most were located in the coastal plains rather than the Sierra Madre and owned by locals rather than newcomers. No one submitted these pseudo-titles to the federal government for verification, but many owners paid property taxes on them as an additional means of asserting their ownership.[47]

It was only with the arrival of Romero and other outsiders in the early 1870s that the public land procedures began to find any takers. Initially, as so many (including Escobar) complained, the process of purchasing public lands was far too lengthy and expensive to make it worth anyone's while. When Romero facilitated the installation of a federal district judge in Tapachula in 1875, he removed some of the hurdles that made the official process so unappealing. While Escobar's violent pushback against federal officials delayed matters, local and newly arrived planters obtained a spurt of titles through legal channels in the early and mid-1880s.[48] As with those landowners who paid Ibarra for a survey, some of these planters had already begun paying taxes on their lands before they held outright title. Many had also already begun cultivating the lands they claimed.[49]

Yet most of the Soconusco remained unsurveyed and unclaimed. Across the 1880s, a number of entrepreneurs tried to capitalize on all this unbounded land. The state and national governments helped incentivize their investments with concessions to do everything from build railroads and piers, to form an agricultural colony, to found a "modernization company" complete with banks, factories, and steamships.[50] As with so many other concessions throughout the country, most granted in Chiapas were never acted upon, but they did leave their mark. An American land company obtained a concession from the federal government to survey and title lands in much of the district in the mid-1880s. Wary of Escobar's continued dominance in and around Tapachula, they bribed the cacique with a monthly salary and a percent of any profits made.[51] The company's activities attracted a trickle of American colonists to the foothills, people like the Humphreys family who opened this book. Yet, due to diplomatic machinations taking place far from the Soconusco, the company quickly failed.[52] In doing so, it left the colonists squatting, hoping that whoever next acquired the rights to the land would recognize their claims and provide legal titles at a discounted rate.[53]

In the early 1890s these squatters and the vecinos of municipalities across the district came face to face with the entity that finally made good on the promise of Díaz's developmentalist policies. Where previous attempts failed, the MLCC succeeded not because of the greater strength of its government or foreign backers, but because the region was by now eager for legally titled property. The 1880s had seen a steady rise in the global price of coffee. Along with the signing of the border treaty and the continued promotion of the region in newspapers and at international expositions, the promise of sizeable profits that those high prices entailed drew an accelerating stream of investors to the Soconusco.[54] Most started their enterprises on untitled lands. As they increased their investments, these new planters began to clamor for clear title that could secure their ownership against usurpation and provide a means to leverage it into more capital.

The MLCC's arrival was thus well-timed for success. It took over its predecessor's concession at the height of coffee's long global market climb. As importantly, by the time its first surveyors made it to Tapachula, Escobar was about to lose his life. In one fell swoop, the company sidestepped the need to pay off the local political boss and found the territorial claims that had inhibited earlier investors lifted. Those colonists left without substantiated land title were among its first clients, particularly those who had already begun planting their stakes with coffee. Just as importantly, locals and earlier arrivals who had relied on murky older documents soon lined up to take advantage of a standardized and supposedly scientific means of documenting their ownership.

As soon as it arrived, the MLCC established a predictable, straightforward, and localized set of procedures for acquiring title. The desired lot was measured out to the ten-thousandth of a hectare, with the price ranging from MX$10 to MX$20 a hectare.[55] Its borders were listed as the neighboring fincas or the general property of the MLCC, and *mojones* or border markers were placed at strategic intervals when naturally occurring landmarks were not clear. The purchaser paid a sixth to a quarter of the price up front and was granted a mortgage for the rest, with the finca serving as collateral. Interest was 6 percent annually, and the term for repayment was negotiated case by case, ranging from one to ten years, usually somewhere around four.[56]

In 1891 the company sold its first properties to locals and other Mexican citizens. By 1895 it had begun selling to foreigners.[57] Sales climbed steadily through the end of the decade, only falling precipitously in 1900 when the impact of the global collapse in coffee prices a few years earlier finally hit the region (see Figure 2). Yet, as with the local economy as a whole, the company recovered quickly. Where it sold 100 properties between 1890 and 1900, the following thirteen years saw it take part in more than 500 land transactions. Despite this seeming boom, the company only ever sold a fraction of the land it received from the government in payment for its work.[58]

The steady climb in sales numbers across the 1890s should not mask the initial conflicts generated by the company's arrival. The land company faced exactly the sorts of contestation that historian Robert Holden points to when discussing the failures of these companies as a whole. Represented by a British engineer named Oliver Herbert Harrison and his Mexican counterpart, a holdover from the previous land company named Plácido Gomez, the MLCC had to overcome difficult terrain, the welter of titling practices described above, recalcitrant villagers, and the continual inability of its clients to cover their costs. Many of these difficulties are visible in the survey map that the MLCC inherited from its predecessor (see Map 5). Gomez had drawn in Cacahoatán's multitude of small properties, representing both fincas and ejido, as the southern bounds of the land company's claim. A couple of large parcels claimed through the Department of Fomento were situated in the center of its territory. The company mostly chose to avoid these earlier claimants with their at least somewhat regularized claims. Early entrepreneurs, though, particularly those who had paid Ibarra for title and the American colonists who had been left high and dry by their sponsor, now found themselves at odds with the MLCC.

Initially enthusiastic about the company's arrival, those without some sort of government-backed title were soon reminded of the dangers of investing in land before acquiring clear ownership of it. As Helen Humphreys put it, "The mere idea that the colonial concession business was about to come back to life put the colonists in quite a flurry of excitement, and no wonder—it had been such a long time laid by."[59] Soon, though, it became clear that the MLCC had no intention of recognizing the Americans' investment of time and capital. In 1892, Harrison and Gomez sued a group of fourteen settlers, accusing them of usurping land legally granted to the MLCC.[60] While some quickly acceded to the company's conditions and paid US$1.50 an acre for the land they had worked for many years, the court forced the holdouts to pay almost double that price.[61] Following this battle,

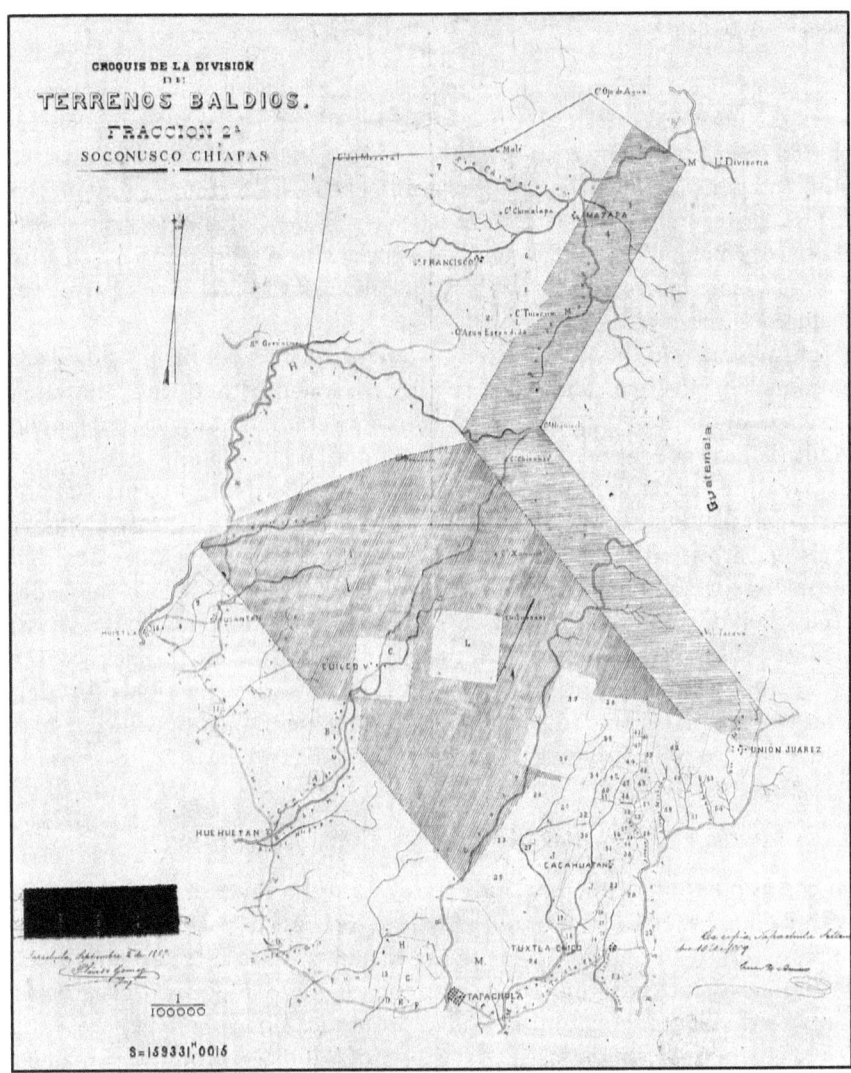

MAP 5. Croquis of the Division of Terrenos Baldíos, 2nd Fraction, Soconusco, Chiapas, 1889. Source: Plácido Gomez, "Croquis de la división de terrenos baldíos, fracción segunda Soconusco Chiapas," 1889. Mapoteca Manuel Orozco y Berra, Colección General, Varilla OYBCHIS01, No. Clasificador 181-06B-7274-A. Reprinted with permission.

a number of local planters and ranchers whose only proof of ownership were the informal titles expedited by Ibarra in the 1870s defensively purchased their own properties from the MLCC.[62] Patience paid off for those who had gone through the time-consuming process of titling land with the federal government, as the company never challenged such official titles. Properties including finca San Juan las Chicharras, represented in Map 5 by a large square labeled with an L and the center of Chapter Five's narrative, endured without issue.

Large-scale landholding patterns were at least as confusing as village commons in late nineteenth-century Mexico. A wide variety of overlapping practices and titles going back to the colonial era butted up against public lands that the government did little to manage. While it had passed a series of laws and regulations across mid-century to ease the survey and sale of these national lands, the central state lacked the capacity to truly facilitate their privatization. Concessions to private land companies provided one means of surmounting this difficulty. Yet such companies could only succeed when demand for their services existed. In the Soconusco, the MLCC arrived at the right time and with the right tools. Even so, it quickly came into conflict with planters who asserted their own property rights through alternate means. It also found its abilities to act curtailed by villagers and municipal councils, bringing us back to Cacahoatán.

The Maintenance of Village Lands in a Time of Transition

As the population of the Soconusco grew and the value of land increased with it, more vecinos began to legally title their portion of the ejidos. The process was still slow. But where the state had failed to force privatization, the influx of coffee capital and the attendant surge in population growth motivated villages to action. Bounded properties slowly spread across the seemingly boundless landscape of the district. Municipal councils remained in charge of the process by which their communal holdings entered into the market for private property. And villagers remained in charge of the lands themselves. As new commercial agriculture made it valuable to do so, municipal councils hired surveyors and oversaw privatization procedures that left lands in the hands of their constituents.

In July of 1894, an official in Tapachula wrote to Cacahoatán's municipal council urging them to provide their municipal titles to aid the MLCC in the rectification of its surveys. This was not the first request for these titles. In fact, the letter arrived as a reminder that the period for submitting such titles had just closed.[63] Despite the official's assertions of urgency, it is unclear that the municipality ever condescended to send its titles along. Instead, the community continued in the repartition and sale of its lands at a steady pace, managed internally, with no evidence of interference from the MLCC. With broad horizons available in the rest of the district, the company had little interest in grappling with the municipality's complex titling history.

Even without the MLCC infringing on community lands, the 1890s did bring a slow uptick in the pace of repartition in the Soconusco. The continued expansion of coffee's hold on the Sierra Madre was largely to blame. Increasingly, those who came before the municipal council in Cacahoatán to purchase title to their lands included mentions of coffee among the crops already growing on the properties they claimed.[64] While many titling lands borrowed legal language around repartition that allowed any head of household—*cabeza de familia*—to be apportioned land for the growing of "grains of first necessity," they also mentioned bananas, sugar cane, coffee, and other market crops in their petitions.[65]

The town's population boom also pushed some to title their lands. In 1892, the town had more than 1,000 residents. By 1900, it had more than 2,500. Unlike earlier periods, no one now suggested that the federal government grant the municipality a new portion of ejidal land. Instead, the council began to grant lots in its *fundo legal*, the town center legally designated for residential and business occupation, for agricultural use. In doing so, it made sure to maintain control over what had once been communally held lands. Based on their understanding of federal laws and their own interest in accommodating a growing town center, the council included clauses allowing itself to reclaim the land if future vecinos wanted to construct buildings or homes on it. State officials who saw these clauses reprimanded the council for their potential to harm poor vecinos without the funds needed to build something on the lot as quickly as the council mandated. Yet the state let the clauses stand, citing the council's commitment to the spirit of progress.[66]

The extant documentation makes it difficult to parse exactly how many titles to ejido lands community members requested each year. That said, the rough timeline of repartition laid out in municipal documents suggests that these activities more or less correlated with local reactions to the global coffee market.[67] Privatization picked up across the 1890s as high coffee prices incentivized investment by both large and small coffee planters. When global coffee prices crashed in the late 1890s, no one seems to have pushed for any new expedition of titles. Only with the local economy's recovery around 1904 did the town again hire someone to act as its agent for the surveying and titling of communal lands.[68] Again, the correlation is rough, but as with the MLCC's activities, it exists. Even though the state continued to issue mandates requiring complete repartition, the municipal council had no problem granting people usufruct rights to land until they had the funds to pay for survey and title. Once they could afford to and the local land market made it seem a reasonable activity, they rectified their claims, formalized earlier land sales, and sometimes expanded their holdings.

While a finquero had been the early driver of Cacahoatán's turn to privatization, most of its council members continued to be smallholders rather than large-scale planters. A very few, like their vanilla-growing counterparts studied by Emilio Kourí in Veracruz, grew quite prosperous from their engagement with export agriculture. They accumulated numerous properties in the now ex-ejidos and purchased lands outside municipal bounds.[69] These were the outliers. Most vecinos, including council members, titled less than ten hectares of land. This cost them less than MX$100, or the equivalent of a year's harvest from 200 coffee bushes or half a year's wages on a nearby finca.[70] Land in Cacahoatán's ejidos was not exactly cheap, but its soils were rich and even a small parcel could produce enough food and market crops to support a family. Privatization enforced the stratification already present within the municipality, but not to the degree that it forced community members off their lands.

This was the case across the Soconusco. Lands that had been ejidos became small properties held by villagers. Most were less than ten hectares when initially surveyed and titled, and vecinos on average paid less than MX$75 to the municipality for the land in question. The process by which municipalities managed repartition differed across the region. In every town, though, it was always the municipal council rather than an outside official that dictated the means by which an ejido was privatized. Tuzantán, a town at the heart of the MLCC's surveying efforts, was the last town in the district to undergo repartition. When it did so, the town council sold the vast majority of ejidal parcels for less than MX$10.[71]

The repartition process was not always a smooth one. In Cacahoatán, Mexican-born villagers occasionally used a neighbor's foreign birthplace to try and push them off a parcel, despite the council's regular defense of its foreign-born vecinos.[72] Elsewhere, villagers' murky legal knowledge sometimes came back to bite them. In Pueblo Nuevo, a municipality in the district's northern reaches, villagers complied with privatization mandates by having one community member purchase a large portion of the ejido using funds collected in equal parts from all his neighbors. The villagers then continued to use the land as they always had, until an unscrupulous interloper took advantage of the "crass ignorance" of the titleholder and used "subterfuge" to purchase the land. He, too, seemed content to let the villagers continue their use of the lands. Only on his death in 1911 did his heir attempt to kick the community out. The town council had forced earlier interlopers to back off without state intervention, seizing lands back from two non-vecinos who claimed them without right and reapportioning them to locals. At this point, with the Mexican Revolution spreading, state intercession apparently seemed an easier means to resolution. Living up to their expectations, the governor quickly ordered local authorities to bring the infringer to justice.[73]

In other municipalities, a careful manipulation of the legislation governing repartition meant that villagers all got their lands without paying. The state's statutes provisioned five free hectares to each head of family whose assets were worth less than MX$200.[74] As Governor Rabasa explained, this provision was intended "to prevent the abuses of the rich" by preferentially granting land to the poor.[75] In some towns, like Huehuetán, every privatized piece of ejido was acquired in this manner, all 159 lots.[76] This was also the case in a newly created town called Frontera Díaz, a colony organized at the request of Guatemalan villagers who wanted to stay in Mexico after fleeing from political violence at home. There, each new colonist received ten hectares, men and women alike. This was despite the fact that the land they claimed was titled to a coffee-growing widow from Tapachula.[77] In Cacahoatán only six individuals registered for poor lots in 1904, and in most other municipalities only a small percentage of lots were apportioned in this manner.[78] Yet even so, the state chastised the Soconusco's municipal authorities for giving away land without following state mandates regarding payment.[79]

This initial pattern of landholding held once newly titled lands entered into broader circulation. Some large-scale landowners, particularly those who complained about being excluded from the repartition process, expressed hope that privatized land would now become accessible. But "los ricos," as Governor Rabasa referred to them, were to be disappointed. Cacahoatán's land market was actually less active than that of other municipalities, despite the early entrance of coffee and its pervasiveness across small and large properties. Even so, at least thirty-four small properties changed hands between 1890 and 1917, a number of them in what had been the town's ejido. Of these, only two were purchased by foreigners, the rest by vecinos of Cacahoatán.[80]

In the earliest sales recorded in the Cacahoatán and the surrounding coffee-intensive municipalities, the average price for a small sale was MX$167, or about MX$21 a hectare. This climbed to around MX$250, or MX$30 a hectare, by 1900. The overall price stayed near that price point for the coming decades, though price per hectare dipped down to MX$25 as coffee prices crashed before recovering by 1910 (see Figure 3). This was still not exorbitantly more than what original owners had paid to the municipal council for the land. Manuel Trinidad Espadas was the buyer in three such small sales in Cacahoatán, and a merchant in neighboring Unión Juárez acquired nine lots from ex-ejiditarios. As with the acquisition of original titles, they were the odd ones out. Instead, most buyers appeared in the records as such only once. Landholding was stable, the land market steady and internally focused. When the 1910 Revolution prioritized land reform and the restitution of ejidos to communities, surveyors sent to the municipality had a difficult time establishing who held outright title to their land, let alone which lands had always been private and which ejidos.[81]

TABLE 1: *Distribution of Small Property Sales by Origin of Purchaser*

		REGION OF PROPERTY SALE				
		Tapachula	Tuxtla Chico	Lowlands	Coffee Highlands	Overall
ORIGIN OF PURCHASER	Soconusco	73%	91%	72%	44%	77%
	Chiapas	7%	2%	7%	6%	5%
	Mexico	9%	3%	12%	26%	8%
	Guatemala	5%	3%	2%	13%	4%
	Foreign	6%	1%	7%	11%	6%
	Total	100%	100%	100%	100%	100%

Based on 934 sales where both origin of purchaser and place of purchase are known.
Source: Archivo del Registro Público de la Propiedad y el Comercio, Tapachula.

Across the Soconusco, municipal councils and former ejiditarios followed Cacahoatán's model of slow privatization and maintenance of an internally oriented property market. As Table 1 illustrates, the coffee highlands where Cacahoatán was located had the highest percent of purchases made by those from outside the Soconusco. Yet even there, 44 percent of purchases were made by those from the Soconusco. In other parts of the district, those born in the Soconusco made more than two-thirds of such purchases. In the district's second largest municipality, Tuxtla Chico, locals made more than 90 percent of purchases. Most of these resales were located in what was alternately labeled the ex-ejidos or the former ejidos of a town. Those doing the purchasing came from the same group who would have had rights to the land before it was privatized.

The vecinos of the Soconusco did not lose their land nor control of their municipal councils. By managing the titling process from within their own administrative bodies, communities resisted intrusion by newcomers. By growing coffee on their lands, villagers acquired the funds necessary to pay for title and taxes and hold onto them. When the MLCC produced a new map of the district documenting its work at the end of its tenure in the district (see Map 6), the space occupied by ejidos and those fincas that had jump-started the coffee economy was completely blank. The plethora of village land claims that had preceded the MLCC's entrance into the region had dictated where this supposedly mighty modernizing actor could take up its work.

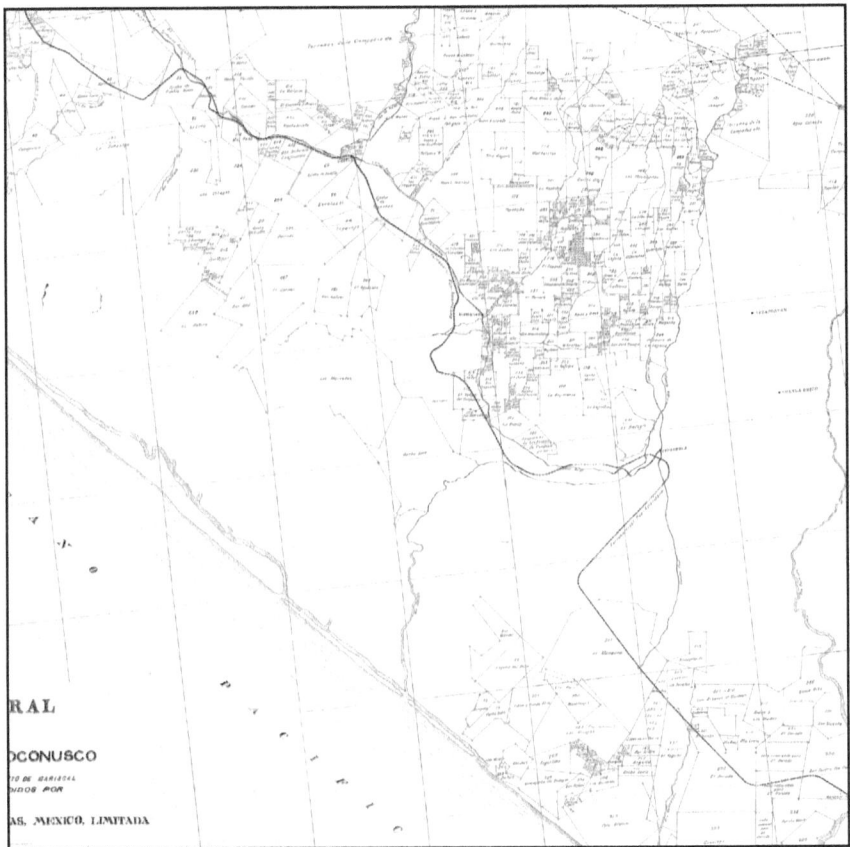

MAP 6. General Plan of the Department of Soconusco by the Mexican Land and Colonization Company, 1913 (Selection). Source: "Plano general del Departamento de Soconusco y la sección segregada para el Departamento de Mariscal indicando los terrenos vendidos por La Compañía de Terrenos de Chiapas, México, Limitada, 1913," Mapoteca Manuel Orozco y Berra, Colección Orozco y Berra, Varilla OYBCHIS02, No. Clasificador 3212-OYB-7274-A-1 y A-2. Reprinted with permission.

The Failed Consolidation of a Plantation Landscape

What about the spaces on this map covered in neatly arranged polygons, the same polygons emphasized by the map that opened the chapter? These irregular but seemingly definitively bounded shapes marched across the landscape in the wake of the MLCC's surveyors and the local and emigrant finqueros who requested them, slowly transforming the tropical forest into regimented columns of coffee bushes. Avoiding battles with villagers, the MLCC and those it served struck out into the wilds of the Sierra. Their expansionism increased the bounds of claimable land, but the hillsides were never occupied as fully as the company's maps tried to portray. Instead, planters continually ran up against the uncertainties that such maps worked to hide. Whether local or foreign, plantation owners squabbled over poorly surveyed property bounds and struggled to bring their large and ill-defined lands into cultivation. The Soconusco and those who had long worked its lands continued to constrain the spaces within which capital-intensive export agriculture could expand.

As with municipal councils' determined control over the implementation of repartition, local interests dictated the direction of the MLCC's activities. Its early contests with American colonists were an irregularity, though the hard-fought conflict left both sides more likely to negotiate going forward. Rather than the land company offering a ready-made list of available parcels, planters generally approached the company with a site in mind. This led to a patchwork of surveyed and unsurveyed lands, as many would-be finqueros had no interest in contesting the bounds of a neighbor's claim.

Planters also claimed lands from the company long before it actually had the right to sell them. According to its concession and the document it cited in every land title filed at the public records office, the Mexican government paid the MLCC for its work with 37,000 hectares of land in 1892. It expanded that payment to 80,003 hectares in 1896.[82] Yet ongoing political battles between elites in central Chiapas forestalled the actual issuance of the company's title to these lands until 1905.[83] Despite this, localized desire for proper titles to back loans and shore up investments motivated the company to begin drawing up deeds of sale as soon as it arrived in the Soconusco.

Unlike the titles drawn up by Ibarra in previous decades, these titles held up and were put to regular use. They were entered into the public records office by the droves, both on initial sale and again when the land was put up as collateral for a loan or claimed by a lender as repayment. Fincas titled by the MLCC were also resold at a steady clip as would-be planters realized their folly or ran out of funds or decided to expand. Commercial agriculture made titles that carried questionable weight outside the district into locally meaningful legal documents. So long as local courts supported their usage, everyone was happy to keep up the pretense.

TABLE 2: *Distribution of Large Property Sales by Origin of Purchaser*

	REGION OF PROPERTY SALE				
	Tapachula	Tuxtla Chico	Lowlands	Coffee Highlands	Overall
Soconusco	24%	41%	26%	13%	24%
Chiapas	8%	30%	14%	5%	11%
Mexico	14%	11%	13%	9%	12%
Guatemala	8%	0%	5%	4%	6%
Foreign	46%	18%	42%	70%	47%
Total	100%	100%	100%	100%	100%

ORIGIN OF PURCHASER

Based on 412 sales where both origin of purchaser and place of purchase are known.
Source: Archivo del Registro Público de la Propiedad y el Comercio, Tapachula.

Unlike the market for land in and around municipal ejidos, the market for MLCC-titled lands was wide open to newcomers (see Table 2). Recent migrants dominated the market for large properties, both in original purchases from the MLCC and in the resale market. Whether from elsewhere in Mexico or from far beyond the country's borders, most were not yet vecinos of the municipalities in which they purchased land. Many would stay for decades, setting up a community that indelibly reshaped the landscape of the Soconusco. These were not the absentee plantation owners of colonial Caribbean nor were they an enclave of expatriates determined to remain apart from those of other nationalities. Foreigners represented just over one third of those who purchased land from the MLCC, another third were from elsewhere in Mexico, and the final third were from the Soconusco itself. Small clusterings of co-nationals did emerge, particularly among the German community at the center of Las Chicharras, the heart of the new coffee zone. Even there, though, Americans, French, Spaniards, and many Mexicans bumped up against fincas called Hamburgo and Nueva Alemania, or New Germany. Helen Humphreys's memories of Christmases with the Swiss couple a few fincas over, invitations to parties thrown by Mexican friends in Tapachula, mountain climbing with the Americans who owned Eureka all attest to the reorientation of identities from nation of origin to shared preoccupation with the coffee harvest.[84]

Buyers named their fincas after hometowns, patron saints, local landmarks, or their hopes and doubts—Quien Sabe (Who Knows) and El Porvenir

(The Future) being classic examples. With a median size of 128 hectares, these fincas were much larger than the properties being bought and sold by villagers but still paled in comparison to the state average of 380 hectares, let alone the national average of 5,600 hectares.[85] In its later years, the company sold at least ten lots that exceeded 3,000 hectares as it attempted to free itself from the quantities of unsold land that were supposed to make it profitable.[86] These sizeable holdings were concentrated in the northern coastal plains and transformed old untitled ranch lands into new sites for investment in rubber cultivation. The rubber enterprises quickly drew new settlements of villagers and part-time workers. These communities in turn established their own municipal councils and carried out their own slow processes of repartition despite, again, the government dictating that the lands were to be privatized immediately.[87]

As with the ex-ejidos of Cacahoatán, the privatization of previously untitled lands was only the first stage in an evolving land market. Unlike in the ex-ejidos of Cacahoatán, even a year's investment could hugely increase the resale price of a large property. In Tapachula, the district seat and center of the MLCC's titling activity, the company sold some eighty properties worth more than MX$500. They averaged just less than 300 hectares, with an average price per hectare of just over MX$11. When those lands as well as a few others previously titled entered into the resale market, the value of a sale averaged about MX$16,000, or MX$64 a hectare.[88] The experiences of Gustavo Scholz, a German finquero who was killed in a fall while returning from a visit to his neighbor, make clear the origins of that added value: coffee. Scholz had invested in substantial coffee plantings immediately upon taking possession and soon imported processing machinery as well. When he died, he had 19,200 coffee plants on his finca, worth in and of themselves MX$9,600. The finca as a whole, which he had purchased for MX$3,350 in 1898, was valued at just over MX$12,000, including the plants. The value of the land was given as just MX$1,750.[89]

These newly created properties, made valuable by the bean that drove the local economy, depended on the reliability and accuracy of the title that the land company provided. Yet the land company favored expediency over precision. The nice straight lines it drew on survey maps hid both slapdash work and the difficulties of turning the Soconusco's undulating terrain into standardized lots. The government investigated the MLCC and its subsidiary real estate companies for shoddy work multiple times across its tenure in Chiapas, eventually leading to the rescinding of its concession. Yet the titles it had expedited endured, even when their owners had to hire new surveyors to clarify bounds.[90]

As Chapter Three discussed, the local courts and the public records office replaced the shotgun as a means of disputing property lines and land claims across the 1890s. Whether a neighbor's cattle wandered in and destroyed some coffee bushes or a finquero sent his workers to pick another man's coffee, planters increasingly turned to the court to defend their holdings. A planter might still draw a pistol in anger, but he then pulled together his papers and hiked to town to file a charge instead of firing his gun. Arbitration created a legible, verifiable record that could be filed for current and future use.[91] Blaming the surveyor for shoddy work also helped deescalate a situation.[92] Everyone knew these engineers' work was haphazard and difficult, so better to just accept that and move forward than come to blows over a misplaced right of way or boundary marker. In any case, court filings, like tax receipts, created a reliable means of proving one's ownership.

The MLCC, inadvertently, also served to reinforce the mixed nature of production in the Soconusco. Having left it to planters to decide where their plantations would be located, the company found itself in possession of many small pockets of land in the Sierra Madre. Its maps were full of rectangles, but their edges did not always meet. Here, the MLCC set up what it called the Indigenous Colony. The effort was meant, as with so many of the state's land distribution projects in the region, to attract a permanent workforce.[93] Instead, it provided a means for villagers and migrant laborers with adequate savings to extend their reach into the heart of the plantation zone.[94]

The five-hectare parcels were more expensive per hectare than larger properties the company sold. Yet they were still more affordable than smaller lots being resold in the ex-ejidos of nearby municipalities. In part because of this, the Indigenous Colony became a site for accumulation by those smallholders who had the means to do so. Over time, a few former smallholders transformed themselves into plantation owners by buying up a parcel at a time from the MLCC.[95]

This sort of consolidation, though, was as much an outlier when it came to MLCC-titled lands as it was in the former ejidos of the district. Counter to the general historiography of the Porfiriato, landholding in the Soconusco remained diversified and dispersed. When consolidation did occur, it was not through outsiders' infiltration of village spaces. Rather, as with the Indigenous Colony, it was locals who did most of the accumulating in the district. A few emigrant finqueros, both Mexican and foreign, did piece together very large plantations through the purchase of neighboring lands.[96] Oliver Herbert Harrison, the MLCC engineer, relayed his connections into a small empire in coffee and rubber. Until his ambition got the better of him, Harrison became the largest landowner in the district aside from his former employer.[97] Yet these accumulators were the odd men and women out.

Of the 1,800 individuals whose property purchases I have record of, 70 percent ever bought only one piece of land. The majority of those 30 percent who did purchase more than one piece of land were smallholders from the Soconusco. Most started with the purchase of a neighboring lot in the ex-ejidos of their municipality, slowly accumulated savings based on market agriculture, and then moved into the market for larger properties. Nicolás Amores and his wife Aurora Caravantes de Amores were the most active participants in the region's property market and accumulated at least forty properties ranging from a few hectares purchased from neighbors to a 426-hectare finca bought from the MLCC. They were both from Tapachula, where Amores served as a municipal official, and they focused their buying there.[98] The Amoreses and other village elites like them were atypical in their multitude of purchases but even so were better representatives of land consolidation in the district than Harrison. Newcomers to the Soconusco were not intruding into the local market for land. Instead, locals were pushing their way into the market for newly available lands beyond the scope of the village commons.

The decades-long process by which the municipal council of Cacahoatán managed the repartition of their ejidos rarely overlapped with the concurrent process of public land sales carried out by the MLCC. But the MLCC and the newly arrived aspirant finqueros it served were most assuredly constrained by the actions of municipal councilors and the villagers they governed. As the survey map submitted by the land company to the national government in 1913 (Map 6) makes clear, there were large swaths of space in the Soconusco where the land company simply could not operate. Along with the map that opened the chapter, this depiction of landholding in the region leaves out the vibrant life of vecinos and other smallholders.

In the map's blank spaces, those who already worked the land engaged the tools of liberal land reform to shore up their livelihoods. Rather than acquiescing to mandates and timetables set out by the state, municipal councils provided their constituents the flexibility of taking up privatization as it became affordable. The process was not without conflict. Municipalities failed to pay surveyors, neighbors contested the vecindad of neighbors, and population growth surpassed the capacity of municipal holdings. Yet through their careful use of repartition and the institutions that facilitated it—courts, surveyors, the public records office—villagers held onto their lands.

When government agents arrived to carry out land reform in the wake of the Mexican Revolution, they encountered a landscape that again resisted easy intervention. The agrarian agent assigned to Cacahoatán complained that the list of holdings sent to him by the municipal president "has privately held fincas mixed up with ejidal possessions, a fact I know from my own personal understanding of all the rustic properties in this municipality."[99] The distinction between the two was not something easily worked out.

As we have seen, many who held land as private property had once been ejiditarios and had little desire to see their land returned to a communal form. In Mazatán, a municipality in the coastal plains to the northwest of Tapachula, the ejidal commission recounted how the ejidos, repartitioned and sold to the vecinos of the town beginning in 1896, were still held by the same purchasers on the commission's arrival in the 1920s. The commission decided that "it is essentially impracticable and impolitic to nullify those titles in order to reconstitute their lands as the possession of the Pueblo and then redistribute them all over again." All this equitability caused consternation amongst the ejidal commission, but, in the end, the villagers were left to their own devices, satisfied with their small private properties.[100]

Those properties and the plantations that they bordered both grew in value across the last decades of the nineteenth century. The availability of proper title facilitated and ensured investments large and small. With clear evidence of ownership, planters could put their properties up as collateral for loans, and villagers could hold neighbors responsible if livestock destroyed coffee bushes. Investments of this sort, though, also opened locals up to the vagaries of the global commodity market. As international coffee prices fluctuated, so too did the property market in this far-off corner of Mexico. Proper title also meant that lands could be seized in payment when debts came due and ruin loomed, a topic I will return to in Chapter Six.

As much as proper title contributed to the transformation of the landscape, it also served to preserve it. Villagers' determined hold on their communal lands slowed and delimited the spread of plantations across the Sierra Madre. While some northern rubber plantations and ranches stretched for thousands of hectares, properties in the district's most populous municipalities remained relatively small. The rich soils of the Soconusco meant that no one needed a huge expanse of land to make a living, and villagers often maintained old practices of mixing forest and farm on their lands. As the next chapter will make clear, villagers' hold on the hillsides meant that labor was always scarce in the Soconusco. Tropical forest continued to impede regimented plantation rows, as no one had an adequate labor force to cultivate all the property they claimed.

5 Scarce Labor and Unrealized Reform

As the coffee harvest began in November of 1892, at least 100 people worked at finca San Juan las Chicharras. The plantation was one of the largest in the Soconusco and took up half of the square in the middle of the land company's 1889 survey map (Map 5 in Chapter Four).[1] Though it stretched over 1,000 hectares, laborers had only managed to clear and plant about one tenth of that land with coffee.[2] Men and women labeled in the account books as *mozos* and *tapiscadores*, or laborers and coffee pickers, passed between the rows of coffee bushes, carefully plucking only the ripe cherries and leaving the rest to continue maturing. At the end of the day, they poured the fruit into measuring boxes and had their harvest carefully noted by the finca manager. A few workers supervised the machinery that separated the cherry from the bean, a few more oversaw the drying patios, replaced in the years to come by gently heated mechanical drums. A number of women spent their days hand-sorting the resulting clean, dry coffee by quality, a task also replaced in the coming years by imported machinery driven by hydraulic power. A few more women oversaw the communal kitchen, and one or two tended subsistence gardens and transplanted coffee seedlings. Most, though, trudged through the endless rows of coffee plants with ever heavier burlap sacks on their backs.[3]

Half of these workers were relatively new hires, recent and likely seasonal migrants from Guatemala and the highland district of Motozintla, which bordered the Soconusco to the east. A recruiter employed by San Juan had advanced them a small amount of money and promised them good wages and access to further credit in return for their trek down from the heights of the Sierra Madre. The manager of the finca, a British man named William Forsyth, was both frustrated by and grateful for their presence on his plantation as harvest got under way. This regional workforce had not been part of his grand plan for the plantation. Instead, he had intended to rely on the labor of 237 men, women, and children he had brought over from the Gilbert Islands in the South Pacific a year before. Tragically, 180 of those migrant workers had died from smallpox in the preceding months. Aside from the monotonous work of tending coffee, the remaining Gilbertese laborers now also cared for their sick and dying family members and tried to negotiate their return home.

The Gilbertese migrants represented an extreme attempt to circumvent local laborers' power to negotiate. Workers in the Soconusco were in scarce supply. Demographics and the land use patterns described in Chapter Four meant few local villagers had any interest in working for wages. Workers from farther afield brought their own expectations and socially embedded labor histories that required navigation. In both cases, those who did turn to plantation work in the Soconusco demanded a multitude of incentives. In return for their toil, they required good wages, regular access to credit, and plots of land to tend for themselves. When a situation did not suit them, workers frequently left a job in the middle of the harvest. Even if they stayed through the harvest, many migrant workers decided not to return the following year, no matter the status of their outstanding accounts. Employers found this system uneconomical at best and ruinous at worst. Yet, despite multiple attempts to legislate and connive and contract their way around local workers, planters in the Soconusco failed to transform the labor system into one that favored their interests.

Though the distance they had traveled was unusual for Mexico, laborers like the Gilbertese migrants were increasingly common across the global tropics. The accelerating circulation of commodities necessitated an accelerating circulation of workers, free and unfree, coerced and cajoled, bound by debt, by custom, and by their own needs.[4] Slavery was only recently abolished in Cuba and Brazil, and indentured servitude of East and South Asian migrants was common practice in much of the Caribbean. In the rest of Latin America, many workers labored within a variety of arrangements that came under the heading of debt peonage. Elites used contract law and land reform to "free" workers from their means of production and force them into wage labor. Debt, backed by liberal doctrine regarding the freedom of contracts, fortified employers' hold on their workforce.[5] Yet, as a large historiography has shown, opponents and advocates alike used the phrase *debt peonage* to describe a spectrum of labor relationships that ranged from coercive to consensual.[6] In the Soconusco, debt peonage was based on incentives and rarely constrained workers' freedom of movement. There was little recourse for employers when it came to collecting on debts, and the sunk costs of the system were high. Because the term debt peonage carries such baggage, I am instead calling this system incentivized contract labor.

This chapter will show how the system of incentivized contract labor endured and expanded despite planters' continual attempts to circumvent or reform it. Advances, access to credit, good wages, and subsistence plots were the norm for laborers in the Soconusco from the time Matías Romero began growing coffee there in the 1870s through the 1910s and beyond. What changed was the scope of this system. Over the course of thirty years, planters brought an exponentially larger number of workers into seasonal employ from across the Soconusco as well as northern Guatemala and the central highlands of Chiapas. Planters may have bemoaned the costs of labor, but they managed to secure the ever-growing number of workers needed to keep their economy growing. Here, I will trace the slow expansion of a relatively resilient labor regime through the case of finca San Juan las Chicharras and elites' ongoing attempts to reform the system in question. Finqueros tried to ease their bottom lines through legislation and attempts to reach beyond the regional labor source. Yet so long as need for workers outpaced the supply of interested laborers, these attempts failed. The informal institutions of incentivized contracts won out over attempts to reform formalized labor relations.

Finding New Workers in a Tight Labor Market

In order to understand the endurance of incentivized contracts in the Soconusco, it is necessary to place the local labor system within a larger context. While land was a localized resource, the people who might serve as plantation labor resided across a much broader geography. In large part this was because the local population, as demonstrated in the prior chapter, held onto its lands. With a relatively small plot, a family could keep itself in staples and cultivate some cash crops to cover any additional needs. Planters had to search farther afield for both permanent and seasonal workers. In doing so, they butted up against long-standing debates about the nature of work in Chiapas as a whole. In the same way that emigrant planters in the Soconusco clashed with Sebastián Escobar over all manner of issues, an emerging export elite in the state's lowlands (including the Soconusco) found itself at odds with well-established hacendados and politicians in the state's highlands. Much of this confrontation centered on access to workers. Highland elites had spent the past centuries securing their hold over indigenous villages that constituted the majority of the state's potential labor pool. Now, newcomers wanted those villagers to work for them as well. Where the Soconusco's planters were able to ignore state politics with regard to other issues, when it came to labor everyone had to take part.

From the colonial era through much of the nineteenth century, the political and economic elites of Chiapas made their home in the central highland city of San Cristóbal de Las Casas. They did so, in large part, because this was the region's indigenous stronghold. While indigenous communities in lowland areas like the Soconusco had suffered tremendous population collapse during the Conquest, the region's higher reaches had provided protection from disease. The crown granted Hispanic elites rights to the labor of these communities through the *repartimiento* system of labor allocation. Even after the abolition of the repartimiento, Hispanic elites used close economic and social ties with the Catholic Church and indigenous leaders to maintain control over the labor of these communities. They espoused a conservative ethos of care and improvement to justify their paternalistic appropriation of laborers for seasonal work on sugar and grain plantations.[7]

Despite their political differences with liberal national politicians, highland elites found reforms related to contract law and land use useful means of institutionalizing their claims to indigenous labor. Across the nineteenth century, they transformed customary labor allocations into individuated contracts based on inescapable debt. Unlike in the Soconusco, highland elites managed to force the privatization of communal lands as a means of depriving villagers of their access to subsistence. They further reinforced villagers' need for wages by demanding the payment of taxes in cash. Mediated by merchants and municipal presidents, this newly institutionalized system secured and legitimized the ongoing provision of migratory seasonal workers for highland elites' sugar, cacao, and grain plantations. By the 1880s, state law dictated that workers were responsible for the cost of their own recapture if they abandoned debts and could be assigned to public works projects as punishment, often without pay. Employers could lend out their laborers at will, debts were inheritable, and workers tied by debt could be sold along with plantations to which they owed labor. This was a system of coercive debt peonage along the lines of that famously described in the muckraking journalism of the day.[8]

Despite the physical and political distance between the Soconusco and San Cristóbal, local ranchers and hacendados like Sebastián Escobar approached labor in much the same way. The lack of available laborers had been an integral factor in the region's turn toward ranching. Yet, even with low labor needs for these enterprises, ranchers made sure to keep a close hold on those workers they did require. In municipal courts, ranchers charged runaways with fraud for breaking their contracts. Judges doled out jail sentences of fifteen to thirty days, adding the costs of recapture to workers' outstanding debts.[9] These cases demonstrate a capacity for enforcement based on close ties between local government and hacendados who tapped a primarily local labor pool.

As quickly became clear, while sufficient for the needs of regionally bounded cattle production, neither the laws nor the labor supply of the

Soconusco could support export agriculture. Coffee plantations required both a substantial year-round workforce and an even larger number of seasonal laborers during the harvest. To meet this need, Escobar and other ranchers-turned-planters shifted what workers they had from cattle to the new crop. They then used their local clout to draw more workers into service through coercion and long-standing social ties. Local elites had no interest in helping emigrant entrepreneurs who might usurp their place and so did little to introduce new arrivals into the social networks that facilitated access to village labor. They also monopolized the means of coercion, both judicial or military, necessary to pursue and punish workers who decided to leave their employ. With villagers also expanding their hold in the foothills, this left few local laborers interested in working for emigrant investors.

As we saw in Chapter One, Romero and other early coffee planters muddled through as best they could. They tried to take the advice of their Guatemalan counterparts and turn the villagers who lived nearby or on the lands they claimed into a labor force, but this rarely worked.[10] Romero tried to orchestrate the importation of permanent workers from as far away as China and seasonal ones from as close as the prisons of San Cristóbal, both to no avail.[11] Growing desperate, early finqueros hired local men to help manage their new fincas in the hopes that these employees could tap into the small regional labor pool.[12] This also proved problematic. Lacking a basic understanding of both the terrain and the work involved in coffee cultivation, Romero and others like him asserted that local managers were not working hard enough, that five or six families should be enough to manage hundreds of hectares of land. "Do not believe us lazy," Romero's work boss wrote to him. So few workers could simply not take on the labor involved in clearing, planting, and tending the lush landscape of the Sierra Madre.[13]

With frequent complaints and suggestions for remedy, newly arrived planters began reaching outside the Soconusco and acquiescing to workers' demands for incentives. Those who arrived with little in the way of funds relied on family labor as long as they had to. Then, like their better-funded neighbors, they turned their eyes east and south, to villagers from along the border and expensive but experienced workers from Guatemala.[14] With the border still porous and coffee a well-established cultivar on its far side, the southern neighbor seemed a natural source of potential laborers. It also had the benefit of villagers in search of work. In the 1870s, prosperous Guatemalan coffee elites enacted labor reforms to incentivize wage work by making it the only alternative to forced labor. Indigenous villagers would have preferred to stay home and work their own lands, but, if they were going to have to toil, they decided to do so on their own terms. Those terms included advance payment of their wages for seasonal migratory labor.[15] Thus, when recruiters hired by planters in the Soconusco arrived, Guatemalan villagers were well accustomed to making demands. With nowhere else to turn, finqueros paid up.

In 1887, the administrator at finca Ixtal Colón laid out two-thirds of October's spending on wages, advances, recruiting, and worker debts. He paid Juan Herrera $8.25 for recruitment in Central America that led to the securing of twenty-three laborers. He paid $155.96 to neighboring fincas to buy the debts of at least nine mozos and transfer them to his finca.[16] He paid at least $75.00 as *habilitaciónes*, or advances, and spent an additional $554.04 on wages.[17] The resultant workforce was a mix of locals, Guatemalans, and those from the *tierra fría*, local phrasing for Motozintla and other neighboring districts in the Sierra Madre de Chiapas. Mozos earned 50 cents a day plus housing and access to credit at the finca store, five to ten times the average wage in much of the state. With the additional barrier of the border to protect them from pursuit, many migrant workers never paid back either their advances or their store accounts.[18]

This was a labor market apart from that of the rest of the state and apart from that of those local ranchers who could still coerce workers into service. The legal tools for securing labor built up by these older employers did not work for new investors. With the local oligarchy losing steam, even its capacity for coercion was waning. New planters, still small in number and without connections, had no such capacity to speak of. Despite planters' complaints and proposals for reform, workers from the Soconusco, the tierra fría, and Guatemala continued to demand and receive incentives from their employers.

A Failed Experiment in Imported Labor

As one of the largest, best-funded, and most globally connected fincas, San Juan las Chicharras and its ongoing difficulties in securing adequate labor make clear the persistent limitations local villagers and regional workers placed on the expansion of the plantation system. As their need for workers pushed them to search further afield, plantation owners and administrators capitulated to laborers' demands and introduced the system of incentivized contracts into parts of Chiapas that had not seen it before. In doing so, they slowly reoriented part of the state's workforce toward coffee production. The details of how labor worked at San Juan—how it was recruited, what it did, and how administrators and mozos grappled over obligations and incentives—demonstrate the ongoing negotiations between workers and their employers. The story of San Juan is one of exceptional violence and tragedy that resulted in the recording of banal, incremental, and yet cumulatively profound shifts in the way labor worked in Chiapas.

In 1892, the administrator of San Juan, William Forsyth, ordered his remaining Gilbertese workers to attack the owner of the plantation, John Magee. Magee had never before visited the Soconusco, instead entrusting Forsyth with his $150,000 investment and overseeing operations from his home in England. When so many of the Gilbertese migrants died of smallpox, Magee grew concerned and decided to check up on his increasingly erratic administrator in person. On arrival, Forsyth chased Magee from the premises, wielding a whiskey bottle and his workers against his partner.[19] Magee immediately filed an all-encompassing case against Forsyth at the local court, charging him with frustrated homicide, abuse of confidence, and fraud.[20] He demanded that the judge embargo the finca, as Forsyth was continuing to sell off its contents, including the debts of his workers.[21]

The importation of the Gilbertese workers had been an extreme attempt to avoid such debts. Forsyth and Magee sought to overhaul the Soconusco in the model of the ideal export plantation grounded on scientific management and careful budgeting. The Mexican government supported their efforts, hoping that capitalistic agriculturalists like them could modernize the countryside.[22] The epitome of this dreamed-of stream of entrepreneurial immigrants, Forsyth and Magee brought with them access to global capital, agricultural knowledge, and management expertise. Yet the modernizers quickly came face to face with their own incapacity to remake the context in which they sought their fortune. The Gilbertese workers were an untenable solution, a temporary mask for the incrementally slow process of accessing and redirecting Chiapas's traditional labor pool.

For a while, Forsyth was able to present the Gilbertese laborers as a brilliant innovation in coffee production in the Soconusco. Finca San Juan was one of the very few plantations with the resources to step outside the burdensome bounds of incentivized contracts. With experience in Latin America as well as in Southeast Asia and Hawaii, the partners attempted to substitute imported labor for local workers.[23]

The workers they turned to were residents of the drought-wracked Gilbert Islands. Ecological disaster and the appealing promise of good wages and a return voyage home had recently drawn the inhabitants of these and many neighboring islands into the accelerating circuit of Pacific plantation labor. Export producers from Hawaii to Peru to Australia used trickery and desperation to draw villagers into coercive labor systems where distance served as an effective means of keeping labor captive.[24] Between 1890 and 1892, more than 1,000 residents of the Gilbert Islands left their homes on three different ships to cross the ocean for Central America.[25] Two hundred thirty-seven of them arrived at San Juan las Chicharras in 1891 with a three-year contract. These newly made laborers expected five pesos a month, room, board, medical care, and small necessities like tobacco and new clothing in return for their work. At the end of their contract, they also expected to be returned to their home islands. Aside from the final promise, San Juan's accounts show that Forsyth more or less upheld the contract. In addition to other staples, he spent enough on meat alone to buy each worker eight pounds of the relative luxury each month.[26]

This would not matter to those who contracted smallpox and died in the fall of 1892. The disease swept across the Soconusco and Guatemala, killing finqueros, merchants, and workers alike. Despite employers' efforts to care for their investments, many Gilbertese laborers died. At San Juan las Chicharras, they went from a community of 237 to only 58. While Guatemalan planters quickly returned the remaining migrants to their home, the San Juan Gilbertese were not so lucky. Magee claimed that his workers had failed to maintain their side of the contract due to illness and laziness. The survivors only made it home again through the intervention of a local Catholic organization.[27]

Magee's reaction was built on Forsyth's own callousness. Forsyth noted the tragedy by renumbering the unnamed migrants in his ledger book and complaining that he had lost his labor force. His records indicate no sympathy for the remaining family members, no provision for their mourning or burial. For Forsyth, the deaths of a large portion of his labor force instead were recorded as a substantial hurdle for the plantation, particularly as the manager had spent 20 percent of the funds Magee forwarded him on the imported workers. Forsyth had done so believing that this circumvention of regional incentivized contracts would free him from any additional labor costs. Yet now he needed more workers.

Capital and connections were not enough to remake San Juan into the prototypical Pacific export plantation Magee and his administrator desired. Forsyth's account books reveal that, despite his best efforts to avoid it, he had already acquiesced to the local system of incentivized contracts. Laborers from Guatemala and the tierra fría were already hard at work at San Juan in 1892. To secure their labor, Forsyth had been employing an *habilitador*, or local recruiter, since 1889. Between then and November of 1892, Forsyth spent $22,965.28 on wages for non-Gilbertese workers who seasonally migrated to the Soconusco. Alongside the surviving Gilbertese, these laborers cleaned and tended the coffee fields, harvested the first cherries, and completed a variety of other household and agricultural tasks, both coffee and subsistence related.[28]

Wages, though, were only one part of the recompense that local workers demanded. If they were going to travel multiple days to toil on his plantation for a few months, regional workers also wanted access to advances and credit. By late 1892, recruitment costs, including the recruiter's expenses as well as advances demanded by workers, had reached $2,505.93. Unlike recruitment costs described in other parts of Chiapas, there was no sense that anyone viewed this payment as anything more than a signing bonus. No worker expected to repay it. Similarly, no one seemed to anticipate repaying their *cuenta corriente*, the account of outstanding debts accrued at the finca store. In October 1892, fifty workers at San Juan owed the finca almost $6,300. Many owed less than a day's work. Others, though, had already managed to borrow what amounted to more than seven month's steady labor. Each month Forsyth noted a small income—between $100 and $250—from credits repaid by mozos, but it was always less than the increases noted in the cuenta corriente.

When the plantation was put in receivership, Forsyth had spent a total of $134,293.51 on the finca. $63,994.37 of that was spent on labor. This was typical for plantations in the area, and outstanding debts in particular weighed heavy on plantation accounts. In the 1890s, workers' debts made up 2 to 19 percent of the value of well-established plantations. In starker terms, an 1897 valuation of debts owed by peons currently or once employed in the region totaled more than MX$467,000, almost half of the MX$1 million estimated value of all the coffee plantations in Soconusco.[29] At San Juan las Chicharras, these outlays had helped plant more than 50,000 coffee bushes. Yet none were yet in harvest, and the plantation was every day more reliant on the local labor system the Gilbertese were intended to circumvent.[30]

Forsyth tried to hide how much he had spent on workers by separating out the various kinds of payment and positing that the effective daily wage on the plantation was much less than the district's norm. Yet despite his creative accounting, it was clear that the costs outlaid to import workers from across the Pacific were another failed attempt to get around the costs of recruiting local labor. Like many a planter before him, Forsyth had found incentivized contracts expensive and unreliable. Unlike many a planter before him, Forsyth and his partner had the resources to try to bring the Soconusco into the labor circuit currently supplying other tropical plantation owners with cheap labor from the drought-prone islands of the South Pacific. Yet even before smallpox killed most of the workers who had traveled to the Soconusco from the Gilbert Islands, Forsyth had come to rely on incentivized contracts. Before the Gilbertese arrived, workers from Guatemala and the tierra fría had done the initial work of clearing the forest and starting to cultivate seedlings. Even when it seemed the Gilbertese would prove a good alternative, regional workers had remained for the good wages and ready credit. With the death of the Gilbertese, the local system of incentivized contracts became the only alternative as the first harvest loomed.

Securing Labor through Insecure Debt

The work of completing that harvest fell to Charles Lesher, an American bookkeeper whom the court appointed as receiver and manager of the finca while Magee's case against Forsyth continued. Lesher had already expressed his doubts about Forsyth's approach to labor recruitment and accounting in letters to Magee sent prior to the owner's arrival. In contrast to Forsyth, Lesher quickly acquiesced to potential workers' demands for incentives. His toolkit for attracting laborers was the same as that used throughout the Soconusco as coffee expanded its reach in the 1890s: good wages, advances, access to credit, and land for subsistence. Tacitly admitting that attempts to circumvent the regional mode of labor recruitment had failed, Lesher expanded access to all of these incentives. Even so, he failed to secure as many workers as he wanted. Those who did take up his offer rarely stayed as long as he would have liked. As was the norm in the district, laborers regularly left San Juan las Chicharras without repaying their debts. As was also the norm, the majority of the land that Lesher managed continued to go uncultivated for lack of an adequate workforce. While the acceptance and improvement of incentivized contracts led to a growing workforce in the Soconusco, recalcitrant and demanding workers meant that coffee could only climb so far into the foothills.

Lesher's task was to recoup the sums that Forsyth had poured into San Juan las Chicharras. He had to do so with much reduced funds. Not only was his salary a measly $125 a month as compared to Forsyth's $200. Lesher also had to justify all his expenditures as receiver to the court so long as Magee's case against Forsyth remained open.[31] Luckily for Lesher, Forsyth and his workers had in fact done much to set the finca up for success. Much of the dilapidation left by Forsyth was superficial. Almost-completed roads needed to be finished, not started; housing and machinery were cleaned up and correctly installed, not built from scratch. Most importantly, once workers cleared the brush from between the rows of bushes, it turned out that coffee was flourishing at San Juan.

Workers, though, once again made themselves scarce. When Forsyth found himself in financial duress after the death of the Gilbertese migrants, most local laborers abandoned the finca. They knew they were unlikely to be paid as promised, the finca store and kitchen were running low on food, and neighboring planters were offering a much better deal. So they left for greener pastures. The few Gilbertese workers who had survived smallpox were nearing the end of their contract. Lesher was faced with 3,500 *cuerdas* of ripening coffee, many times the amount a village family could harvest on their own. If he was to have anything to pay himself and the remaining workers, Lesher had to find someone to help him bring in the harvest and get it to market.

German agronomist Karl Kaerger has long been historians' authoritative guide to southern Mexico's turn-of-the-century agricultural economy. Based on his calculations, a dozen male laborers, supported by their families and working at a steady pace of at least one *tarea* or task (here defined as an assigned amount of coffee to be picked) a day, should have been able to bring in the coffee grown at San Juan las Chicharras.[32] Any finquero in the Soconusco would have laughed at this assertion. Account books from fincas near San Juan indicate that while some laborers worked more than fourteen tareas in a two-week period, most recorded fewer. In a three-week period, the forty laborers on finca San Carlos worked 280 tareas, nowhere near the more than 1,000 Kaerger would have suggested they complete in the same period.[33] Women also earned their own wages on fincas in the Soconusco, casting doubt on Kaerger's assumption that a man's wage covered his entire family's labor. San Juan las Chicharras was much larger than San Carlos, and so Lesher's labor force would have to be equally greater. When he was forced off the plantation, Forsyth had employed fifty local laborers and fifty-eight Gilbertese migrants. When Lesher returned the finca to Magee four years later, his ledgers indicated that he had advanced more than MX$18,000 to secure the labor of at least 229 workers from Guatemala and the tierra fría.[34]

Where Forsyth had tried to get around the advances that attracted most laborers to work in the Soconusco, Lesher embraced them. Desperation in the face of the huge quantities of coffee about to be lost likely forced his hand. Unable to wait for labor or attempt to negotiate better deals, he paid up. By 1896, Hilario Roblero and Pedro Bernardo had drawn $50.10 and $57.88 on account from the plantation's funds. This was the rough equivalent of 100 tareas of work and was at the lower end of sums owed by the finca's resident workforce. Many workers had borrowed $100, $150, or more than $200. José Tenorio would probably never be able to pay off the $404.49 he had been advanced by the finca. Tapiscadoras—women workers—tended to owe much less. With debts ranging from 5 to 20 pesos, their inclusion again indicates that women were employed apart from their partners, but these lower debts also suggest that families or employers still addressed family units as a whole when it came to matters of credit, with only one member racking up an account. Those who worked at the finca year after year tended to have more access to credit and less inclination to repay it.[35] These debts only make sense if examined as part of an incentivized contract, essentially functioning as a promise of continued support if a worker upheld his or her side of the bargain.

Aside from credit, workers like Robledo, Bernardo, and Tenorio also had access to small houses with a plot of land where they could cultivate subsistence crops. José Borraz was not the only one to take part of his pay in lime used to improve soil quality. San Juan was a large plantation for the region—more than 1,000 hectares—but its coffee groves only comprised 174 hectares of that total. On average, fincas in the region cultivated 25 percent of their total land with coffee by 1899. The rest of that land was available for the workers' own use or remained forested, and planters acknowledged that the provisioning of garden plots was a regular means by which they could maintain a loyal workforce.[36]

Two other factors also demonstrate that these debts were noncoercive. Firstly, advances did not inextricably tie laborers to the plantation. The overlap between the list of mozos from 1892 and 1896 is minimal. Only twenty-two people, less than half of the labor force, remained in residence across those four years. This turnover is in line with labor patterns on other fincas, where only about 40 percent of workers appear on the books for more than one month.[37] At San Juan, the plantation actually owed back pay to a few of the workers who had remained across the years. Most, though, had borrowed even more from the finca. Camilo Bravo owed the finca 25 cents in 1892; by 1896 he owed almost $90. Four others had also increased their debts by more than ten times. Of the twenty-eight laborers no longer working at the plantation, only six had accounts outstanding. The rest had either worked off the loans they had taken, most under $100, or been released from their obligations as part of Lesher's attempt to start anew. Either way, their debts to the finca did not keep these laborers attached to it four years later.

Secondly, many newly hired workers also left the finca without repaying their advances and without pursuit. Despite being recognized as a competent administrator and friend to numerous finqueros in the region, Lesher lacked the physical and political clout to enforce the labor laws of the state. He was an honest accountant and took pains to note down the money lost in advances never repaid. By the time he handed the finca back over to Magee, 145 workers had decided not to return to the plantation despite their outstanding debts. Together, these debts totaled almost $7,000, ranging from Carnaciana Méndez's debt of 13 cents to Juan Bartolón's $250.43. Nothing in Lesher's statements to the court makes it seem as though he was apologetic for these losses or that he had done anything to pursue their repayment. This was how things worked: if you wanted labor, you had to incentivize contracts with extensions of credit and accept the risks those credit lines entailed.[38]

The accounts of other fincas point to similar levels of unamortized advances among laborers. It was common to see the phrase *deudas de mozos* or "workers' debts" included in the value of fincas being sold.[39] When the court inventoried a finca on the death of its owner or its embargo during default, outstanding accounts were listed as active credits, either attributed to specific workers or generalized into a round lump sum. The more coffee cultivated, the more outstanding advances accumulated. These unpaid debts often constituted more than 15 percent of a plantation's value.[40] When wages alone could make up more than 90 percent of a mature finca's outlays during harvest season, this kind of additional, unenforceable advance lay heavy on the accounts of plantations worth far less than San Juan las Chicharras.[41]

Most laborers did not receive these credits as cash, for currency was in scarce supply in the Soconusco. Rather, they drew on their accounts to purchase food and wares from finca stores and the *cocinas de solteros*, or single-men's kitchens. Fincas were isolated endeavors, roads were bad, and town was far away, so some sort of store was necessary if an owner did not want to feed and clothe his laborers outright. Supply lists included food and basic supplies, and assessed values generally matched those of stores in town.[42] Some plantations simply paid part of their employee's wages in corn or goods, as with those mozos who drew pay in lime and food at San Juan las Chicharras. Some finqueros went further and extended credit in the form of tokens minted for use in their store alone. Desperate to keep those workers they could attract, planters did anything they could to keep laborers attached to their plantations from year to year. This meant that even when wages received in cash would have covered a worker's unpaid debts, that worker was allowed to collect his money and leave his account outstanding if he wished.[43]

Workers were paid what they were owed by fincas, without deductions made to cover what they owed to fincas. Most debts were between $15 and $100, but every finca seemed to have at least one or two laborers who utilized their credit with impunity, some owing more than $500.[44] The amount of debt accrued on a monthly basis was generally less than 10 pesos, and it was only that small percentage of workers who worked on the same fincas for years on end, either seasonally or year-round, who amassed large sums. Despite the profligate use of the courts to prosecute fellow finqueros, cases making use of the laws regulating the pursuit of indebted peons were almost nonexistent.[45] One of the very few involving labor was brought, not by the finquero, but by an employee trying to collect back wages before he changed employers.[46] We cannot generalize from a single case, but the judge's willingness to hear the laborer's argument demonstrates that the legal noose conveyed by the term debt peonage was not so constrictive in the Soconusco as it was elsewhere. Extensions of credit were certainly a means to secure labor, as in so many parts of the world, but they were not a means to keep it.

An Ineffectual Attempt to Reform the State Labor Pool

By the mid-1890s, with Lesher's tenure at San Juan in full swing, the coffee elite in the Soconusco had become entrenched. A former worker had killed Sebastián Escobar a few years before, the Mexican Land and Colonization Company was selling titled properties at an accelerating pace, and the region's coffee exports were about to break MX$1 million. Finqueros had taken up positions on a number of local municipal councils. Yet while planters like Lesher had managed to expand their labor pool by giving in to workers' demands, they were running out of options. Efforts to import workers like the Gilbertese migrants had failed. The rising price of coffee made landed villagers in the Soconusco even less interested in wage labor than before. Attempts to attract new permanent workers through initiatives like the MLCC's Indigenous Colony backfired when new landowners simply started growing coffee of their own. Feeling both desperate in the face of shortages and emboldened by growing economic clout, finqueros in the Soconusco turned to the state's emphatically liberal governor for aid. With his legislative help, they hoped to gain access to some of the indigenous workforce controlled by highland elites in and around San Cristóbal. Despite their best attempts and most high-minded rhetoric, legal reform failed to overcome the entrenched norms governing labor in the state.

As part of the shift toward more concerted state consolidation explored in Chapter Three, President Porfirio Díaz began to take aim at the highland elites of Chiapas beginning in the early 1890s. Governor Emilio Rabasa, born in the lowlands, started this process with the replacement of jefes políticos and the movement of the state capital from highland San Cristóbal to lowland Tuxtla Gutiérrez. Aside from its political aim, this move was also intended to recognize the growing importance of tropical export agriculture in the state.[47] The reallocation of indigenous labor away from highland hacendados and toward lowland planters was a key part of this gambit. Rabasa faced stark challenges as he tried to overcome the established debt peonage system. Highland hacendados had already mobilized the usual liberal arsenal of vagrancy laws, contract reforms, land privatization, and increased taxes—many borrowed from Guatemalan legislation—to their own benefit. When Rabasa tried to repurpose these tools for coffee planters in the Soconusco and elsewhere, he instead only reinforced highlanders' hold on "their" villages.[48]

Rabasa's successor, Francisco León, tried further administrative means to dislodge San Cristóbal's elites by creating a new highland district called Chamula. Where political elites and hacendados in San Cristóbal had previously overseen the management of the villages in this region, residents now fell under direct gubernatorial control. Yet highland municipal presidents, still selected locally rather than through appointments, continued to serve as gatekeepers to their constituents' labor. León's attempt to free villages from the "voracious vampires" who ruled the highlands had also failed as most indigenous municipal presidents continued to work for the highland elites to whom they were accustomed.[49] Until locals bought in, no amount of reform could remake labor in the state.

Public calls for change accompanied administrative reform. Positioning themselves in opposition to exploitative highland hacendados, lowland export producers like those in the Soconusco argued fiercely for an end to debt peonage and the introduction and enforcement of free wage labor. They masked their own desire for cheap, reliable workers behind overblown liberal and moralistic language. This language had its roots in a discourse that used the language of individual rights enshrined in the 1857 Constitution to denigrate debt peonage on both economic and moral grounds.[50] Jurist José Maria Lozano was among the first to take up the case of labor in Chiapas, Yucatán, and Tabasco as a demonstration of the contradictions between Mexico's Constitution and its daily practices.[51] Lozano's basic arguments about the ties between democracy and the inherent rights of the individual came to form the basis for many further arguments against debt peonage. Journalists in Chiapas detailed the evils of their state's labor system, and newspapers in Mexico City soon picked up their stories.[52] Not long after, the American press caught onto the tale as well.

According to both national and foreign papers, the plantation owners of Chiapas made their workers get up at two or three in the morning on the pretext of praying before starting the day's work. When a laborer tried to liquidate his account and leave service, the employer would calculate his *faltas*, or deficits, at 25 cents per day, when he only made two pesos a month.[53] "The black slave of Havana," one editorial went so far as to write, "is much happier than the Indian of our countryside."[54] Each account was more lurid than the last. As foreign investment in Chiapas, to be discussed in the next chapter, grew, so too did foreign concerns over the evils of its labor system. Papers from the *Washington Post* to the *Los Angeles Times* decried the debt peonage that tied laborers into interminable, inescapable servitude. While emphasizing its ills, American journalists also defended those masters—particularly foreigners—who treated their servants well. They also held President Díaz and his plans for overhauling the education system in special regard. Agreeing with the unnamed liberal politicians they quoted, these articles proceeded from the assumption that only a reform of the indigenous population would free them from the slavery of debt peonage.[55]

Governor León, one of the most progressive of President Díaz's appointees, took these stories as his call to arms. Yet in calling for an Agricultural Congress to debate the issue of debt peonage, he also made clear that the issues at hand were as much economic as moral. In his letters to Díaz and his announcement of the Congress in 1895, León intertwined the humanitarian issues of labor abuses with the economic impediments that labor concentration represented. Unlike the lowland planters who complained continually about recalcitrant workers, León insisted that workers were people who deserved a say in their employment. He also, though, acknowledged that export agriculture was the state's lifeblood and needed more workers if it was to continue expanding.[56] León asserted that the system of mozos as it stood was detrimental to both the "human progress" of laborers and the overall growth of Chiapas. Planters might be resistant, he wrote, but it was time to give voice to the indebted workers.[57]

The country's press responded with laudatory editorials and reportage. While some were dubious as to how successful the Congress would prove, the majority applauded León for taking a positive step toward resolving a shameful situation that benefited neither employer nor employee.[58] They were right to direct their praise at the governor—this was his personal project, one that he championed on the same moral grounds which journalists had utilized for the past decades.

The planters who had first written to complain of the scarcity of labor and the costs of debt peonage quickly took up the governor's project and repeated his language. They in many ways envied the secure hold that highland hacendados had on their workforce and would do what it took to loosen it. Planters in the Soconusco and other lowland export regions had tried to co-opt the old system of debt bondage to their own use. They had tried to make the liberal reform of contract law work for them in the same way that highland hacendados did. Yet, for the most part, they had found it costly and ineffective. Given that the old rules had not worked, they might as well try to write new ones.

Yet they came up against an entrenched and uninterested coalition of highland elites. While the economic power of the lowlands was growing across the 1890s, their tax contributions still paled in comparison with the regions controlled by these older, well-established highlanders. León's "voracious vampires" prospered on the fruits of traditional goods like sugar and tobacco. Many had also taken up new crops like coffee. With these incomes, highland elites were able to pay indigenous municipal presidents whatever they demanded in return for securing the needed labor. And while both Rabasa and León had done their best to disrupt these political and commercial ties, money continued to win out.

The strength of the highland elites was on clear display at León's Agricultural Congress. The highlanders' disdain for both the governor and the president went untempered by fear of retribution. Other historians have mostly invoked the Congress as a further ineffectual attempt at reform, full of lawyers blowing hot air without any real hope for change.[59] Yet the framing of arguments and the alliances that emerged capture the dissonance between existing labor institutions and the shifting economic geography of the state. Though Díaz and his proxies in the state and national governments had inscribed private property and contractual agreements into law, only local action could make that legislation meaningful. As it stood, the state still lacked the means to enforce its agenda. The Agricultural Congress of 1896 in the end only made this disconnect clearer.

The Soconusco sent three men to the Congress to represent the interests of the district as a whole.[60] Nicolás Bejarano, Bernardo Mallen, and Gustavo Scholz traveled to Tuxtla Gutiérrez in April of 1896 as the voice of the growing number of finqueros, like Magee and his various administrators, in desperate need of a steady supply of labor. All three men had personal experience with the coffee economy and the scarcity of labor, having themselves invested heavily in the costs of attracting workers. All three were also migrants to the region, Bejarano from Veracruz, Mallen from Sinaloa, and Scholz from Germany. As such, they lacked the ties to local towns or state politicians that would have eased entry into customary labor markets. Each, though, had also become relatively prosperous thanks to coffee and owned land and small luxuries that marked them as successful finqueros.

Scholz appears only briefly in the archives but is notable in being one of the very few non-Mexicans who attended the Congress in an official capacity. When he died four years later, his estate was worth about MX$12,000, mostly based on the value of the 19,600 coffee bushes planted on his finca Morelia, rather than the large library he had brought with him from Oschersleben, Germany.[61]

Bejarano, who came to the region with his brother, had married into a local elite family soon after his arrival. According to an article in a Mexico City newspaper, in the decade since, he had built up a fortune of at least MX$60,000.[62] When he died intestate just a year after the Agricultural Congress, his estate was worth almost $25,000, casting doubt on that previous sum. Nonetheless, he was assuredly well off. He had four gold pocket watches, a pearl tie pin, and cuff links studded with diamonds. He had a number of houses, both in Tapachula, in the "suburbs," and on his fincas, which were also numerous. He had a great deal of livestock and 25,000 coffee bushes on the finca San Andrés. He was also owed CySA$4,786.31 by thirty-seven workers.[63]

Mallen, who had also migrated to the Soconusco with a brother, was one of the early converts to coffee in the Soconusco, arriving sometime in the early 1870s. By 1880, he had been elected municipal president of Unión Juárez and was known to Matías Romero as a prominent local figure and potential ally in his struggles against General Sebastián Escobar.[64] That said, like Bejarano, he had married into a local elite family connected to the cacique. Mallen acquired and resold numerous fincas over the following decades, forming an important node in the credit market explored in Chapter Six. He bought coffee from his neighbors and resold it in Tapachula and abroad, advancing sums to other planters in return for promises of coffee harvests to come.[65] Mallen was one of the victims of the global coffee crisis of the late 1890s, losing some of his fincas to foreclosure in 1900. Yet because of his local clout, he was able to renegotiate with his lenders and keep some properties in the hope that he might recoup some of his losses.[66] This bet proved a poor one, and Mallen left the Soconusco in ruin a few years later. He then moved to Tabasco and took up bananas instead. All this was in the future at the time of the Congress, which he attended wealthy and well respected.[67] As with Bejarano, Mallen's workers also owed him considerable sums. When his wife passed away early in 1891, the debts of seventy-one workers made up 10 percent of her fincas' value. Given the growth Mallen's holdings saw in the years between her death and the Congress, he must have been owed a great deal more by 1896.[68]

Of the seventy-six men representing seventy municipalities and eleven districts at the Congress, only a few had the chance to speak and have their opinions recorded. Bejarano and Mallen were among that select few. They were rousing advocates for reform, both economic and humanitarian, and their demands were taken up by a good number of Congress attendees. Yet despite their vocal promotion of new labor laws, an even more vocal conservative element within the Congress repeatedly and raucously called for the preservation of the system as it stood. The conflict between this highland cohort and lowlanders like Mallen and Bejarano led to a cacophonous Congress that ground to a halt numerous times. The delegates only came to a rather milquetoast final proposal for reform through the intervention of the governor himself.

The seriousness with which these two sides approached the issue can be seen in the length and detail of their proposals to their fellow delegates. The Congress was organized around a series of questions posed by various commissions. Highland delegates tended to keep their questions short and to the point. They knew what they wanted—the status quo—and there was no need to go into the nuances of the economics or morality of the labor system as it stood. In contrast, lowland planters tried to push their fellow delegates into careful conversations about the rights of laborers and the need for fiscal responsibility to promote economic development. They had no qualms in taking up the charges of slavery from the Mexico City and foreign press because they considered themselves the victims of debt peonage as much as any indebted worker.

As it came time to answer these questions, Bejarano took the lead in promoting reform. The committee he sat on declared that the system in question was not slavery, despite outsiders' accusations, and the debt contracts that governed it were in fact constitutional. Yet, he and his fellows stated, these debts bound up a great deal of capital in the state and clogged the wheels of progress. They pleaded with their fellow delegates to abolish the system and promote the civilizing effects of wage labor. By providing the "indios infelices" with savings banks, government-run pawn shops (*montes de piedad*), schools for both boys and girls, books and manuals, public conferences, agricultural banks, roads and other communication projects, and prohibiting child labor, the committee felt that the state could use the lessons of the economic sciences to overcome its labor problem.[69] Bejarano's cause was taken up by a number of other delegates, also lowland planters, who further detailed the means by which debt- and incentive-based labor could slowly be converted into wage labor in line with the country's civil code.[70] This was the liberal progressive program in action, a regional manifestation of the positivist program Díaz and his technocrats were promoting across the country.

The opposition rebutted this argument by asserting that debt labor served as a civilizing tool and would someday naturally give way to wage labor.[71] Their arguments went on for hours and pages, detailing the moral obligations of Hispanic elites to their indigenous peons. Yet, at base they were no more nuanced than "if it ain't broke, don't fix it." Despite the detail and heft of the lowland planters' positions, the highland elites held strong. Chiapas was far from Díaz's seat of power, and though the turn to exports was giving liberals greater sway, the locus of political and economic might in Chiapas remained with the highlands. As the conservative highlanders well knew, real change could only be effected by local action. When it came time to vote on a final resolution, the highland leader declared, "The current system of service by indebted servants should be tolerated until changes in economic circumstances themselves extinguish it. In consequence, the occasion [to do so] has not arrived." Twenty-four of the fifty some delegates still in attendance at the end of the Congress voted in his favor.[72]

As this proposal was diametrically opposed to Governor León's understanding of the system and wishes for its prohibition, León, through the auspices of the Congress's secretary, moved against the highlanders. The Congress secretary fervently asserted that there had been an irregularity in the proposed resolution and threw out the vote.[73] Acting on behalf of León, the secretary proposed a new, three-part resolution to abolish the current system, substitute daily wages, and amortize debts through discounted payments.[74] The delegates were dismissed for the day after admonitions to help move Chiapas toward a world where "progress will not be anathema for the indebted servant, for the unhappy Indian." On their return the next morning, they passed the secretary's resolution thirty-two to sixteen, with fully a third of the original delegates having bowed out.[75] Of those who remained, an entire third held their ground against the obvious desires of the governor, himself likely seen as a proxy for the president. Subsequently, they blocked any resolutions as to how the state's legislature might go about enforcing the measure they had just passed.

Money Moves What the Law Cannot

The 1896 Agricultural Congress was followed a year later by a new labor law passed by the state legislature. Both were celebrated from afar, but neither had much impact within Chiapas. Most in the Soconusco and other lowland plantation areas saw the new law as toothless. Once again, local practice trumped any sort of state-mandated reform. Nonetheless, finqueros in the Soconusco tried to implement the new rules and comply with the law's spirit, in the hopes that through perseverance and reference to liberal ideals they could free themselves from the costs of incentivized contracts. Workers had little of it. With coffee climbing ever further up the Sierra Madre, the scarce workforce was well positioned to continue making demands. Increased incentives to both workers and recruiters, rather than any sort of legal work-around, slowly redirected some labor from the highlands near San Cristóbal down to the Soconusco. Yet highland elites continued to maintain a firm hold on many of the indigenous villages in central Chiapas. Thus, Guatemala and the tierra fría remained key sites of labor recruitment for planters in the Soconusco. Labor remained a scarce resource, and the incentives that workers demanded continued to constrain coffee's expansion, even as planters in the Soconusco broadened the reach of their recruiting efforts.

Despite the governor's best efforts and wording that suggested major reforms, the labor laws that eventually emerged from the Agricultural Congress changed little. In May 1897, the new statute went into effect, limiting advances to two months' salary and mandating that all indebted mozos and their employers register outstanding debts with the local jefe político. Only a certificate issued by the jefe político could serve as legal proof of the debt, and that certificate had to be passed from one employer to another if the debt was to continue to be recognized. Mozos were to be protected from fraud or double entry in the debt registers. As the state legislature explained it, this law would promote a gradual abolition of the system as it stood, allowing for the substitution of wage labor through the introduction of a "dike" to hold back the creation of new indebted workers. It respected the debts that stood, as it respected property rights, and only attacked the future creation of additional debts.[76]

Journalists in Mexico City and Tuxtla Gutiérrez celebrated the law's passage, lauding the government of Chiapas for fighting slavery in the republic.[77] Other states reprinted the law as an example of what they might pursue in their own legislatures.[78] Yet within Chiapas, opinions regarding the possibilities for change were muted. Most recognized that reform at the state level was meaningless unless given shape by those who it governed. In this case, highland hacendados had little incentive to take part. In the Soconusco, planters took the law in stride, seeing it as the weak legislation that it was but nonetheless abiding by the ruling, at least on paper. As it did little to ameliorate the labor shortage, they, like planters throughout the state, increasingly adapted the system of debts institutionalized by highland planters to their own needs. As a journalist reminded readers of the local newspaper in Tapachula, the abolition of debts did little to solve the problem of acquiring new labor. He went on to suggest that only higher wages or the recruitment of workers from points unknown could ease that scarcity.[79] As planters in the region well knew, legislation could do little to undermine an entrenched social and political arrangement that benefited many.

Yet, through acquiescence to laborers' demands and to the constraints of the system in place, practice was already slowly shifting. Through the extension of incentives to both recruiters and workers themselves, lowland planters were beginning to pull some of the highland workforce away from its traditional routes. Money did what the law could not. Good pay for both recruiters and workers in the highlands slowly opened the flow of labor. Planters regularly paid highland recruiters, many closely tied to municipal governments, a monthly salary of MX$100. They further sweetened the deal by ensuring that seasonal migrant workers would return with cash in hand, an important promise given that many recruiters had ties to merchants and tax collectors in the workers' hometowns.[80] The workers coming from the highlands often had little say in the matter. Some chose to take the week-long walk to the coast, recognizing the potential benefits of freeing themselves from the cycles of debt that governed communities in the highlands. Other workers, though, were pulled into plantation labor through a medley of trickery and debt. Secured through outstanding tax bills, debts left from political and religious *cargos,* or obligations, and the usual arsenal of enticements and advances and trickery—one cannot write about debt peonage without mentioning alcohol—indigenous highlanders slowly made their way down to coffee plantations in the Soconusco.[81]

The good wages, though, and the ongoing use of incentivized contracts, was not primarily in service of highland recruiters or workers. Rather, this system endured because planters still relied on workers from elsewhere. Highland recruiters were still primarily responsible to the elites who had always governed their activities. They also increasingly found their workers in demand in other export-oriented regions of the state like the northern lowland district of Palenque.[82] For many planters in the Soconusco, the costs of highland recruiters were simply too much. Thus, most workers in the Soconusco continued to come from the tierra fría and Guatemala. Because of this, incentives remained a necessary part of recruitment as escape back into the Sierra Madre or across the border was always an alternative to a poorly remunerated position. Well into the twentieth century finqueros complained about the advances they were forced to lay out and the workers who left before fulfilling their obligations.[83]

Despite this, and despite a crash in global coffee prices in 1897, coffee harvests grew exponentially across the turn of the century. Exports more than doubled between 1896 and 1900 and did so again roughly every five years through 1920.[84] With this growth came an ever-greater need for both seasonal and permanent workers to plant and maintain the ever-expanding coffee orchards.

In 1909, one source reported that 10,000 workers had been sent as seasonal migrants from the state's highlands to the Soconusco.[85] Whether or not this number is exaggerated, these workers were a supplement rather than a substitute for the regional sources of labor long cultivated with incentives.[86] In 1897, before planters had access to highland labor, the state reported 6,500 indebted servants in the Soconusco, the highest concentration in Chiapas.[87] Three years later 9,476 out of a total population of 36,500 lived on coffee fincas.[88] An American couple admired the district's sizeable Guatemalan workforce when they passed through in 1901.[89] By 1910, the district had 54,000 inhabitants, 15,855 of whom were peons and wageworkers in agriculture. No one in the district spoke Tzotzil or Tzeltal, the languages of those 10,000 workers supposedly sent down from the highlands. But 11,000 of the district's residents had been born in Guatemala, more than five times the 2,000 who had lived there in 1900.[90]

At the same time as efforts were being made to mobilize highland labor for lowland use, politicians were also working with planters to enlarge the regional pool. Government officials at all levels worked to facilitate Chiapaneco and Guatemalan migration to the Soconusco. As we saw in Chapter Two, the jefe político and planters alike offered Guatemalans who crossed the border in the wake of internal political turmoil in 1897 incentives to stay.[91] As we saw in Chapter Three, planters worked with municipal governments to improve the roads from the coffee zones of the Soconusco to Motozintla and the tierra fría and facilitate the movement of workers.[92] As we saw in Chapter Four, the Mexican Land and Colonization Company sold lots of land in its Indigenous Colony to Guatemalans and locals in the hopes of creating a permanent workforce in the midst of the coffee zone.

None of this eliminated the outstanding debts that burdened planters' account books. Instead, it facilitated the spread of this system of incentives far beyond the bounds of the Soconusco. While the 1897 labor law outlawed advances and amortized old debts, it was, in the end, another example of the distance between paper and practice. Planters concealed advances from the state, referencing them only in glancing asides within estate inventories and receivership account books.[93] Recruiters' whose wages and expenses emerged in these mentions worked primarily within the Soconusco, the tierra fría, and, in one case, the central lowland district of Comitán. None of the account books I have access to mentions payments to highland recruiters.[94] All of these arrangements required incentives because coercion was still not an option. Though planters were economically dominant, lack of coordination within the coffee elite and the dispersed nature of the workforce left them without the political clout or judicial capacity needed to enforce contracts.[95] Incentives instead had to serve.

It could be said that Charles Lesher saved finca San Juan las Chicharras by embracing and expanding the use of incentivized contracts. Alternately, that success could be attributed to workers from across Chiapas and Guatemala who took up Lesher's offer of land, high wages, and easy access to credit. Through their toil, they made the finca boom. When Lesher took on management in 1892, the plantation was worth $50,000. Four years and $18,000 in loans to workers later, an assessor placed its value at $376,000. While John Magee, the finca's owner, took these outstanding credits as cause for a fraud suit, the judge and other finqueros in the region dismissed such claims and rewarded Lesher's success.[96] Magee never returned to the Soconusco, but Lesher found new employment at a series of ever-larger fincas, building up capital and connections, and purchased his own plantation in 1910.[97] Where Magee had called foul, those with more experience in the district saw what had come to be good sense. Workers demanded incentives, and, by 1900, planters across the Soconusco had recognized that this system was the only means to secure the labor they needed.

Just as Lesher saved San Juan las Chicharras from ruin by embracing indebted labor, so too did the planters of the Soconusco secure the future expansion of the coffee economy by bowing to the custom of contracts and advances. That is not to say that they did not attempt to reform the system as it stood. The Agricultural Congress of 1896, though, was a clear demonstration of the inability of the state and legal statutes to create real change. The economic and political heft of highland elites and their deeply ingrained linkages with indigenous villagers kept most of those villagers from traveling to the southern coast for work. No legal or administrative reform could unseat this system. Only a gradual expansion of incentivized contracts and costly payments would slowly redirect some of that labor to the Soconusco.

When representatives of Mexico's revolutionary government arrived in Tapachula for the first time in 1914, they brought with them another new labor law. This one again mandated the elimination of debt and added a requirement that wages be paid weekly in cash. Planters protested that this would take away the small amount of leverage they had over their workers, as it was only the promise of pay at the end of the harvest that kept laborers working through the season. They suggested instead that they deposit the weekly payments in a bank where laborers could retrieve them once work was done.

Workers again threatened to simply depart if they did not receive their cash up front. As always, the menace of coffee rotting on the bush was a convincing one. Fined for not depositing wages, finqueros protested to the new government that they would rather acquiesce to worker demands and keep their labor force than embrace the untested insurance offered through deposit. Implicit in these worries was concern over the eliminations of those incentives hidden from state view since the passage of the 1897 labor reforms. Now, in order to avoid fines and additional scrutiny, larger plantations began inscribing advances as wage bonuses in the books, eliminating the pretext that these sums of money were ever going to be repaid.[98]

Credit and debt were the only means by which planters could secure and keep workers on their plantations. Despite multiple attempts at reform, incentives remained an integral part of labor in the Soconusco. Over the course of forty years, planters had learned that workers would abandon ship on even the suggestion of eliminating credit. When presented with the opportunity to do so in 1914, they quickly backed away. As the next chapter will show, the gradual acceptance of customary, informal, and flexible regulation of credit was not limited to labor alone. As much as formalized institutions around property proved a boon to all involved in export production, so too did the preservation of less rigorous institutions around lending and borrowing.

6 *The Circulation of Codes and Commerce*

Everyone owed a debt to the widow Bado. Very few had cash to pay it. Her husband, Antonio Bado, had arrived in the Soconusco from Gibraltar with his brother in the early 1870s. Soon after, he married Herlinda Rosales, the daughter of a local elite family. The Bados together served as a key intermediary between locals and the global market. They moved coffee out of the Soconusco and manufactured goods and capital into it. In Antonio Bado's name, they slowly built up a mercantile business, first investing in lighter barges to carry goods from ship to shore, then building a warehouse in the port, then opening a general store in Tapachula. Along the way, they also started growing coffee. Almost all of their business relied on credit. When Antonio passed away during the smallpox outbreak in 1898, his commercial enterprises were valued at more than CYSA$400,000. Of that, CYSA$183,405.49 took the form of debts owed to the business. Herlinda Rosales, now viuda, or widow, de Bado, and her five children had little in the way of liquid assets to cover the business's own outstanding debts of almost CYSA$200,000. Constituted on the basis of a multitude of transactions with people down the street and across the world, these debts represented the deep integration of the local and the global in the Soconusco.[1]

The Soconusco's economy grew based on its connections with global markets. Yet growth also required the intimacy of personal relationships based on trust. This book has telescoped its focus as needed, moving from the broad scope of international diplomacy and national politics to the particularities of the land itself and the intermediary sphere of regional labor migration. Commerce and capital provide a means to look at how these circuits overlapped and intersected. By examining how money and goods moved in, around, and out of the Soconusco, we also see how local actors adopted and adapted the ideas and institutions that facilitated global integration.

Economic reformers in nineteenth-century Mexico intended their work to broaden and deepen the scope of the country's commercial activity. As in much of Latin America, guild law limiting commercial activity to specific families and collectives had long set the bounds of economic life. Much as liberal land reform targeted collective landholding, so too did liberal commercial reform target the corporate privileges left over from colonial times. With new civil and commercial codes issued in the 1850s and revised through the end of the century, the nation's regulated, official commercial life expanded to include many who had long been excluded.[2] Liberal reformers worked to redefine progress for their modernizing nation by broadening the scope of who could take part in formal economic endeavors.[3]

Yet until the late nineteenth century, these reforms had little resonance beyond major economic centers. Institutional creditors and modernizing bureaucrats remained concentrated in Mexico City. Local lenders and promoters only slowly took up the work of interpreting and implementing reform beyond the capital. Only gradually did commerce prove to be one of the most effective vectors for the spread of liberal norms during this era. That said, those participating in this new liberal legal and economic culture also had great bearing on the shape it took and the activities it governed.[4] As the coffee economy grew, people in the Soconusco increasingly made use of state-sponsored institutions to secure and promote their investments. Through their use, local actors built these institutions into meaningful and durable parts of the economy.

In large part, this chapter is about credit. In a place where cash was scarce and incomes cycled with the harvest, credit made the wheels of the economy spin. Short- and long-term credit, loans for both working and consumption capital, mortgages and advances, IOUs and buying on account all served to ease the flow of goods, labor, and investment. The Bados' books capture the complexity of these flows and the ways in which local actors engaged with the increasingly diverse array of commercial institutions that made the globalizing economy run. Lacking formal credit institutions, individual lenders in the Soconusco worked to make Mexico's new civil and commercial regulations protect their interests and move the region's coffee out onto world markets. At the intersection of local production and global trade, merchants and other lenders in the Soconusco selectively implemented the liberal commercial project in a way that suited their needs.

Through these commercial relationships, this chapter also illuminates the material life of the Soconusco and the way those invested in export agriculture engaged international discussions of the meaning of modernity. Just as colonial cacao producers traded for pottery from China, so too did this new boom in export production introduce international goods into the region. Whether machinery or tinned foods or, again, fine china, these imported goods were an international means of representing prosperity. Producers from the Soconusco also sent their goods out of the region, as both commodities and as a means of attracting investment. Samples sent to consulates and international expositions were a physical way to supplement editorials and newspaper articles that advertised the region's potential and progress. Just as the slow formalization of credit instruments cemented liberal practices in daily life, so too did the flow of commercial goods and information enmesh local actors in global practices.

The Bado family, as owners of an import-export firm, general store proprietors, and coffee finqueros in their own right, made use of the entire gambit of commercial institutions available to residents of the Soconusco. This chapter will use their engagement with commerce to illustrate how local use of regulation and promotion evolved to meet the needs of an increasingly globally integrated economy. The chapter begins with an examination of everyday credit and the ways in which people adopted the language of new commercial regulation to secure even the smallest amounts of money. In so doing, they created a liberal economic vernacular to govern quotidian transactions. Next, the chapter moves to examine the development of parallel vernacular institutions for governing the more complex credit arrangements that undergirded the expansion of plantations and large import-export businesses. A decade of easy access to informal interpersonal credit led to massive losses as the century turned. Learning from experience, commercial actors like the Bados drew on the civil and commercial codes to build a more regulated and normalized system of mortgages and advance contracts in the early 1900s. Throughout, the chapter emphasizes the increasing material and institutional integration of the region into the global economy. In doing so, it also shows how the expansion of the global economy relied on local actors' engagement with and interpretation of its essential institutions.

Drawing on Liberal Legislation to Regulate Everyday Debt

In any economy, credit optimally circulates in a multitude of forms, serving a multitude of needs. In examining the expansion of commerce in the modern era, historians tend to focus on what can be thought of as capital, that is, loans made available for the initiation of a new endeavor or the expansion of an old. I will return to capital investments later, as they are vital to understanding the macroscale economic expansion that occurred across rural Latin America during the export boom. First, though, it is important to consider everyday forms of credit. Before credit cards and payday lenders, people in the Soconusco shopped on credit and borrowed small sums of cash from friends and family. This borrowing allowed people to meet quotidian needs when cash was scarce and the harvest still months away. In the 1870s and

1880s, this type of everyday incremental lending lacked much in the way of formalization. Businesses were rarely constituted as legal entities in their own right, meaning that heirs could lose everything if a proprietor died in debt.[5] As the new century approached, borrowers and lenders in the Soconusco increasingly turned to Mexico's civil code to formalize and standardize these everyday forms of credit and commerce. Though there was no legal obligation to do so, individuals constituted business entities and filed their small loans at the local court to secure them against fraud or failure. In doing so, they turned abstract liberal legalese into a concrete and useful vernacular.

Everyday purchases were as integral to the growth of the export economy as the once-in-a-lifetime purchase of a finca or the annual securing of an advance contract for that year's harvest. From tinned sardines to champagne, Tapachula's stores held a variety of local and imported goods to tempt those nostalgic for home and those looking for a treat. Stores also sold the new tools, new seeds, and new supplies that the export economy required.[6] As the introductory note on units indicated, cash, particularly Mexican pesos, was scarce in the Soconusco. While most businesses were happy to accept Guatemalan pesos, even these were rarely abundant.[7] Small-scale consumer credit was the answer. Procured through merchants, neighbors, friends, and family members, loans allowed for the circulation of capital and goods based on the expectation of future income. Generally repaid with coffee and other cash crops, these loans also helped move smallholders' harvests out of the Soconusco.

Small-time credit was nothing new in the late nineteenth century. Buying on account, lending a few pesos to a neighbor, paying up front for part of an order to be delivered later, agreeing to pay for damages done to a property over time—all were traditional and relatively unregulated parts of economic life.[8] As a part of the push for legibility and centralized administration that began to emerge mid-century, the new commercial and civil codes of the 1850s through 1870s, revised again in the 1880s, regulated all such transactions. Officially, though, transactions involving less than MX$500 did not need to be written down or registered to be binding. Agreements were validated through simple mutual consent by two competent parties.[9] The new codes did mandate that merchants maintain up-to-date ledgers of daily business, purchases on account, and inventory, all of which had to be provided to the court or interested parties as needed.[10] Lenders, borrowers, and the state benefited if all those individuals entering into the commercial sphere could prove and enforce their agreements through standardized and substantiated means.[11]

The use of consumer and short-term credit expanded during the export boom as more people had both access to and need for consumer goods. Lenders and borrowers made use of liberal reforms to make their relationships increasingly uniform and legible. While even the richest finqueros ran up tabs at the general store, these small loans represent an opportunity to understand the economic lives of those without recourse to the types of capital usually addressed. In these transactions we see how villagers and farmers got by. We also see how they capitalized on and reworked the strictures of liberal economic reform.

THE LIMITS OF SELLING ON CREDIT

On her husband's death in 1898, Herlinda Rosales viuda de Bado inherited a tangle of commercial and personal obligations. She also inherited a busy general store and mercantile operation, neither of which would have functioned without that mess of credit and debt. In her attempts to unravel the knot of obligations, it is possible to see both how and why people borrowing and lending small amounts of money made use of the new civil and commercial codes. The widow Bado's inability to recoup her extensions of credit, including short-term consumer credit, made it impossible for her to save her business. Yet her family's careful compliance with the commercial code meant she kept her home and agricultural lands.

Herlinda Rosales was born and raised in Tapachula. She married Antonio Bado in 1881, and together they had six children and created a small commercial empire.[12] Though early contracts were signed in Antonio Bado's name, by the mid-1880s he had constituted a commercial firm called Sres. A. Bado y Cía that protected his personal interests from the risks he took with his growing business.[13] Import-export houses like theirs, which imported goods from national and foreign commercial enterprises and exported coffee in turn, were key intermediaries between the Soconusco and the world. As Bado's wife, Rosales de Bado had no legal standing without Bado's permission, no legal authority with regard to contracting or borrowing.[14] Yet the alacrity with which she took up the many threads of his enterprises suggests that she was a partner, if not always an equal one, in what was a family business.[15]

Once widowed and granted both the liberties that came with that legal status and the obligations that came with her inheritance, Rosales de Bado reconstituted her former husband's commercial operations under her own name as the Casa Viuda de Bado. Unfortunately for her, Antonio's death coincided with a global decline in coffee prices that wreaked havoc on the region's export economy. The Bados' had allowed customers to buy everything from luxury imports like cashmere to necessities like burlap sacks on credit. Whether celebrating with fine wine or mourning with new black clothes, the Bados' store provided for all needs. As a result, though, the widow Bado now had a carefully annotated pile of difficult-to-collect IOUs and unrecoverable sales on account. Within a year of establishing her own commercial house, Rosales de Bado filed to liquidate her business.[16]

This was despite the fact that the Bados had run their business as mandated by the commercial code. As she herself pointed out, her business was worth—and was owed—far more than the sum of its own outstanding debts. The widow Bado could tally up what was owed to her because she and her husband had carefully maintained code-mandated ledgers of both running tabs, or *cuentas corrientes*, and IOUs, or *pagarés*. These ledger books were the most basic of credit instruments. They were the point at which most individuals entered into contact with the growing body of law governing contracts and commerce. Each entry in a merchant's ledgers constituted a contract between the buyer and seller for the amount of the purchase made.[17]

Despite taking great care to prevent fraud on the part of merchants, the codes paid little attention to the enforcement of debts noted in these ledgers. While other countries had specific statutes governing these accounts, Mexico did not.[18] The code did not mandate terms for their repayment, and merchants were left responsible for their collection. These loans were also given least priority if a debtor entered into bankruptcy.[19] Merchants would sometimes employ a notary or go before a judge to formally register an account if it grew too large and required a structured repayment scheme. Most accounts, though, remained solely within ledgers and thus were difficult to enforce.[20] This was the crux of Rosales de Bado's financial mess.

Rosales de Bado could have attempted to collect from each of the customers who together owed her company almost CYSA$100,000, mostly in sums of less than CYSA$100. If she did so, it would have become apparent that these customers also owed money to many other creditors. Accounts from other local stores make clear that the practice of buying on credit was the norm in Tapachula, as it was across Mexico. Finca owners, smallholders, and those who lived in town purchased everything from imported ginger ale and liquor to rough cloth and keys on credit.[21] When claims were laid against a finca or a store on its owner's death or financial collapse, local merchants were almost always among the assembled creditors.[22] Most debtors repaid their tabs in cash or in kind—here often in coffee—but when a business went belly up, these small but necessary extensions of everyday credit were hard to redeem.

The downturn in coffee prices and the attendant stagnation of the local economy impeded the usual slow repayment of day-to-day debt. By 1898, coffee was worth half what it had been a few years before, reducing the ability of producers to repay their short-term loans. It does not appear that Rosales de Bado even tried to collect what she was owed. As her own creditors began to come after her, she instead turned to the civil code to save her family. Having established her own commercial firm to separate her affairs from those of the business, Bado had also made herself and her children into its creditors themselves.[23] As such, she and her family, along with the foreign and local creditors who had advanced the company goods and cash on account, now received the debts contained in the ledger books as payment. According to the code, each of these outstanding debts constituted a contract with real value. It could be used to pay off the company's own obligations.[24]

While her customers may not to this point have noticed their engagement with Mexico's commercial code, they suddenly became aware of its presence in their lives. Instead of owing money to the widow Bado, they now owed money to a German merchant or a commercial house in Mazatlán. With a key node snipped from the web of regional, national, and international credit that kept the economy of the region going, the separation between local and global suddenly collapsed.[25] Other Tapachula-based merchants—Spanish, German, Chinese, Mexican—soon stepped in to again facilitate the percolation of global goods and capital into the local economy. Business remained tight for a few more years, with repayment periods renegotiated, belts tightened, but everyone still needed rope and wagon wheels and an occasional bottle of whiskey or *aguardiente*. As the economy recovered and coffee harvests swelled, they needed new dresses and fine linens and wine from home to celebrate success. Running accounts continued to accumulate their small incremental contracts, the ledger books tallying up and checking off the never-ending small loans that eased the movement of goods and services necessary to the region's economy. No one figured out a better means to conduct everyday consumption with scarce cash, but the backstop of the commercial code meant business could continue.

COLLOQUIALIZING CONTRACT LAW IN THE LIBROS DE CONOCIMIENTO

While buying goods on account was the most common credit practice in the Soconusco, local ranchers, villagers, and homemakers had always needed more than what shopkeepers could offer from their wares. Sometimes what was needed was cash to pay workers, funds to buy a piece of land or a neighbor's horse, means to expand the fields under cultivation, time to cover past obligations, help in recouping the costs of natural disasters. A small, well-connected community had long been all the assurance necessary for a credit network of this sort. Moderated by informal, interpersonal agreements, these types of lending were necessarily limited in their scope. As the community grew beyond the bounds of interpersonal enforcement, the formalized mechanisms of contract law substituted for neighborliness.[26] The local magistrate opened his court to register interpersonal loans, and residents of Tapachula showed up in a steady stream.

Embracing the language of the civil code, they turned informal lending into formalized manifestations of small-time engagement with the tenets of liberal commerce. In time, these tenets became implicit in the everyday business of lending and borrowing.

The growth of both the Soconusco's population and its economy in the late nineteenth century expanded the pool of capital available for borrowing. It also undermined the relationships of trust that had earlier facilitated short-term, small-time lending. The new civil code set out a means by which such loans could be enforced. Interpersonal lending fit within the bounds of the *préstamo con mutuo simple*, or simple mutual loan. This statute covered the lending of fungible money or goods with or without interest for a specific time period.[27] The code's regulations were flexible, permitting the appending of clauses to cover the mode and timing of repayment, the inclusion of a guarantor, penalties and obligations, and, for the first time, allowing for the charging of interest of 6 percent or more annually. Repayment was enforceable through the courts, and, if a debtor could not pay in cash, his or her current and future goods were subject to seizure.[28] This regulation was to be universal, whether or not a contract was registered with the government or even written down, and formalization by a notary or public official was only required for agreements pertaining to more than either MX$300 or MX$500 depending on the circumstances.[29] No matter the form such an agreement took, it was subject to the precepts of the law and could be enforced through the court system if either party failed in their obligations.[30]

Villagers, workers, housewives, and farmers in the Soconusco did not trust in those implied precepts. Wary of being cheated by someone not bound by familial or community norms, they began to enter their contracts into government ledgers. Elsewhere, as had been customary deep into the colonial era, borrowers and lenders turned to notaries to keep track of these small loans and other day-to-day contracts. In the Soconusco, they turned to the municipal court, itself already a customary site for enforcing if not initially registering such agreements.[31] There, in what were labeled *libros de conocimiento*, people set down on paper the business of borrowing and lending.[32] Signed by the municipal judge or an *alcalde,* as well as two witnesses, these contracts served to standardize older forms of debt.

No one mandated this engagement with the new liberal language of contracts. Instead, individuals who were neither merchants nor investors found in the direct usage of liberal regulations a reliable means of facilitating and regulating the movement of even the smallest amounts of capital. Antonio Bado and his company signed a number of these contracts over the years to cover deliveries of goods and other unspecified credits.[33] The vast majority, though, involved parties without the Bados' commercial experience or elite status. A horse that Catarina Mejía borrowed from Vicente Lara died while in her care and she was unable to immediately pay the $25 she owed for lost property.[34] Januario Salvador promised to deliver 800 pieces of planed timber to Delfino Lopez and received the $16 they were worth in advance.[35] Jeronima Bermudes gave Federico Ibarra food, drink, and cash worth $9, to be paid back when he could.[36] These were small everyday debts that lenders might previously have scratched out at home if the parties involved were literate. Most, though, were verbal, rarely witnessed, and hard to find in the archive. Beginning in the late 1870s, they began to be inscribed on a regular basis.

Even though filing a contract at the local court required the payment of a small fee, the security that came with having a contract in writing and witnessed by a judge was apparently worth the cost.[37] Sixteen extant libros de conocimiento from Tapachula record the business of everyday credit between 1877 and 1913. Men and women from the town registered loans at least a few times a week. Most borrowers only appear in the registers once, while at least a quarter of creditors loaned money multiple times. Despite the legalization of interest up to 6 percent, only four contracts filed at the municipal court include provision for interest to be paid. Most lenders also ignored the other new tenets of the civil code related to guarantors or collateral.[38] People wanted the assurance of an inscribed contract, but did not necessarily find the more complex aspects of the code particularly useful.

The number and median value of loans fluctuated year to year, only very roughly correlating with global coffee prices. Loans were generally for less than CYSA$30 to be repaid in between a few weeks and a few months. They were recorded in Guatemalan rather than Mexican pesos. To the region's finqueros and foreign merchants, this amount would have appeared piddling. To its villagers and workers it represented a month's wages, a down payment on a plot of land, or a new cow.

While the value and number of debts betray no clear pattern, the types of contracts included in these ledgers and the language used by the court's clerks shifted over the years as the civil code went from useful innovation to accepted norm. As people became used to the language of the civil code, they ceased to explicitly copy that language in their contracts. The vast majority of contracts contained few specifics as to the purpose of the sums lent. In the 1870s and 1880s, labor agreements and those concerning the future delivery of goods were the most numerous among those that did specify their intent.[39] Early years reflect the embrace of new contractual regulations with clear restatements of the civil code's terms and phrases, though contracts rarely cited specific articles. Those drawing up the documents explicitly laid out the requirement that borrowers cover not only the sum borrowed but any "daños y perjuicios"—harm and damages—incurred in late payment. Similarly, clerks often copied out phrasing indicating that the creditor could pursue the debtor and his current and future belongings if the debt went unpaid.

The explicit outlining of these tenets of contract law peaked in the late 1890s as commercial activity in the Soconusco boomed. People wanted the security of contract writ and registered. The economic difficulties that caused the widow Bado's liquidation in 1898 correlated with the height of legalistic specifics, as well as with other reassurances like collateral or guarantors. Through their repeated invocation, borrowers and lenders made these tenets customary. As they became an entrenched part of the local institutions surrounding credit, they no longer had to be written out. By the early 1900s, it was rare for a contract to indicate anything more than the amount of a loan and the repayment period. They also rarely indicated the purpose of the loan. Instead, contracts simply indicated the extension of a certain value in return for a promise of future repayment by a specific date. Whether because reference to provisions for penalties was no longer seen as necessary or because the courts had become busier places with little time for elaborate annotations of now basic civil precepts, contracts became bare bones.

Many of the widow Bado's former customers registered loans in the court's ledgers after she went out of business. People like Apolinar Coutiño loaned cash to others for unspecified use. As always, terms of repayment were within a few months, no interest was charged, no guarantor or collateral was indicated. Coutiño appears four times in the ledgers, twice as creditor, twice as debtor. Those with whom he contracted were locals, as was he, and all were relatively anonymous, with only one appearing in the records of other official spaces.[40] As with his purchases on credit from the widow Bado, Coutiño was taking advantage of the multiplicity of ways in which small amounts of credit flowed around a region without banks or much ready cash. Having figured out how best to tap into liberalized commercial and civil codes to ensure their interests, Coutiño and his neighbors relied on the regularized and now customary application of liberal financial regulation instead of its explicit invocation.

Through the use of the commercial and civil codes, everyday borrowers and lenders secured their interests and made the language of liberal commerce into a vernacular of accessible credit. Small loans between friends and tabs at corner stores had long been the way of making ends meet in the Soconusco. In the late nineteenth century, the formalization of these loans through the use of contract law facilitated the expansion of the local economy by granting all involved the protections of the court. Even when the commercial code failed to provide a means to collect outstanding consumer loans, it secured people like Herlinda Rosales viuda de Bado against the loss of personal property by separating business interests from those belonging to private individuals. Officials at the Department of Fomento hoped that export agriculture would provide a means for all Mexicans to prosper through engagement with liberal commercial culture and scientific innovations.[41] In a roundabout way, with little credit granted to the Mexican government, here was evidence of producers on all scales taking on that mission themselves. In doing so, people far from the capital built up the capacity of the state by making use of its tools. People borrowing and lending very small sums of money—as little as a few days' wages—used state institutions and legal language to ensure against fraud and bad luck. In doing so, they cemented liberal norms of contract law in the quotidian experience of the Soconusco.

Standardizing and Institutionalizing Long-Term Lending

Shopping on credit and lending some cash to a neighbor were enough to keep the day-to-day workings of a regional economy going. They were not enough to facilitate the growth of that economy. While a loan of 50 pesos could finance the cultivation of a few hectares of coffee, it could not finance the thousands of hectares needed to make the Soconusco a player in the global coffee market. Banks and government lenders did not arrive in the district until after 1903. Instead, planters relied on a web of interpersonal lending to supply their capital needs during the first decades of the coffee boom. Though initially scarce, access to credit expanded as coffee prices soared and clearly titled properties provided ready collateral during the first half of the 1890s. Planters and merchants drew on newly liberalized regulations to slowly standardize a variety of credit instruments that met their needs. This rapid expansion turned disastrous for many when global coffee prices collapsed in that decade's final years. Despite increased use of legal language and the administrative offices discussed in Chapter Three, enthusiasm for a booming market and ignorance as to its particulars had made it easy for planters to overleverage their properties. This experience laid the groundwork for a more moderated, formalized embrace of financial regulations in the years that followed.

Many tropical export crops, coffee included, require years to provide any income. This leads to a greater need for both working and investment capital as compared to staples like grains or even cattle. The institutional lenders, particularly banks, that facilitated the expansion of commercial enterprises in the United States and Britain were absent from most of nineteenth-century Latin America because of national financial regulations and a paucity of liquid assets. Most elites held their wealth in land at mid-century, a form not easily converted into lending capacity. While the Church had served as a steady source of credit for the upper echelons of society in the colonial era, its activities were now curtailed by liberal reforms.[42] Instead, those looking to begin a new venture or expand their plantation had to rely on individuals or, at best, commercial enterprises as sources of capital.

This interpersonal lending could severely limit access to credit. In the wheat fields of Argentina and the tobacco plantations of Veracruz, only those with the right connections and well-established reputations could borrow. Merchants and other hacendados based their lending practices on their own familiarity with potential borrowers and local markets, limiting new entrants and burdening small producers with higher interest rates and stricter terms.[43] Elsewhere, though, a few scholars have found that interpersonal lending was much more flexible. Historians like Juliette Levy and Eugene Wiemers have found that a wide variety of planters accessed credit from a wide variety of lenders.[44] This was also the case in the Soconusco. While certain types of credit were limited to those with extensive, established properties, most who wanted it could find adequate access to the money they needed. Given the number of defaults and bankruptcies recorded when global coffee prices plunged, credit was, if anything, too abundant in southern Mexico in this moment.

Like local villagers in need of small, short-term amounts of credit, planters strung together pieces of the new commercial and civil codes to meet their needs. The following section will examine the credit instruments most in use and how they evolved as crises made many lenders more cautious. In the process, elites cemented the use of the civil and commercial code as a means of shoring up their interests against fraud and catastrophe. They brought the credit institutions of the Soconusco in line with international commercial norms, while maintaining a degree of responsiveness and flexibility that suited the needs of their export economy.

MOVING CAPITAL INTO THE SOCONUSCO AND COFFEE OUT

The earliest form of large-scale lending to emerge in the Soconusco was the advance purchase or futures contract. This was the way that most coffee grown on plantations, rather than village smallholdings, was exported from the district. A merchant like Antonio Bado would pay a planter a sum of money in the spring, to be paid back with coffee from the following harvest. In this way, the planter had enough capital to maintain his or her finca and cover the year's costs. The merchant, in turn, was guaranteed delivery of a substantial amount of coffee, usually at better than market prices. Merchants acted either on their own, independently securing commodities to sell abroad, or as representatives for commercial houses in Germany and London. Dependent on weather conditions and global commodity prices, these contracts could be risky for all parties involved. Because of this, the form went through a multitude of changes across the decades as both sellers and buyers tried to deploy legal tools to best protect their interests.

Early futures contracts were short-term, inflexible, and relatively uncomplicated. As we saw in Chapter One, Matías Romero was the first to register such a contract with the local court. A few years later, Antonio Bado took up this new form and began to standardize its usage in the region. Contracts signed by Romero in 1874 and Bado in 1881 combined the civil code's language regulating sales contracts with that regulating loans to create a form that backed advance purchase with collateral.[45]

In form and language, these contracts looked much like the loans registered in the libros de conocimiento discussed earlier. Namely, the buyer paid for a set amount of coffee at a set price to be delivered on a set date. In January 1881, Bado agreed to buy 400 quintals of coffee from Timoteo de León for nine pesos per quintal, delivered by the end of January 1882. In guarantee of that delivery, de León offered his current and future belongings as collateral, echoing the same civil code language as his less prosperous neighbors.[46] Unlike those village neighbors, de León put up a specific property as collateral for his debt. Though not explicitly outlined as a possibility in the civil code's regulations of sales contracts, de León agreed to be subject to all "legal vigor" with regard to mortgage regulations should he not fulfill his end of the contract. When he delivered only 330 of the promised 400 quintals, Bado returned to the district judge and filed a *juicio hipotecario*, or foreclosure filing, to recoup not only the missing quintals but also the additional losses Bado had suffered due to a rise in coffee prices from 9 to 12 pesos. These were the "costs and damages" so often referred to in such contracting. Instead of immediately pursuing the next legal step, the two men agreed to extend the terms of repayment for another year. When de León had still not met his obligations a year later, Bado filed to embargo his finca and begin the process of auctioning it off to cover the amount owed.[47]

This was the benefit of using the language of the new civil code and registering a contract with the court. When something went wrong, it was clear how recourse might be achieved and who should stand as arbiter if renegotiation was not possible. The involvement of property in the agreement made registration legally mandatory, as did the value of most such contracts. It was also in the interest of both parties to take advantage of the legitimacy bestowed by engagement with the administrative state, even if it was still governed by an often hostile cacique. A number of the early contracts explicitly stated that they were registering private agreements in order to give them "the entire force" of an official bond.[48]

The 1890s brought a wave of emigrant planters and capital to the Soconusco. They were drawn by ongoing advertisements of the district as a site for investment and the new availability of easy land title via the Mexican

Land and Colonization Company. Government incentives offered in the form of tax exemptions and other subsidies also eased the way.[49] Matías Romero had not been the only one to celebrate the district as a place to experiment with new types of agriculture. Planters in the Soconusco started sending examples of their products to international expositions in the 1880s, first to New Orleans and later to Paris.[50] By the early 1890s, Carlos Gris, the planter chased off his plantation by Sebastián Escobar's lackeys in Chapter Three, had become the butt of jokes in the Mexico City press for his continual overblown prose regarding the promise of the Sierra Madre's fertile foothills.[51] His laudatory remarks were repeated in only slightly more tempered form by other journalists who regularly reported on the district and its potential to provide returns for both individual entrepreneurs and the Mexican modernizing project as a whole.[52] Fearing that profits were going to foreigners rather than Mexicans, writers charged their fellow citizens with moving south and investing.[53] While Mexico's attempts to attract foreign colonists were not an overwhelming success, the Soconusco was one place where the Department of Fomento could celebrate some strides forward.[54]

With interest and investment increasing, both merchants and planters sought new, more flexible means to get capital into the district and coffee out. Alongside aspiring coffee finqueros, foreign commercial agents also moved to the Soconusco during these years. While local merchants like the Bados continued to act as middlemen for smaller-scale producers, foreign commercial houses now sought to buy directly from those producers who owned more extensive plantations. Based in the Mexican port city of Mazatlán, as well as London and Hamburg, these commercial houses had years of experience writing contracts that protected them from the fluctuations of commodity markets. The contracts their agents drew up with planters included a number of elements not before seen in the district. Firstly, they added either monthly or annual interest to most advanced sales contracts, one of the earliest and easiest incentives to lending provided for in the new codes.[55] Not long after, advance contracts began to mandate that producers deliver coffee sufficient to cover not just the advance and attendant interests, but also processing costs, taxes, tariffs, shipping, and insurance. This placed the majority of the risks inherent in agricultural production and transportation in the hands of planters, rather than purchasers. To further secure their investment, contracts signed with foreign commercial houses indicated that the coffee's value was to be determined on delivery. This protected merchants if the price of the commodity fell between when the contract was signed and when it was fulfilled.[56] Locally based merchants like Bado soon followed suit. By 1894, Bado had adopted the now common language of repayment in "sufficient coffee."[57] By the end of the 1890s, buyers further amended contracts to set the value of coffee at a peso or two below local market prices.⁵⁸

Newly standardized to the benefit of merchants, advance contracts spread across the Soconusco and increased in value as global coffee prices rose across the early 1890s. The rapid uptick in property sales by the Mexican Land and Colonization Company provided ample collateral to back these contracts. As properties grew larger, so too did the promised deliveries of coffee and thus the advances extended. In the 1880s, most planters borrowed at most MX$1,000. By the late 1890s, half of all contracts exceeded MX$10,000 (see Figure 4). To repay this amount, a planter had to deliver about 2,000 quintals of coffee, the harvest of at least 120 hectares of mature coffee bushes.⁵⁹ Despite the fact that few planters actually cultivated enough of their property to produce this much coffee, the German marks, British pounds, and U.S. dollars flooded in.⁶⁰

Large-scale advance contracts with foreign merchants were not a form of credit available to everyone. A very few companies supplied a limited number of planters with futures contracts worth more than MX$10,000. Foreign commercial companies were only interested in grappling with the hassle of transnational contracting and transportation when substantial quantities of

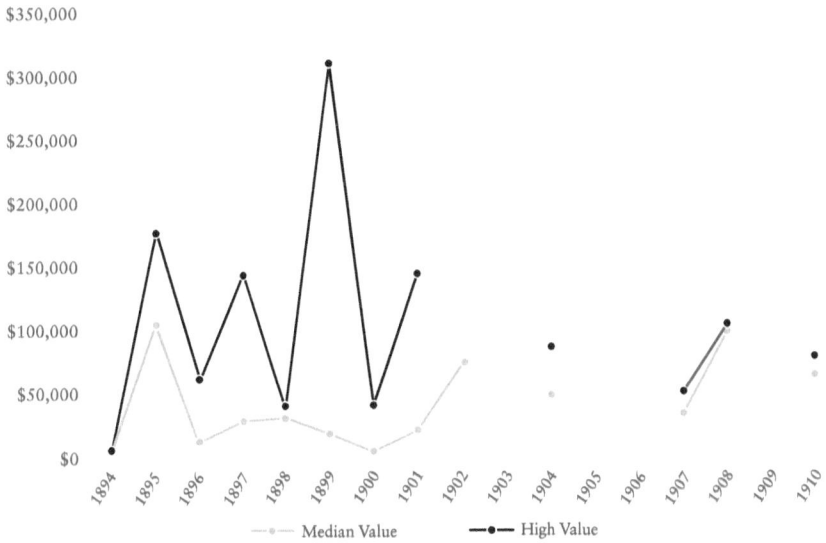

FIGURE 4. Median and High Values for Advance Contracts in MX$, 1894–1910. Figure only includes years for which I have access to at least three advance contracts. Source: Archivo del Registro Público de la Propiedad y el Comercio, Tapachula, Chiapas.

the beans were involved. Because of this, such companies did little business with finqueros cultivating less than 100 hectares. They signed no contracts with villagers planting coffee alongside their subsistence plots.

Instead, a dozen or so merchants and planters based in Tapachula supplied smaller producers with credit. 80 percent of advance purchases worth less than MX$10,000 involved merchants or planters based in Tapachula.[61] The Bados and their German, Spanish, and Mexican merchant neighbors each signed a few such contracts. To acquire enough coffee to make export worthwhile, they supplemented prearranged purchases by taking repayment in coffee for the everyday loans discussed above and buying additional sacks of coffee brought in at the end of the harvest.

Some planters also signed advance contracts with their neighbors. In many cases, these planter-purchasers had themselves signed advance contracts with foreign commercial houses. Their local purchases likely helped them meet the terms of their own agreements. Contracts between neighboring finqueros remained much simpler than those signed by foreign houses. Proximity and shared commercial customs likely served in the stead of elaborate legal language. That said, most still included language about collateral and damages, but few went so far as to specify insurance, transport, or the cost of export duties.[62]

Whether the purchaser was based locally or abroad, most advance contracts had a term of at most two years. Most were granted to already established planters who could demonstrate at least some ability to deliver the promised coffee. Aspiring finqueros still lacked the sort of funds that would facilitate entry into this growing economy. The predominance of general store owners, export merchants, and agents for foreign commercial houses as expediters of these contracts speaks to the continued substitution of local knowledge for more formalized risk assessment. That said, local enthusiasm for the coffee economy often blinded those who should have known best to potential risks. Absent personal wealth, would-be planters patched together bits and pieces of financing and frugality in the form of store accounts and continually renegotiated futures contracts until the same actors who engaged in such lending finally felt comfortable enough to engage in longer term credit.

LONG-TERM CREDIT IN A MATURING EXPORT ECONOMY

The final types of credit to emerge in the Soconusco were those we most commonly associate with growing industries: long-term, relatively low interest loans that served as working capital. These were the instruments of an economy local and foreign lenders judged to be mature, an economy seen to be a dependable source of returns. As with advance contracts, these capital investments melded global commercial customs with the language of Mexico's legal codes. Introduced during the boom of the late 1890s, complex, mortgage-backed loans combined with advance contracts to lead the local economy to the brink of collapse.

Like a number of her colleagues, Herlinda Rosales viuda de Bado moved capital into the local economy through both everyday credit and long-term formalized loans. As with their early embrace of futures contracts, locally based merchants like the Bados served as key sources of capital for those looking to get into the coffee business. While she restricted most customers to running up tabs at the store, she and her husband also signed a variety of long-term mortgage-backed loans with select finqueros. These the Bados formalized before a notary and registered at the public records office. When Rosales viuda de Bado filed for the liquidation of her business, it was these formalized loans, like the MX$115,000 taken out by a planter from Guanajuato named Rafael Ortega, that were seen as her most valuable assets.[63]

Ortega was an innovative and expansive user of mortgage-backed credit. Between 1889 and 1898, he secured more than MX$500,000 in credit by mortgaging his plantations to a number of Tapachula-based merchants and planters. While he arrived in the Soconusco with some capital in hand, he shored up his standing with a marriage to Sara Salas, daughter of an important local family. Through these connections, he bought a massive property from Sebastián Escobar, naming it Tonintaná las Chicharras. Even after he sold half of it to John Magee—the planter at the heart of Chapter Five—Ortega's property covered more than 1,000 hectares.[64] It was this property and the exploitation of newly liberalized lending practices that facilitated the expansion of his enterprises.

While contract law was important to standardizing and guaranteeing contracts, the legalization of interest above 6 percent and the regularization of collateral truly opened the door for credit markets in Mexico.[65] At the heart of these reforms was the basic tenet of real rights backing real obligations, recorded in a regulated, enforceable manner.[66] Ortega quickly embraced what would become an enduring precept of mortgage-backed lending: more property meant more capital. As one massive piece of property, Tonintaná las Chicharras did him little good in terms of accessing credit. While the civil code allowed for multiple mortgages on a single property, lenders were less willing to take their place in line as third or fourth claimant in case of default.[67] So Ortega subdivided his land into a number of smaller but still extensive lots. With his connections established and sureties in hand, Ortega seemed a safe bet for experimentation with new types of lending. By 1898, Ortega had at least six mortgages outstanding with six different merchant- and planter-lenders. Three were backed by Tonintaná itself. Smaller subdivided portions of the original property backed the others.[68]

This profusion of mortgages was common in the 1890s. As the global coffee market boomed, and for a few years after it crashed, lenders and borrowers went mortgage crazy in the Soconusco.[69] In 1895, planters registered four mortgage-backed loans, the largest for just over MX$3,000. In 1898 they registered at least twenty-five loans, the largest of which came in at more than MX$145,000 (see Figure 5). For the next few years, both the number and size of loans continued to grow. Just as coffee prices were collapsing around the world, just as Herlinda Rosales viuda de Bado filed to liquidate her business because of the troubled local economy, mortgage-backed capital poured into the Soconusco.

As with futures contracts, larger planters got larger loans and most of the largest loans came from commercial companies based abroad. Most of the large-scale debtors, though, were Mexican. They were part of the first generation of planters who had migrated in Romero's footsteps, acquired title

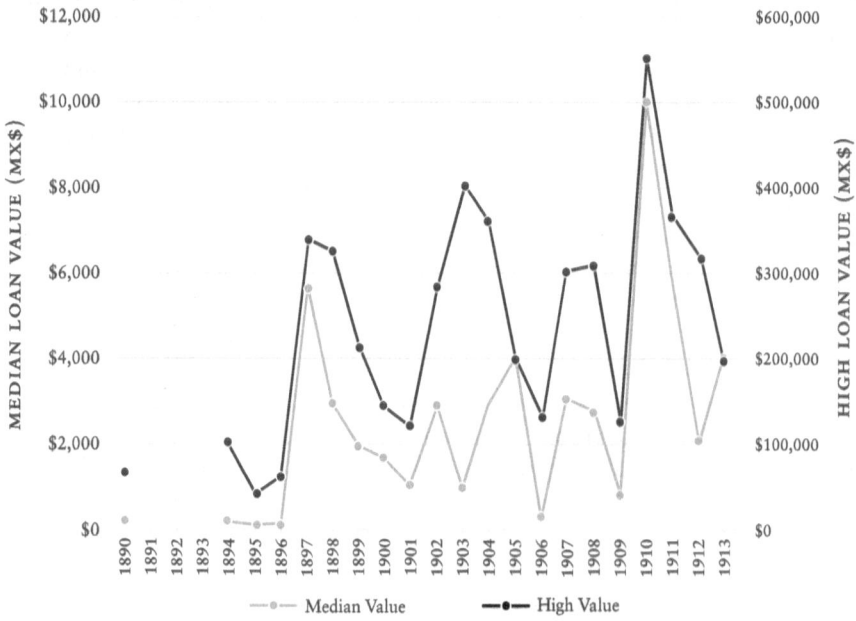

FIGURE 5. Median and High Values for Mortgage-Backed Loans in MX$, 1890–1913. Figure only includes years for which I have access to at least three mortgage-backed loans. The number of loans recorded each year is not included because the preservation of the archive is not uniform year to year. Source: Archivo del Registro Público de la Propiedad y el Comercio, Tapachula, Chiapas.

through various means, and already had coffee to harvest.⁷⁰ Like Ortega, a number used multiple pieces of property to back multiple mortgages. Again, this was working capital, meant to be invested in improving the properties that backed it. It was to be paid back in cash, not coffee, over a period of at least two years, often more, with interest set between 6 and 12 percent annually.

Less well-established planters also had ready access to smaller amounts of credit in the 1890s. As Figure 5 demonstrates, the value of the median mortgage-backed loan stayed below MX$10,000 across the period in question. In fact, three quarters of the loans made before 1901 were for less than MX$10,000. Almost half of those were made for less than MX$1,000. Here, lenders were as diverse as their borrowers. A few acted in both capacities. As with futures contracts, foreign commercial houses had little interest in contracting with those with less than 100 hectares of land. Planters and merchants living in the Soconusco stepped up instead.

Mexicans, particularly those from the Soconusco itself, made up the majority of debtors. While foreigners tended to borrow from their countrymen, Mexicans borrowed from everyone. Even without impersonal institutional lenders, the local credit market moved past the need for close personal ties that had previously governed lending practices. Backing their debts with small fincas, houses, or lots in what had been the ejidos, borrowers promised to repay within one to five years with interest at reasonable rates.

In summary, credit was flowing. Between 1895 and 1901, planters in the Soconusco borrowed at least MX$1.7 million. Banks and other formalized credit institutions had no involvement in this lending. Instead, the administrators, clerks, and other local representatives of the slowly spreading administrative state discussed in Chapter Three had to scramble to keep up with demand.⁷¹ About one quarter of the credit in circulation came from foreign commercial houses. The rest came from merchants and planters based in Tapachula. Noninstitutional lending between acquaintances, neighbors, shop owners and their customers, and family members more than met the needs of the growing economy. Most contracts were light on legal language. Lenders and borrowers registered them at the public records office, affixed the proper stamps, and noted the lien placed on their property. Occasionally they included language regarding the timing of payments, but they rarely invoked legal precepts governing damages and costs. Everyone seemed sure of what they were doing, eager to capitalize on the booming demand for coffee, the rapid spread of proper land titles, the final arrival of easy capital. The faster capital could get into circulation and start earning interest, the better. Not infrequently, contracts noted that the borrower had already received the cash prior to notarization, to his or her "complete satisfaction."

REINING IN EASY CREDIT IN THE WAKE OF CRISIS

That complete satisfaction did not last. Global coffee prices collapsed in the late 1890s, and with that collapse came a veritable flood of foreclosures. Numerous finqueros lost their livelihoods, as did the merchants who had loaned them money. The clear dangers of overabundant credit led to a reorganization of local commercial institutions in the early 1900s. Access to capital did not disappear. Rather, borrowers and lenders became more farsighted and cautious in the way they applied the possibilities enshrined in Mexico's civil and commercial code. They worked to tame the enthusiasm for global market integration that had led to disaster and instead delimited new commercial customs that provided flexible, negotiable access to capital.

Between 1895 and 1898, the average price of a pound of coffee on the global market fell by half.[72] Suddenly, planters had to produce twice as much coffee to cover their futures contracts. The enthusiastic influx of working capital slowed to a trickle. As Herlinda Rosales viuda de Bado wrote, "The commerce of this place is paralyzed . . . the life of commerce is essentially null." Tapachula had once been in "bonanza"; now it was lifeless, waiting.[73]

The distances implied by global trade and the hope that prices might quickly recover delayed the full force of the downturn. 1898 and 1899 saw the most lending yet. Many of these loans were second or third mortgages, last-ditch attempts to save the finca by using a new loan to pay off the interest on an old loan.[74] The liquidation of Casa Viuda de Bado in 1899, though, marked a turning point. Juicios hipotecarios—civil suits that led to the embargo and eventual auction of the mortgaged property in cases of default—took up most of the local civil court's time by 1900. Borrowers and lenders became thoroughly familiar with the civil and commercial codes as they renegotiated loans and futures contracts. Wherever possible, both parties tried to forestall foreclosure through reductions in principle, the discounted sale of mortgages, or the consolidation of multiple loans.[75]

Most of these attempts failed. Twice as many mortgage-backed loans signed between 1895 and 1901 ended in default as were repaid.[76] Half of the futures contracts signed during the same period ended in court.[77] The result was a huge turnover in finca ownership. Some finqueros fled the Soconusco, abandoning their properties and their debts.[78] Others attempted to recoup some of their costs by flouting embargos and selling off what coffee or other goods they had.[79] In turn, the enforcement of embargos and the rapid inventorying and auctioning of fincas upon the filing of a default claim became de rigueur. It was unclear if the local export economy could endure.

A flood of foreclosed fincas, some well-developed, some as-yet forested hillside, washed over the land market. Judicial sales of plantations at auction occurred on a regular basis, and a few new investors acquired extensive lands at a steal. In many cases, though, no purchaser stepped forward and creditors were left holding halfway-developed land. Put into receivership, some of these fincas floundered and were allowed to go dormant. Others, along with properties purchased by savvy newcomers and fincas whose owners had not overextended their borrowing, formed the basis for a sturdier, less volatile mortgage-backed credit market soon to emerge.

Low prices continued to dampen the global market for coffee through the next decade. Yet by 1902 the Soconusco was already on the way to a resurgent, if reorganized and rather more staid, engagement with the global market for capital and commodities. On the ground, things did not yet look sunny. On October 24, 1902, the Santa María volcano erupted just across the border in Guatemala. The eruption was distant enough to prevent fatalities, but the planters of the region were nonetheless distraught and fled en masse to Tapachula to escape the darkened skies and temblors.[80] Planters petitioned the president for relief, and the governor suggested, if nothing else, exemption from property and sales taxes for the coming few years.[81]

Despite the quite literal gloom and seeming doom, Helen Humphreys's mother could have been writing of the economy as a whole when she assured her daughter that "coffee trees are so tough.... They are bent but not broken."[82] The century's turn was a nadir for the local economy, but while many planters abandoned the region, village production and a determined clique of finqueros provided the basis for rebuilding. Crisis led to the development of new credit institutions and instruments to better undergird sustainable growth on a finca-by-finca basis. While the government eventually had a small role to play in this reset, it was planters and merchants who managed the transition from heady recklessness to more reliable returns. Before 1902, only one in three mortgage-backed loans and futures contracts ended in repayment. After 1902, almost three contracts were repaid in full for every one that ended in court.

This remarkable turnaround in lending outcomes was the result of borrowers and lenders restructuring how they conducted their businesses rather than an overall reduction in lending. While total lending bottomed out at MX$171,000 in 1903, it returned to between MX$300,000 and MX$500,000 a year by 1904. Lenders and borrowers, though, became more studied in their practices. Planters with well-established fincas and experience in the district came to dominate the coffee economy. These men, and a few women, were local ejiditarios, former ranchers from the coastal plains, the few emigrant planters who survived the crash, and plantation managers who took advantage of the glut of foreclosed properties to become finqueros. Many organized their new undertakings as agricultural companies, again making use of the protections between private and corporate property enshrined in the commercial code.[83] Having benefited from their predecessors' risky behavior, these new planters took on very few second and third mortgages.

Lenders learned more about the timeline of coffee cultivation and drew up terms of repayment that were longer and more flexible. They also frequently renegotiated contracts to give borrowers more time to repay.

After 1903, both foreign commercial companies and local finqueros quickly reentered the local credit market. They did so in ways that allowed them to better secure their investments while providing a variety of credit instruments to planters. Foreign commercial houses combined advance contracts with mortgage-backed working capital loans to extend credit in the long term. They signed contracts that promised up-front as well as ongoing infusions of capital over two to ten years. This was money that could be used to buy land, hire laborers, import processing machinery, build a new home for a finquero and his family, and, in general, invest in the long-term success of a plantation. In return, borrowers promised preferential rights to the coffee they grew. Borrowers only received those profits remaining once costs for transport and the loan itself were covered. Under these arrangements, planters controlled the day-to-day working of their fincas, but distant capitalists controlled their long-term finances.[84]

In contrast, local planter-lenders doled out credit in monthly installments and required repayment in cash over terms of a few years. They no longer contracted for future deliveries of coffee. Drawing on their intimate knowledge of local conditions and local residents, they kept a close watch on their investments to ensure repayment. They made sure neighbors were not using their capital to buy lavish furnishings or travel abroad. A small holiday party or sending a child to school back in Germany was all well and good, but no one wanted to lend to someone known for taking things too far. That said, connections of kinship or strong social ties were not necessary for lending to take place. The finquero community was still relatively small—the jefe político listed only thirty principal coffee producers in the district in 1907—and matches between those with money to lend and those in need were likely easy to make.[85] Whether the loan was 300 Guatemalan cachucas (about MX$240) between two neighbors in the ex-ejidos of Tapachula, or 3,000 pounds sterling (about MX$29,000) between a British finquero and his Mexican business partner, those who worked the land were best situated to judge the possibilities for solid returns.[86]

Merchants based in Tapachula also continued to serve a variety of intermediary roles in the circulation of coffee and capital. Like Antonio Bado and Herlinda Rosales de Bado before them, emigrants from Spain, Germany, and Britain dominated in this group. Most started their businesses with small everyday lending. They held on through the crisis by renegotiating terms, exporting coffee, acquiring properties from defaulting debtors for later resale, taking a cut of contracts they orchestrated for commercial houses abroad, and doing their own share of borrowing. As the economy recovered, they continued to lend sums through a variety of instruments, in quantities from a few hundred pesos to more than one hundred thousand. Merchants loaned less mortgage-backed capital than either of the groups discussed above. When they did, they moved away from contracts for specific amounts of coffee and instead embraced the model of exclusive purchasing rights in return for flexible lines of credit.[87]

A number of these locally based merchants also came to serve as branch presidents and local representatives for the banks that finally arrived in the wake of the global coffee crisis. This fit in with their more generalized investment in a variety of modernizing projects across the district. Across the 1900s, groups of merchants and merchant-planters founded a local electrical company, an ice factory, and a local theater.[88] Banks were a natural addition to this modernizing portfolio. The Banco de Chiapas opened a branch in Tapachula in 1903, and was joined soon after by a branch of the Banco Nacional de México and representatives for similar institutions based in Mexico City, Guatemala City, and London.

Yet little changed for most coffee growers in the region. Planters had written to President Díaz a few years before, one of the only times they did so, pleading for a bank to save them from "the hands of the agiotistas," or loan sharks, who they claimed were charging usurious rates.[89] Yet, in looking at their activities, it is clear that the entrance of banks did almost nothing to free up credit for most coffee planters. If anything, banks charged higher rates of interest than merchant- and planter-lenders. They also limited their lending to only well-established, well-propertied planters who could provide guarantees of substantial returns.

The formal, inflexible mode of lending employed by banks also tended to drive their borrowers to ruin. Banks, including the Caja de Préstamos para Obras de Irrigación y Fomento de la Agricultura, the country's first government-run development bank, injected more than MX$2 million into the local economy between 1903 and 1913. This was the largest sum of any single type of lender.[90] All that capital went to only twelve borrowers. Other types of creditors served more than 250 different planters, villagers, and merchants. Banks were generally repaid in full and more or less on time, as their contracts often mandated preferential repayment. This lack of flexibility drove borrowers into crisis. Individuals who borrowed from banks were more likely than any others to find themselves in default to their other creditors. At least eight of the twelve individuals and companies that borrowed from banks lost properties to foreclosure after doing so.

The Spanish merchant José Revuelto committed suicide in 1916. Like Antonio Bado, he left his heirs a tangle of credit and debt obligations. Those who owed him money included some of the most important finca owners in the region, including the former regional head of the MLCC, Oliver Herbert

Harrison. Harrison had invested heavily in both coffee and rubber across the Soconusco but had done so through the singular usage of limited liability corporations organized in the United States. When his companies went belly up, he was safe.[91] Revuelto, though, was not protected from Harrison's poorly timed and ill-advised investment in Mexican rubber. Having borrowed at precipitous terms from the Banco Nacional de México in an attempt to shore up Harrison's failing enterprises and thus his own fortunes, Revuelto was left without liquid assets by 1916. As with the widow Bado, his debts more or less equaled the credits owed him, but the scale was now much larger. The merchant felt he had way no way to go on.[92]

As opposed to the crisis that followed the widow Bado's liquidation of her business, Revuelto and Harrison's failures were not indicative of a generalized crisis. Their defaults were in fact quite unusual, outliers in this era of more studied lending and borrowing. The greater flexibility, frequent renegotiation, and recombination of credit instruments that followed the crisis of the late 1890s led to the quick recovery of the Soconusco's coffee economy. Most borrowers took on obligations of less than MX$10,000. Most repaid their debts on time or within a reasonable term after their initial due date. As the first section of this chapter demonstrated, lending registered in merchants' ledger books and the municipal court's libros de conocimiento continued unabated into the twentieth century. Credit was available in a multitude of forms, backed by flexible but reliable interpretations of the country's new civil and commercial codes. The spectacular failures of those like Bado, Revuelto, and Harrison catch the eye, but the endurance and expansion of the coffee economy was based on the widespread availability of small amounts of capital backed by regular engagement with the new civil and commercial codes.

In 1908, the government of Chiapas reported that foreigners had invested more than MX$4.4 million in the Soconusco, more than double the amount invested in any other district in the state.[93] While impressive, this sum in no way captures the even more vibrant picture of capital circulation painted in this chapter. Foreign purchases of land and investments in these new properties were only one part of the complex local economy. The number does nothing to capture lines of credit recorded at local shops, nor does it include the borrowing and lending of sums as small as two or three pesos registered in the libros de conocimiento. It may encompass some of the complex mortgage-backed credit arrangements and futures contracts that supported large-scale fincas, but it does not touch on the loans made between neighbors or in-laws or acquaintances to support smaller-scale planting and harvesting. Over the entire period covered by this chapter, the archives account for

MX$7 million loaned or advanced by foreigners and backed by a mortgage. Mexican mortgage-backed lending added at least MX$4 million more to that pot. Add to that the smaller sums daily extended as consumer capital and the loans registered at the municipal court, plus the multitude likely agreed to without resort to legal registration, and the investment captured by the state's records pales in comparison.

That we can account for the circulation of so much capital in this far corner of Mexico attests to the increased usage of legalistic instruments and institutions across the late nineteenth century. While investment in large-scale agriculture unquestionably ballooned during the period in question, the corpus of registered lending agreements also points to the ballooning usage of the country's civil and commercial codes as a means of ensuring one's investments. As the region's population grew, so too did the pool of lenders and borrowers and the social distance between them. Custom and the intervention of community elites could no longer be counted on to enforce agreements. Contract law, as laid out by liberal legislators in Mexico City, came to serve in their place. Initially cited explicitly, with obligations and consequences laid out in detail by court officials and contracting parties, the tenets of contract law were slowly made implicit. Outsiders, especially foreign commercial houses and banks, continued to weight down their contracts with highly specific and specialized language. Those living within the region instead relied on shared understanding of the commercial institutions they had built together through failure and success.

It was the combination of all the types of credit explored in this chapter that allowed for expansion of the region's coffee economy. Planters at all scales, whether growing a few coffee bushes alongside their subsistence crops or covering thousands of hectares in the bright red cherries, used credit instruments of all sorts. They engaged with state bureaucrats to back up their claims, paid their taxes, and affixed 50-cent stamps to their contracts. In the process, they drew the trappings of global commerce, both institutional and material, into their everyday lives. They ate off imported plates, drank imported wine, and read imported books. In return, they shipped out ever more coffee to be consumed in cafés and homes across the United States and Europe.

Merchants, planters, commercial agents, bankers, villagers, and shopkeepers drew on Mexican legal codes to meet their own needs. By engaging with these codes, they enshrined the tenets of liberal economic ideology in their daily practice. They ingrained contract law and the sanctity of private property in the minds and actions of those participating in the Soconusco's coffee economy. Local actors took up the language and activities of the modernizing state and put them into action. Through use, they made the aspirations of faraway technocrats into reality.

Conclusion

This was how an export economy was built. In fits and starts, failures and collapses, booms and busts, lawsuits and countersuits, contracts and trust, murders and marriages, emigration and running away. By villagers, merchants, laborers, judges, families, municipal councilors, planters, notaries, entrepreneurs, surveyors, caciques, and adventurers. Everyone had a role to play in determining the Soconusco's engagement with global markets. International trade, foreign investors, and national policy reform provided the context for this engagement. Yet these external forces could not dictate how their projects would be taken up. Instead, actors on the ground—and the ground itself—resisted, adopted, adapted, interpreted, and translated outside imperatives to suit local needs and conditions.

Between 1870 and 1920, the incremental and often stumbling turn to export commodities and the commercial institutions that facilitated their movement transformed the Soconusco. The population of the district more than quadrupled, from about 17,000 to more than 72,000. Producers went from exporting just a few quintals of coffee a year to sending over 11,000 metric tons of the bean abroad in 1919. A region once best traversed by foot or mule now had a railroad, bridges, and a highway. Rubber trees in orderly ranks marched across the northern plains, and coffee bushes climbed the foothills in carefully tended rows.

Yet those rows, like the bounds of the properties on which they grew, only superficially appeared straight and true. Even though fincas and smallholdings blanketed the landscape, much of the terrain remained untrammeled. The railroad was rickety, the bridges required constant refurbishment, the telegraph and telephone lines only extended so far. The landscape that provided such possibility also bounded that possibility. The people who planted and tended the new export crop also determined how far it could extend.

By growing coffee themselves, villagers both cemented the commodity as a staple of the regional economy and delimited the spaces, the intensiveness, and the institutions of that new economy.

The participation of so many different actors helps us understand the speed with which export agriculture spread across the Latin American countryside in the second half of the nineteenth century. It also helps us understand the consolidation of liberal economic institutions during the same era. Registering both the threat and the possibilities presented by participation in export production, local actors seized the tools available to secure their livelihoods. In many cases, these were the same tools promoted by those seeking to smooth the way for Latin America's deeper integration into the global economy. Border negotiations could be sites for local justice as well as international reputation building. The spread of bureaucracy could provide nonviolent means of arbitration as well as centralize state control. Property titles could be used to protect land as well as to purchase it. Labor contracts could ensure access to credit as well as a workforce. Standardized lending regulations could facilitate loans of a few pesos as well as those of a few hundred thousand. Each of these tools also served to dispossess villagers of their homes, their labor, and their wealth. Yet throughout this book we have seen how local appropriation of liberalism's trappings mediated and constrained their use by outside actors.

While this book has focused on the Soconusco, it is not only about the Soconusco. By 1911, Mexico was supplying world markets with more than seventy different agricultural goods. These ranged from plantation crops like henequen and sugar to cash crops like garbanzo beans, vanilla, and fruit, easily grown alongside subsistence goods.[1] The national value of such export commodities increased from less than four pesos per capita in 1870 to more than forty by 1920.[2] Much of the rest of Latin America saw similar engagement with a newly expanded market basket. Producers small and large sent rubber, bananas, guano, spices, fibers, sugar, grains, beans, beef, and so on to their own urban centers as well as to the United States and Europe. To fulfill the demands of industry and a growing consumer class, villagers, ranchers, plantation owners, and laborers remade the Latin American countryside.

An extensive literature on coffee's spread across Latin America has provided a solid foundation for exploring this multisided transformation. Scholarship on popular political liberalism has overwhelmingly shown how many types of people took up the new ideology and cemented it in their approach to government. Histories of finance and banking make clear that negotiation was a constant when it came to the implementation of new commercial reforms. Beyond Latin America, scholars have also begun to push toward an understanding of this era of global integration that incorporates local as well as international actors.[3]

Yet the plantation remains the totemic institution of the export boom. Foreign investors and regional elites remain its primary protagonists. This book has set out one model for reevaluating the spread of export crops and the consolidation of new economic institutions that accompanied them. By drawing together the multiple facets of the evolving economy, by looking at how local actors overcame, worked around, or muddled through the hurdles that stood in the way of growth, this book has demonstrated that much is lost by focusing solely on plantations. Instead, it has shown how a diverse group of producers used their engagement with export agriculture to negotiate and constrain state centralization and global economic integration.

Here, I have sought to advance a history of the export boom that understands late nineteenth-century globalization through the activities of all those involved in production. I have walked us through the process by which people in the Soconusco negotiated or doubled down on impediments to new types of economic activity. I have shown how their engagement with state projects for modernization and consolidation cemented those projects in local practice, but on a timeline and in a manner that had much more to do with local need than the desires of higher authorities. This stilted, sometimes stumbling manner of building new legal and commercial institutions may have impeded future economic development. Yet as the nineteenth century slipped into the twentieth, it facilitated the continued involvement of a large swath of local society in export production.

This book closes in the midst of the Mexican Revolution. Wherever possible, I have drawn each chapter into the 1910s, tracing the continuities of production and commerce that marked that tumultuous decade. In the same way that places like the Soconusco have long been absent in narratives of the export boom, so too have they been left out of general histories of the Mexican Revolution. Yet, as John Womack reminded us almost forty years ago, the "Mexican economy functioned from 1910 to 1920."[4] In that functioning, we are reminded that revolts like the Mexican Revolution, often presented as the ultimate rebuke to the export boom, were only one set of responses to global commercial integration.

As a Mexico City journalist wrote of the Soconusco in 1911, "There is no need to talk to them of politics: they are too busy." With so much to do, people were "not only not inclined to sedition, but must in fact be its enemy."[5] Elsewhere in the country agrarian displacement, political disenfranchisement, and a sense of unequal access to the benefits promised by Díaz's modernizing state had fermented into a series of strikes, riots, and outright revolt.[6] In the Soconusco, people got on with business. In 1911, the district exported 8,000 metric tons of coffee worth MX$4.5 million in addition to a variety of other tropical goods. By 1920, the harvest had expanded to over 10,000 metric tons.[7]

Economic functionality of this sort was not evenly dispersed either geographically or temporally. Regional economies ebbed and flowed across the revolutionary decade. Labor supply for the country as a whole was diminished by war, disease, and displacement, but in industrial regions, the number of workers in fact increased. Financial systems experienced massive upheavals and new investments in infrastructure were temporarily halted, but business in no way stopped. The global context of World War I provided ongoing demand for many of Mexico's exports, though war both external and internal also interrupted transit routes. Oil, a newly discovered and newly valuable resource, further boosted the country's trade.[8] No region remained immune to the political upheaval of the decade, nor to the social change the new Constitution of 1917 attempted to legislate. Many though, experienced the Revolution as an import or, as Gilbert Joseph titled his book on the Yucatán, Mexico's largest export producing region, a *Revolution from Without*. While high levels of coercion and dependency explain peons' and peasants' failure to join the Revolution in some places, the diverse productivity of the Soconusco provides another possible rationale for sitting out the violence.[9]

It was not that people in the Soconusco did not know of the promises and threats the Revolution represented. German finqueros wrote to their representatives in Mexico City asking for extra protections, terrified of the coming "bands of agitated Indians" they had heard rumor might be marching out of the Sierra Madre. Even their consul was quick to reassure the planters that such activity was unlikely—the massacre of Germans was not a top priority for anyone.[10] So they got on with business. They registered contracts, sold properties, and planted coffee.

Workers traveled down from the highlands or traversed the frontier to harvest beans as they ripened, demanding advances on their wages and access to credit. When the first revolutionary forces arrived in Tapachula in 1914 and tried to eliminate these debts, both planters and workers themselves rebelled. Laborers threatened to leave in the midst of the harvest, and planters declared they would rather pay fines than lose their workforce.[11] A few years later, the Constitutionalists' revolutionary rhetoric did resonate with some seasonal workers who went on to found the Socialist Party of Chiapas (*Partido Socialista Chiapaneco*) in 1920 in Motozintla. While later important in state politics, the party did little to push for change along the coast.[12]

The story of land reform in the Soconusco is also one of indifference and belated partial embrace. The Agrarian Archive in Mexico City has extensive files on the confusing cases that their agents took up starting in

1917. On arrival, agrarian agents confronted the mix of small and large holdings that formed the basis of the coffee economy. This patchwork left many befuddled, as they had anticipated a landscape ripe for redistribution. Instead, repartition, as carried out by municipal councils on their own timelines, had left former ejiditarios still in control of their land.[13] In some places, it was workers who had invaded plantations and carved out parcels for their own purposes, rather than the reverse.[14] Most communities had no interest in the agents' offers to reconstitute old collective holdings. In the 1930s, the local affiliate of the Socialist Party did help seasonal workers claim parcels of unworked land, both private and public, as new ejidos in the Sierra Madre.[15] Again, though, local interests overrode the strictures of national policy. Many of these new ejiditarios had been born Guatemalan and as foreigners had no rights to land reform. Yet, taking advantage of the lack of proper demographic registration, they turned themselves into Mexican citizens and claimed their revolutionary inheritance.[16] As they had with privatization mandates in the 1890s, villagers and workers engaged state programs for land management in a mode that suited their interests.

The Revolution in the Soconusco was rarely marked by outright violence. Constitutionalist troops remained quartered along the frontier, guarding against the reactionary forces of Felix Díaz who had, as so many before, taken refuge across the border in Guatemala.[17] Reactionaries and federal forces both threatened Tapachula on occasion, but no one ever carried through. Some laborers joined up with various factions, again endangering the harvest by abandoning their contracts. Their commanders extorted finqueros for as much as MX$10,000 in return for protection. When a planter refused to pay the demanded sum, sacks of coffee went missing from warehouses and train cars, despite complaints from both German and American officials.[18] For one young German-American girl, the Revolution was only remembered as the American Intervention. The landing of U.S. troops in Veracruz caused her family and other American expatriates to temporarily flee to Guatemala for fear of retribution.[19]

Each of these, though, was a momentary experience, soon overcome. Within a few months the Americans were all back on their fincas, finding a few vases broken, a few toys scattered, but no permanent damage done. It was not that the Revolution did not eventually reach the Soconusco, but rather that the Soconusco never reached out for the Revolution. Nor, truly, did anyone in the region ever take up its banners. Anticipatory fears were much more notable than actual harm taken by planters or triumph achieved by the villagers who elsewhere became the era's heroes. Most in each group simply kept chugging along, much like the rickety but reliable train that continued to carry their coffee to market.

In these stories of minimal engagement with the Revolution, from either above or below, the Soconusco makes clear that not everyone in Mexico saw a need for insurrection. Much research remains to be done on those regions that remained quiescent during the Revolution. Scattered throughout post-revolutionary histories of many of Mexico's agricultural regions, from Veracruz to Michoacán to the cotton regions of the northern border, are unquestioned asides about the difficulties of finding adherents for new revolutionary social reforms.[20] In these reluctant villagers, historians need to continue looking for those who engaged the liberal reforms of the export era on their own terms.

It is not likely that Helen Humphreys would recognize the city of Tapachula, seat of a municipality that is now home to more than 300,000 people. Population growth and the further march of global demand has filled in all the empty spaces and uncultivated lands she once traversed on visits to neighbors. The city itself would overwhelm her with traffic, Guatemalan shoppers in town for the day, and Central American migrants stymied and left destitute on their journeys to the United States. Heading into the Sierra Madre, Helen could no longer ignore the village ejidos that fill in stretches between private fincas. Coffee bushes march down hillsides and encroach on the highways that wind from small town to small town. In 2012, production reached 110,000 metric tons, more than ten times what the Soconusco produced when Helen sailed back to California in 1905.[21]

Depart from the main arteries, though, or peek behind the bushes, and much looks the same. Finqueros' elegant homes still look out over the machine sheds and small cabins where seasonal laborers sleep. During harvest, sitting on the veranda or standing by the finca administrator, Helen could watch migrant laborers trudge past. She would easily recognize the measuring boxes awaiting their large canvas sacks of fresh picked coffee cherries, boxes that still determine their daily pay. The machinery for processing all those beans is now driven by electricity rather than hydraulic power, but many of the depulpers and drying drums on large properties are the same ones installed in the 1910s.

Most of the workers are still Guatemalan. Local labor remains scarce because land remains in the hands of local villagers. Ejidatarios and smallholders grow their own coffee in greater quantities than ever. Across Mexico's southeast, 82 percent of the land planted in coffee is parceled out in lots of less than five hectares.[22] Many villagers employ drying patios and process their coffee by hand. Others are part of cooperatives that formed in the wake of the national coffee board's collapse in the late 1980s and use collectively owned processing plants to clean and dry their beans. Such small-scale production has inspired its own conflicts. During the Zapatista uprising in 1994, many co-op members refused to support the insurgents. As they had during the Mexican Revolution, the Soconusco's producers found little appeal in the promised social reforms.[23]

As always, the vast majority of coffee leaves the Soconusco, primarily in the hands of foreign export companies employing local agents. Dependent as always on the fluctuations of the global coffee market, planters large and small in the Soconusco have found their ways to buffer themselves. Villages have formed cooperatives, planters have entered into corporate partnerships with export firms, everyone experiments with supplementary crops and tourism. Climate change presents its own threats through coffee rust, drought, and floods. As they always have, planters large and small are using diversification as insurance against adversity. Soy, rambutans, papayas, mangos, and numerous other new export goods have joined traditional crops like sugar cane, bananas, timber, and cacao on both ejidos and fincas across the department.[24] Coffee has led to as many failures as it has successes, but the descendants of the locals and migrants who made it their business in the last decades of the nineteenth century continue to believe in the fragrant bean. This place has long tied its fortune to the fecundity of its soil, and those who export from it continue to invest in the prosperity that they hope the landscape can bring.

APPENDIX 1
Coffee Exports from the Soconusco and Mexico, 1867–1920

Year	Total Coffee Exports from the Soconusco (metric tons)	Total Coffee Exports from Mexico (metric tons)	Total Value Coffee Exports from the Soconusco (MX$)	Total Value Coffee Exports from Mexico (MX$)
1867		420		
1868		140		
1869		120		
1870		240		
1871		860		
1872		930	$17,000	$532,649
1873		1330	no data	$705,427
1874		1250	no data	$588,587
1875		2470		
1876		3270		
1877	86	4300	$24,686	$1,242,041
1878		7060	$10,861	$2,230,097
1879		6760	$9,334	$1,984,472
1880	40	8700	$150,306	$2,243,782
1881	47	10448	$144,588	$2,414,538
1882	61	8557	$12,851	$1,717,190
1883	61	6918	$12,820	$1,579,020
1884	350	5824	$80,417	$1,201,673
1885	none listed	8386		$1,699,723
1886	1226	8326	$404,715	$2,627,477
1887	632	6528	$145,759	$2,431,024
1888	487	9243	$183,671	$3,886,033
1889	335	10010	$198,228	$4,811,000
1890	363	14657	$201,328	$6,150,358
1891	372	11058	$184,761	$5,514,355
1892	665	14510	$461,935	$8,727,119
1893	760	20210	$483,629	$11,766,090
1894	767	16510	$526,020	$12,670,783
1895	937	11464	$691,128	$8,103,302
1896	1220	14820	$914,220	$9,876,532
1897	1630	20360	$1,076,941	$10,649,119
1898	1450	17700	$721,376	$7,936,908
1899	2370	28860	$1,099,513	$10,898,678
1900	3140	15380	$805,000	$10,499,737
1901	3330	15573		$6,973,272
1902*	3000	22565	$750,000	$10,552,313
1903	2220	18460		$8,576,239
1904	5780	18265		$8,501,573

1905	5630	19260	$989,987	$9,288,623
1906	5800	14160		$7,237,529
1907	7000	14160	$2,800,000	$6,979,562
1908	10120	21460	$4,840,000	
1909	6720	26690		
1910	7728	18680		
1911	7896	18860		$24,385,012
1912	9128		$4,525,120	$21,078,333
1913	8904	20950		
1914	9912			
1915	7728	22690		
1916	8008	25080		
1917	8232	23570		
1918	7280	13610		$13,685,958
1919	11312	17400		
1920	10360	15950		

*1902 was the year of a volcanic eruption in Guatemala that blanketed the region in ash not long before the harvest. Sources: México, Secretaría de Hacienda y Crédito Público, Noticia de la exportación de mercancías; México, Secretaría de Hacienda y Crédito Público, Exportaciones en el año fiscal; México, Ministerio de Hacienda y Crédito Público, Boletín de estadística fiscal; México, Secretaría de Hacienda y Crédito Público, Comercio exterior; México, Secretaría de Fomento, Colonización e Industria, Anuario estadístico de la República Mexicana; México, Importación y exportación de la República Mexicana; Ludewig, Veinte años, appendix; Bynum, The World's Exports of Coffee; Waibel, La Sierra Madre de Chiapas, 199; Colegio de México, Estadísticas económicas del Porfiriato.

APPENDIX 2
Population of the Soconusco and Its Municipalities, 1778–1930

	1778	1838	1880	1892	1900	1910	1921	1930
Total Soconusco	6,894	11,465	17,828	20,928	36,477	54,691	72,545	97,481
Acacoyagua	145	164	317	374	512	757	1,415	1,654
Cacahoatán	46	26	924	1,996	2,666	4,475	5,082	7,313
Escuintla	1,171	1,172	1,733	1,267	2,741	5,184	4,854	7,868
Frontera Hidalgo (formerly Frontera Díaz)					1,818	1,996	1,232	
Huehuetán	833	449	949	1,369	2,057	2,835	4,378	5,023
Huixtla	56	254	594	760	880	1,613	4,342	8,511
Mazatán	308	568	923	895	1,460	1,753	2,237	2,253
Metapa	106	262	241	589	676	702	751	646
Suchiate	142	151	408				552	1,970
Tapachula	1,556	3,605	5,285	7,091	15,154	21,672	26,469	36,742
Tuxtla Chico	1,892	3,369	4,721	4,356	6,323	6,891	9,971	11,154
Tuzantán	273	775	402	481	992	2,617	3,131	4,111
Unión Juárez		902	1,200	2,176	2,560	4,255	4,865	

Table only includes municipalities mentioned in this book and those that grew coffee but are not specifically discussed herein. The difference between the total for the district and the sum of each column is made up for by unincorporated areas and other municipalities in the coastal plains. Source: Juan Pedro Viqueira Albán, "Indios y ladinos, arraigados y migrantes en Chiapas. Un esbozo de historia demográfica de larga duración," online appendix.

Notes

INTRODUCTION

1. "Soconusco" in *Annual Series of Trade Reports*.
2. This and the following all from Humphreys Seargeant, *San Antonio Nexapa*, 1–19, 243.
3. "Colonization in Mexico," *San Francisco Chronicle*, April 4, 1882.
4. For an early example of the sale of a small subsistence plot planted with coffee, see Arrevillaga and Mallen, Feb. 12, 1880, APJS 1° Civil Soconusco, 1873–1879; for even earlier evidence of coffee growing by villagers, see Gasco, "Soconusco Cacao Farmers Past and Present," 331.
5. Almost all coffee grown in the Soconusco was of the *Coffea arabica* species. Until 1900 or so, most was of the Typica variety, at which point some planters in higher elevations also began to grow Bourbon varietals. Coffee can grow to as tall as nine meters, but most plants in the Soconusco were pruned to heights between two and three meters to ease the harvest. Horticulturally, coffee of this size is a shrub, rather than a tree, though the term bush can also be applied. For more on growing coffee in the Soconusco, see Romero, *Cultivo del café en la costa meridional de Chiapas*; Kaerger, *Agricultura y colonización en México en 1900*.
6. Kuntz Ficker, *Las exportaciones mexicanas durante la primera globalización 1870–1929*, 132.
7. In 1899, coffee finqueros estimated that 3,055 hectares of the 14,680 hectares that they owned were producing coffee. Karl Kaerger, a German agronomist who traveled through the Soconusco in that same year, found great variation in the productivity of fincas depending on altitude, age, and management. Using his estimate of average productivity, production for 3,055 hectares would be about 1,285 metric tons. Exports from the Soconusco that year totaled 2,370 metric tons. This means that someone else—namely smallholders—were producing at least 1,085 metric tons of coffee that year. It is also likely that not all of the 3,055 hectares registered as under cultivation with coffee were yet productive; much land had been purchased in the previous few years, and coffee takes at least four years to come into harvest. "Exposición de París de 1900: Chiapas—Estadística Agrícola," AGN, Fomento: Exposiciones Exteriores, caja 52, exp. 4; Kaerger, *Agricultura y colonización en México en 1900*, 97–98, 109; Mexico. Secretaría de Hacienda, *Comercio exterior*.
8. There have been a number of studies of the Soconusco and its foreign landowners, the majority of which are based in newspaper, published, and state and national sources. Absent the local sources that form the base of this book, these works for the most part hew to the traditional narrative of exploitative, expropriative export development in the hands of a small group of foreign elites. Baumann,

"Terratenientes, campesinos y la expansion de la agricultura capitalista en Chiapas, 1896–1916"; Spenser, "Soconusco: The Formation of a Coffee Economy in Chiapas"; Benjamin, *A Rich Land, a Poor People*; Renard, *El Soconusco*; Villafuerte Solís and Betancourt Aduen, *El café en la frontera sur*; Gudiño, "Finqueros extranjeros en el Soconusco, legislación y colonización, 1875–1910"; Nolan-Ferrell, "El desarrollo de una región sin una identidad nacional; Nolan-Ferrell, *Constructing Citizenship*, Ch. 1.

9. For examples of this traditional narrative, see Ch. IV, "Emergence of a Neocolonial Order," and Ch. V, "Maturity of a Neocolonial Order," in Halperín Donghi, *The Contemporary History of Latin America*; also Topik and Wells, *The Second Conquest of Latin America*.

10. In Mexico, see Brading, "Liberal Patriotism and the Mexican Reforma"; Hamnett, "Liberalism Divided"; Green, Thomson, and Lafrance, "Patriotism, Politics, and Popular Liberalism in Nineteenth-Century Mexico"; Chassen de Lo?pez, *From Liberal to Revolutionary Oaxaca*; Guardino, *The Time of Liberty*; Caplan, *Indigenous Citizens*; Schaefer, *Liberalism as Utopia;* Francois, *A Culture of Everyday Credit*. Elsewhere, see Thurner, "'Republicanos' and 'La Comunidad de Peruanos'"; Méndez G., *The Plebeian Republic*; Sanders, *Contentious Republicans*; Larson, *Trials of Nation Making*; Adelman, "Liberalism and Constitutionalism in Latin America in the 19th Century"; Premo, *The Enlightenment on Trial*.

11. For a definition of *institutions*, I rely on Douglass North, as do many new economic historians. Institutions, in this conception, are humanly devised constraints that include both formal (laws, regulations, property regimes, constitutions) and informal (taboos, social norms, customs) limitations on political, economic, and social interactions and relationships. North, "Institutions." One of the few to look at economic institutions as avenues for engagement with liberalism is Carmagnani, "Vectors of Liberal Economic Culture in Mexico."

12. For an overview of these reforms in Mexico, see Bortz and Haber, *The Mexican Economy, 1870–1930*. For the rest of Latin America, see Glade, "Economy, 1870–1914"; Palacios, *Coffee in Colombia, 1850–1970*, Ch. 1; Hale, "Political and Social Ideas in Latin America, 1870–1930"; Gootenberg, *Imagining Development*.

13. There is a growing environmental history of this push that looks to how both the landscapes and modes of such production relied on and reshaped such spaces. For example see Adelman, *Frontier Development*; Santiago, *The Ecology of Oil*; Grandin, *Fordlandia*; Cushman, *Guano and the Opening of the Pacific World*; Cribelli, *Industrial Forests and Mechanical Marvels*.

14. The new history of capitalism, particularly American capitalism, has demonstrated how, as Walter Johnson wrote, it makes more sense "to think about the political economy of the eighteenth- and nineteenth-century Atlantic as a single space, its dimensions defined by flows of people, money, and goods, its nested temporalities set by interlocking (though clearly distinct) labor regimes, cyclical rhythms of cultivation and foreign exchange, and shared standards of calculability and measurement." Johnson, "The Pedestal and the Veil," 304; Tutino, *Making a New World*; see also Sklansky, "The Elusive Sovereign"; Beckert, *Empire of Cotton*; Topik and Wells, *Global Markets Transformed*.

15. For example, by 1911 Mexico was exporting more than seventy different agricultural goods, not including meat, oil, minerals, or manufactures. Mexico. Ministerio de Hacienda y Crédito Público, *Boletin de estadística fiscal. Jul. 1910–Jun. 1911 (no. 366)*, 86–89.

16. During this time, exports of commodities other than precious metals increased both as a part of Mexico's GDP and in terms of its per capita wealth. Prior to 1870, these export commodities were valued at less than $2 per capita; by 1920 their value was almost $20 a person. Similarly, while they had represented an insignificant percentage of the GDP prior to the 1860s, export commodities accounted for 11 percent of national wealth by 1920. While this is a significant growth, it bears reminding that, compared to Cuba and Argentina, where per capita exports exceeded $60 per person, Mexico's prosperity was less dramatic. Compared to the North Atlantic, growth was even less impressive. Mexico began the nineteenth century with a national per capita income of about half that of the United States, and its total income was similarly calculated. By 1877, these measures had fallen to just over one-tenth and one-fiftieth respectively. The current scholarly consensus is that this "falling behind" can be blamed on the failure to create reliable institutions around finance, infrastructure, and legal norms. Coatsworth, "Obstacles to Economic Growth in Nineteenth-Century Mexico," 82–83; Topik and Wells, *Global Markets Transformed*, 40–41; Cardoso, *Historia económica de América Latina*; Cardoso and Faletto, *Dependency and Development in Latin America*; Cosío Villegas, *La vida económica*; Rosenzweig, *El desarrollo económico de México, 1800–1910*; Coatsworth, *Los orígenes del atraso*; Haber, "Assessing the Obstacles to Industrialisation"; Haber, *How Latin America Fell Behind*; Knight, "Review of How Latin America Fell Behind"; Gootenberg, *Imagining Development*; Kuntz Ficker, *El comercio exterior de México en la era del capitalismo liberal, 1870–1929*.

17. This is a particularly contentious issue in Mexico. The absence of a complete cadastral survey for the country makes this issue difficult to study. Preliminary results from a study of landholding surveys completed in advance of the 1899 Paris Exposition suggest that the median size of properties reported was 120 hectares, with only 40 hectares under cultivation, much lower than the usual narratives of giant haciendas ascribed to the era despite the surveys' bias toward large properties. For an overview of the current state of the historiography, see Escobar Ohmstede and Butler, "Introduction;" "Exposición de París de 1900, Estadística agrícola," AGN, Fomento: Exposiciones Exteriores, cajas 51–53.

18. Liberalism in Latin America did not loyally hew to the European schools of thought out of which it grew. Numerous scholars have explored the varied trajectories of the history of liberalism in Latin America and the ways in which national and local politicians and thinkers remade, recombined, and abandoned tenets of European liberalism to suit their own contexts. See, for example, Love and Jacobsen, *Guiding the Invisible Hand*; Hale, *The Transformation of Liberalism in Late Nineteenth-Century Mexico*; Gootenberg, *Imagining Development*; Sábato, "On Political Citizenship in Nineteenth-Century Latin America"; Gudmundson, *Central America, 1821–1871*; Jaksic and Posada Carbó, *Liberalismo y poder*; Suarez-Potts, *The Making of Law*, Introduction; Posada-Carbó and Jaksic, "Shipwrecks and

Survivals"; Adelman, "Liberalism and Constitutionalism in Latin America in the 19th Century"; Schaefer, *Liberalism as Utopia*.

19. Kuntz Ficker, *El comercio exterior de México en la era del capitalismo liberal, 1870–1929*, 76; Topik and Wells, *The Second Conquest of Latin America*, 10.

20. The literature on elites in the export boom is large, but for some clear examples, see: Wells, *Yucatán's Gilded Age*, 1985; Joseph, *Revolution from Without*; Gootenberg, *Between Silver and Guano*; Bieber, *Power, Patronage, and Political Violence*; Striffler and Moberg, *Banana Wars*; Bucheli, *Bananas and Business*; for the more generalized problems that export involvement could wreak on a national economy, especially one heavily committed to one particular export, see the introduction to Topik and Wells, *The Second Conquest of Latin America*; or Gunder Frank, *Capitalism and Underdevelopment in Latin America*.

21. Wells, *Yucatán's Gilded Age*, 1985; Pineda, *Industrial Development in a Frontier Economy*; Hanley, *Native Capital*; Font, *Coffee and Transformation in São Paulo, Brazil*; Tenorio-Trillo, *I Speak of the City*; see also Overmyer-Velázquez, *Visions of the Emerald City*; Beatty, *Technology and the Search for Progress in Modern Mexico*.

22. This is the median size of properties I have recorded as coffee fincas. The median size of fincas valued at over MX$500 at the time of sale was 128 hectares. The median size of properties already cultivating coffee at their time of sale was only 104 hectares. All of these numbers are relatively small compared to the average size of coffee plantations in Latin America. It is also small compared to Mexican plantations in general, though we still lack a clear understanding of Mexico's rural landscape during the late nineteenth century. The differentiation between property categories as taxed by the Mexican government—*hacienda* and *rancho* being the key terms—seemed to have been defined locally. In the north, haciendas could extend over tens or hundreds of thousands of hectares, and nationwide the average hacienda comprised 5,600 hectares. In Chiapas, haciendas averaged 360 hectares. Benjamin, *A Rich Land, a Poor People*, 48–49.

23. Ortiz Hernández, "Formación histórico-política de la región del Soconusco."

24. In 1910, the Soconusco had 854 residents born elsewhere in Mexico. As a percentage of total population this was comparable to or even less than other districts in Chiapas with growing export sectors. Mexico, *Tercer censo de población*.

25. Holloway, *Immigrants on the Land*; Buchenau, "Small Numbers, Great Impact"; Moya, "A Continent of Immigrants."

26. Misawa Saito, "La colonia Enomoto de Chiapas."

27. This does not include 11,000 Guatemalan migrants, the majority of whom were laborers. Mexico, *Tercer censo de población*.

28. See the origins of the rubber boom in Brazil or the vanilla boom in Veracruz for examples. Weinstein, *The Amazon Rubber Boom, 1850–1920*; Kourí, *A Pueblo Divided*.

29. Examples of this localized political and economic life are myriad, but for one particular iteration of the discussions that surround it, see the varied ways in which local Andean communities interacted with the fights for independence from

Spain. Thurner, "'Republicanos' and 'La Comunidad de Peruanos'"; Mallon, *Peasant and Nation*; Méndez G., *The Plebeian Republic*.

30. Communities engaged in production were in no way the closed corporate entities once codified by anthropologists. Instead, my exploration of the export boom provides insights into how villagers, indigenous or otherwise, connected to and shaped broader worlds. Wolf, "Closed Corporate Peasant Communities in Mesoamerica and Central Java"; Wolf, "The Vicissitudes of the Closed Corporate Peasant Community"; Patch, "Imperial Politics and Local Economy in Colonial Central America."

31. In Mexico, the cases of sugar in Morelos and henequen in Yucatán are emblematic. The transformation of the Guatemalan countryside is another case often brought up, as well as the clearing of the Argentinian pampas. Womack, *Zapata and the Mexican Revolution*; Wells, "From Hacienda to Plantation"; Hart, *Bitter Harvest*; Zuleta Miranda, "Hacienda pública y exportación henequenera en Yucatán, 1880–1910"; Cambranes, *Coffee and Peasants*; McCreery, *Rural Guatemala, 1760–1940*; Adelman, *Frontier Development*; Bechis, "La 'organización nacional' y las tribus pampeanas en Argentina durante el siglo XIX."

32. Lauria-Santiago, *An Agrarian Republic*; Charlip, "So That Land Takes on Value"; Kourí, *A Pueblo Divided*; Soluri, "Bananas Before Plantations"; Smith, "Rewriting the Moral Economy."

33. Viqueira Albán, "Indios y ladinos, arraigados y migrantes en Chiapas."

34. The district had grown by almost 50 percent since 1900. A few districts in Mexico City had grown by more than 100 percent, but Mexico as a whole had only grown by about 11 percent and very few districts exceeded 20 percent growth. See Appendix 2 for population data. Mexico, *Tercer censo de población*, "Población, área, y densidad por distritos, partidos o cantones, de las entidades federativas."

35. It is generally understood that the 1910 census was not carried out with a great deal of precision, particularly in rural regions. When it comes to estimating the number of individuals involved in coffee production, its occupational categories are not very helpful. The census lists 20,000 or so children without occupation, almost 16,000 male peons or day laborers, and 15,500 housewives. All were likely involved in coffee in some regard, despite the descriptors, as finqueros valued children and women's small fingers for coffee harvesting and sorting. The number of laborers seems quite high, even if it was taken at the height of the harvest. Kaerger stated that most fincas had 40 or 50 families in residence, supplemented at harvest time by another 200 or so seasonal laborers. The agronomist tended to overestimate based on the fact that he spent most of his time on large German fincas. Records for average-sized fincas that went into receivership indicate closer to 20 families in residence year round, with an additional 15 to 20 families during the harvest. Based on an estimate of about 100 fincas active by 1900, Kaerger's numbers would give us 4,500 families permanently living on fincas, plus an additional 10,000 families traveling to the region for the harvest, or about 15,000 families total, the same as estimated by the 1910 census. Estimates based on local documents would lead to a permanent laboring population of closer to 2,000 families, plus an additional 2,000 families or so at harvest time, or 4,000 families total. This

is more in line with the 9,500 individuals living on coffee fincas in the 1900 census. Mexico, *Censo general de la República Mexicana verificado el 28 de octubre de 1900*; Mexico, *Tercer censo de población*; Viqueira Albán, "Indios y ladinos, arraigados y migrantes en Chiapas"; Kaerger, *Agricultura y colonización en México en 1900*, 104; "Cuentas de administración de las fincas secuestradas a Don Rafael Ortega correspondientes al mes de Enero," Jan. 31 1901, APJS 1° Civil Soconusco 1901, 251–300.

36. The 1910 census includes only 759 men in the category of *agricultor*, or farmer, a number I consider to be low if it is supposed to account for the total number of landowners in the region, high if it is only counting finca owners. My estimate of 2,000, likely a conservative estimate, is drawn from the total number of land sales worth less than MX$500 (1,231) as well as the incomplete registration of those who bought land from their town councils during the privatization of ejidos (555). Given that most of these landholdings were between half a hectare and five hectares and planted with subsistence crops as well as coffee, this estimate brings us much closer to the amount of land that would need to be under cultivation to achieve the district's export numbers. See Chapter Four for more details on the land transactions and, for the ejido numbers, see "Concentración de los documentos de todos los Ejidos," AHCH, Fondo de Gobierno, Fomento, 1908, vol. 2, exp. 12.

37. Womack, "Mexican Political Historiography."

38. As Centeno and López-Alves put it, "Why not treat Latin America as simply an alternative development, with its own probabilities and variances?. . . . Our job is not to find what is 'wrong' with a patient but to understand how the body works." Centeno and López-Alves, "Introduction," 10.

39. Beatty, *Institutions and Investment*; Maurer, *The Power and the Money*; Suarez-Potts, *The Making of Law*; Gómez Galvarriato, *Industry and Revolution*; Beatty, *Technology and the Search for Progress in Modern Mexico*.

40. Haber, *How Latin America Fell Behind*; Knight, "Review"; Hanley, *Native Capital*; Pineda, *Industrial Development in a Frontier Economy*; Cushman, *Guano and the Opening of the Pacific World*; Cribelli, *Industrial Forests and Mechanical Marvels*.

41. The literature on coffee is quite rich and varied; most of these studies, though, focus on one type of cultivation in one particular region, though they might allude to the variety of production that made up a national economy. Stein, *Vassouras*; Bergquist, *Coffee and Conflict in Colombia, 1886–1910*; Palacios, *Coffee in Colombia, 1850–1970*; Cambranes, *Coffee and Peasants*; Gudmundson, "Peasant, Farmer, Proletarian"; Samper K., "Los paisajes sociales del café"; Roseberry, Gudmundson, and Samper K., *Coffee, Society, and Power in Latin America*; Yarrington, *A Coffee Frontier*; Lauria-Santiago, *An Agrarian Republic*; Topik, "Coffee Anyone?"; Clarence-Smith, Gervase, and Topik, *The Global Coffee Economy in Africa, Asia and Latin America, 1500–1989*; Charlip, *Cultivating Coffee*; Córdova Santamaría, *Café y sociedad en Huatusco, Veracruz*; Gallini, *Una historia ambiental del café en Guatemala*; Fowler-Salamini, *Working Women, Entrepreneurs, and the Mexican Revolution*; Akaki, "Los siglos XIX y XX en la cafeticultura nacional."

42. Holden, *Mexico and the Survey of Public Lands*; Schryer, "Peasants and the Law"; Escobar Ohmstede and Rojas Rabiela, *Estructuras y formas agrarias en México*; Purnell, "With All Due Respect"; Chassen de López, *From Liberal to Revolutionary Oaxaca*; Kourí, *A Pueblo Divided*; Fenner, "Los deslindes de terrenos baldíos"; Escobar Ohmstede and Butler, "Introduction"; Smith, "Rewriting the Moral Economy."

43. The plantation complex as defined by Philip Curtin was centered on the production of tropical goods through slave labor. While the abolition of the slave trade across the nineteenth century undermined the plantation's preeminence, Curtin also points to the structure's transformation and continuance through other forms of labor both in the Caribbean and in new European colonial holdings in South and Southeast Asia and Africa. Latin America, too, had its share of plantations from the colonial era onward, generally termed *haciendas* or *fazendas*, and the southern United States, of course, relied on this organization of production for centuries. The predominance of the plantation has been at the heart of much recent literature on the consolidation of global capitalism, though discussions of the interdependencies between capitalism and unfree labor have much deeper roots. Williams, *Capitalism and Slavery*; Wolf and Mintz, "Haciendas and Plantation in Middle America and the Antilles"; Solow and Engerman, *British Capitalism and Caribbean Slavery*; Curtin, *The Rise and Fall of the Plantation Complex*; Topik and Wells, *Global Markets Transformed*; Follett, *Plantation Kingdom*.

44. Mexico, Secretaría de Hacienda y Crédito Público, *Noticia de la exportación de mercancías*.

45. Mexico, Secretaría de Hacienda y Crédito Público; Secretaría de Hacienda, *Exportaciones en el año fiscal de 1890 a 1891*.

46. Tutino, *From Insurrection to Revolution in Mexico*.

47. Womack Jr., "The Mexican Economy during the Revolution 1910–1920."

CHAPTER ONE: AN UNCULTIVATED EDEN

1. Romero quit his position as minister in June of 1872, visited the Soconusco in September and October of that year, and moved to Tapachula in February of 1873. Romero, *Refutación de las inculpaciones hechas al c. Matías Romero por el gobierno de Guatemala*, 12–13.

2. Romero was focused on the Soconusco but always looking for other possibilities. He spent far more time on the road than he had to—more than two months on the initial journey to Tapachula—so that he might scope out additional sites for investment. On all his future journeys he traveled by steamship down the Pacific coast, making use of the shipping line he helped secure for the Soconusco. For Romero's complete itinerary see "Itinerario del viaje de 1872," Nov. 15, 1872. AHMR, Correspondencia enviada, vol. 19, pp. 166–70. For future journeys, see correspondence with his wife, Matías Romero to Lucretia Allen de Romero, Oct. 8, 1872. AHMR, Correspondencia enviada, vol. 19, pp. 94–95.

3. Romero to Allen de Romero, Sept. 13, 1872. AHMR, Correspondencia enviada, vol. 19, p. 63; Antonio Arreola to Matías Romero, May 7, 1873. AHMR, Correspondencia recibida, f. 18696; José Pantaleón Domínguez to Matías Romero, May 13, 1873. AHMR, Correspondencia recibida, f. 18697.

4. Cosío Villegas's two pieces on Romero's time in the Soconusco both use the word adventure in their titles and, while crediting the minister with some semblance of a plan, posit him as a somewhat hapless participant in diplomatic intrigues far beyond his abilities. Cosío Villegas, *La vida política exterior*, 3; Cosío Villegas, "La aventura de Matías."

5. This chapter draws its structure from Romero's correspondence as well as two classics on Mexico's economic stagnation in the late nineteenth century. The complaints and pleas penned by those hoping to make the Soconusco prosper resonate quite closely with the works of Coatsworth and Haber. Coatsworth, "Obstacles to Economic Growth in Nineteenth-Century Mexico"; Haber, *How Latin America Fell Behind*.

6. Liberalism in Mexico combined aspects of French-inflected positivism with more doctrinaire British liberalism, creating space for state intervention in the economy and society in general. For more on the particularities of Latin American liberalism in general and Mexican liberalism in particular, see Hale, *The Transformation of Liberalism*; Rodríguez O., *The Divine Charter*; Posada-Carbó and Jaksic, "Shipwrecks and Survivals."

7. Gomez et al., "Early Formative Pottery Production, Mobility, and Exchange on the Pacific Coast of Southern Mexico," 336; Blake and Neff, "Evidence for the Diversity of Late Archaic and Early Formative Plant Use in the Soconusco Region of Mexico and Guatemala," 47; Michaels and Voorhies, "Late Archaic Period Coastal Collectors in Southern Mesoamerica"; Voorhies, *Postclassic Soconusco Society*; Lesure, "Early Social Transformations in the Soconusco," 14.

8. Archaeologists have provided a number of comprehensive descriptions of the Soconusco's environment. See, for example, Coe and Flannery, *Early Cultures and Human Ecology in South Coastal Guatemala*, 9–15; Lowe, *Izapa*, 55–62.

9. For more see Helbig, *El Soconusco y su zona cafetalera en Chiapas*, 43–44.

10. For more on the curious story of Mormonism and the rich archaeological scholarship on the Soconusco, see Wade, "How a Mormon Lawyer Transformed Archaeology in Mexico—and Ended up Losing His Faith."

11. Wild cacao is native to the Amazon but was present across much of Mesoamerica by this point. Powis et al., "Cacao Use and the San Lorenzo Olmec"; Gasco, "Soconusco Cacao Farmers Past and Present," 325.

12. While others use the word groves, Gasco's work has made clear that the monocrop agriculture implied in that term is misleading. Rather, cacao was grown in what she calls "forest plots" or "forest gardens," that is, interspersed among existing trees, with perhaps only a few trees cut down to make a little extra room for the cacao. Gasco, "Soconusco Cacao Farmers Past and Present," 326; Gasco, "Cacao and Commerce in the Late Postclassic Xoconochco."

13. Borrás, "Soconusco"; Voorhies, "Whither the King's Traders"; Voorhies and Gasco, "The Ultimate Tribute," 75–78; Orellana, *Ethnohistory of the Pacific Coast*, 43–45; Chinchilla Aguilar and Gasco, "La Provincia de Soconusco desde la Conquista hasta 1700," 673; Gasco, "Consolidation of the Colonial Regime," 56.

14. MacLeod, *Spanish Central America*, 71; Viqueira Albán, "Indios y ladinos, arraigados y migrantes en Chiapas."

15. MacLeod, *Spanish Central America*, 77–79, 146–49; Solórzano,

"Haciendas, ladinos y explotación colonial," 111; Gasco, "Indian Survival and Ladinoization in Colonial Soconusco," 309–10; Gasco, "Linguistic Patterns, Material Culture, and Identity in Late Postclassic to Postcolonial Soconusco."

16. Patch, "Imperial Politics and Local Economy in Colonial Central America," 84–87, 98.

17. For classic examples, see Gibson, *The Aztecs under Spanish Rule*; Spalding, *Huarochirí, an Andean Society under Inca and Spanish Rule*; Lockhart, *The Nahuas after the Conquest*.

18. Ladino would later come to mean "non-indigenous" in much of Central America, but was initially used to describe those indigenous individuals who took up some aspects of Spanish culture, particularly the language. Gasco, "Indian Survival and Ladinoization in Colonial Soconusco," 310–14.

19. MacLeod, *Spanish Central America*, 147–48; Gasco, "Consolidation of the Colonial Regime: Native Society in Western Central America," 58.

20. Cahill, Tovías, and Gasco, "Beyond the Indian/Ladino Dichotomy: Shifting Identities in Colonial and Contemporary Chiapas, Mexico," 123–24; Gasco, "Consolidation of the Colonial Regime: Native Society in Western Central America," 58–59; MacLeod, *Spanish Central America*, 77–79, 146–49.

21. Multi-cropping is still a common strategy to protect against economic or natural disaster, and Gasco surmises that coffee likely arrived in the Soconusco in much the same way that cacao had centuries before: a traveler or migrant brought a few plants from somewhere already growing the bean, and through neighborly gossip and seed sharing, the new crop spread slowly across the landscape. Gasco, "Soconusco Cacao Farmers Past and Present," 328–30; Gasco, "Cacao and Economic Inequality in Colonial Soconusco, Chiapas, Mexico," 393–94.

22. Romero, *Bosquejo histórico*, I, 1821–1831: Parte III; Larráinzar, *Chiapas y Soconusco*, 25–27; Buchenau, *In the Shadow of the Giant*, 4; Castillo, Toussaint Ribot, and Vázquez Olivera, *Espacios diversos, historia en común*, 28–33; Vázquez Olivera, *El Imperio Mexicano y el Reino de Guatemala*.

23. Ortiz Hernández, "Formación histórico-política de la región del Soconusco."

24. Romero, *Bosquejo histórico*, I, 1821–1831: Parte III; Larráinzar, *Chiapas y Soconusco*, 25–27; Buchenau, *In the Shadow of the Giant*, 4; Castillo, Toussaint Ribot, and Vázquez Olivera, *Espacios diversos, historia en común*, 28–33; Vázquez Olivera, *El Imperio Mexicano y el Reino de Guatemala*.

25. For more on the importance of vecindad in nineteenth century Central America, see Valerio-Jiménez, "Neglected Citizens and Willing Traders"; Herzog, *Defining Nations*; Dym, "Citizen of Which Republic?"

26. Ortiz Hernández, "Formación histórico-política de la región del Soconusco," 35.

27. This is a large and growing literature. For some key examples, see Thomson, "Popular Aspects of Liberalism in Mexico, 1848–1888"; Mallon, *Peasant and Nation*; Green, Thomson, and Lafrance, "Patriotism, Politics, and Popular Liberalism in Nineteenth-Century Mexico"; Guardino, *The Time of Liberty*; Caplan, *Indigenous Citizens*.

28. This is a subject deserving of further study; the municipal archive is rich

with electoral records that have not yet been studied. The representativeness of these elections and the alliances they manifested is not the subject of this study, but could provide a fruitful avenue for examining state-building at the periphery during a particularly turbulent era of Mexican politics. AMT, caja 1, Presidencia Municipal 1837–1853.

29. Oficios de los autoridades del Departamento, 1852–1853. AMT, caja 1, Presidencia Municipal 1837–1853, exp. s/n.

30. Noticias de sirvientes prófugos, 1854. AMT, Presidencia Municipal, caja 1, 1837–1853, exp. 20; AMT, Oficios de los autoridades del Departamento, 1852–1853. AMT, Presidencia Municipal, caja 1, 1837–1853, exp. s/n; Padrón de Cosechero de maiz, frijol, arroz, 1854. AMT, Presidencia Municipal, caja 2, 1846–1940, exp. 27.

31. Diario de las reses y cerdos picados en el presente año, 1855. AMT, Presidencia Municipal, caja 1, 1837–1853, exp. 6; Comunicaciones, 1851. AMT, Presidencia Municipal, Caja 1, 1837–1853, exp. s/n; Petición para prohibir que pasten el ganado bovino, caballar, y mular en terrenos del ejido, 1851. AMT, Presidencia Municipal, caja 1, 1837–1853, exp. 23; Legajo de comunicaciones del Juzgado de 1a Instancia, 1847. AMT, Presidencia Municipal, caja 1, 1837–1853, exp. 2; Comunicaciones de las autoridades departamentales, 1847. AMT, Presidencia Municipal, caja 1, 1837–1853, exp. 1; Comunicaciones de la prefectura, 1849. AMT, Presidencia Municipal, caja 2, 1846–1940, exp. s/n.

32. Sánchez-Albornoz, "Population."

33. AGA, Asunto: Dotación, Estado: Chiapas, Municipio: Cacahoatán, exp. 408, legajo 7.

34. Ortiz Hernández, "Formación histórico-política de la región del Soconusco," 38–42.

35. The ruling families of the Soconusco owned some 72,000 hectares by 1880, most of it in the coastal plains, but this represented at most a tenth of the region's total territory of about 5,475 square kilometers. Escobar, *Informe de los recursos agrícolas*, 12–13; Ortiz Hernández, "Formación histórico-política de la región del Soconusco," 22–31.

36. During the War of the Reform, Escobar came to national attention as he helped to quash the raids that his conservative, separatist half-brothers José María and Manuel de Jesús Chacón led from across the border. His alliance with ousted President Benito Juárez and the liberals was short-lived and, as was always the case with Escobar, contingent on his own interests. When the Conservatives consolidated power with French aid, installing Maximilian of Austria as the head of a new government, Escobar joined their cause. Not long after, he hedged his bets by refusing to pick sides and claiming a new neutrality for his home district. Ortiz Hernández, "Formación histórico-política de la región del Soconusco," 45–48.

37. This political expediency and use of alliances to undergird local autonomy is out of step with much writing about popular liberalism in mid-nineteenth century Mexico. It will be further explored in Chapter Three, as will the idea of the cacique. Thomson, "Popular Aspects of Liberalism in Mexico, 1848–1888"; Brading, "Liberal Patriotism and the Mexican Reforma"; Hamnett, "Liberalism Divided."

38. *Jefe político* literally translates as "political chief" or "boss." The rank's

exact position in the political hierarchy of Mexico shifted across the nineteenth century and depended on location as much as historical moment, as will be further discussed in Chapter Three. At this point in time and in Chiapas, the position signified supervision of a district within the state. I will use the term jefe político throughout the book, as political boss or chief carries more unofficial rather than hierarchical connotations in English. For an overview, see Schaefer, *Liberalism as Utopia*, 165–66.

39. Romero's first publication, written before his departure for Washington, was an examination of the current state of Mexico's international economic relations with gestures toward a future in which his country could stand strong in the face of foreign threats, both military and economic. In her examination of his three terms as Minister of Hacienda, Graciela Márquez Colín emphasizes the importance of Romero's time in the United States in the formation of his economic outlook and understanding of planning and policy. For more on Romero's life, see: Bernstein, *Matías Romero, 1837–1898*; MacGregor, "Introducción," 13–26; Márquez Colín, "La administración hacendaria de Matías Romero."

40. Juliette Levy writes that the 1870 Civil Code was in fact a "hastily republicanized version" of the codes and laws instituted by Maximilian. Levy, *The Making of a Market*, 38.

41. Lurtz, "Developing the Mexican Countryside."

42. For an overview of this transformation, see Topik and Wells, *Global Markets Transformed*.

43. Mexico, Secretaría de Hacienda, *Las medidas propuestas*, 3.

44. I was not able to find a specific letter in which someone suggested Romero turn his eye toward the Soconusco, but he began searching about for investment projects as soon as he returned to Mexico City. He had taken up a correspondence about coffee in Chiapas by early 1868. See Matías Romero to Teofilo Orantes, Sept. 1868. AHMR, Correspondencia enviada, vol. 4, p. 381.

45. Romero explicitly wrote that he left the Soconusco because Guatemalan opposition to his presence in the district meant that he could not secure workers or land where he desired. He also wrote that by 1875 he felt that he could better serve the district's interests by taking up the role of congressional representative to which he had been elected in 1873. Romero, *Refutación de las inculpaciones hechas al c. Matías Romero por el gobierno de Guatemala*, 76–77.

46. Matías Romero to Sebastián Escobar, Oct. 17, 1870. AHMR, Correspondencia enviada, vol. 12, p. 513.

47. Sebastián Escobar to Matías Romero, Jan. 9, 1871. AHMR, Correspondencia recibida, f. 12853.

48. For a general overview of the various everyday experiences of violence in nineteenth century Mexico, see the essays in Katz, *Riot, Rebellion, and Revolution*. On banditry in particular, see Vanderwood, *Disorder and Progress*; Frazer, *Bandit Nation*.

49. For other examples in both Mexico and the Americas more broadly, see Slotkin, *Regeneration through Violence*; Bieber, *Power, Patronage, and Political Violence*; Holden, *Armies without Nations*; Fowler, *Forceful Negotiations*; Falcón, *El jefe político*.

50. Bieber, *Power, Patronage, and Political Violence*; Pérez Meléndez, "The Business of Peopling"; Hanley and Lopes, "Municipal Plenty, Municipal Poverty, and Brazilian Economic Development, 1836–1850."

51. Chowning, "Nineteenth-Century Mexican Agriculture."

52. The examples of Tlaxcala-Puebla conflicts and Tabasco's ongoing struggles over its frontier are telling. Sumner, "National Autocracy, Regional Governance," 96–99; Rugeley, *The River People in Flood Time*. For a comprehensive history of state boundaries, see O'Gorman, *Historia de las divisiones territoriales de México*.

53. Concerns about tax evasion and contraband were raised on both sides of the border. Patricio León to Matías Romero, Sept. 4, 1868. AHMR, Correspondencia recibida, f. 2749; Romero, *Refutación de las inculpaciones hechas al c. Matías Romero por el gobierno de Guatemala*, 230; Comisión Guatemalteca de Límites con México, *Memoria sobre la cuestión de límites entre Guatemala y México*, 91.

54. Identified by their towns of origin, it is unlikely that these villagers saw themselves as belonging to either one nation or the other. Romero, *Refutación de las inculpaciones hechas al c. Matías Romero por el gobierno de Guatemala*, 21.

55. The winter and spring of 1853 saw a slew of missives related to Guatemalan incursions as conflict led to the defection of troops and attempted prison breaks. Oficios de los autoridades del Departamento, 1852–1853. AMT, caja 1, Presidencia Municipal 1837–1853, exp. s/n

56. Carlos Gris, "Departamento de Soconusco," *El Telégrafo*, Mexico City, Jan. 18, 1882.

57. Palmer, "Central American Union or Guatemalan Republic?"; Karnes, *The Failure of Union: Central America, 1824–1960*.

58. Arciniega to the Ministerio de Relaciones Exteriores, July 6, 1870. AHMR, Correspondencia recibida, f. 11325-A; Romero to Escobar, June 1, 1871. AHMR, Correspondencia enviada, vol. 14, p. 381; Escobar to Romero, April 10, 1871. AHMR, Correspondencia recibida, f. 13668; Escobar to Romero, June 18, 1871. AHMR, Correspondencia recibida, f. 14286-A.

59. For a few examples, see Avendaño to Romero, Oct. 7, 1869. AHMR, correspondencia recibida, f. 7816; Domínguez to Romero, Oct. 26, 1869. AHMR, Correspondencia recibida, f. 8154; José Encarnación Ibarra to Matías Romero, Jan. 15, 1871. AHMR, Correspondencia recibida, f. 12924; José Luis León to Matías Romero, April 25, 1871. AHMR, Correspondencia recibida, f. 13777; Daniel Córdova to Matías Romero, April 25, 1871. AHMR, Correspondencia recibida, f. 13781; Escobar, *Informe de los recursos agrícolas*, 16.

60. Escobar to Romero, April 10, 1871. AHMR, Correspondencia recibida, f. 13668; Escobar to Romero, April 25, 1871. AHMR, Correspondencia recibida, f. 13779; Escobar to Romero, Feb. 18, 1872. AHMR, Correspondencia recibida, f. 17059.

61. Ibarra to Romero, Jan. 22, 1871. AHMR, exp. 12990; Escobar to Romero, July 18, 1871. AHMR, Correspondencia recibida, f. 14633.

62. Flavio Paniagua, "Soconusco bloqueado por Guatemala," *La Brújula: Periódico Independiente y Progresista*, Sept. 23, 1870.

63. For examples of pushback against national consolidation, see descriptions of regional rebellions during the Restored Republic in Katz, "Mexico: Restored

Republic and Porfiriato, 1867–1910"; Hamnett, "Liberalism Divided"; Falcón, "El estado liberal ante las rebeliones populares. México, 1867–1876."

64. Carmagnani, "El Federalismo liberal mexicano," 152–57; Hamnett, "Liberalism Divided"; Fowler, *Forceful Negotiations.*

65. Abraham Poumián to Matías Romero, July 18, 1871. AHMR, Correspondencia recibida, f. 14642.

66. Romero to Escobar, April 20, 1871. AHMR, Correspondencia enviada, vol. 14, p. 184; Salas to Romero, Feb. 17, 1870. AHMR, Correspondencia recibida, f. 9970; Romero, *Refutación de las inculpaciones hechas al c. Matías Romero por el gobierno de Guatemala,* 79.

67. Maldonado to Ponce de León, May 7, 1875. AHMR, Correspondencia recibida, f. 18923; Plutarco Rodas to Matías Romero, May 9, 1875. AHMR, Correspondencia recibida, f. 18924; Fermín Maldonado to Matías Romero, May 13, 1875. AHMR, Correspondencia recibida, f. 18925.

68. The neo-institutional turn in economic history encompasses a large number of scholars, but for the key arguments, see Acemoglu, *Why Nations Fail*; Coatsworth, "Desigualdad, instituciones y crecimiento económico en América Latina"; Engerman and Sokoloff, *Economic Development in the Americas since 1500*; see also the growing field of environmental history in Latin America, e.g. Miller, *An Environmental History of Latin America.*

69. Carmagnani, *Estado y mercado*; Mirow, *Latin American Law.*

70. Locals requested aid in the form of duty-free importation of flour and corn. Cristóbal J. Salas to Matías Romero, March 4, 1870. AHMR, Correspondencia recibida, f. 9936; Ismael Salas to Matías Romero, March 23, 1870. AHMR, Correspondencia recibida, f. 10135.

71. The Soconusco totals some 547,500 hectares or 5,475 sq. km. Escobar, *Informe de los recursos agrícolas,* 12–13; Ortiz Hernández, "Formación histórico-política de la región del Soconusco," 22–31.

72. See, for example, the history of the municipality of Cacahoatán as documented many years later and discussed in Chapter Four. AGA, Asunto: Dotación, Estado: Chiapas, Municipio: Cacahoatán, exp. 408, legajo 7.

73. Holden, *Mexico and the Survey of Public Lands,* 7–8; see also Craib, *Cartographic Mexico*; Appelbaum, *Mapping the Country of Regions*; Palacios, *Coffee in Colombia, 1850–1970,* Ch. 8.

74. Romero to Escobar, June 1, 1871. AHMR, Correspondencia enviada, vol. 14, p. 381.

75. Letters from Teófilo Orantes, the local man Romero partnered with in his first attempt at coffee cultivation, indicate that no one had managed to begin the titling process. Orantes was himself planting coffee on neighboring lands, and he promised to make sure that Romero got the best lands that were to be had. Matías Romero to Juan Avendaño, Jan. 20, 1870. AHMR, Correspondencia enviada, vol. 10, p. 104; Teófilo Orantes to Matías Romero, May 16, 1868. AHMR, Correspondencia recibida, f. 2548.

76. Escobar to Romero, June 26, 1871. AHMR, Correspondencia recibida, f. 14417.

77. Romero, May 30, 1875. AHMR, Correspondencia enviada, vol. 12, caja 2.

78. The majority of titles claimed through Fomento were expedited in the mid to late 1880s. AGN, Fomento y Obras Públicas: Colonización (Baldíos), cajas 1–13.

79. This will be further discussed in Chapter Four. See the scans of 53 of these hand drawn titles on "El Soconusco Cervantino: Cartografía de una encomienda imaginaria," CD-Rom. Archivo General de la Nación, México.

80. Alejandro Arreola to Matías Romero, June 25, 1871. AHMR, Correspondencia recibida, f. 14384.

81. See Appendix 2 for population data. Viqueira Albán, "Indios y ladinos, arraigados y migrantes en Chiapas." Other sources from the era set the population of the district at 11,465 in 1842, with 3,605 in Tapachula; at 11,218 in 1857 with 3,408 in Tapachula; at 12,959 in 1861, with 4,093 in Tapachula; at 9,376 in 1869, with 4,769 in Tapachula; and at 17,110 in 1871, with 3,000 in Tapachula. The disparities in these numbers make them difficult to use, and so despite their tempting proximity to my dates of interest, I will be relying on Viqueira's recent study. Pineda, *Descripción geográfica*, 9; *El Espíritu del Siglo*, t. I, núm 5, 9 de marzo de 1861 and *La Brújula*, t. I, núm 23, septiembre 24 de 1869, cited in cited in Ortiz Hernández, "Formación histórico-política de la región del Soconusco," 80–81; Secretaría de Hacienda, *Las medidas propuestas*, 9–10.

82. Legajo de comunicaciones del Juzgado de 1a Instancia, 1847. AMT, Presidencia Municipal, caja 1, 1837–1853, exp. 2; Comunicaciones de las autoridades departamentales, 1847. AMT, Presidencia Municipal, caja 1, 1837–1853, exp. 1; Comunicaciones de la prefectura, 1849. AMT, Presidencia Municipal, caja 2, 1846–1940, exp. s/n; AGA, Asunto: Dotación, Estado: Chiapas, Municipio: Cacahoatán, exp. 408, legajo 7.

83. Carlos Gris, "Departamento de Soconusco," *El Telégrafo*, Mexico City, Jan. 18, 1882.

84. For an overview of these reforms, see Rus, "Coffee and Recolonization," 261–66; Washbrook, "Una Esclavitud Simulada"; for more on theories of labor coercion see Acemoglu and Wolitzky, "The Economics of Labor Coercion."

85. Comunicaciones recibidas en el Juzgado 1°, Aug. 5, 1871. AMT, Juzgado 1o Municipal, caja 3, exp. 23; Libro de juicios verbales del Juzgado 1°, 1878. AMT, Juzgado 1° Municipal, caja 3, exp. 26 (29).

86. Demanda interpuesta por el C. Mont Ysmael Salaz en contra de su sirviente Rito Rodriguez, March 27, 1872. AMT, Juzgado 1° Municipal, caja 3, exp. 5.

87. Gibbings, "'The Shadow of Slavery,'" 77. For more on this ongoing debate over the realities of debt peonage elsewhere in Latin America, see Bauer, "Rural Workers in Spanish America"; Knight, "Mexican Peonage"; Knight, "Debt Bondage in Latin America"; Loveman, "Critique of Arnold J. Bauer's 'Rural Workers in Spanish America'"; Brass and Linden, *Free and Unfree Labour*; Hagan and Wells, "Brassed-Off"; McCreery, "Coffee and Indigenous Labor in Guatemala, 1871–1980"; Dore, "Patriarchy from Above, Patriarchy from Below"; Charlip, *Cultivating Coffee*; Gonzales, "Capitalist Agriculture and Labour Contracting in Northern Peru, 1880–1905"; Peloso, *Peasants on Plantations*.

88. While I take issue with Katz's description of labor conditions in Chiapas,

he provides a valuable overview of the variety of working conditions that emerged across Mexico. Katz, "Labor Conditions on Haciendas in Porfirian Mexico."

89. Romero, *Cultivo del café en la costa meridional de Chiapas*, 17.

90. Escobar to Romero, Jan. 9, 1871. AHMR Correspondencia recibida, f. 12853; Escobar to Romero, March 12, 1872. AHMR, Correspondencia recibida, f. 17362.

91. Charles H. Currier to Matías Romero, Aug. 2, 1871. AHMR, Correspondencia recibida, f. 14842; Miguel Pritchard Gamboa to Matías Romero, March 18, 1876. AHMR, Correspondencia recibida, f. 19104.

92. For more information on the "Caste War," see Rus, "Whose Caste War? Indians, Ladinos, and the 'Caste War' of 1869." The degree to which the fighting in the highlands permeates Romero's letters from these years suggests there may be more to examine with regard to the intensity of the war, which Rus suggests was actually only a few skirmishes, instigated by the *coleto* elites. Domínguez to Romero, March 14, 1871. AHMR, Correspondencia recibida, f. 13458; Matías Romero to José Pantaleón Domínguez, July 13, 1871. AHMR, Correspondencia enviada, vol. 14, p. 677; Domínguez to Romero, July 30, 1871. AHMR, Correspondencia recibida, f. 14795; Escobar to Romero, March 16, 1872. AHMR, Correspondencia recibida, f. 17429; Escobar to Romero, May 1, 1872. AHMR, Correspondencia recibida, f. 18056.

93. McCreery, "Coffee and Indigenous Labor in Guatemala, 1871–1980."

94. "Mis trabajadores, todos con fuertes deudas, mirando que no hay justicia para mi, se han fugado, y es inútil perseguirlos, porque nadie me escucharía contra ellos." Carlos Gris, "Departamento de Soconusco," *El Telégrafo*, Jan. 11, 1882.

95. Maldonado to Ponce de León, May 7, 1875. AHMR, Correspondencia recibida, f. 18923.

96. Arreola to Romero, June 26, 1871. AHMR, Correspondencia recibida, f. 14384.

97. Escobar, *Informe de los recursos agrícolas*, 5.

98. These types of arrangements appear in the local record from the mid-1870s onward. The municipal court served as a site for registering all sorts of contracts, as will be discussed further in Chapter Six.

99. For some examples of the limited scope of similar entrepreneurial elites elsewhere in Mexico, see Wiemers, "Agriculture and Credit in Nineteenth-Century Mexico"; Chowning, "Nineteenth-Century Mexican Agriculture"; Corbett, "Republican Hacienda and Federalist Politics"; Chowning, *Wealth and Power in Provincial Mexico*; Tutino, *Making a New World*.

100. Romero formed a company to pursue the building of a railroad in the early 1870s that included a number of North American investors, Ulysses S. Grant among them. The company never laid a single rail, and its concession lapsed by 1880. Molina Pérez, *Por los rieles de Chiapas*, 22–23; see also Kuntz Ficker, "Los ferrocarriles y la formación del espacio económico en México, 1880–1910"; Garner, "The Politics of National Development in Late Porfirian Mexico."

101. Romero sent a survey team south to try to find a better location for the port, but its efforts were delayed for more than a year because it did not have a suitable boat. After multiple attempts to secure a boat locally, the team turned

to the consul in San Francisco, California, for assistance. The consul was able to send a boat south, but it did not arrive for months. Miguel M. Ponce de León to Matías Romero, Aug. 8, 1871. AHMR, Correspondencia recibida, f. 14916; Escobar to Romero, July 28, 1871. AHMR, Correspondencia recibida, f. 14728; Ponce de León to Romero, Aug. 12, 1871. AHMR, Correspondencia recibida, f. 14969; Ponce de León to Romero, Nov. 8, 1871. AHMR, Correspondencia recibida, f. 15939-B; Escobar to Romero, Feb. 18, 1872. AHMR, Correspondencia recibida, f. 17059; Escobar to Romero, April 29, 1872. AHMR, Correspondencia recibida, f. 18025; Ponce de León to Romero, May 5, 1872. AHMR, Correspondencia recibida, f. 18112.

102. As Sandra Kuntz Ficker demonstrates, the late 1860s was an era in which numerous ports were opened to both national and international trade, though, as with San Benito, the simple legal distinction did not necessarily do much to regularize shipping there or improve the port facilities. Kuntz Ficker, *El comercio exterior de México en la era del capitalismo liberal, 1870–1929*, 103–7. When the port finally opened, Romero received letters of thanks from the governor and various others, all of whom more or less paraphrased Ibarra's gratitude to "el padre y protector de estos pueblos." "Parte oficial," *El Siglo Diez y Nueve*, June 24, 1869; Domínguez to Romero, Jan. 7, 1870. AHMR, Correspondencia recibida, f. 12835; Salas to Romero, Jan. 16, 1871. AHMR, Correspondencia recibida, f. 12928; Escobar to Romero, Jan. 22, 1871. AHMR, Correspondencia recibida, f. 12983; Ibarra to Romero, Jan. 23, 1871. AHMR, Correspondencia recibida, f. 12999.

103. Romero never got his free trade zone at the border, likely in part because it countered his general promotion of import duties as a substitute for internal tariffs. Márquez Colín, "La administración hacendaria de Matías Romero."

104. Ibarra to Romero, Jan. 22, 1871. AHMR, Correspondencia recibida, f. 12990; Escobar to Romero, July 18, 1871. AHMR, Correspondencia recibida, f. 14633. Romero, *Refutación de las inculpaciones hechas al c. Matías Romero por el gobierno de Guatemala*, 80.

105. Matías Romero, Feb. 2, 1872. AHMR, Correspondencia recibida, f. 16902. Pacific Mail took over the route by the 1880s. Secretaría de Hacienda, *Las medidas propuestas*, 162; Romero, *Refutación de las inculpaciones hechas al c. Matías Romero por el gobierno de Guatemala*, 79.

106. "Un puerto de deposito, un nuevo arancel, y el departamento de Soconusco," *El Siglo Diez y Nueve*, Feb. 21, 1868.

107. Salvucci, *Politics, Markets, and Mexico's "London Debt," 1823–1887*.

108. Wiemers, "Agriculture and Credit in Nineteenth-Century Mexico"; Sweigart, *Coffee Factorage and the Emergence of a Brazilian Capital Market, 1850–1888*; Adelman, "Agricultural Credit in the Province of Buenos Aires, Argentina, 1890–1914"; Marichal, "Obstacles to the Development of Capital Markets in Nineteenth-Century Mexico"; Triner, "Banks, Regions, and Nation in Brazil, 1889–1930"; Passananti, "Managing Finance and Financiers"; Riguzzi, "The Legal System"; Hanley, *Native Capital*; Levy, *The Making of a Market*.

109. Difficulties immediately arose, as no one in Tapachula was accustomed to or able to use American dollars, if, in fact, the money could get there at all given the unreliability of local transport. The company eventually arranged for someone

to collect and convert the money for Romero in either Acapulco or Puerto Ángel and ship it on to him in San Benito. Felix M. de Nemegyei to Matías Romero, April 12, 1873. AHMR, Correspondencia recibida, f. 18685; Nemegyei to Romero, Dec. 19, 1873. AHMR, Correspondencia recibida, f. 18748; Nottebohm and Company to Matías Romero, Dec. 30, 1873. AHMR, Correspondencia recibida, f. 18751; Colonia Hewith to Matías Romero, Feb. 8, 1874. AHMR, Correspondencia recibida, f. 18783; Hoadley & Co. to Matías Romero, Jan. 31, 1876. AHMR, Correspondencia recibida, f. 19069; Thomas Sell to Matías Romero, March 4, 1876. AHMR, Correspondencia recibida, f. 19084; Sell to Romero, March 8, 1876. AHMR, Correspondencia recibida, f. 19090; Sell to Romero, March 13, 1876. AHMR, Correspondencia recibida, f. 19097.

110. Unmarked, March 5, 1874, APJS 1° Civil, Soconusco 1864, 1865, y 1869; Matías Romero, March 24, 1874. AHMR, Correspondencia recibida, f. 18813.

111. Romero renegotiated the contracts, but neither planter ever delivered anywhere near the contracted amount. That said, because of Romero's willingness to negotiate, both remained in the coffee business for decades to come. Matías Romero, April 7, 1875. AHMR, Correspondencia recibida, f. 18918.

112. Romero did deliver some of the coffee he promised, but his debts remained outstanding for many years to come. Hoadley & Co. to Matías Romero, Jan. 31, 1876. AHMR, Correspondencia recibida, f. 19069; Thomas Sell to Matías Romero, March 4, 1876. AHMR, Correspondencia recibida, f. 19084; Sell to Romero, March 8, 1876. AHMR, exp. 19090; Sell to Romero, March 13, 1876. AHMR, Correspondencia recibida, f. 19097.

113. In later letters, Romero and Escobar would argue over the disposition of both the local and the district court. Romero to Escobar, March 7, 1876. AHMR, Correspondencia enviada, vol. 23, p. 197.

114. Carlos Gris to Matías Romero, Nov. 15, 1876. AHMR, Correspondencia recibida, f. 19146-B; Gris to Romero, Jan. 28, 1877. AHMR, Correspondencia recibida, f. 19216.

115. The list only includes those fincas with over 50 cuerdas of coffee planted or ready to plant. Malacate, the finca that Romero had hoped to buy from Barrios, is included in this list, with some 1,000 cuerdas of coffee to be planted on a part of it previously not cultivated. No indication is given as to how much property was currently planted with coffee. Romero, *Cultivo del café en la costa meridional de Chiapas* and "Progreso del cultivo de café en Soconusco," *El Cultivador*, Nov. 1, 1874.

116. Orantes to Romero, June 16, 1870. AHMR, Correspondencia recibida, f. 11034.

CHAPTER TWO: FIXING THE BORDER

1. This and the following from Mexico, Secretaría de Relaciones Exteriores, *Correspondencia diplomática* 1882, 625–26.

2. Literature on the use of terms like *frontier* and *borderland* is vast, though primarily centered in the territory that would become the United States. Borrowing only slightly anachronistically from Adelman and Aron, I use the term *borderland* to refer to the political understandings of the Soconusco as a space of confrontation

between two nations (as opposed to empires) within which some peoples were "afforded room to maneuver and preserve some element of autonomy." I do use the term *frontier* elsewhere in this work but primarily to refer to the region's lack of economic and institutional incorporation into the state. Adelman and Aron, "From Borderlands to Borders," 816.

3. Mexico et al., *Legislación mexicana*, 262–63.
4. Castillo, Toussaint Ribot, and Vázquez Olivera, *Espacios diversos, historia en común*, Ch. 2.
5. Rebert, *La Gran Línea*; Craib, *Cartographic Mexico*, Ch. 1.
6. Manuel Orozco y Berra, quoted in Craib, *Cartographic Mexico*, 32.
7. Craib, 24; Hobsbawm, *Nations and Nationalism since 1780*.
8. Sahlins, *Boundaries*. For further extrapolations on Sahlins's conceptualization of borderlands and nationality, see Baud and Van Schendel, "Toward a Comparative History of Borderlands"; Wilson and Donnan, *Border Identities*; Adelman and Aron, "From Borderlands to Borders"; Hart, "Culture, Civilization, and Demarcation at the Northwest Borders of Greece"; Herzog, *Defining Nations*; Brubaker, "Migration, Membership, and the Modern Nation-State." Cartography was also a vital part of imperial expansion during this era. For a short overview of this historiography, see Burnett, *Masters of All They Surveyed*, 8–13. For Latin American construction of identities in the wake of border disputes and treaties, see Skuban, *Lines in the Sand*; Kraay and Whigham, *I Die with My Country*.
9. Craib, *Cartographic Mexico*, 51–52; Anna, *Forging Mexico*.
10. García Cubas, "Carta General de La República Mexicana."
11. Craib, *Cartographic Mexico*, 23.
12. Toussaint Ribot and Vázquez Olivera, *Territorio, nación y soberanía*, 73–75; Cosío Villegas, *La vida política exterior*, 46–49.
13. Arciniega to the Ministerio de Relaciones Exteriores, July 6, 1870. AHMR, Correspondencia recibida, f. 11325-A.
14. Escobar to Romero, April 10, 1871. AHMR, Correspondencia recibida, f. 13668; José Luis León to Matías Romero, April 25, 1871. AHMR, Correspondencia recibida, f. 13777; Daniel Córdova to Matías Romero, April 25, 1871. AHMR, Correspondencia recibida, f. 13781; Escobar to Romero, June 18, 1871. AHMR, Correspondencia recibida, f. 14286-A.
15. Castillo, Toussaint Ribot, and Vázquez Olivera, *Espacios diversos, historia en común*, 104–05.
16. Pichardo Hernández and Moncada Maya, "La labor geográfica de Antonio García Cubas en el Ministerio de Hacienda, 1868–1876"; Lurtz, "Developing the Mexican Countryside."
17. Craib, *Cartographic Mexico*, Ch. 2.
18. Matías Romero to Sebastián Escobar, Gral. Felix Dias, Manuel L. Orozco, Mariano Saldgado, José Victoria Araujo, Abraham Bumian, José Pantaleón Domínguez, Teófilo Orantes, José Tovilla, Ismael Salas, José Encarnación Ibarra, and Leandro Soto, May 20, 1871. AHMR, Correspondencia enviada, vol. 14, p. 313.
19. Ponce de León to Romero, April 28, 1872. AHMR, Correspondencia recibida, f. 18017.

20. Matías Romero to Justo Rufino Barrios, Aug. 31, 1875. AHMR Correspondencia enviada, vol. 21, p. 23; Romero to Barrios, Sept. 7, 1873. AHMR, Correspondencia enviada, vol. 21, pp. 39–41; Romero to Barrios, Oct. 20, 1873. AHMR, Correspondencia enviada, vol. 21, pp. 164–165; Romero, *Refutación de las inculpaciones hechas al c. Matías Romero por el gobierno de Guatemala*, 16, 22.

21. Matías Romero to Juan José Ramírez, March 13, 1875. AHMR Correspondencia enviada, vol. 23, p. 29; Testamento de Matías Romero, Feb. 10, 1880. AHMR, exp. 29910.

22. Romero to Barrios, Aug. 31, 1875. AHMR Correspondencia enviada, vol. 21, p. 23; Romero to Barrios, Sept. 7, 1873. AHMR, Correspondencia enviada, vol. 21, pp. 39–41; Romero to Barrios, Oct. 20, 1873. AHMR, Correspondencia enviada, vol. 21, pp. 164–65; Romero, *Refutación de las inculpaciones hechas al c. Matías Romero por el gobierno de Guatemala*, 16, 22.

23. Toussaint Ribot and Vázquez Olivera, *Territorio, nación y soberanía*, 73–75; Cosío Villegas, *La vida política exterior*, 13–17.

24. Cosío Villegas, *La vida política exterior*, 23.

25. Romero, *Refutación de las inculpaciones hechas al c. Matías Romero por el gobierno de Guatemala*.

26. "Queja del Señor Don Matias Romero relative a devoulción de terrenos de su propiedad en territorio de Guatemala," Año de 1888. AGN, Fondo Relaciones Exteriores, Siglo XIX, caja 26, exp. 2.

27. Fermín Maldonado to Antonio Ponce de León, May 7, 1875. AHMR, exp. 18923.

28. "El pueblo de Tajmulco . . . " June 12, 1875, *La Estrella de Occidente*, San Marcos, Guatemala; Romero, *Refutación de las inculpaciones hechas al c. Matías Romero por el gobierno de Guatemala*; Toussaint Ribot and Vázquez Olivera, *Territorio, nación y soberanía*, 76.

29. Romero, *Bosquejo histórico*.

30. Romero, *Refutación de las inculpaciones hechas al c. Matías Romero por el gobierno de Guatemala*.

31. Katz, "Mexico: Restored Republic and Porfiriato, 1867–1910."

32. Craib, *Cartographic Mexico*; Castillo, Toussaint Ribot, and Vázquez Olivera, *Espacios diversos, historia en común*, Introduction.

33. Cambranes, *Coffee and Peasants*; McCreery, *Rural Guatemala, 1760–1940*.

34. See Stefania Gallini's work on a map commissioned by the Guatemalan government in 1876 that depicted the Soconusco as an anomalous extension of Mexican territory into Guatemalan lands. Gallini, "Coffee Grounds"; Vázquez Olivera, "¿Repúblicas hermanas?," 86.

35. Castillo, Toussaint Ribot, and Vázquez Olivera, *Espacios diversos, historia en común*, 114.

36. Castillo, Toussaint Ribot, and Vázquez Olivera, 113–14.

37. Buchenau, *In the Shadow of the Giant*, Ch. 2.

38. Harris, "The Global Construction of International Law in the Nineteenth Century."

39. Castillo, Toussaint Ribot, and Vázquez Olivera, *Espacios diversos, historia en común*, 115.

40. *A Report of Secretary of State*; Buchenau, *In the Shadow of the Giant*, 33–38; see also Findling, *Close Neighbors, Distant Friends*.

41. For example, *La Voz de México* had a multi-issue serial regarding the border question that lasted from the fall of 1881 through the spring of 1882. For select editions, see "México y Guatemala," *La Voz de México*, Oct. 21, 1881, 1; "Cuestión con Guatemala," *La Voz de México*, Dec.11, 1881, 1; "Cuestión con Guatemala," *La Voz de México*, March 23, 1881, 1; "Cuestión con Guatemala," *La Voz de México*, June 1, 1882, 1.

42. Mexico, Secretaría de Relaciones Exteriores, *Correspondencia diplomática 1882*, 629–34.

43. Exteriores, 818–19; *A Report of Secretary of State*.

44. See also the Guatemalan foreign minister's references to the "conquest" that would take place as a result of Guatemala not being able to pay indemnities when it lost if the two countries were to go to war. *A Report of Secretary of State*, 18–19, 33.

45. See, for example, Dardón, *La cuestión de límites entre México y Guatemala*, Introducción.

46. *A Report of Secretary of State*, 26, 69.

47. See correspondence between the Guatemalan and American ministers *A Report of Secretary of State*, 46–47, 60–87; Buchenau, *In the Shadow of the Giant*, 33.

48. *A Report of Secretary of State*, 3, 38.

49. Romero, *Refutación de las inculpaciones hechas al c. Matías Romero por el gobierno de Guatemala*, 21.

50. Mexico, Secretaría de Relaciones Exteriores, *Correspondencia diplomática 1882*, 621–22.

51. "México y Guatemala," *El Siglo Diez y Nueve*, Feb. 16, 1882, 1.

52. Castillo, Toussaint Ribot, and Vázquez Olivera, *Espacios diversos, historia en común*, 114–18.

53. *Manifestaciones de los poderes del Estado de Chiapas y de los representantes del mismo en el Congreso Federal con relación a la cuestión de límites pendiente entre México y Guatemala*. Mexico: Imprenta del Gobierno, 1881. AGN Fondo de Gobierno, Folletería, caja 35, folleto 917; *Manifestaciones de los poderes del Estado de Chiapas y de los representantes del mismo en el Congreso Federal con relacion a la cuestion de límites pendiente entre México y Guatemala*. Mexico: Imprenta del Gobierno, 1882. AGN, Fondo de Gobierno, Folletería, caja 35, folleto 918.

54. See, for example, translations of memos from Mariscal with detailed accounts of assassination attempts against Mexican surveyors and destruction of boundary markers, as well as further violence against villages and fincas. *A Report of Secretary of State*, 41–46, 53–58.

55. *A Report of Secretary of State*, 67.

56. *A Report of Secretary of State*, 68–87.

57. Comisión Guatemalteca de Límites con México, *Memoria sobre la cuestión de límites entre Guatemala y México*, 134.

58. Montúfar, *Reseña histórica de Centro América*.

59. In fulfillment of his campaign promises of no reelection, Díaz ceded the presidency in 1880 after his first four-year term. He took up a variety of positions during the following four years but never entirely handed over power to González, his hand-picked replacement. He then ran again and won in 1884. Coerver, *The Porfirian Interregnum*.

60. For a comparable moment on the northern border, see Adelman and Aron, "From Borderlands to Borders," 838.

61. Tratado sobre límites entre México y Guatemala, celebrado en 1882, Mexico-Guatemala, Sept. 27, 1882.

62. Cruz, *La verdad histórica*; Comisión Guatemalteca de Límites con México, *Memoria sobre la cuestión de límites entre Guatemala y México*, 149–52.

63. At one point Mexican officials called for a local vote as to whether a region was part of Mexico or Guatemala. "A plebiscite! What a strange idea! We are not in the times of the Roman Republic!" the Guatemalan press cried in response. This had, though, been the means by which Chiapas first joined Mexico. Worries about Guatemalan annexation or sale of this area would continue into the twentieth century, including a momentary panic in 1910 when the departure of an engineer for the Petén led the Mexican representative in Guatemala City to frantically write to the Secretary of Foreign Relations regarding rumors that Guatemala and the United States were in talks about the sale of the region. It turned out the engineer was in debt and was going to the frontier to help settle disputes with British settlers in Belize in order to pay off some of his obligations. *La zona comprendida entre los Ríos Chixoy y Santa Isabel*, 38; Mexico, Secretaría de Relaciones Exteriores, *Correspondencia diplomática* 1882, 175, 186, 187; "Colonización en la Frontera con Guatemala," 1910, SRE 27-3-105.

64. Romero to Martínez, July 29, 1877. AHMR, Correspondencia enviada, vol. 25, p. 292.

65. Guatemalan authorities had attempted to lay claim to the lands as early as 1878, when some of the villagers living on his property worked with Guatemalan surveyors to delimit various properties within it. Carlos Hausler to Matías Romero, Dec. 1878. AHMR, Correspondencia recibida, f. 28706.

66. "Queja del Señor Don Matías Romero relativa a devoulción de terrenos de su propiedad en territorio de Guatemala," Año de 1888. AGN, Fondo Relaciones Exteriores, Siglo XIX, caja 26, exp. 2.

67. Adelman and Aron, "From Borderlands to Borders," 837–38.

68. O'Gorman, *Historia de las divisiones territoriales de México*, 142–43.

69. For contrasting cases, see Sahlins, *Boundaries*; Skuban, *Lines in the Sand*.

70. Tratado sobre límites entre México y Guatemala, celebrado en 1882, Mexico-Guatemala, Sept. 27, 1882.

71. This law was a remnant of the secession of Texas and the Mexican American War. Aspiring emigrant planters, supported by local citizens of note, wrote careful letters describing both their bona fides and the land they hoped to purchase and, generally, were quickly granted permission to do so. See "Extranjeros que desean adquirir bienes raíces en el Estado," AHCH, Fondo de Gobierno, Fomento, 1907, vol. 6, exp. 16; "Agencia de Terrenos Baldíos," AHCH, Fondo de Gobierno, Fomento, 1909, vol. 1, exp. 1.; Augustine-Adams, "Constructing Mexico."

72. Debates over the types of citizenship and belonging available in Central America were as old as the countries in question. See Dym, "Citizen of Which Republic?"

73. The outcome of the Pérezes' case is unclear; I have not been able to find out if they were granted damages or reparations of any sort.

74. Romero to Barrios, Aug. 31, 1875. AHMR Correspondencia enviada, vol. 21, p. 23; Romero to Barrios, Sept. 7, 1873. AHMR, Correspondencia enviada, vol. 21, pp. 39–41; Romero to Barrios, Oct. 20, 1873. AHMR, Correspondencia enviada, vol. 21, pp. 164–65. Romero recounted this advice in a more bitter tone a few years later when the resident Guatemalans began causing problems. Romero, *Refutación de las inculpaciones hechas al c. Matías Romero por el gobierno de Guatemala*, 16, 22.

75. Salvador Mota to Porfirio Díaz, Oct. 22, 1896. CGPD, vol. 55, exp. 5974; Francisco León to Porfirio Díaz, April 17, 1897. CGPD, vol. 56, exp. 1524; León to Díaz, April 14, 1899. CGPD, vol. 58, exp. 1508; Mexico, Secretaría de Fomento, *Memoria 1897–1900*, 20.

76. Mauro Cándano to Porfirio Díaz, Oct. 9, 1897. CGPD, vol. 56, exp. 4820; Cándano to Díaz, Oct. 13, 1897. CGPD, vol. 56, exp. 4910.

77. Nolan-Ferrell explores this population and its lack of clear nationality further in her recent book. As she illustrates, citizenship only really began to matter once land reform passed in the wake of the Revolution. Many of those who had resided in the frontier region claimed Mexican birth in order to benefit from repartition. Identity was flexible based on what each country offered and legally mutable because of ongoing confusion over the nationality of towns and the scarcity of birth certificates. Mexico, *Censo general de 1900*; Nolan-Ferrell, *Constructing Citizenship*.

78. Pichardo Hernández and Moncada Maya, "La labor geográfica de Antonio García Cubas en el Ministerio de Hacienda, 1868–1876."

79. *Censo general de la República Mexicana, verificado el 20 de octubre de 1895.*

80. Hernández, *Mexican American Colonization*.

81. Buchenau, "Small Numbers, Great Impact."

CHAPTER THREE: FROM BULLETS TO BUREAUCRACY

1. Gris, *Sebastián Escobar*, 7.

2. Gris to Romero, March 24, 1877. AHMR, Correspondencia recibida, f. 19291.

3. Gris to Romero, Nov. 15, 1875. AHMR, Correspondencia recibida, f. 19150-B; Miguel Lavalle to Matías Romero, Nov. 11, 1877. AHMR, Correspondencia recibida, f. 23538; Gris to Romero, Aug. 27, 1878. AHMR, Correspondencia recibida, f. 27171; Santiago Keller Rigaud to Matías Romero, July 8, 1880. AHMR, Correspondencia recibida, f. 29839.

4. Gris, *Sebastián Escobar*, 6.

5. These began with a piece detailing his attempts to find justice in the local courts in 1880 and continued through 1882 in multiple newspapers. "Juzgado de

Distrito de Soconusco," *El Foro,* Jan. 10, 1880, 1; "Departamento de Soconusco," *El Telégrafo,* Jan. 4, 1882, 2; "Carta," *La Patria,* July 11, 1882, 2.

6. Gris, *Sebastián Escobar,* 11.

7. Gris and Mallen, Sept. 7, 1880, APJS 1º Civil Soconusco, 1873–1879; Carlos Gris, Cafetal Magdalena, July 2, 1880, APJS 1º Civil Soconusco, 1873–1879.

8. He wrote so glowingly of coffee that he was even made the subject of caricature in certain papers and compared to Jules Verne. Gris, "L'avenir des terres chaudes," *Le Trait de Union,* Sept. 2, 1890; "Carlos Gris," *El México Gráfico,* Oct. 12, 1891, 7.

9. He purchased some properties from a land company and some from the municipal government. MLCC to Gris, Feb. 25, 1905, ARPPC Doc Priv 1906; MLCC to Gris, May 14, 1910, ARPPC Doc Priv 1910: Sección 2a Hipotecas; Gris to Junta Calificadora, Dec. 20, 1914, APP: Lesher y Gris.

10. "Poder General conferido por la sociedad Lesher y Fisher a Don Manuel Gris," March 23, 1915, APP, loose papers.

11. He repeatedly served as executor for estates as well as witness to other people's contracts, as well as signing many of his own. See, for example, "Ab—intestato Carlos H. Adams," May 28, 1907, APJS 1º Civil Soconusco 1907, 01-50.

12. B. Acosta to P. Díaz, Dec. 21, 1909. CGPD, vol. 34, exp. 19428.

13. Gris to Jefe Político, 1914 (?), APP: Lesher y Gris.

14. "Testimonio de la escritura de disolución de la sociedad Lesher y Gris y aplicación de la Finca Peru a Don Manuel Gris," Oct. 17, 1933, APP: Documentos Legales de Fincas Peru y Paris.

15. Cosío Villegas, *La vida política interior,* xx.

16. North's work is extensive, as is its invocation by economic and legal historians. For the original paper and overviews of its use in Latin American historiography and the new history of capitalism, see North, "Institutions"; Adelman, "Institutions, Property, and Economic Development in Latin America"; Beck, "Legal Institutions and Economic Development."

17. For example, José Esperón to Matías Romero, Aug. 31, 1875. AHMR, Correspondencia recibida, f. 18995; Tomás de Rojas to Matías Romero, Sept. 3, 1877. AHMR, Correspondencia recibida, f. 21920; Antonio Bado to Matías Romero, Sept. 10, 1878. AHMR, Correspondencia recibida, f. 27351.

18. Carlos Gris reiterated this accusation repeatedly in his letters to the national press. Gris, *Sebastián Escobar.*

19. The literature on caciquismo, caudillismo, and coronelismo in Latin America is vast. Patronage, political bossism, and violence have long been seen as essential to both the consolidation of governance in independent Latin America and its fragmentation. The term is sometimes applied too broadly, but as many writing about Escobar in the period in question explicitly referred to him as a cacique, I will do so as well. For key writings on the phenomenon, see Brading, *Caudillo and Peasant in the Mexican Revolution*; Falcón, *Revolución y caciquismo*; Graham, *Patronage and Politics in Nineteenth-Century Brazil*; Lynch, *Caudillos in Spanish America, 1800–1850*; De la Fuente, *Children of Facundo*; Knight and Pansters, *Caciquismo in Twentieth-Century Mexico.*

20. Hamnett, "Liberalism Divided"; Hale, *The Transformation of Liberalism in Late Nineteenth-Century Mexico.*

21. Carmagnani, "El Federalismo liberal mexicano," 152–57; Hamnett, "Liberalism Divided."

22. The best description of this turn is probably Scott, *Seeing like a State*, Ch. 3. See also Raat, *El positivismo durante el Porfiriato, 1876–1910*; Corr, "The Enlightenment Surfaces in Nineteenth-Century Mexico."

23. For one example of the increasing reach of bureaucracy, see Lurtz, "Developing the Mexican Countryside"; for Romero's role in this, see Márquez Colín, "La administración hacendaria de Matías Romero"; for continuities between the Juárez and Díaz regimes, see Perry, *Juárez and Díaz.*

24. Gris, *Sebastián Escobar*, 8. Italics in original.

25. Fowler, *Forceful Negotiations*; Fowler, *Celebrating Insurrection.*

26. "Plan político regenerador de las libertades y garantías en Chiapas," *El Siglo Diez y Nueve*, Sept. 6, 1875, 3.

27. Escobar and his allies, using guns provided by the Mexican government to shore up the southern border and by the Guatemalan president to help defeat that government, chased the governor from his home before federal reinforcements could arrive. When state forces defeated the rebellion, the governor offered amnesty for all participants and gave Escobar the opportunity to plead his case in Mexico City. Instead, Escobar escaped to Guatemala. The entire saga was captured in the Mexico City press because of Barrios's involvement. As the previous chapter demonstrated, tensions at the border were riding high, and the Guatemalan president's intervention in Mexican state politics did not bode well for Mexican authority in the south. "Chiapas—Últimas noticias," *El Monitor Republicano*, Aug. 29, 1875, 4; "Oficial: Ministro de Relaciones—Sección de Américas," *El Siglo Diez y Nueve*, Oct. 6, 1875, 2; "Decreto de Gobernador J. Pantaleón Domínguez: Revolución acuadillada por Julian Grajales y Sebastian Escobar," Nov. 25, 1875. AHCH, Fondo Documental Fernando Castillo Gamboa, exp. 514; "Todo indica . . . ," *El Siglo Diez y Nueve*, Jan. 1, 1876, 1.

28. During this time, Matías Romero attempted to get Díaz to invest in any number of new enterprises along the lines of what he himself was doing in the Soconusco.

29. Hamnett, "Liberalism Divided," 687–88; Garner, *Porfirio Díaz.*

30. Juan G. Puron, "Un Alcance del Imparcial," *El Combate*, Feb. 10, 1878.

31. Gris to Romero, March 3, 1877. AHMR, Correspondencia recibida, f. 19080; Gris to Romero, Dec. 18, 1876. AHMR, Correspondencia recibida, f. 19161-A; Gris to Romero, March 24, 1877. AHMR, Correspondencia recibida, f. 1929; José Martínez to Matías Romero, April 15, 1877. AHMR, Correspondencia recibida, f. 19306; Martínez to Romero, July 18, 1877. AHMR, Correspondencia recibida, f. 20725.

32. Gris to Romero, Nov. 20, 1876. AHMR, Correspondencia recibida, f. 19150-B.

33. For examples of recent scholarship that elucidates this ongoing negotiation, see Wasserman, *Capitalists, Caciques, and Revolution*; Falcón, "Esplendor y ocaso de los caciques militares"; Falcón and Buve, *Don Porfirio presidente*; Aguilar

Rivera, *Las elecciones y el gobierno representativo*; Sumner, "National Autocracy, Regional Governance"; Baud and Parra, "Respuestas, resistencias y acomodos a los procesos modernizadores en América Latina."

34. Bravo Regidor, "Elecciones de gobernadores durante el Porfiriato," 265–67.

35. Thomson, "Porfirio Díaz y el ocaso del partido de La Montaña."

36. Wasserman, *Capitalists, Caciques, and Revolution*.

37. Rendón Garcini, *El prosperato*; Sumner, "National Autocracy, Regional Governance."

38. See the case of the state of Mexico in Falcón, *El jefe político*, 69–73.

39. This was how almost all governors came to power in the wake of Tuxtepec. Aside from two who completed their electoral terms, the rest took power through military means and collaboration with Díaz and were later confirmed to their positions via special elections. Crisóstomo Lara to Porfirio Díaz, March 2, 1877. CGPD, vol. 2, doc. 1449; Lara to Díaz, May 12, 1877. CGPD, vol. 2, exp. 735; Bravo Regidor, "Elecciones de gobernadores durante el Porfiriato," 263–64.

40. Escobar was an outsider to the conservative elites who had long ruled Chiapas from the highland capital of San Cristóbal de las Casas. He was also removed from the mounting tensions between those entrenched highland oligarchs and the emerging cadre of newly wealthy planters in the state's central lowlands. Benjamin, *A Rich Land, a Poor People*, Prologue.

41. This double claim to the governorship presaged the tumult of leadership in Chiapas across the Porfiriato. More than twenty men claimed the governor's seat in the next thirty years, sometimes simultaneously and not always with Díaz's support. Lara to Díaz, March 2, 1877. CGPD, vol. 2, doc 1449; Lara to Díaz, May 12, 1877. CGPD, vol. 2, exp. 735.

42. Manuel M. Sánchez to Matías Romero, Aug. 7, 1877. AHMR, Correspondencia recibida, f. 21529; Tomás de Rojas to Matías Romero, Sept. 3, 1877. AHMR, Correspondencia recibida, f. 21920; Crecensio Escalona to Matías Romero, Dec. 16, 1877. AHMR, Correspondencia recibida, f. 23970; J. P. de los Rios, "Estado de Chiapas—Abusos," *El Monitor Repúblicano*, Sept. 18, 1877; "Al Diario Oficial," *La Bandera Nacional*, Dec. 15, 1877.

43. Unknown to Matías Romero, 1878. AHMR, Correspondencia recibida, f. 28784.

44. Martínez to Romero, July 12, 1877. AHMR, Correspondencia recibida, f. 20568.

45. Lavalle to Romero, Nov. 17, 1877. AHMR, Correspondencia recibida, f. 23538.

46. Notas oficiales del juzgado, 1878. AMT, Tapachula, Juzgado 1º Municipal, caja 3, exp. 13.

47. Lavalle to Romero, Nov. 17, 1877. AHMR, Correspondencia recibida, f. 23538.

48. Quote from J. P. de los Rios, "Estado de Chiapas—Abusos," *El Monitor Repúblicano*, Sept. 18, 1877.

49. "Chiapas," *El Combate*, June 2, 1878; Sebastián Escobar, "La administración local de Chiapas," *La Patria*, Aug. 7, 1877.

50. "Editorial—al *Diario Oficial*," *La Bandera Nacional*, Dec. 15, 1877.

51. Clemente Villaseñor, "Editorial: Chiapas," *La Patria*, March 5, 1878.
52. Sebastián Escobar to Porfirio Díaz, March 14, 1878. CGPD, vol. 3, exp. 301.
53. Similar negotiations happened across Latin America. See Centeno and Ferraro, "Republics of the Possible," 15–16.
54. Porfirio Díaz to Sebastián Escobar, April 3, 1878. CGPD, vol. 3, exp. 301-A.
55. Díaz to Escobar, April 16, 1878. CGPD, vol. 3, exp. 298; Díaz to Escobar, April 24, 1878. CGPD, vol. 3, exp. 296.
56. Rodas to Romero, Aug. 8, 1879. AHMR, Correspondencia recibida, f. 29542.
57. "Jurisprudencia federal," *El Foro*, Jan. 10, 1880.
58. Juan G. Puron, "Por qué atacamos al Gobierno de Escobar," *El Combate*, Aug. 22, 1878, 2.
59. Keller to Romero, Jan. 19, 1880. AHMR, Correspondencia recibida, f. 29747.
60. Avelino Villareal to Matías Romero, May 17, 1878. AHMR, Correspondencia recibida, f. 25925.
61. Matías Romero to José Martínez, March 25, 1878. AHMR, Correspondencia enviada, vol. 28, p. 202.
62. Neufeld, *The Blood Contingent*.
63. Vanderwood, "Mexico's Rurales."
64. It is unclear why Escobar did not take on the role of jefe político himself, but writers in the region and in Mexico City regularly labeled him the regional cacique and acknowledged that he could cause problems for the district and the regime if not kept happy.
65. The transfer of the finca Plancitada in El Rodeo, Guatemala, from Sebastián Escobar to Isidoro Betanzos in 1879, as far as I can tell, removed Escobar's last direct link to coffee production. Aug. 2, 1879, AJPS 1° Civil Soconusco, 1873–1879.
66. Avelino Villareal to Matías Romero, May 17, 1878. AHMR, Correspondencia recibida, f. 25925; Carlos Gris, "Departamento de Soconusco," *El Telégrafo*, Jan. 18, 1882; Gris, *Sebastián Escobar*.
67. Even though the local branch of the society was shuttered, the national organization's weekly bulletin, published under the auspices of the Department of Fomento, continued to publish regular updates on the region's coffee economy. Keller to Matías Romero, Jan. 19, 1880. AHMR, Correspondencia recibida, f. 29747; Keller to Romero, April 15, 1880. AHMR, Correspondencia recibida, f. 29795; Keller to Romero, July 8, 1880. AHMR. Correspondencia recibida, f. 29839; "Efectos de la baja del café en Soconusco," Boletín de la Sociedad Agrícola Mexicana 21: 45 (Dec. 1897), 719.
68. Carlos Gris, "Departamento de Soconusco," *El Telégrafo*, Jan. 18, 1882.
69. Salvador Vázquez, "Interior—Corresponencia particular de la Patria," *La Patria*, Nov. 19, 1880; "Editorial," *El Telégrafo*, Jan. 20, 1882.
70. Ortiz Hernández, "Formación histórico-política de la región del Soconusco."
71. It was not that Tapachula was unsuited to coffee or was lacking in lands.

The municipality stretched from shore well into the Sierra Madre, and most of its residents lived in and around the town itself or in the plains. In total, the Soconusco had about 18,000 residents in 1880, spread between fourteen municipalities. Tapachula and neighboring Tuxtla Chico were the largest at around 5,000 apiece, while the rest were home to between 150 and 1,000 individuals. Ramón Fernández Jesús Guzmán, "Orografía de la Región del Soconusco," 1889. MMOB, Colección General, Varilla CGCHIS06, No. Clasificador 22335C-CGE-7274-B; Romero, *Refutación de las inculpaciones*, 307–09; Viqueira Albán, "Indios y ladinos, arraigados y migrantes en Chiapas."

72. Keller to Romero, Jan. 19, 1880. AHMR, Correspondencia recibida, f. 29747.

73. It is somewhat confusing that no one else became certified as a notary during this period, but as business was still relatively limited and the certification was another arena in which Escobar could likely exert control, perhaps it is to be expected. The first evidence I have of another notary working in town comes from 1892, in a document attesting to the concession granted to the Mexican Land and Colonization Company to be discussed in Chapter Four. "1881 Notaría Pública de José Ibarra: Testimonio," Feb. 16, 1881, APJS 1° Civil Soconusco 1881 01-50; "Compañía Mexicana de Terrenos y Colonización," Feb. 17, 1892, APJS 1° Civil Soconusco 1892, 01-50.

74. Haussler had previously had a run in with the tax collector with regard to annual property taxes, which amounted to some $275, a high fee he had only paid because they threatened to take away the finca. He wrote to Romero after paying the taxes, insisting that it should be Romero, not he, making the payments and griping about the additional sums he had put into the finca without recompense. It is unclear whether or not Romero responded, but this prelude likely predisposed him to the tax collector's machinations. "Promovido por Don Carlos C. Haussler relativamente a la finca "Juárez" de la propiedad de Don Matías Romero," April 14, 1880, APJS 1° Civil Soconusco 1880; Carlos Haussler to Matías Romero, April 27, 1880. AHMR, Correspondencia recibida, f. 29801; Keller to Romero, Aug. 7, 1880. AHMR, Correspondencia recibida, f. 29860.

75. F. M. Peñaloza to Porfirio Díaz, Jan. 19, 1886. CGPD, vol. 11, exp. 1304. See also complaints of mismanagement of the customs office made in the local court in 1880: Aduana Maritima encargado por Hipólito Rebora, July 1880, APJS 1° Civil Soconusco, 1873–1879.

76. P. Jímenez, et. al. to Porfirio Díaz, Jan. 1, 1889. CGPD, vol. 14, exp. 6434.

77. For more on the ways commerce changed legal systems in Latin America, see Adelman, *Republic of Capital*, Part III; Mirow, *Latin American Law*, Part II; essays in Centeno and Ferraro, *State and Nation Making in Latin America and Spain*.

78. A number of these were for members of the Escobar family, but at least a dozen others, primarily concentrated outside of Tapachula, were completed for newcomers to the region. AGN, Fomento y Obras Públicas: Colonización (Baldíos), cajas 1–13.

79. Those making insurance claims were all foreigners whose interests were insured abroad. For example: A. Horn and Compañía Señores Thomlonsen San

Francisco, Oct. 26, 1879, APJS 1° Civil Soconusco, 1873–1879; "Información seguida a solicitud del Señor Antonio Bado y Compañía," 1887, APJS 1° Civil/Penal Soconusco 1873.

80. For example Bado and León, Jan. 29, 1880, APJS 1° Civil Soconusco, 1873–1879; Mallen and Rafaeles, April 28, 1880, APJS 1° Civil Soconusco, 1873–1879.

81. "Solicitud del C. Estanislao Rafales para deslinde de su terreno S. Gerónimo," Feb. 25, 1880, APJS 1° Civil Soconusco 1880.

82. "Feliz Hernández contra Bruno Pérez por reclamación de un terreno," Sept. 4, 1879, APJS 1° Civil Soconusco, 1873–1879.

83. "Juicio verbal hipotecaria instaurado por el C. Bernardo Mallen contra el de igual clase Teodosio Reynoso," Oct. 24, 1879, APJS 1° Civil Soconusco, 1873–1879.

84. Fermín Romero to Matías Romero, Nov. 25, 1883. AHMR, Correspondencia recibida, f. 31342.

85. A brief telegram from Rabasa to Díaz regarding Escobar's interference with elections is suggestive of the power that the cacique had. Elections during the Porfiriato are generally understood as political theater, with the president's political machine controlling results from the lowest level up, especially as an increasing number of positions, including jefe político, were converted to appointments. Yet, in August of 1892, Rabasa complained that Escobar had done all he could to impede elections in the Fifth District, keeping electors away in order to prevent a valid vote from taking place. Escobar and his allies frequently called appointees at the District Court to task, especially one Miguel Lira y Lira, the district attorney, who multiple letter writers accused of drunkenness and collusion. Emilio Rabasa to Porfirio Díaz, Aug. 15, 1892. CGPD, vol. 51, exp. 6122; Lauro Candiani, Tapachula, to Porfirio Díaz, Jan. 12, 1891. CGPD, vol. 16, exp. 266; Citizens of Escuintla to Porfirio Díaz, Jan. 1, 1889. CGPD, vol. 14, exp. 6434; J. Reyes Spindola to Porfirio Díaz, April 13, 1891. CGPD, vol. 16, exp. 4226.

86. Emilio Rabasa, Sebastián Escobar, Emilio Velarca, June 19, 1893, APJS 1° Civil Soconusco 1883, 51–100.

87. Plutarco Rodas to Porfirio Díaz, Oct. 10, 1890. CGPD, vol. 15, exp. 12745.

88. Mexico. Secretaría de Hacienda y Crédito Público, *Noticia de la exportación de mercancías*.

89. Bravo Regidor, "Elecciones de gobernadores durante el Porfiriato," 273.

90. Katz, "Mexico: Restored Republic and Porfiriato, 1867–1910," 36; Garner, *Porfirio Díaz*, 100–02; Falcón, *El jefe político*, 213–14.

91. "El asesinato del General Escobar," *El Siglo Diez y Nueve*, Oct. 5, 1893.

92. Hale, *Emilio Rabasa and the Survival of Porfirian Liberalism*.

93. Benjamin, *A Rich Land, a Poor People*, 43.

94. Lauro Candiani to Porfirio Díaz, Jan. 12, 1891. CGPD, vol. 16, exp. 266.

95. Rabasa to Díaz, Dec. 11, 1891. CGPD, vol. 50, exp. 6781; Candiani to Díaz, Dec. 12, 1891. CGPD, vol. 50, exp. 6710; Escobar to Díaz, 1891. CGPD, vol. 50, exp. 6809; Escobar to Díaz, Jan. 5, 1892. CGPD, vol. 17, exp. 509.

96. Rabasa to Díaz, Jan. 9, 1892. CGPD, vol. 17, exp. 1153; Rabasa to Díaz, March 2, 1892. CGPD, vol. 17, exp. 4546.

97. "El asesinato del General Escobar," *El Siglo Diez y Nueve*, Oct. 5, 1893.
98. Rabasa to Díaz, Oct. 14, 1893. CGPD, vol. 18, exp. 15335; Teodomiro Palacios to Porfirio Díaz, Nov. 1, 1893. CGPD, vol. 18, exp. 16432.
99. Rabasa to Díaz, Oct. 14, 1893. CGPD, vol. 18, exp. 15335; Palacios to Díaz, Nov. 1, 1893. CGPD, vol. 18, exp. 16432.
100. Lauro Candiani was followed in late 1892 by Manuel Figueroa. He was replaced not long after by Isaac de Jesús Salas, himself replaced early in 1896 by a military commander, Colonel Julián Hornedo. Hornedo only held the position for a year before being replaced by his subordinate, Mauro Cándano. Cándano would hold his post until the end of the decade, when Plácido Gomez, who had once worked as a surveyor for a foreign-owned land company doing business in the Soconusco, took over. He held the post until 1906, when Leopoldo Salazar was appointed to the post. He was the first locally born jefe político in fifteen years. See *El Periodico Oficial del Estado de Chiapas* for the names of officials. See Plácido Gómez, *Croquis de la división de terrenos baldíos fracción 1ª Soconusco, Chiapas*, Map 1889. MMOB, Servicio de Información Agroalimentaria y Pesquera, SAGARPA, Colección General, No. Clasificador 408-CGE-7274-A, Varilla CG-CHIS03, for Gómez's prior employment.
101. There was a spate of complaints about Mauro Cándano, the jefe político in 1898, again regarding corruption and blatant abuse of powers against both locals and migrants. When the governor decided not to force Cándano's resignation, a number of local and foreign planters thanked him for leaving the jefe político in place. Sarah Washbrook includes the incident in her dissertation, basing her account on the master's thesis of María de los Angeles Ortíz Hernández, but neither know what to make of it, as Cándano was connected to both the Mexican Land and Colonization Company and many of the important local families. Because no one would come forward to support the claims of the primary complainer—Joaquín Rodas y Martínez, a member of a local merchant family—it is possible that there was a personal conflict at the base of the charges, though Rodas y Martínez's list of abuses committed by Cándano was incredibly specific, particularly with regard to harm done to lower class locals. Francisco León, the governor who appointed Cándano to his position, admitted to Cándano's greediness and possible graft but let him remain in power. J. Rodas y Martínez to Porfirio Díaz, July 2, 1898. CGPD, vol. 23, exp. 9874; León to Díaz, Oct. 19, 1898. CGPD, vol. 23, exp. 13550; León to Díaz, Aug. 5, 1898. CGPD, vol. 57, exp. 2843. Washbrook, "Exports, Ethnicity and Labour Markets," 283–84.
102. People appearing in court had previously invoked aspects of the civil code, but most doing so had been foreigners and they had done so only occasionally.
103. Taboada and Robledo, May 11, 1894, APJS 1º Civil Soconusco Varios Años.
104. Ortega and Martínez, April 3, 1889, APJS 1º Civil Soconusco 1889.
105. Cárdenas v. Moya de Ramírez, May 17, 1897, APJS 1º Civil Soconusco 1887.
106. For example, see "Interdicto promovido por Desiderio Rivera contra Gerónimo Quiterio," Sept. 5, 1887, APJS 1º Civil Soconusco 1887; "Interdicto de recuperar la posesión entablado por los Ciudadanos Juan Albarado, José María

Vergudo y Mauricio Lopez, contra el Señor Francisco Garcia," July 13, 1892, APJS 1° Civil Soconusco 1892, 01-50; Lopez v. Lopez, July 7, 1905, APJS 1° Civil Soconusco 1905, 01-50.

107. Mexico, *Censo general de 1900*.

108. AGN, Fomento, Obras Públicas, y Colonización, caja 10, exp. 1072, folleto 2356; "Providencia precautoria solicitada por el Señor Pedro del Cueto," Feb. 3, 1898, APJS 1° Civil Soconusco 1888; Cueto y Cia v. Brewer in "Registro de Hipotecas 1899," July 19, 1899, ARPPC Varios Doc Privados 1889; "Ejecutivo Mercantil Retor Guillermo Henkel, Demandado Luis Brewer," Sept. 18, 1901, APJS 1° Civil Soconusco 1901, 201–250; Brewer v. Harrison, Aug. 10, 1903, APJS 1° Civil Soconusco 1903, 01-50; Brewer and Isaac and Samuel of London, July 21, 1899, ARPPC Varios Doc Privados 1889: Registro de Hipotecas 1899; "Hipotecario Actores Isaac Samuel Rio, Luis R. Brewer, Guillermo Henkel," Aug. 30, 1899, APJS 1° Civil Soconusco 1899; "Testimonio de la acta de protesta de una letra expedido a favor del Señor Alvino Schulze como tenedor de aquello," Sept. 7, 1901, APJS 1° Civil Soconusco 1901, 251–300; "Ejecutivo Mercantil Retor Guillermo Henkel, Demandado Luis Brewer," Sept. 18, 1901, APJS 1° Civil Soconusco 1901, 201–250; Kaerger, *Agricultura y colonización en México en 1900*, 118; "Oton Marth pide que el juzgado declare en estado de quiebra al Señor Luis R Brewer," Aug. 2, 1899, APJS 1° Civil Soconusco 1899; Brewer and Isaac and Samuel of London, March 30, 1905, ARPPC Varios Doc Privados 1889: Registro de Hipotecas 1899.

109. The exact opening date for the Registro Público de la Propiedad y el Comercio is unclear but falls sometime in 1893 or 1894. Such offices were mandated by the civil code of 1870, but at least in the Soconusco, the fulfillment of their duties was carried out at the civil court until that point. For clarity's sake, I am translating this phrase as public records office rather than public property registry. *Código civil del Distrito Federal y territorio de la Baja-California*, Título XXIII.

110. There were at least four notaries at work in the Soconusco by the 1900s. Escobar's buddy José Encarnación Ibarra stops appearing as such in the early 1890s. Manuel Salvador Elorza (from Mexico City), who appears most frequently, Enoch Paniagua (origins unknown), Teofilo Figueroa (a lawyer from Tapachula), and Juan Felix Zepeda (origins unknown) took on the work of officiating documents across the 1890s and early 1900s. This is still a relatively small number for a region with the Soconusco's level of economic activity. I have not found a good explanation for why more did not take up this potentially lucrative work. For comparison, see Juliette Levy's work on the proliferation of notaries in the early years of the Yucatán's henequen economy. Levy, *The Making of a Market*.

111. See Chapter Six of this book.

112. For the prototypical example, see Womack, *Zapata and the Mexican Revolution*.

113. Keller to Romero, Jan. 19, 1880. AHMR, Correspondencia recibida, f. 29747.

114. "Ayuntamientos en el Estado," AHCH, Gobernación 1909, vol. 1, exp. 2.

115. B. Acosta to P. Díaz, Dec. 21, 1909. CGPD, vol. 34, exp. 19428; Compañía de Teatro de Tapachula," Jan. 9, 1907, ARPPC Doc Priv 1900 y 1907: Registro de Comercio 2° Auxiliar Libro No 3, Sociedades y Poderes Año 1907; Telegrama

to R. Rabasa, Jan. 21, 1909, AHCH, Fondo de Gobierno, Fomento, 1909, vol. VI, exp. 23: Agricultura.

116. Alejandro Trejo represented the Soconusco from sometime before 1885 until 1887. He may have had ties to the ranching families in the lowlands of the Soconusco, as he proposed legislation related to the slaughter of cattle, but he himself seems to have been from central Chiapas. Those who followed him were similarly tied more to the coastal ranchlands rather than the foothills of the region. Only in the late 1890s did Ángel María Pérez, who at least owned land in the coffee zone of Tapachula, come to serve as the district's delegate. "Sesión del día 12 de Noviembre de 1884," *Periódico Oficial del Estado de Chiapas*, July 4, 1885, 3; "Segunda junta," *Periódico Oficial del Estado de Chiapas*, Oct. 9, 1897, 6; MLCC to Ángel María Pérez, April 6, 1899, ARPPC Varios Doc Privados 1889.

117. The labor and fraud case that makes up the meat of Chapter Five was one such instance.

118. This is the most frequent type of document pertaining to the Soconusco in the state archive. Federal law required foreigners interested in buying lands in the "zona fronteriza con Guatemala" to petition for permission to do so in the interest of national security. See, for example, A. Aldasor al Gobernador, Feb. 26, 1907, AHCH, Fondo de Gobierno, Fomento, 1907, vol. VI, exp. 16: Extranjeros que desean adquirir bienes raices en el Estado.

119. Agustín Farrera, a member of a prominent family in Tuxtla Gutiérrez, briefly represented a group of planters from the Soconusco, including Germans, Mexicans, Brits, and an American. Through his auspices they petitioned the president for improved treaties with Guatemala, the expansion of banking services, and the lowering of tariffs. Coffee planters across the nation did benefit from a suspension of export tariffs when global coffee prices collapsed in the same period, but it is unclear that the advocacy of Soconusco planters had anything to do with this. "La exportación del café," *Boletín de la Sociedad Agrícola Mexicana* 23:44 (Nov. 1899), 877; Agustín Farrera to Porfirio Díaz, Oct. 12, 1899. CGPD, vol. 24, exp. 15132; Bernardo Mallen to Agustín Farrera, March 16, 1900, CGDP, vol. 25, exp. 2870.

120. Haber, *Crony Capitalism and Economic Growth in Latin America*; Passananti, "Dynamizing the Economy in a Façon Irréguliére."

121. Guerra, *México*, 315–18.

122. Colonists were exempt from military service, all taxes except those collected at the municipal level, import tariffs on equipment and plants for their land and housing, export tariffs on their production, and fees on legal documents from consulates. Mexico. Secretaría de Fomento, *Memoria 1892–1896*, 11–12.

123. It is difficult to tell how often and in what degree finqueros were underreporting the value of their property for tax purposes. I only have a few cases where I was able to find both a tax receipt and a valuation of a finca for the purposes of serving as collateral, but in those cases, valuations for tax purposes are generally lower. Nonetheless, the Soconusco was still generating more revenue in taxes than most other districts. "Tesorería y dirección general de rentas . . . ," *Periódico Oficial del Estado de Chiapas*, Jan. 10, 1897, 5; "Tesorería y dirección general de rentas . . . ," *Periódico Oficial del Estado de Chiapas*, Feb. 22, 1902, 5; "Tesorería

y dirección general de rentas . . . ," *Periódico Oficial del Estado de Chiapas*, Feb. 4, 1905, 7; "Tesorería y dirección general de rentas . . . " *Periódico Oficial del Estado de Chiapas*, Feb. 10, 1912, 7.

124. Washbrook, *Producing Modernity in Mexico*, 116–17; Benjamin, *A Rich Land, a Poor People*, 46.

125. Pawson, *Transport and Economy*; Guldi, *Roads to Power*; Hanley and Lopes, "Municipal Plenty, Municipal Poverty, and Brazilian Economic Development, 1836–1850."

126. As Mexico City's bureaucracy grew, regulation of railroads and other public works projects was eventually siphoned off from Fomento and transferred to a new department. Until that point, Fomento's reports to Congress contained pages on pages of updates on myriad road and bridge projects, railroad concessions, port modernization, and the drainage of the Valley of Mexico. The topic deserves a great deal more research, but the best done thus far can be seen in Coatsworth, *Growth Against Development*; Garner, "The Politics of National Development in Late Porfirian Mexico"; Kuntz Ficker and Riguzzi, *Ferrocarriles y vida económica en México, 1850–1950*; Connolly, *El contratista de Don Porfirio*; Connolly, "Introducción a obras públicas"; Van Hoy, "La Marcha Violenta?"; Zuleta, *De cultivos y contribuciones*; Passananti, "Dynamizing the Economy in a Façon Irréguliére"; Garner, *British Lions and Mexican Eagles*; Candiani, *Dreaming of Dry Land*; Bess, "Revolutionary Paths"; Mexico, Secretaría de Fomento, *Memoria 1883–1885*, Vol. II.

127. Romero had gone so far as to form a railroad company with a number of American investors including Ulysses S. Grant. Another concession was given to a British man, Edward C. Wise, in 1881, to build a railway connecting the port of San Benito to Tapachula, along with the respective telegraph lines and an improved pier in the port, but this, too, failed to go anywhere. Molina Pérez, *Por los rieles de Chiapas*; Coatsworth, *Growth Against Development*, 37–41.

128. Márquez Colín, "La administración hacendaria de Matías Romero"; Beatty, *Institutions and Investment*, 36–38; Aboites and Jáuregui, *Penuria sin fin*; Guerra, *México*, 316.

129. For a comparative case on another coffee frontier, see Hanley and Lopes, "Municipal Plenty, Municipal Poverty, and Brazilian Economic Development, 1836–1850."

130. Washbrook, *Producing Modernity in Mexico*, 168–69.

131. It is important to note that while the rail network was growing, it never approached the density of equivalent networks in the United States or Great Britain. Many agricultural regions across Mexico continued to rely on mules or human cargo bearers to transport their goods to market. Bado v. Fetens, Dec. 12, 1879, APJS 1° Civil Soconusco, 1873–1879; Bado v. Brewer, Nov. 5, 1889, APJS 1° Civil Soconusco 1889: Libro 4° Registro de Sentencias; Manuel Carrascosa to Porfirio Díaz, Nov. 9, 1889. CGPD, vol. 14, exp. 12215; Molina Pérez, *Por los rieles de Chiapas*, 25, 28–30.

132. Another road, from Motozintla to Tuzantán was in the works in 1907, with many of the costs covered by the jefe político of Motozintla, while the salaries of thirty day laborers—$0.37 a day, plus $1.00 a day for the supervisor—were

covered by the state treasury. Similarly, there are other indications of the state covering some repair costs, though generally as a reimbursement to the local officials rather than outright payments. After 1907, no further indications of state involvement in road construction or repairs appear through 1913. León to Díaz, Jan. 13, 1897. CGPD, vol. 57, exp. 576; AHCH, Fondo de Gobierno, Fomento, 1907, vol. III, exp. 10: Construcción y reparación de caminos.

133. Leopoldo Salazar to Ramón Rabasa, Feb. 12, 1907, AHCH, Fondo de Gobierno, Fomento, vol. 9, exp. 30–33: Puentes; Dirección General de Telegrafos to Flavio Guillen, Jan. 15, 1913, AHCH, Fondo de Gobierno, Fomento, 1913, vol. 2, exp. 16; Agenor Culebro to Secretarío General de Gobierno, March 26, 1913, AHCH, Fondo de Gobierno, Fomento, 1913, vol. 2, exp. 16.

134. "El Ferrocarril Panamericano," *El Sur de México*, April 28, 1907.

135. Molina Pérez, *Por los rieles de Chiapas*.

136. According to one American visitor, the humid climate of the coast soon caused the cane seats to crumble, as well as the railroad ties, leading to frequent derailments. The crew and the passengers would clamber out and help guide the train back onto the tracks. Pollard, *A Busy Time in Mexico*, 55–58.

137. Planters and merchants switched their shipping allegiances so quickly that by 1911 the Spanish merchant who held a controlling interest in the company that ferried goods between the shore and ships in San Benito had to dissolve the company. "Since the establishment of the Pan American Railroad," he wrote, "the business of this company has declined to such a degree that this past year there was essentially no income."

138. Pablo Hinze to Esteban Figueroa, Sept. 29, 1911; Juan Monribot to Figueroa, Sept. 8, 1911; and Guillermo Kahle to Figueroa, Sept. 26, 1911. AHCH, Fondo de Gobierno, Fomento, 1911, vol. 2, exp. 14.

139. Wasserman, *Capitalists, Caciques, and Revolution*; Wells, *Yucatán's Gilded Age*, 1985; Katz, "Mexico: Restored Republic and Porfiriato, 1867–1910," 36; Wasserman, *Pesos and Politics*.

CHAPTER FOUR: THE LANDSCAPE OF PRODUCTION

1. Isaac de Jesus Salas v. Unión Juárez, "1896 No. 161 fojas 91 Copia," 1896, APJS 1° Civil Soconusco 1896.

2. *Memoria que presenta el Ciudadano Manuel Carrascosa*, x-4.

3. "Documentos en que se funda la contestación de Don Teófilo Acebo a la demanda de Don Manuel Sánchez Deleón," Nov. 12, 1891, APJS 1° Civil Soconusco 1883, 51–100.

4. As Antonio Escobar Ohmstede and Matthew Butler point out in the introduction to a recent collection of essays on Mexican agrarian history, the country had plenty of land at the turn of the century. The challenge for the government was in rationalizing and normalizing and taxing that land. Escobar Ohmstede and Butler, "Introduction," 34.

5. A rich historiography of cartography and our reading of maps related to the colonial period takes seriously not only the relations of power that went into mapmaking, but also the real constitutive powers of maps themselves. Scholarship on the modern era has also embraced these ideas and further demonstrated how maps

could both set the foundation for later coercive capabilities as well as undermine state's real knowledge of their territories and inhabitants. Lopes, "Historias de la Cartografía de Iberoamérica"; Dym, "Taking a Walk on the Wild Side"; Mundy, "The Images of Eighteenth-Century Urban Reform in Mexico City and the Plan of José Antonio Alzate"; Craib, *Cartographic Mexico*; Dym and Offen, *Mapping Latin America*; Scott, *Seeing like a State*.

6. This followed an earlier, quite successful forcible sale of much of the Catholic Church's holdings in the country.

7. There is a rich historiography on both large-scale and small-scale landholding in nineteenth-century Mexico, but rarely have historians attempted to address the intersection of the two processes of privatization going on during the era. For some key examples of this historiography, see Brading, *Haciendas and Ranchos in the Mexican Bajío, León, 1700–1860*; Wells, "Family Elites in a Boom-and-Bust Economy"; Joseph, *Revolution from Without*; Lindley, *Haciendas and Economic Development*; Wasserman, *Capitalists, Caciques, and Revolution*; Wells, "From Hacienda to Plantation"; Chowning, *Wealth and Power in Provincial Mexico*; Gómez Serrano, *Haciendas y ranchos de Aguascalientes*; Escobar Ohmstede and Schryer, "Las Sociedades agrarias en el norte de Hidalgo, 1856–1900"; Purnell, "With All Due Respect"; Escobar Ohmstede, Falcón, and Buve, *Pueblos, comunidades y municipios frente a los proyectos modernizadores en América Latina, siglo XIX*; Kourí, *A Pueblo Divided*; Mendoza García, *Los bienes de comunidad y la defensa de las tierras en la Mixteca oaxaqueña*; Escobar Ohmstede and Butler, *Mexico in Transition*.

8. Kourí, "La invención del ejido."

9. See Washbrook, *Producing Modernity in Mexico*, Ch. 2.

10. See, for example, Womack, *Zapata and the Mexican Revolution*; Tutino, *From Insurrection to Revolution in Mexico*; Hu-DeHart, *Yaqui Resistance and Survival*; Craib, *Cartographic Mexico*; Kourí, *A Pueblo Divided*; Mendoza García, *Los bienes de comunidad y la defensa de las tierras en la Mixteca oaxaqueña*.

11. For discussion of emigration and colonization policies elsewhere in the Americas, see Sábato, *Agrarian Capitalism and the World Market*; Adelman, *Frontier Development*; Nugent, "New World Frontiers"; Pérez Meléndez, "The Business of Peopling."

12. States had previously been in charge of the division of baldíos; only in the 1850s did they become the purview of the national government. Holden, *Mexico and the Survey of Public Lands*, 9.

13. Holden, 15–16; for a specific case, see Fenner, "Los deslindes de terrenos baldíos."

14. Within the context of the history of coffee, the colonization process that played out in the Soconusco seems to point to a combination of various experiences in other countries. The maintenance of local title found in Costa Rica and El Salvador here accompanied the colonization efforts and frontier expansionism of São Paulo. Gudmundson, "Peasant, Farmer, Proletarian"; Lauria-Santiago, *An Agrarian Republic*; Holloway, *Immigrants on the Land*.

15. See, for example, the concession described by Jesus María Muñoz in his

defense of Unión Juárez's lands. Isaac de Jesús Salas v. Unión Juárez, "1896 No. 161 fojas 91 Copia," 1896, APJS 1° Civil Soconusco 1896.

16. Federico Baker to Matías Romero, Sept. 20, 1877. AHMR, Correspondencia recibida, f. 22293.

17. Mexico. Secretaría de Hacienda y Crédito Público, *Comercio exterior*.

18. See the arguments of new institutionalists like Douglass North and Stephen Haber. North, *Institutions, Institutional Change, and Economic Performance*; Haber, *The Politics of Property Rights*.

19. Originally called the International Company of Mexico and later renamed the Land Company of Chiapas, Mexico, Ltd.

20. According to the law governing public lands, the Department of Fomento set the price and published a schedule of costs by state and territory every two years. Land companies could set their own prices and tended to charge more per hectare for small lots of land than for large lots. For example, the Mexican Land and Colonization Company (MLCC) regularly charged between MX$25 and MX$30 a hectare for lots of around five hectares, while lots over 100 hectares went for between MX$2 and MX$12 a hectare. Mexico, *Legislación de terrenos baldios*, 4.

21. It is worth noting that 128 hectares is not a large piece of land. Because of limited mechanization, coffee in the nineteenth century had little economy of scale and is thus unusual in the diversity of landholding patterns that it engendered, as discussed in Chapter Two. Even so, 128 hectares is on the low side for coffee production. Within Mexico, this size of property would in no way be regarded as *latifundia*, or overly expansive landholding, and the application of the term *hacienda* is even potentially problematic. Thanks to Steven Topik for reminding me of this fact. The analysis of large, also called public or notarized, land sales (over MX$500) in this chapter is based on the integration of deeds of sale and incomplete indices from the Registro Público de la Propiedad y el Comercio for the Soconusco, information gleaned from local judicial records, and Justus Fenner's database of about 450 sales made by the MLCC in the department, resulting in a database of about 1,000 notarized property sales between 1870 and 1918. The analysis of small or private sales (under MX$500) is based on equivalent documentation for about 1,900 sales between 1890 and 1918. With regard to small sales, complete indices for the years 1894, 1899–1901, 1904–1905, and 1910–1912 are available and form the base for the majority of my analysis of cross-time shift in the market. I include sales of rural land but not *potreros* (land dedicated to grazing) or urban lots that indicate residential rather than agricultural usage.

22. This section is drawn from the three volumes of municipal documents submitted to the national government in the 1930s during the post-revolutionary land reform and reconstitution of ejidos. AGA, Asunto: Dotación, Estado: Chiapas, Municipio: Cacahoatán, exp. 408, legajo 7.

23. Kourí, *A Pueblo Divided*, 144; Kourí, "La invención del ejido."

24. Tuxtla Chico and Tapachula both expanded their ejidos in the late 1840s. Legajo de comunicaciones del Juzgado de 1a Instancia, 1847. AMT, Tuxtla Chico, Presidencia Municipal 1837–1853, caja 1, exp. 2; Comunicaciones de la prefectura, 1849. AMT, Tapachula, Presidencia Municipal 1846–1940, caja 2, exp. s/n, año.

25. This made Cacahoatán a midsized municipality for the region. Tapachula and Tuxtla Chico had 5,200 and 4,700 residents respectively, but most other municipalities had somewhere between 200 and 400 in 1880. A few others—Huehuetán and Mazatán, towns with similar pre-Columbian roots—also had about 900 residents. Viqueira Albán, "Indios y ladinos, arraigados y migrantes en Chiapas."

26. AGA, Asunto: Dotación, Estado: Chiapas, Municipio: Cacahoatán, exp. 408, legajo 7.

27. Romero only listed fincas with at least fifty cuerdas of land under cultivation. According to a German agronomist who traveled through the region in later years, a hectare was about twenty-three cuerdas of cultivated land. Romero, *Refutación de las inculpaciones hechas al c. Matías Romero por el gobierno de Guatemala*, 306–09; Kaerger, *Agricultura y colonización en México en 1900*, 109.

28. Keller to Romero, Jan. 19, 1880. AHMR, Correspondencia recibida, f. 29747.

29. Keller to Romero, July 8, 1880. AHMR, Correspondencia recibida, f. 29839.

30. The law recognized the confusion of ownership practices in the state, mentioning lands assigned to towns as ejidos, lands measured for towns without particular designation, towns where no ejidos had been designated or measured, land that had already been claimed by a head of household, and so on. It also laid out the means by which repartition would be carried out. Surveyors chosen by the state would work with a representative designated by the *ayuntamiento* or municipal council of the town where the ejidos were located to put together a map of lots, to which they would extend title to the residents of the lot so long as the proper fees had been paid on the value of the land. That value would be decided based on current land prices designated by the government. Mexico, *Legislación de terrenos baldios*, 33–34.

31. Ibarra to Romero, Aug. 30, 1871. AHMR, Correspondencia recibida, f. 15173.

32. It is unclear how the quality of the land was determined, and this may be another instance in which the municipal council manipulated state regulations to ease the fiscal burden on their constituents. AGA, Asunto: Dotación, Estado: Chiapas, Municipio: Cacahoatán, exp. 408, legajo 7, Jan. 1880.

33. Ibid.

34. Keller to Romero, Aug. 7, 1880. AHRM, Cartas recibidas, exp. 29860.

35. AGA, Asunto: Dotación, Estado: Chiapas, Municipio: Cacahoatán, exp. 408, legajo 7, March 27, 1881.

36. Keller to Matías Romero, Jan. 19, 1880. AHMR, Correspondencia recibida, f. 29747.

37. AGA, Asunto: Dotación, Estado: Chiapas, Municipio: Cacahoatán, exp. 408, legajo 7, Feb. 1882.

38. AGA, Asunto: Dotación, Estado: Chiapas, Municipio: Cacahoatán, exp. 408, legajo 7, Nov. 26, 1881.

39. Ibid.

40. Romero, having recently lost his friend José Martínez to Escobar's violent

retribution, was quick to lay blame at the cacique's feet. Augusta Rigaud Keller to Romero, April 29, 1882. AHMR, Correspondencia recibida, f. 30426.

41. "Acta de transaccion celebrada entre los acredores de la testamentaria de D Santiago R Keller," July 10, 1883, APJS 1° Civil Soconusco 1883.

42. Gris, *Sebastián Escobar*, 47.

43. AGA, Asunto: Dotación, Estado: Chiapas, Municipio: Cacahoatán, exp. 408, legajo 7, 1886; Dec. 1889.

44. AGA, Asunto: Dotación, Estado: Chiapas, Municipio: Cacahoatán, exp. 408, legajo 7, Feb. 23, 1889.

45. *Memoria que presenta el Ciudadano Manuel Carrascosa*, x-4.

46. In October of 1889 Camilo Canel, born in France but long resident in Cacahoatán, petitioned to expand his ejidal holdings into land claimed by a local man, Toribio Sandoval. Canel asserted his rights as the head of a large family who would put the land to better use than Sandoval, who only used it to graze cattle. AGA, Asunto: Dotación, Estado: Chiapas, Municipio: Cacahoatán, exp. 408, legajo 7, Oct. 1889.

47. See fifty-three of these hand drawn titles on "El Soconusco Cervantino: Cartografía de una encomienda imaginaria," CD-Rom. Archivo General de la Nación, México; *Memoria que presenta el Ciudadano Manuel Carrascosa*, x-4.

48. AGN, Fomento y Obras Públicas: Colonización (Baldíos), cajas 1–13.

49. When they purchased land from the Department of Fomento, they paid 50 or 75 cents a hectare, even if they had already reported the value of the land in question as higher when they paid taxes on it. *Memoria que presenta el Ciudadano Manuel Carrascosa*, x-4.

50. Multiple plans to build a railroad along the Pacific coast were shuttered across these decades. Another scheme led to the ousting of Governor Manuel Carrascosa when shady dealings with government bonds came to light. The grandest plan for modernizing Chiapas through private investment and management was dreamed up by José Mora, a Chiapaneco politician, and his partner in New York. The prospectus for this company is impressive in its breadth of ambition and its expressions of what modern economic development would mean in Chiapas, all funded on the back of one thousand Mexican colonists for whom they would receive government subsidies. See "The Chiapas Company," "Prospectus," (no date), MCP: box 1, folders 20–22 and José Mora to John Morris, July 25, 1888, MCP: box 1, folder 10. Research done by José Angel Hernández puts this emphasis on Mexican colonists in perspective. While historians have long focused on the language of "whitening" that circulated throughout the Americas in the nineteenth century, little to none of this ideology was codified in Mexico. Rather, Mexican policy focused on shoring up its borders with both native, especially indigenous, and foreign settlers. Hernández, "From Conquest to Colonization: Indios and Colonization Policies after Mexican Independence." For more on the various railway concessions see: Molina Pérez, *Por los rieles de Chiapas*, 22–33; for more on the Porfirian practice of granting concessions, see Connolly, *El contratista de Don Porfirio*.

51. Emilio Rabasa, Sebastián Escobar, Emilio Velarca, June 19, 1893, APJS 1° Civil Soconusco 1883, 51–100.

52. The International Company of Mexico (ICOM) was initially headed by a well-connected German, Louis Huller, but backed by American financing. Huller reached out to Escobar, attempting to negotiate a deal with the cacique wherein he would be paid MX$150 per month plus 2.5 percent of the profits from land sales to, essentially, stay out of the company's way. Escobar agreed to the terms, as Governor Rabasa pointed out in a letter to the cacique in 1893, just before his death. Based on the timing, it is likely that Escobar never saw any of the promised profits. The company itself was flummoxed by the region's difficult terrain as well as Mexico's shifting political environment. Just as it finished its preliminary surveys, Díaz forced its American-backed owner into selling the concession. Díaz, determined to balance American interests with more European investment, used legal and political manipulation to eventually force Huller's arrest and near-bankruptcy. ICOM's unfulfilled concessions were transferred to the British-backed MLCC in 1889. Fenner, "Los deslindes de terrenos baldíos," 131, 135, 167–74.

53. See "Colonization in Mexico," *San Francisco Chronicle*, April 4, 1882, and Humphreys Seargeant, *San Antonio Nexapa*, 15–17.

54. See Chapter Six of this book.

55. Interestingly, the moment the MLCC began selling property is also the moment that annotations of Mexican as opposed to Central and South American pesos began to prevail in legal filings. That said, complaints about the scarcity of Mexican currency continued, so it is unlikely that the MLCC was actually collecting Mexican currency. It may, in fact, have been paid in multiple currencies, as those to whom it sold land were from across the globe. Yet in the interest of saving face and presenting formal accounts, it noted all contracts in Mexican pesos.

56. For a standard early sale, see Bejarano v. Catlin, Jan. 13, 1893, APJS 1° Civil Soconusco 1884 or MLCC to Widmaier Hnos., March 16, 1895, ARPPC Doc Priv 1894, 1895, 1899–1900: Registro Público de la propiedad Año de 1895.

57. Alfredo Moody for Mexican Land and Colonization Company, Dec. 18, 1907, ARPPC Doc Priv 1900 y 1907; MLCC to Carlos Auerbach, Feb. 13, 1895, ARPPC Doc Priv 1894, 1895, 1899–1900: Registro Público de la propiedad Año de 1895.

58. The data on MLCC sales has been gathered from multiple sources. Fenner's work includes a list of 450 fincas surveyed and sold by the MLCC between 1889 and 1916 based on documents filed by the various iterations of the company with the government. My own research has amended and added another 300 sales to this list, and I will be referring to both Fenner's appendix and the original deeds of sale that I have found filed at the Registro Público de la Propiedad in Tapachula, as they provide more detailed information than the Fenner data and include a number of sales not noted in his appendix. See "Anexo 9-3: Lista de fincas vendidas en Chiapas," in Fenner, "Los deslindes de terrenos baldíos" and specific documents as noted.

59. Humphreys Seargeant, *San Antonio Nexapa*, 113.

60. Compañía Mexicana Limitada de Terrenos y Colonización, Sept. 4, 1892, APJS 1° Civil Soconusco 1880. The planters charged were Alejandro Córdova, Santiago Catlin, Enrique Schellanger, Federico Quinby, Archie Vallance, Federico Kraul, Juan Sarriente, Carlos Lesher, José Figueroa and Julian Figueroa in Las

Chicharras in the municipality of Tapachula and Blas Zamora, Crecencio Galvez, Jesus Anzueto and Francisco Rodriguez in Cuilco Viejo in Huehuetán.

61. Humphreys Seargeant, *San Antonio Nexapa*, 120–21.

62. See, for example, MLCC to Alejandro Córdova, July 1, 1908, ARPPC Doc Priv 1902, 1908: 1908 Registro Público Sección 2a Hipotecas; MLCC to Ramón Toledo, Nov. 18, 1904, ARPPC Doc Priv 1902, 1908: Año de 1904 sección segunda Hipotecas.

63. AGA, Asunto: Dotación, Estado: Chiapas, Municipio: Cacahoatán, exp. 408, legajo 7, July 31, 1894.

64. AGA, Asunto: Dotación, Estado: Chiapas, Municipio: Cacahoatán, exp. 408, legajo 7, 1896, "Colector de Rentas," various.

65. AGA, Asunto: Dotación, Estado: Chiapas, Municipio: Cacahoatán, exp. 408, legajo 7, Epitacio Hernández, Nov. 26, 1892.

66. AGA, Asunto: Dotación, Estado: Chiapas, Municipio: Cacahoatán, exp. 408, legajo 7, Ireneo Espinoza, Aug. 10, 1892; AGA, Asunto: Dotación, Estado: Chiapas, Municipio: Cacahoatán, exp. 408, legajo 7, Nov. 10, 1905; AGA, Asunto: Dotación, Estado: Chiapas, Municipio: Cacahoatán, exp. 408, legajo 7, Secretaría General de Gobierno, Feb. 19, 1906.

67. See AGA, Asunto: Dotación, Estado: Chiapas, Municipio: Cacahoatán, exp. 408, legajo 7 as well as "Concentracción de los documentos de todos los Ejidos," AHCH, Fondo de Gobierno, Fomento, 1908, vol. 2, exp. 13; AHCH, Fondo de Gobierno, Fomento, 1909, vol. 2, exp. 12.

68. Municipal councils were notoriously bad at paying these surveyors on time. By 1904, Virgilio Figueroa, the state surveyor who had charge of the Soconusco starting in 1895, was owed more than MX$32,000 in back pay. The state apparently set up a payment plan to cover the money owed to him at the rate of MX$50 monthly, which it raised to MX$150 monthly in 1901. In 1910, the Contador Encargado al Secretario General de Fomento in Tuxtla Gutiérrez passed along a report on the outstanding balance due to Figueroa for his work in the department, which came to MX$31,189.54. The state treasury and local ejidal agents had paid parts of his salary along the way, but only in the amount of MX$8,906.18. His total pay for these six years of work, then, was some MX$40,000 of which he had been paid less than a quarter. AHCH, Fondo de Gobierno, Fomento, 1910, vol. 6, exp. 28; AHCH Fondo de Gobierno, Fomento, vol. 3, exp. 12.

69. "Apeo y deslinde de la finca La Reforma," June 12, 1909, APJS 1º Civil Soconusco 1909; AGA, Asunto: Dotación, Estado: Chiapas, Municipio: Cacahoatán, exp. 408, legajo 7; Kourí, *A Pueblo Divided*.

70. "Concentración de los documentos de todos los Ejidos," AHCH, Fonde de Gobierno, Fomento 1908, vol. 2, exp. 12.

71. AHCH, Fondo de Gobierno, Fomento, 1909, vol. 2, exp. 12; "Concentración de los documentos de todos los Ejidos," AHCH, Fondo de Gobierno, Fomento, 1908, vol. 2, exp. 12.

72. "Interdicto de recuperar promovido por el Sr. Margarito Perez contra el Sr Teodomiro Garcia," AMT Juzgado 1a Instancia caja 2, exp. 18, Año 1892.

73. AHCH, Fondo de Gobierno, Fomento, 1911, vol. 2, exp. 12; "Impersonal," in AHCH, Fondo de Gobierno, Fomento, 1913, vol. 5, exp. 25.

74. Chiapas and Moguel, *Nueva colección de leyes de hacienda vigentes en el estado de Chiapas*, 109.

75. Rabasa was writing to Díaz to explain that a letter the president had received petitioning for the suspension of repartition in Unión Juárez had actually been written by a local planter who had "at the least $100,000." The vecinos of the town had been the ones to request a surveyor to begin the privatization process, and the planter worried that he would lose out to the poor, who received their lots preferentially. Rabasa to Díaz, May 21, 1894. CGPD, vol. 19, exp. 7417.

76. "Concentración de los documentos de todos los Ejidos," AHCH, Fondo de Gobierno, Fomento, 1908, vol. 2, exp. 12.

77. P de Pananá to Porfirio Díaz, Nov. 28, 1895. CGPD, vol. 54, exp. 6833; Salvador Mora to Porfirio Díaz, Oct. 22, 1896. CGPD, vol. 55, exp. 5974; Mora to Díaz, May 27, 1898. CGPD, vol. 57, exp. 1745; León to Díaz, April 14, 1899. CGPD, vol. 48, exp. 1508.

78. In 1904, six individuals registered for "lotes de pobres" in Cacahoatán, but none of the titles included in a 1908 overview of titles expedited included reference to the practice. "Concentración de los documentos de todos los Ejidos," AHCH, Fondo de Gobierno, Fomento, 1908, vol. 2, exp. 12; AGA, Asunto: Dotación, Estado: Chiapas, Municipio: Cacahoatán, exp. 408, legajo 7, 1904, "Registro de los individuos que se han inscrito como pobres para el reparto de lotes de terreno en el Ejido de esta poblacion."

79. AGA, Asunto: Dotación, Estado: Chiapas, Municipio: Cacahoatán, exp. 408, legajo 7, March 9, 1909.

80. Various documents from the ARPPC.

81. AGA, Asunto: Dotación, Estado: Chiapas, Municipio: Cacahoatán, exp. 408, legajo 7, April 27, 1916, July 26, 1917.

82. MLCC v. varios, Sept. 4, 1892, APJS 1° Civil Soconusco 1880, 1873–; MLCC to Bado and Ampudia Chavero, Aug. 5, 1897, APJS 1° Civil Soconusco 1884.

83. Fenner has demonstrated that much of the conflict that arose between the MLCC and the government was instigated by a small group of well-connected actors in the central and northern departments of the state. There, individuals and companies in Palenque and Chilón, as well as across the state border in Tabasco, with interests in timber and coffee prompted intervention in the allocation of surveyed lands to the ICOM/MLCC in payment for its surveying work. See the fourth chapter of Fenner's dissertation, "Los deslindes en Palenque-Chilón y Soconusco: dos experiencias distintas," as well as the end of the previous chapter for further discussion of the differences in surveying practices within Chiapas. Fenner, "Los deslindes de terrenos baldíos."

84. Humphreys Seargeant, *San Antonio Nexapa*.

85. This is the median size for lots sold by the MLCC for more than MX$500. The majority of lots sold for less than MX$500 were purchased by those from the Soconusco and Guatemala or were *anexos*, small add-ons to large properties. If these are included, the median size for a sale by the land company was eighty-five hectares. As American consul Albert Brickwood, based in Tapachula, noted in 1911, "Chiapas is unique among the states of Mexico for the number of small

holdings and peasant farmers," a quote most historians studying the region have chosen to dismiss out of hand. Cited in Benjamin, *A Rich Land, a Poor People*, 48–49.

86. This strategy made the Soconusco one of the only parts of the country where a land company managed to sell the majority of the land it was granted. Holden, *Mexico and the Survey of Public Lands*, 56–60, Conclusion.

87. In 1912 in Acacoyagua, a community like Cacahoatán that was both ancient and newly formed, the municipal council seized part of a neighboring land grant to a Japanese company as part of its ejidos. The company complained to the state government, which ordered the council to stop its repartitions and respect the Japanese company's titles. The municipal president of Acacoyagua then wrote back at length to explain how, in fact, the Japanese company, despite direct orders to the contrary, had colluded with an earlier state official to push the villagers off their lands, destroy their cacao, banana, and sugar fields, and turn the whole area to ranching. The jefe político of the district, trying to resolve the issue, discovered that the lands in question had been legally purchased from "sons of the town" after an earlier round of titling that had taken place in 1904. As he understood it, the municipal council in Acacoyagua was now taking advantage of revolutionary rhetoric to try and expand its holdings. He admitted that he might be entirely wrong about the matter and was, in part, passing on rumors circulating locally about mysterious interests at work riling up villagers around the region. Villagers confirmed his belief when they wrote not long after to ask the governor to kick out their municipal president as he was going after their lands as well. AHCH, Fondo de Gobierno, Fomento, 1913. vol. 3, exp. 6; AHCH, Fondo de Gobierno, Fomento, 1911, vol. 2, exp. 12; Henderson, "Modernization and Change in Mexico"; Schell, "American Investment in Tropical Mexico."

88. I have records for 437 resale transactions for the whole department between 1880 and 1917. The average size of these resales was 380 hectares; the average price was MX$11,391. The median property was 112 hectares, the median price MX$2,330. Medians for Tapachula were MX$2,000 and 93 hectares.

89. "Sección 1 del Inicio al intestato de Don Gustavo Scholz," March 22, 1898, APJS 1° Civil Soconusco 1892; "2a sección del juicio de intestado de Gustavo Scholz," July 5, 1900, APJS 1° Civil Soconusco 1900, 201–50 (1904).

90. Sometimes this led to more business for the MLCC. Unknowingly, or through willful ignorance, a finquero sometimes began the cultivation of land outside his legal holdings. Too, finqueros whose titles preceded the MLCC sometimes found that the titles they had been granted by the national government were as inaccurate as any expedited by the land company. In either case, the improperly claimed and worked land was generally still technically public lands, and so the MLCC was again able to step in and sell it to the finquero in question as an *anexo* or *excedencia*. See, for example, Anexo a Irlanda, Feb. 22, 1910, ARPPC Doc Priv 1902, 1910, 1912. At least thirty of the MLCC's sales were for anexos.

91. See, for example, "Apeo y deslinde de los terrenos San Gregorio Suchiate promovido por José Pinzon," Jan. 18, 1898, APJS 1° Civil Soconusco 1898.

92. Fault for lack of reliable bounds was generally placed at the feet of the surveyor, whether those working for the MLCC or previous surveyors like Ibarra.

Bejarano v. Catlin, Jan. 13, 1893, APJS 1° Civil Soconusco 1884; Chol v. Kilehsen, June 12, 1906, APJS 1° Civil Soconusco 1906, 101–150; Cruz v. Castrejon, Aceves, and Salas Iturbe, Jan. 18, 1910, APJS 1° Civil, Soconusco 1864, 1865, 1869.

93. It was also intended to help fulfill the colonization clause of the company's concession, which required them to not only survey but also to populate the land in question. Property sales thus also included requirements that purchasers cultivate the land and not produce alcohol without the company's explicit permission. These colonists were important to both the company and the federal government and, when the company's fulfillment of its contract came into question, special efforts were made to clarify the titles of these colonists and ensure that they were able to stay on the land. MLCC to Gálvez, "Registro Público de la propiedad Año de 1895," May 2, 1895; ARPPC Doc Priv 1894, 1895, 1899–1900; "Remite a esta Secretaría un estudio sobre colonización del Estado de Chiapas, presentado por el Abogado Consultor de la Secretaría de Fomento," 1912, SRE, 11-2-141.

94. Guatemalans had to petition the government for permission to buy these lots, as they were located within the border zone. See "Extrangeros que desean adquirir bienes," AHCH, Fondo de Gobierno, Fomento, 1911, vol. 1 exp. 1.

95. See, for example the sale of 129 hectares within the Indigenous Colony sold by a man from the Soconusco in 1912. Robledo to Valle, March 5, 1912, ARPPC Doc Priv 1902, 1910.

96. Subdivision of land was also common, with many finqueros carving up extensive plantations into more manageable pieces, either to pay off debts or because their eyes were bigger than their stomachs. I will return to this in Chapter Six.

97. Harrison organized his enterprises as limited liability companies in the United States. When overtapping, disease, and the maturation of rubber plantations in Malaysia drove his companies into bankruptcy, he left the Soconusco and retired to Marin County, California. A number of his employees received the plantations they had managed for him in payment of outstanding salaries, returning the lands to Mexican hands. For more on Harrison's rubber investments in the Soconusco, see Fisher v. Hidalgo Plantation Company, April 18, 1917, ARPPT Doc Priv 1917; "Testimonio de la escritura de préstamo de dinero garantizada con hipoteca celebrado por los Señores Guillermo S. Fisher y F Glur y Compañía," 1922, APP; Henderson, "Modernization and Change in Mexico"; Olsson-Seffer, *Report on Hidalgo Plantations and Impressions of La Zacualpa Rubber Plantation*; Olsson-Seffer, *Rubber Planting in Mexico and Central America*.

98. For examples of their purchasing, see the spate of purchases made by Caravantes de Amores in 1894 in ARPPC: Doc Priv 1894, 1895, 1899–1900; and various sales to Amores including M. Rodas to Amores, July 22, 1908, ARPPC Doc Priv 1903: Suplemento al Libro de la Sección 1°; Land Company of Chiapas (LCC) to Amores, June 21, 1909, ARPPC Doc Priv 1909; Madrid viuda de Farfán to Amores, Feb. 3, 1911, ARPPC Doc Priv 1911.

99. AGA, April 27, 1916, Estado: Chiapas, Municipio: Cacahoatán, exp. 9, legajo 408.

100. The ejidal commission in Cacahoatán had similar difficulties, though there small portions of fincas that bordered the municipality as well as remaining portions of national lands were transformed into ejidos for laborers who desired land.

This also happened around Tuzantán and in the upper reaches of Tapachula. AGA, Asunto: Dotación, Estado: Chiapas, Municipio: Mazatán, Manuel Lazos, exp. 43, legajo 4; AGA, Asunto: Dotación, Estado: Chiapas, Municipio: Cacahoatán, exp. 408, legajo 7; AGA, Asunto: Dotación, Estado: Chiapas, Municipio: Tapachula, El Naranjo, exp. 599, legajo 4.

CHAPTER FIVE: SCARCE LABOR AND UNREALIZED REFORM

1. Now owned by an English investor, it had originally been titled by Sebastián Escobar, who then sold the parcel to a recent emigrant from Guanajuato. "Juicio Hipotecario promovido por Julian J. de Urruela contra Rafael Ortega," Aug. 8, 1899, APJS 1° Civil Soconusco 1899; Juicio hereditario Juana Benonie de Magee, March 16, 1905, APJS 1° Civil Soconusco 1905, 201–50.

2. In 1896, 3,000–3,500 cuerdas or roughly 125 hectares of San Juan las Chicharras's land was planted with coffee. In 1899, 168 out of its total 1,000 hectares were under cultivation. "Exposición de París de 1900: Chiapas—Estadística Agrícola," AGN, Exposiciones Exteriores, caja 52, exp. 4; Kaerger, *Agricultura y colonización en México en 1900*, 104.

3. The Gilbertese laborers were generally referred to as "Kanakas" in the documents, a pejorative term used throughout the Pacific to refer to migrant island laborers. I have chosen the more specific and hopefully less freighted geographic descriptor related to their place of origin for use here. Details in this section drawn from "El Señor Juan Magee acusa criminalmente a su consocio Guillermo José Forsyth," Dec.15, 1892, APJS 1° Civil Soconusco 1892, 01-50; "Juicio ordinario provido por Don Carlos Lesher contra Don Juan Magee, por honorarios de depósito de la finca San Juan Las Chicharras," 1896, APJS 1° Civil/Penal Soconusco 1873.

4. For more on the global implications of this reorganization, see Melillo, "The First Green Revolution."

5. For a detailed study of nineteenth-century Mexican ideals of labor organization, see Suarez-Potts, *The Making of Law*. Contract labor secured by debt was perfectly in line with late nineteenth-century liberal ideas of acceptable labor practices. See the work of David Northrup, e.g., Northrup, "Free and Unfree Labor Migration, 1600–1900."

6. Katz, "Labor Conditions on Haciendas in Porfirian Mexico"; Bauer, "Rural Workers in Spanish America"; Loveman, "Critique of Arnold J. Bauer's 'Rural Workers in Spanish America'"; Knight, "Debt Bondage in Latin America"; Gibbings, "'The Shadow of Slavery.'" The case of coffee has been particularly illustrative of the variety of modes of export production. See: Bazant, "Peones, arrendatarios y aparceros"; Cambranes, *Coffee and Peasants*; Dore, "Patriarchy from Above, Patriarchy from Below"; McCreery, "Coffee and Indigenous Labor in Guatemala, 1871–1980"; Stein, *Vassouras*; Holloway, *Immigrants on the Land*; Palacios, *Coffee in Colombia, 1850–1970*; Lauria-Santiago, *An Agrarian Republic*; Roseberry, "La Falta de Brazos"; Charlip, *Cultivating Coffee*. For the accepted history of labor in Chiapas, see Rus, "Coffee and the Recolonization"; Washbrook, *Producing Modernity in Mexico*.

7. These relationships were based on colonial *repartimiento* practices that had

never fallen out of use. Rus surmises that indigenous village leaders continued to fulfill the requisitions made by highland hacendados in order to maintain a degree of political and social autonomy within their communities. Rus, "Coffee and the Recolonization," 261.

8. Turner, *Barbarous Mexico*; Rus, "Coffee and the Recolonization," 261–66; Washbrook, "Una Esclavitud Simulada," 273; Washbrook, *Producing Modernity in Mexico*, 268; Rus, "Revoluciones contenidas," 62.

9. In the 1870s and 1880s, labor contracts were often recorded in the municipal court's *libros de conocimiento*, the court contract registers further explored in Chapter Six. These contracts included advances on wages, specific terms for repayment, and numerous clauses protecting against the flight of laborers before their debts were repaid. In a few cases, illiterate laborers even signed away their legal rights and agreed to be imprisoned if they left before the term of their contract was up. Almost none of those registering labor contracts in this forum were from outside the Soconusco. For an example of a planter pursuing a worker who abandoned his debt, see Dn Joaquin Gallegos demanda a unos mozos fugos, July 12, 1881. AMT, Juzgado 1° Municipal, caja 4, exp. 18. For examples of contracts, see Córdova and De los Santos, July 15, 1881, AMT, Juzgado 1° Municipal, caja 4, exp. 1; Cárdenas and Madrid, Jan. 14, 1890, AMT, Juzgado 1° Municipal, caja 5, exp. 2.

10. Romero to Barrios, Aug. 31, 1875. AHMR Correspondencia enviada, vol. 21, p. 23; Romero to Barrios, Sept. 7, 1873. AHMR, Correspondencia enviada, vol. 21, pp. 39–41; Romero to Barrios, Oct. 20, 1873. AHMR, Correspondencia enviada, vol. 21, pp. 164–165. Romero recounted this advice in a more bitter tone a few years later when the resident Guatemalans began causing problems. Romero, *Refutación de las inculpaciones hechas al c. Matías Romero por el gobierno de Guatemala*, 16, 22.

11. Charles H. Currier to Matías Romero, Aug. 2, 1871. AHMR, Correspondencia recibida, f. 14842; Miguel Pritchard Gamboa to Matías Romero, March 18, 1876. AHMR, Correspondencia recibida, f. 19104; Romero to Domínguez, July 13, 1871. AHMR, Correspondencia enviada, vol. 14, p. 677.

12. See the correspondence between Romero and his local manager regarding the complaints and demands made by workers and the constant need for more hands: Hipólito Flores to Matías Romero, Dec. 30, 1874. AHMR, Correspondencia recibida, f. 18896; Flores to Romero, Feb. 11, 1875. AHMR, Correspondencia recibida, f. 18907; Flores to Romero, Feb. 23, 1875. AHMR, Correspondencia recibida, f. 18913.

13. Flores to Romero, Feb. 20, 1875. AHMR, Correspondencia recibida, f. 18911.

14. See, for example, the Humphreys family's experience. Starting with just family labor, they added two resident families after a few years and then began traveling to the tierra fría themselves to recruit seasonal workers a few years later. Humphreys Seargeant, *San Antonio Nexapa*, 74–76, 168, 301.

15. Seasonal migratory labor brought with it myriad issues for the workers' hometowns including a drain of locally needed workers during harvest time and a

rash of disease and alcoholism, but it also infused cash into local institutions. McCreery, "Coffee and Indigenous Labor in Guatemala, 1871–1980," 199, 203.

16. The sale of mozo debts to other finqueros is often pointed to as another sign of the coercive nature of these labor arrangements. Prior to the mid-1890s, there is evidence of planters acquiring laborers by buying their debt off of other planters. As of 1895 or so these transactions disappear, to be replaced by increasing *cuentas corrientes*, or running tabs, and outlays on recruitment.

17. "Juicio hereditario intestado de Manuel Colón, Sección 3a," 1887, APJS 1° Civil/Penal Soconusco 1873. Other estate accounts indicate that these were normal outlays and usual means. Credits beyond the habilitación, which are not explicitly indicated in these accounts, become apparent in estate inventories for this early era. Recording 73, 25, and 17 mozos owing $1,957.43, $445.22, and $531.18 respectively, the fincas inventoried were on the larger, better-developed side, and were all already harvesting coffee. "Partición de los bienes que a su fallecimiento dejaron Don Francisco Palacios y su esposa Doña Manuela Córdoba," April 26, 1887, APJS 1° Civil Soconusco 1888; "Juicio Intestamentario de Petrona Palacios," Feb. 15, 1891, APJS 1° Civil Soconusco 1891; "Juicio testamentario de la que fue Doña Concepción Escobar de Mallen," Jan. 24, 1891, APJS 1° Civil Soconusco 1891.

18. Wage laborers, or *jornaleros*, in the rest of the state earned more than mozos—between 18 and 30 cents—but still less than workers in the Soconusco. Washbrook, *Producing Modernity in Mexico*, 263.

19. *Litígio entre Juan Magee y Guillermo José Forsyth*, 41–42.

20. Baumann, "Terratenientes, campesinos y la expansion de la agricultura capitalista en Chiapas, 1896–1916," 30.

21. Forsyth's control over the dispositions of his partner's funds was unusual, as most finca owners oversaw operations themselves. Many hired employees to help with the running of the finca, and a diverse group of young men with Anglophone, Hispanic, and Germanic names are found as salaried employees in finca books, counter to assertions that three quarters of plantations in the region were either owned or managed by Germans. Baumann, "Terratenientes," 30.

22. Porfirio Díaz to Manuel Carrascosa, May 1, 1891. CGPD, vol. 16, exp. 4665; Mexico. Secretaría de Fomento, *Memoria* 1883–1885, ix–x.

23. Forsyth and Magee had met in the early 1880s when Magee was serving as the British Vice-Consul in Guatemala and Forsyth, a tropical agronomist, was looking for a new project. Magee helped Forsyth find work in developing quinine production for the country, and a decade later, Forsyth turned to Magee with his idea to invest in coffee just north of the border. *Litígio entre Juan Magee y Guillermo José Forsyth*, 2; Forsyth, *Journal of W. J. Forsyth*, 89.

24. For more on the recruitment of Southern Pacific Islanders as labor, see Howe, "Tourists, Sailors and Labourers"; Cushman, *Guano and the Opening of the Pacific World*, Ch. 4.

25. McCreery and Munro, "The Cargo of the Montserrat," 273–74.

26. "El Señor Juan Magee acusa criminalmente a su consocio Guillermo José Forsyth," Dec. 15, 1892, APJS 1° Civil Soconusco 1892, 01-50.

27. McCreery and Munro, "The Cargo of the Montserrat," 284–86.

28. "El Señor Juan Magee acusa criminalmente a su consocio Guillermo José Forsyth," Dec. 15, 1892, APJS 1° Civil Soconusco 1892, 01-50.

29. This is likely a low estimate of finca value, as valuations for mortgage and inheritance purposes carried out around the same time were often higher. Even if the true value of coffee fincas was double or triple, mozo debt would still represent a significant percentage of total value. "Inscripción de Mozos," *Periódico Oficial del Estado de Chiapas*, July 30, 1898; "Exposición de París de 1900: Chiapas—Estadística Agrícola," AGN, Fomento: Exposiciones Exteriores, caja 52, exp. 4.

30. See "Juicio hereditario Intestado de Manuel Colón, Sección 3a," 1887, APJS 1° Civil/Penal Soconusco 1873 and "El Señor Juan Magee acusa criminalmente a su consocio Guillermo José Forsyth," Dec. 15, 1892, APJS 1° Civil Soconusco 1892, 01-50.

31. The fight between Forsyth and Magee was vicious. Knowing that Magee's experience would get back to other potential investors, many local notables testified against Forsyth. The court decided that he was responsible for the almost $100,000 difference between what Magee had invested and the value assigned by the court assessor. Forsyth tried to countersue, charging that Magee's inflexibility and unwillingness to forward further funds broke their contract, but when that failed he resorted to appealing the case to the state court. They, too, decided in favor of Magee, but it is unclear whether Forsyth ever repaid any of the funds. "El Señor Juan Magee acusa criminalmente a su consocio Guillermo José Forsyth," Dec. 15, 1892, APJS 1° Civil Soconusco 1892, 01-50; "Juicio ordinario provido por Don Carlos Lesher contra Don Juan Magee, por honorarios de depósito de la finca "San Juan Las Chicharras," 1896, APJS 1° Civil/Penal Soconusco 1873; *Litígio entre Juan Magee y Guillermo José Forsyth*, 50.

32. Kaerger, *Agricultura y colonización en México en 1900*, 106–7, 116.

33. "Cuenta de administración de la finca Vergel de San Carlos correspondiente al mes de Agosto," Aug. 1899, APJS 1° Civil Soconusco 1899.

34. "Inventario de la finca San Juan Las Chicharras," Jan. 18, 1896, APJS 1° Civil Soconusco 1896.

35. Ibid.

36. "Exposición de París de 1900: Chiapas—Estadística Agrícola," AGN, Fomento: Exposiciones Exteriores, caja 52, exp. 4; *Pan American Magazine* 6, no. 6 (1908).

37. Based on five different fincas in receivership between 1898 and 1906. Mozo debts were only reported sporadically in these accounts. "Cuenta de administración de la finca rústica Guanajuato," Aug., Oct., 1899, Jan., May–Dec. 1901, Jan. 1902; "Cuenta de administración de las fincas Concepción, Buenavista, Tonintaná Chico, y Blas Blen o Chemeta," Jan.–Aug. 1900; "Cuenta de administración de la finca Vergel de San Carlos," Aug. 1899–Jan. 1900; "Cuentas de San Carlos, San Antonio El Zapote," Dec. 1889–April 1901; "Incidente de cuentas de Administración de la finca El Talisman," Feb. 1900–Feb. 1906. APJS 1° Civil Soconusco.

38. "El Señor Juan Magee acusa criminalmente a su consocio Guillermo José Forsyth," 15 Dec. 1892, APJS 1° Civil Soconusco 1892, 01-50; "Inventario de la finca San Juan Las Chicharras," Jan. 18, 1896, APJS 1° Civil Soconusco 1896.

39. This goes back to the earliest deeds of sale for coffee fincas and endures through the early twentieth century. See, for example, "Un cuaderno de actas levantadas por el Juez Residencial Joaquín Rodas," June 2, 1883, APJS 1° Civil Soconusco 1883; "Jurisdicción voluntaria licencia para vender la finca Argovia," Oct. 30, 1913, APJS 1° Civil Soconusco 1913, 51–100.

40. "Juicio Intestamentario de Petrona Palacios," Feb. 15, 1891, APJS 1° Civil Soconusco 1891; "Juicio testamentario de la que fue Doña Concepción Escobar de Mallen," Jan. 24, 1891, APJS 1° Civil Soconusco 1891; "Cuenta de administración que como Albacea de la testamentaria del Sr Juan Francisco Sarrien siguió la Señora Carmen Frenco viuda de Sarrien," March 18, 1899, APJS 1° Civil Soconusco 1899; "Sección segunda del juicio intestamentario de Don Nicolas Bejarano," April 3, 1897, APJS 1° Civil Soconusco 1899.

41. "Cuenta de administración de la finca Vergel de San Carlos," Aug. 1899–Jan. 1900; and accounts for Refugio in "Cuentas de San Carlos, San Antonio El Zapote, Agosto 1901," APJS 1° Civil Soconusco Varios Años.

42. For a store inventory, see: "Juicio testamentario de la que fue Doña María Paz Chacón," Aug. 27, 1897, APJS 1° Civil Soconusco, 1897.

43. "1a Sección Juicio Testamentario del Señor Christian J Widmaier," April 17, 1906, APJS 1° Civil Soconusco 1906, 51–100; "Cuenta de administración de la finca Vergel de San Carlos," Aug. 1899–Jan. 1900, APJS 1° Civil Soconusco 1899.

44. "Sección segunda del juicio intestamentario de Don Nicolas Bejarano," April 3, 1897, APJS 1° Civil Soconusco 1899.

45. Even then, of the five or so cases extant in the archive, three were the result of a vendetta between two finqueros rather than the actions of the mozos themselves. "Juicio verbal por Alejandro Córdova contra Juana Bonifacia Sánchez," Nov. 8, 1898, APJS 1° Civil Soconusco 1898; "Juicio verbal promovido por Don Alejandro Córdova contra Margarita Velázquez," Nov. 6, 1898, APJS 1° Civil Soconusco 1883; "Juicio verbal por don Alejandro Córdova contra Atamacio Bravo," Nov. 23, 1898, APJS 1° Civil Soconusco 1898.

46. "Juicio verbal entre Casimiro García y Isaac de J Salas," April 16, 1894, APJS 1° Civil Soconusco 1894, 01–50.

47. Rabasa to Díaz, Aug. 23, 1892. CGPD, vol. 17, exp. 14534.

48. Rus, "Coffee and the Recolonization," 275–76.

49. Rus, 280–82. León to Díaz, April 10, 1896, CGPD, vol. 21, exp. 5530.

50. Suarez-Potts, *The Making of Law*.

51. Lozano, *Estudio del derecho constitucional patrio en lo relativo a los derechos del hombre*, 5, 9–15, 587.

52. "Artículos de Angel Pola," in García Cantú, *El socialismo en México, siglo XIX*, 378–402.

53. "Abusos en Chiapas," *El Monitor Republicano*, July 22, 1890; "Los pueblos esclavos y los gobierno tiranos," *El Siglo Diez y Nueve*, Feb. 1, 1893.

54. "La esclavitud en México," *El Siglo Diez y Nueve*, March 3, 1896.

55. See "Fortunes in Coffee," *Washington Post*, Oct. 12, 1890; "Making Money in Mexico," *Washington Post*, Nov. 4, 1895; "Foreign Capital in Mexico," *New York Times*, April 1, 1891; "About Chiapas: Rubber Enterprise is Defended," *Los Angeles Times*, Oct. 9, 1900; "Mexico's System of Peonage," *Chicago Tribune*,

Jan. 1, 1891; "Peon Slaves in Mexico," *Chicago Tribune*, Aug. 17, 1896; "The Peon in Mexico," *Los Angeles Times*, Nov. 12, 1899.

56. León wrote to Díaz of the different wages that workers received in different parts of the state, from six centavos a day in Chamula to over a peso in the Soconusco, and the different costs affiliated with taking a job in different parts of the state. He recognized that cattle ranchers did not need as many workers as finqueros. More than any other state leader, León had a grasp on the diversity of his state's economy and the necessity of a flexible labor system. León to Díaz, April 7, 1896. CGPD, vol. 21, exp. 5541; León to Díaz, Dec. 20, 1898. CGPD, vol. 23, exp. 17495.

57. Chiapas, *Documentos relativos al congreso agrícola de Chiapas*, iv.

58. "Proyecto importante," *El Foro*, Feb. 11, 1896; "Reglamento para un Congreso Agrícola," *El Siglo Diez y Nueve*, Feb. 14, 1896, ; "Un Congreso Agrícola," *Semana Mercantíl*, Feb. 17, 1896; "Los sirvientes en Chiapas—Congreso agrícola," *La Patria*, Feb. 18, 1896; "Los grupos agrícolas," *La Patria*, March 2, 1896; "La esclavitud en México," *El Siglo Diez y Nueve*, March 3, 1896.

59. Baumann, "Terratenientes, campesinos y la expansión de la agricultura capitalista en Chiapas, 1896–1916," 5–13; Benjamin, *A Rich Land, a Poor People*, 61–64; Washbrook, "Una Esclavitud Simulada," 370–72.

60. Most of the delegates at the Congress were there to represent one or two municipalities, not entire districts. Some highland delegates represented municipalities in both the highlands and in the lowlands where they also owned plantations.

61. "Intestado de Gustavo Scholz," May 15, 1900, APJS 1° Civil Soconusco 1900, 151–200.

62. "Las maravillas del café," *La Tierra*, Aug. 31, 1895. Bejarano also published a few articles in the same newspaper.

63. "Sección segunda del juicio intestamentario de Don Nicolas Bejarano," April 3, 1897, APJS 1° Civil Soconusco 1899.

64. Keller to Romero, Jan. 19, 1880. AHMR, Correspondencia recibida, f. 29747.

65. Mallen y Hermano and Stein Haack y Cia, June 2, 1884, APJS 1° Civil Soconusco 1884: Sección 2a Hipotecaria; Mallen v. Martínez, Oct., 17, 1879, APJS 1° Civil Soconusco, 1873–1879; Mallen and Rafales, April 28, 1880, APJS 1° Civil Soconusco, 1873–1879; Taboada v. Mallen, March 21, 1881, APJS 1° Civil Soconusco 1892.

66. "Juicio Hipotecario promovido por Albino Schulze apoderado de los Señores Koch Hagmann y Companía de Hamburgo contra Bernado Mallen," April 3, 1900, APJS 1° Civil Soconusco 1900, 51–100.

67. In 1904, he also wrote a volume to be circulated at the St. Louis World's Fair called *Mexico Yesterday and Today, 1876–1904*, celebrating President Díaz and his modernization projects. "El oro vegetal," *El Eco de Tabasco*, May 9, 1909; Mallen, *Mexico Yesterday and To-Day, 1876–1904*.

68. "Juicio testamentario de la que fue Doña Concepción Escobar de Mallen," Jan. 24, 1891, APJS 1° Civil Soconusco 1891.

69. Chiapas, *Documentos relativos al congreso agrícola de Chiapas*, 67–72.

70. Chiapas, 84–87.

71. Chiapas, 88–89.
72. Chiapas, 73.
73. Chiapas, 73.
74. Chiapas, 74.
75 Chiapas, 82.
76. "Cronica Parlamentaria," *Periódico Oficial del Estado de Chiapas*, June 26, 1897.
77. "La esclavitud en la República: El gobierno de Chiapas la combate," from *La Nacional*, republished in the *Periódico Oficial del Estado de Chiapas*, July 17, 1897.
78. "La Servidumbre en Chiapas," *El Horizonte*, San Juan Bautista, Tabasco, republished in the *Periódico Oficial del Estado de Chiapas*, Sept. 4, 1897.
79. "Proyecto de ley sobre sirvientes adeudados," *Periódico Oficial del Estado de Chiapas*, June 6, 1897.
80. While workers resisted the recruitment system in the highlands, they did not voice complaints about the conditions in the Soconusco. Rus, "Coffee and the Recolonization," 283–84.
81. According to some, Guillermo Kahle, a German planter, was the first in the Soconusco to turn to highland-based *enganchadores*, a frequently used term for labor recruiters, though Kaerger had written about similarly employed men by 1900. Rus, 279–84; Washbrook, *Producing Modernity in Mexico*; Pozas, "El trabajo en las plantaciones de café y el cambio sociocultural del indio," 34; Kaerger, *Agricultura y colonización en México en 1900*, 105.
82. Washbrook, *Producing Modernity in Mexico*, 299, 303, 313, 328.
83. German finqueros complained frequently about outstanding debts and runaways, stating that two-thirds of workers left before their contracts were up and organizing among themselves to limit debts. Complaints also made their way into international publications like the *Pan American Magazine*. *Pan American Magazine* 6, no. 6 (1908): 506; Rus, "Coffee and the Recolonization," 284; Benjamin, *A Rich Land, a Poor People*, 84.
84. Mexico, Secretaría de Hacienda y Crédito Público, *Exportaciones de los años fiscales de 1890–1895*; Mexico, Secretaría de Hacienda y Crédito Público, *Comercio exterior*; Mexico, Secretaría de Hacienda y Crédito Público, *Boletin de estadística fiscal. Años 1900–1911*; Waibel, *La Sierra Madre de Chiapas*.
85. Rus, "Coffee and the Recolonization," 282; Benjamin, *A Rich Land, a Poor People*, 89.
86. In the 1950s when cultivation was even greater, the anthropologist Ricardo Pozas reported that of the 34,000 seasonal workers in the Soconusco, only 10,000 came from the highlands. Pozas, "El trabajo en las plantaciones de café y el cambio sociocultural del indio," 48.
87. Incomplete figures in the state newspaper reported 3,997 indebted workers with an average debt of $117.05, the third highest in the state. Benjamin reports 6,500 total though does not explain the basis for his estimation beyond the official newspaper report. *Periódico Oficial del Estado de Chiapas*, July 30, 1898; Benjamin, *A Rich Land, a Poor People*, 65.
88. Mexico, *Censo general de 1900*.

89. Colburn, *An Interesting and Authentic Description of a Mule-Back Ride Through the Quaint, Little-Known Department of Soconusco, Mexico*, 25; Nolan-Ferrell, *Constructing Citizenship*.

90. The 1910 census is notoriously spotty, and the language statistics are especially suspect, as despite listing 11,000 Guatemalan-born residents, only 686 were listed as speaking a language native to Guatemala. For more on this see footnote 35 in the Introduction. Mexico, *Tercer censo de población de los Estados Unidos Mexicanos*.

91. Cándano to Díaz, Sept. 28, 1897. CGPD, vol. 56, exp. 4635; Cándano to Díaz, Oct. 9, 1897. CGPD, vol. 56, exp. 4820; Cándano to Díaz, Oct. 1897. CGPD, vol. 56, exp. 4827; Cándano to Díaz, Oct. 13, 1897; CGPD, vol. 56, exp. 4910.

92. León to Díaz, Jan. 13 1897. CGPD, vol. 57, exp. 576; AHCH, Sección de Fomento, 1907, vol. III, exp. 10: Construcción y reparación de caminos.

93. Seven estate inventories from after 1897 include mozo debts; three place their value at a round $5,000, including that completed on Magee's death. Receivership accounts from the era occasionally slipped up and indicated ongoing unpaid advances. "Cuenta de administración que como Albacea de la testamentaria del Sr Juan Francisco Sarrien siguió la Señora Carmen Frenco viuda de Sarrien," March 18, 1899, APJS 1° Civil Soconusco 1899; "Sección 2a de la Sucesión del Sr Dr Neftalí Palomeque," June 10, 1901, APJS 1° Civil Soconusco 1901, 51–100; Magee and Benonie du Tiel viuda de Magee, May 23, 1901, ARPPC Doc Priv 1906; "Juicio intestamentario de quien fue Walter Von Bodecker," Dec. 29, 1905, APJS 1° Civil Soconusco 1905, 151–200; "1a Sección Juicio Testamentario del Señor Christian J Widmaier," April 17, 1906, APJS 1° Civil Soconusco 1906, 51–100; "Escritura de poder que otorgaron los Sres Urbano y Felipe Jacoby en favor de Don Albino Schulze," May 24, 1909, APJS 1° Civil Soconusco 1909, 151–200; "Incidente de cuentas de la finca Guanajuato," Sept. 1901, APJS 1° Civil Soconusco 1901, 251–300.

94. "Cuentas presentadas por Guadalupe Garcia correspondiente al mes de Mayo," May 31, 1900, APJS 1° Civil Soconusco 1900, 301–350; "Incidente de cuentas de la finca Guanajuato," Sept. 1901, APJS 1° Civil Soconusco 1901, 251–300.

95. Washbrook emphasizes complaints made by Germans against local officials to demonstrate the lack of consolidated political power, but non-German finqueros remained important and many of them had connections to local government that they were still unable to leverage into coercive capacity. Washbrook, *Producing Modernity in Mexico*, 337–38.

96. "Cuaderno de pruebas del actor señor Carlos A. Lesher en el juicio que sigue a don Juan Magee por pago de honorarios," March 18, 1897, APJS 1° Civil Soconusco, 1897; Lesher v. Magee, Sept. 20, 1897, APJS 1° Civil Soconusco 1897.

97. "Juicio hereditario Juana Benonie de Magee," March 16, 1905, APJS 1° Civil Soconusco 1905, 201–250; Land Company of Chiapas, Mexico to Hidalgo Plantation and Commercial Company, Feb. 27, 1909, ARPPC Doc Priv 1909; Land Company of Chiapas, Mexico to Charles Lesher, Escrituras Públicas de 1912, Feb. 22, 1910, ARPPC Doc Priv 1902, 1910, 1912.

98. In looking at the particular ramifications of the law on the region's rubber plantations, Henderson notes that the Zacualpa Rubber Plantation Company converted what had been credit advances of five to ten pesos to on-the-books pay increases. SRE, 1915, 16-4-145; Henderson, "Modernization and Change in Mexico."

CHAPTER SIX: THE CIRCULATION OF CODES AND COMMERCE

1. "Jurisdición Voluntaría: Doña Herlinda R viuda de Bado pide autorización para vender bienes de sus hijos menores Victor y Carlos Bado," Dec. 24, 1903, APJS 1° Civil Soconusco 1903, 51–100.

2. Those governed by the commercial code were, by definition, also governed by the civil code; the reverse was not necessarily true, as the commercial code designated only merchants as its subjects. Yet across the second half of the nineteenth century, the law became more universal and the separation of the two spheres was increasingly blurred. By 1870, the commercial tribunals institutionalized in the 1854 commercial code, vestiges of the self-governing and privileged mercantile *gremios*, or guilds, of the colonial era, were eliminated and adjudication of the code was handed over to civil courts. Similarly, while neither purchases for direct consumption nor farmers selling their products directly to consumers were governed by the commercial code, anyone who had a transaction with a merchant was the beneficiary of the new regulations governing that merchant. Mexico, *Código de comercio de México*, 242–45; Mexico, *Proyecto de código mercantil*, 12; Carmagnani, "Vectors of Liberal Economic Culture in Mexico," 290.

3. Lurtz, "Developing the Mexican Countryside."

4. Carmagnani, *Estado y mercado*; Carmagnani, "Vectors of Liberal Economic Culture in Mexico."

5. For example, Concepción Becerra de Solís lost her properties to repay her husband's business debts on his death in 1887 because he had never separately incorporated his company. "1° sección del intestado de Don Luis L. Solis," March 28, 1887, APJS 1° Civil Soconusco 1887.

6. See, for example, the inventory of Bernabé Acosta's store carried out in 1898. "Sección 2a del juicio intestamentario de los Señores Alonso y Eutimio Acosta," Jan. 20, 1898, APJS 1° Civil Soconusco 1898.

7. This was an issue not only in the Soconusco but throughout Chiapas. It continued to be a problem through the 1900s, even after most transactions recorded at the public records office started being noted in Mexican pesos. Pánfilo Grajales to Porfirio Díaz, Feb. 14, 1911. CGPD, vol. 36, exp. 2909; "Memoria de la Comisión de Cambios y Moneda," *La Iberia*, Nov. 2, 1909.

8. Bunker, *Creating Mexican Consumer Culture*; Francois, *A Culture of Everyday Credit*.

9. *Código civil del Distrito Federal y territorio de la Baja-California (1870)*, Libro Tercero, Título I, Capítulo I, art. 1392, pp. 237–38.

10. Mexico, Código de comercio de México (1854), 12.

11. Mexico, Código de comercio de México (1854), Libro I, Título III, Sección II, 14–22; Mexico, *Proyecto de código mercantil*, Libro I, Título II, Capítulo

I, 13–17; *Código de comercio de los Estados Unidos Mexicanos (1884)*, Título Segundo, Capítulo IV, 20–24.

12. "Testimonio del testamento público abierto otorgado por Don Antonio Bado," Sept. 28, 1897, APJS 1° Civil Soconusco 1894, 01-50.

13. Sres. A. Bado y Cía and Victor Robledo, July 4, 1883, APJS 1° Civil Soconusco 1883.

14. Her citizenship and connections to the local oligarchy, though, had likely smoothed the way for her foreign husband's acquisition of property. Various laws impeded noncitizens from acquiring properties in Mexico's border zones. Mexican proxies, including Mexican wives, were often used to get around these restrictions. See Augustine-Adams, "Constructing Mexico."

15. Married women had to have their husband's permission to take up commerce, but once that permission was granted, it was difficult to rescind and women were given great autonomy to act with regard to signing contracts, mortgaging their property, and buying and selling. Unmarried women and men under the age of twenty-five needed their father's permission to engage in commerce, as they were still legally minors, but so long as they were above twenty years of age, later dropped to eighteen, could do so with similarly broad license. These precepts were kept almost intact for the revised 1883 commercial code. Mexico, *Código de comercio de México (1854)*, 5–6; Mexico, *Proyecto de código mercantil*, 12–13; Mexico, *Código de comercio de los Estados Unidos Mexicanos (1884)*, 4–5.

16. "Liquidación judicial solicitada por la Señora Herlinda Rosales Viuda de Bado," May 4, 1899, APJS 1° Civil Soconusco 1899.

17. The 1883 code went so far as to specify the type of binding required for these ledgers and prohibit the erasure or removal of pages. Mexico, *Proyecto de código mercantil*, 14; Mexico, *Código de comercio de los Estados Unidos Mexicanos (1884)*, 23.

18. Vallés y Pujals, *El contrato de cuenta corriente*, 283.

19. Escriche et al., *Diccionario razonado de legislación y jurisprudencia*, 1152.

20. See, for example, Lorenza Arévalo to Maria Briceño, July 21, 1888, AMT, Juzgado 1° Municipal caja 5, exp. 7, Año 1888, Libro de conocimientos.

21. For more on commercial extensions of credit in Mexico and Latin America as compared to Europe, see Bunker, *Creating Mexican Consumer Culture*, 119–20. For a typical example of credit in the Soconusco, see, "Sección 2a del juicio intestamentario de los Señores Alonso y Eutemio Acosta," Jan. 20, 1898, APJS 1° Civil Soconusco 1898 and "Sección II Juicio de intestado de los Señores Juan Biscarría y Gertrudis Morales de Biscarria," Jan. 9, 1898, APJS 1° Civil Soconusco 1899.

22. For example, see "Cesión de bienes hecha por el albacea de la sucesion de Neftalí Palomeque," March 12, 1902, APJS 1° Civil Soconusco 1902, 01-50.

23. "Liquidación judicial solicitada por la Señor Herlinda Rosales Viuda de Bado," May 4, 1899, APJS 1° Civil Soconusco 1899.

24. Unless a contract was being litigated, the 1870 civil code permitted debts to be transferred from one creditor to another, with or without the consent of the debtor. Since, in this case, the debts being litigated were those with Rosales de Bado's creditors rather than her debtors, this transfer was permissible. *Código civil del Distrito Federal y territorio de la Baja-California*, Libro Tercero, Título IV, Capítulo VIII, 285.

25. It is unlikely that many foreign merchants willingly took on credits listed in the cuenta corriente, but given the total value of the ledger as compared to the mortgages or other more formalized credit documents contained in the business's inventory, they may have well had to take on the risk and annoyance of collecting on accounts as small as six pesos. "Jurisdicción Voluntaría: Doña Herlinda R viuda de Bado pide autorización para vender bienes de sus hijos menores Victor y Carlos Bado," Dec. 24, 1903, APJS 1° Civil Soconusco 1903, 51–100; "Liquidación judicial solicitada por la Señor Herlinda Rosales Viuda de Bado," May 4, 1899, APJS 1° Civil Soconusco 1899.

26. For more on how institutions come to substitute for trust, see Zucker, "Production of Trust"; Cook, *Cooperation without Trust?*; Hanley, "Is It Who You Know?"

27. The statutes regarding préstamos were maintained almost verbatim in the 1884 civil code. *Código civil del Distrito Federal y territorio de la Baja-California (1870)*, Libro Tercero, Título XVI; (Mexico), *Código civil del Distrito federal y territorios de Tepic y Baja California (1884)*, Libro Tercero, Título XVI.

28. *Código civil del Distrito Federal y territorio de la Baja-California (1870)*, Libro Tercero, Título I, Capítulo V, 243–244; Título VI, 296; Título IX, Cap. 1, Art 2054, 332.

29. Contracts worth more than MX$500 had to be registered; those worth less did not. The only exception to this was the transfer of land, which, no matter the value, had to be recorded at the public records office, though transactions worth less than MX$500 could take place without a notary or official present so long as the paperwork was later filed. Mexico, *Código civil del Distrito Federal y territorio de la Baja-California (1870)*, Libro Tercero, Título VII, Cap. II, Art. 1928, 312; Títiulo VIII, Cap. IV, 326; Título XVIII, Cap. X, 471; Título XXIII, Cap. II, 507; Mexico, *Código civil del Distrito federal y territorios de Tepic y Baja California (1884)*, Libro Tercero, Título XVIII, Cap. XI, Art. 2923, P. 565; Título XXIII, Cap. II, 611.

30. *Código civil del Distrito Federal y territorio de la Baja-California (1870)*, Libro Tercero, Título I, Capítulo VI, 244; Título III, Capítulo I, 257.

31. I do not know why they did not turn to notaries, other than that there were very few notaries in the Soconusco. I have found evidence of only one for the early period and just a few more by the 1900s. I cannot say why, as the general understanding is that notaries appear where they are needed, given the lucrative nature of the position. Levy, *The Making of a Market*; Chowning, *Wealth and Power in Provincial Mexico*.

32. I have yet to find reference to this specific type of record in any other historical works, nor can I find explicit mention of it in the legal codes of either the Mexican government or the state of Chiapas. The term *libro de conocimiento* is a generic one that carried over from colonial Spanish law to designate any number of registers officials were required to keep. By 1863, state law in Chiapas permitted municipal magistrates and councilors to validate and record agreements when a town lacked notaries or others with the power to do so. Other historians, working earlier in the nineteenth century, have found evidence of villagers making use of municipal courts to enforce this sort of agreement. In Guanajuato, San Luis Potosí,

and Sonora, villagers and workers made use of municipal courts to pursue unpaid debts and unmet contracts throughout the decades that followed independence, though neither Shelton nor Schaefer points to the use of courts for the registration of agreements later broken. Again, this form may have come about because of the lack of notaries, but its endurance into the twentieth century, once a number of notaries had taken up work in the region, suggests that it was a less expensive and more accessible means of making use of the law for those without the capital or access to take advantage of other forms of registration. Sánchez, *Colección de Pragmáticas*, 384, 442; Islas, *Codificación de la República Mexicana*, 133; Schaefer, *Liberalism as Utopia*, Chapter 1; Shelton, *For Tranquility and Order*, 104.

33. The Bados appear five times in these records, twice registering advance payment for future deliveries of wood, and three times without indicating the specifics behind the contract beyond who owed money to whom.

34. Vicente Lara to Catarina Mejia, July 20, 1900, AMT, Juzgado 1° Municipal, caja 7, exp. 3, año 1900, Libro de Conocimientos del Juzgado 1°.

35. Delfino Lopez to Januario Salvador, Aug. 20, 1894, AMT, Juzgado 1° Municipal, caja 6, exp. 3, Año 1894, Libro de conocimientos.

36. Jeronima Bermudes to Federico Ibarra, March 28, 1888, AMT, Juzgado 1° Municipal, caja 5, exp. 7, Año 1888, Libro de conocimientos.

37. Taxed at 2 cents for every 20 pesos in question, private obligations including advances and *pagarés* became a small but steady source of income for the federal government. While these taxation codes were complex and frequently amended and republished, local use of them was straightforward and seemingly dismissive of the bureaucratic muddle they entailed. The 1876 code covered pagarés as part of private contracts, where any amount between ten and one hundred pesos was charged three cents. Mexico, *Ley del timbre reformada*, 37; Mexico, *Ley del timbre*, 17, 33; Mexico, *La nueva ley de la renta federal del timbre*, 16, 25.

38. I have also integrated these names with those recorded as buying or selling land, but only about one sixth of the participants show up in the land transaction data, a reminder that while my information is representative, it is in no way a complete registry of landholding in the region and favors rural over urban property information. It also suggests that the municipal court was a space primarily used by non-elites. Only about 3 percent of loans included language about guarantors, and about 7 percent of loans included mention of either specific property put up as collateral or a more general statement about "present and future goods" backing a loan. For contracts that included interest, see Corzo and Parlange, July 18, 1886, AMT, Juzgado 1° Municipal, caja 4, exp. 39; Córdova and Ramírez, Aug. 9, 1888, AMT, Juzgado 1° Municipal, caja 5, exp. ; Sumuano and Flores, Aug. 4, 1899, AMT, Juzgado 1° Municipal, caja 6, exp. 1; Maldonado and de los Reyes, Jan. 26, 1900, AMT, Juzgado 1° Municipal, caja 7, exp. 3.

39. Of those contracts that specified their purpose, labor and the future delivery of goods were most common. Out of the 960 loans for which I have records, 90 pertained to labor. Sixty-four of those occurred before 1890. Seventy-seven agreements for the delivery of agricultural or basic manufactured goods were present in the records I have access to, peaking from the early 1880s through the mid-1890s. For examples, see Becerra and Solis, June 8, 1888. AMT, Juzgado

1° Municipal, caja 5, exp. 7, Año 1888, Libro de conocimientos and Elorza and Osuna, May 2, 1888. AMT, Juzgado 1°Municipal, caja 5, exp. 7, Año 1888, Libro de conocimientos.

40. Coutiño and Ramirez, April 9, 1894, AMT, Juzgado 2° Municipal, caja 5, exp. 2, Año 1894, Libro de Conocimientos; Coutiño and Rincón, April 5, 1899, AMT, Juzgado 2° Municipal, caja 5, exp. 1, Año 1899, Libro de Conocimientos; Servin and Coutiño, July 14, 1899, AMT, Juzgado 2° Municipal, caja 5, exp. 1, Año 1899, Libro de Conocimientos; Iza and Coutiño, May 14, 1900, AMT, Juzgado 3a Municipal, caja 5, exp. 33, Año 1900, Conocimientos.

41. Lurtz, "Developing the Mexican Countryside."

42. Ridings, "Class Sector Unity in an Export Economy"; Quiroz, *Banqueros en conflicto*; Adelman, "Agricultural Credit in the Province of Buenos Aires, Argentina, 1890–1914"; Haber, "Industrial Concentration and the Capital Markets"; Sikkink, *Ideas and Institutions*; Oñate, *Banqueros y hacendados*; Adelman, *Frontier Development*; Maurer, "Banks and Entrepreneurs in Porfirian Mexico"; Passananti, "Managing Finance and Financiers"; Riguzzi, "Sistema financiero."

43. Greenow, *Credit and Socioeconomic Change in Colonial Mexico*; Lindley, *Haciendas and Economic Development*; Adelman, "Agricultural Credit in the Province of Buenos Aires, Argentina, 1890–1914"; Gómez Serrano, *Haciendas y ranchos de Aguascalientes*; Hanley, *Native Capital*.

44. Wiemers, "Agriculture and Credit in Nineteenth-Century Mexico"; Levy, *The Making of a Market*.

45. The commercial code qualified any sale by a laborer or rancher of the products of his work as not mercantile. The code alluded to *compras a plazo*, or advance purchase, a phrase very occasionally used in these contracts, but most were registered as *compraventas*, or sales. Toledo v. Rosales, Sept. 12, 1883, APJS 1° Civil Soconusco 1883; Mexico, *Proyecto de código mercantile*, Libro III, Título III, Sec. I, Art. 957, 177.

46. de León and Romero, March 5, 1874, APJS 1° Civil, Soconusco 1864, 1865, y 1869 (Tapachula Paquete 2); Libro de ocursos, March 24, 1874, APJS 1° Civil Soconusco 1864, 1865, y 1869 (1865–1875) (Paquete 2).

47. Bado and de León, Jan. 29, 1880, APJS 1° Civil Soconusco, 1873–1879; Bado v. De León, Feb. 16, 1881, APJS 1° Civil Soconusco 1881, 01-50.

48. Bado and Garcia, March 21, 1882, APJS 1° Civil Soconusco 1882, Escritos sueltos de varias personas; "Protocolo de instrumentos públicos del Juzgado de 1 Instancia del Departamento de Soconusco," Aug. 6, 1881, APJS 1° Civil Soconusco 1881, 01-50.

49. Mexico. Secretaría de Fomento, *Memoria 1892–1896*, 11–12.

50. As early as 1884, Bernardo Mallen personally took coffee and other goods from the Soconusco to the international exposition in New Orleans. "Soconusco en la Exposición de Nueva Orleans," *La Patria*, Nov. 18, 1884, 2; "Lo que México remitirá a la Exposición de París," *La Defensa Católica*, Aug. 15, 1888, 3. For more on Mexico's participation in these types of expositions, see Tenorio-Trillo, *Mexico at the World's Fairs*.

51. "Carlos Gris," *El México Gráfico*, Oct. 12, 1891, 7; "Alucinaciones Agrícolas," *Semana Mercantil*, May 14, 1894, 232–33.

52. For example: "Tabasco y Chiapas," *El Siglo Diez y Nueve*, Dec. 20, 1892, 2; "Agricultura, industria, y comercio," *Semana Mercantil* Aug. 5, 1895, 365; "Un gran abono," *La Tierra*, Aug. 31, 1895, 128.

53. "La Cuestión palpitante," *Semana Mercantil*, Oct. 30, 1893, 1–3; "Cultivo del café," *La Patria*, Sept. 13, 1893, 3.

54. Hernández, *Mexican American Colonization*; Lurtz, "Developing the Mexican Countryside," 445–48.

55. Locally based merchant buyers tended to charge 1 to 2 percent monthly, as they were able to capitalize on a regular basis. Purchasers based abroad—more on this momentarily—tended to charge interest of 6 to 10 percent on an annual basis, better suited to their less frequent contact with finqueros. Bado v. Chavez, Jan. 21, 1894, APJS 1° Civil Soconusco 1894, 01-50, Luis R. Brewer, Isaac y Samuel de Londres, July 21, 1899, ARPPC Varios Doc Privados 1889, Registro de Hipotecas 1899.

56. For a boilerplate contract, see "Documentos en que se funda la contestación de Don Teófilo Acebo a la demanda de Don Manuel Sanchez Deleón," Feb. 24, 1898, APJS 1° Civil Soconusco 1883, 51–100.

57. Stein Haack y Cía and Mallen, 2a Sección Hipotecaria, June 2, 1884, APJS 1° Civil Soconusco 1884; Bado v. Chavez, Jan. 21, 1894, APJS 1° Civil Soconusco 1894, 01-50.

58. For example, Giesemann and Sanchez Deleón, May 15, 1901, ARPPC Doc Priv 1906.

59. Sixty of the eighty futures contracts for which I have records come from after 1890. The median value of these loans was MX$16,000, whereas the median loan for the period before 1890 was MX$950. Kaerger writes of a German finca that, at the height of its productivity, produced 3,000 quintals on 3,000 cuerdas, or 129 hectares, of land planted with 120,000 coffee bushes. Usual production, though, he writes, would have been lower, closer to 2,000 quintals for 3,000 cuerdas. The finca in question would have been much larger than 129 hectares, as much land was left forested or dedicated to *milpa* or pasturage. Kaerger, *Agricultura y colonización en México en 1900*, 97–109.

60. Only a third of the loans valued at over MX$10,000 were issued in local currency.

61. Half of the advance contracts registered between 1890 and the crisis that followed the price collapse of the turn of the century were for less than MX$10,000, half were for more, with the largest single contract for this period valued at more than MX$300,000, the smallest at MX$350.

62. For a few typical examples of these contracts, see Acosta, Robledo González, and Robledo, April 27, 1907, ARPPC Doc Priv 1900 y 1907, Registro Público Sección 1, Num. 3 1907; Giesemann and Bejarano, Registro de Hipotecas 1900, April 11, 1900, ARPPC Varios Doc Privados 1889.

63. Some of the overdue loans were based on direct contracts between Ortega and those pursuing repayment, but the documentation also includes debts of unspecified origin. "Juicio Hipotecario promovido por Julian J. de Urruela contra Rafael Ortega," Aug. 8, 1899, APJS 1° Civil Soconusco 1899.

64. Ortega and Forsyth, April 2, 1901, ARPPC Doc Priv 1900 y 1907: Sección Primera del Registro Público, 1900.

65. Juárez repealed the ban on usury in 1861, and the civil codes of the 1870s and the 1880s explicated and diversified mortgage regulations in the following decades. Levy, *The Making of a Market*, 38.
66. *Código civil del Distrito Federal y territorio de la Baja-California (1870)*, Título Octavo, Capítulos IV–VI. These statutes remained essentially the same through the various iterations of the civil code ratified under Díaz.
67. *Código civil del Distrito Federal y territorio de la Baja-California (1870)*, Libro III, Título VIII, Capítulo I, p. 314.
68. He also signed two futures contracts, both with foreign finqueros in the Soconusco. Haack y Compañía and Ortega, Jan. 18, 1892, APJS 1° Civil Soconusco 1892, 01-50; Taboada and Ortega, March 30, 1897, ARPPC Doc Priv 1894, 1895, 1899–1900: 1900 Legajo de cédulas hipotecarias; Thomalen y Cia v. Ortega, Aug. 2, 1899, APJS 1° Civil Soconusco 1899; Koch Hagmann y Cía and Ortega, 1898, ARPPC Varios Doc Privados 1889: Indice de hipotecas; Hernández Mendía y Cía and Ortega, 1898, ARPPC Varios Doc Priv 1889: Indice de hipotecas; Gándara and Ortega, 1899, ARPPC Varios Doc Priv 1889: Indice de hipotecas; "Juicio ordinario de Francisca A Viuda de Cerdio contra Adolfo Giesseman," June 18, 1901, APJS 1° Civil Soconusco 1901, 01-50; A. Viuda de Cerdio v. Giesemann, April 4, 1909, APJS 1° Civil Soconusco 1911, 01-50; "Juicio Ordinario por cobro de pesos seguido por don Benito Taboada contra don Rafael Ortega," July 25, 1901, APJS 1° Civil Soconusco 1899.
69. All values have been converted to Mexican pesos. As in Chapter Four, these data have been compiled by inserting data gleaned from court cases at the APJS into indices and original registration documents from the ARPPC. Almost all of the mortgages found in the judicial archive were also present in the various indices transcribed. Most of the entries from the ARPPC come from an alphabetical index dated 1899 that includes 349 entries for mortgages registered between 1889 and 1912; 237 of these are for mortgages offered by creditors other than the MLCC. The rest come from periodic and incomplete monthly or yearly indices, many of which are missing pages and personal details about the parties involved. As was noted in Chapter Four, the ARPPC did not open until around 1894; therefore any data from before that date is especially spotty. As in Chapter Four, I will look at change over time using those years for which my data is comparably comprehensive and at the general make up of the market using all of the data, assuming that damage to and losses from the archive have been random. The fact that all but one of the mortgages mentioned in a 1908 review of the still-active debts are included in my data is reassuring. Documents from the judicial archive will be cited as appropriate. The indices used are: "Indice de hipotecas," Año 1899, ARPPC Varios Doc Privados 1889; "Indice alfabética de las nombres de los dueños de las fincas gravadas en la Sección 2a," 1887–1908, ARPPC Doc Priv 1903; "Noticia de la operaciones de Registro vigentes habidas en este oficio desde el año de 1883 hasta la fecha Sección II," 1883–1901, ARPPC Doc Priv 1902, 1910, 1912; "Movimiento del Registro Público," 1907, ARPPC Doc Priv 1900 y 1907; "Cuadros que manifiestan el movimiento habido en este Registro," 1908, ARPPC Doc Priv 1903; "Cuadros que manifiestan el movimiento habido en este Registro," 1909, ARPPC Doc Priv 1909; "Cuadros que manifiestan el movimiento habido en este Registro,"

1910, ARPPC Doc Priv 1903; "Indices de 1912," 1912, ARPPC Doc Priv 1902, 1910, 1912.

70. Records of 147 loans exist for the period between 1895 and 1901. Thirty-six of these were for more than MX$10,000, 91 for less than MX$10,000, and 20 records did not include a value. Two-thirds of those borrowing more than MX$10,000 during this period were Mexican in origin.

71. Both the district court and the public records office had employees with remarkably poor penmanship considering that they were primarily hired to write. By the early 1900s the region had a second notary and soon two more, but for many years one man took on much of the work. He may well have assisted in connecting potential buyers with potential lenders, as was the case in the Yucatán according to Juliette Levy, but I have not been able to find his papers and document this. Levy, *The Making of a Market*.

72. Samper K. et al., "Appendix: Historical Statistics of Coffee Production and Trade from 1700 to 1960," 451.

73. "Liquidación judicial solicitada por la Señora Herlinda Rosales Viuda de Bado," May 4, 1899, APJS 1° Civil Soconusco 1899 (1868, 1878, 1896, 1904, 1915).

74. For example, "Córdova contesta la demanda interpuesta en so contra Melcher Sucs de Mazatlán," Aug. 27, 1901, APJS 1° Civil Soconusco 1901, 101–150.

75. Cuek and Córdova, April 13, 1900, ARPPC Varios Doc Privados 1889: Registro de Hipotecas 1900; "Tercería excluyente de preferencia por L. Thomalen y Compañía," 1898, APJS 1° Civil Soconusco 1900, 01-50 (1899, 1901); Estrada v. González Galván, Dec. 19, 1910, APJS 1° Civil Soconusco 1910, 101–150; Hutoff and Acosta, July 8, 1904, ARPPC Doc Privados 1904.

76. Fifty-nine of the 147 mortgages for which I have records for this period either appear in juicios hipotecarios in the court of first instance or have "cédula hipotecaria" or "embargado" noted by their entry in one of the indices. Thirty-one others are either annotated as having been paid in full, sold to another creditor, or canceled without note of how. I do not know the result of the remaining 57 mortgages.

77. Twenty-one of forty-three futures contracts for this period ended with court proceedings. That said, the turning point for rethinking futures contracts occurred a few years before lenders and borrowers reworked the general terms for mortgage-backed loans. Almost all advances signed after 1900 completed to the satisfaction of all involved parties. Finqueros with more than one mortgage were more likely to go into default. Those who had taken on large debts were no more or less likely to go into default than those who had taken on smaller amounts. About one third of each group—over and under MX$10,000—are recorded as having gone into default. That said, the cases involving large-scale borrowers were much more dramatic. Louis Brewer, discussed in Chapter Three, was the epitome of this type. "Hipotecario Actores Isaac y Samuel Rio, Luis R. Brewer, Guillermo Henkel," Aug. 30, 1899, APJS 1° Civil Soconusco 1899 (1905); "Providencia precautoria solicitada por el Señor Pedro del Cueto," Feb. 3, 1898, APJS 1° Civil Soconusco 1888.

78. Garlick v. Keller, Dec. 19, 1900, APJS 1° Civil Soconusco Varios Años.

79. "Juicio hipotecario por Guillermo Henkel contra León y Santos Almengor," Feb. 22, 1899, APJS 1° Civil Soconusco 1899.

80. Eisen, "The Earthquake and Volcanic Eruption in Guatemala in 1902."

81. Governor Pimentel recommended against suspending taxes on alcohol and personal contributions—the head tax—because "it would be difficult and cause much disgust if we were to reestablish them." Pimentel to Díaz, Nov. 11, 1902. CGPD, caja 27, exp. 13628: B. Melgor to Díaz, Nov. 5, 1902. CGPD, caja 27, exp. 13936.

82. Humphreys Seargeant, *San Antonio Nexapa*, 335.

83. For typical language constituting such a company, see, for example, Luttman and Edelman, Jan. 28, 1901, ARPPC Doc Priv 1900 y 1907: Sección Primera del Registro Público, 1900.

84. For examples of these types of contracts, see Cotesworth y Powell and Harrison, June 7, 1902, ARPPC Doc Priv 1906, Nottebohm y Cía and Luttmann y Kahle, 1904, ARPPC Doc Priv 1902, 1908: Año de 1904 sección Segunda Hipotecas, or M. M. Warburg y Cía and Sociedad Ad Giessemann y Cía, Dec. 26, 1913, ARPPC Doc Priv 1913.

85. AHCH, Sección de Fomento, 1907, vol. II, exp. 7: Leopoldo Salazar, Nov. 1, 1907.

86. Garcia and Garcia viuda de Urrutia, 1905, Indice alfabética de las nombres de los dueños de las fincas gravadas en la Sección 2a, 1887–1908, ARPPC Doc Priv 1903; Christy and Acosta, Feb. 4, 1907, ARPPC Doc Priv 1900 y 1907, Sección Segunda—Hipoteca—Enero a Abril de 1907.

87. The processing plant had once been owned by John Magee, the owner of San Juan las Chicharras, but by the early 1900s was in the hands of a new owner whom I have not been able to identify. "Sección II del Intestado de Cenobio Rodas," June 11, 1898, APJS 1° Civil Soconusco 1898.

88. When listing their occupations in the foundational documents of these companies, almost all the investors called themselves merchants. "Compañía de Luz Eléctrica y Fuerza Motríz de Tapachula, Sociedad Anónima," July 1, 1906, ARPPC Doc Priv 1906; Huthoff and Wohler Bartning y Suc., Dec. 3, 1906, ARPPC Doc Priv 1906; "Compañía de Teatro de Tapachula," Jan. 9, 1907, ARPPC Doc Priv 1900 y 1907: Registro de Comercio 2° Auxiliar Libro No 3, Sociedades y Poderes Año 1907.

89. The letter writers complained of rates as high as 24 percent annually, though none of the loans I have seen charged anywhere near that. Manuel Bejarano to Porfirio Díaz, Dec. 10, 1898. CGPD, vol. 23, exp. 17857. Tenenbaum, "Agiotista."

90. The Caja de Préstamos was a partnership between the government and the country's four biggest banks to supply tens of millions of pesos to rapidly develop unirrigated lands. Plantations, particularly rapidly expanding cotton fields, rather than smallholders, were the general beneficiaries, as the paperwork and legal requirements for obtaining such a loan were complex and costly. Oñate, *Banqueros y hacendados*, 35–36; Walsh, *Building the Borderlands*.

91. Fisher and Harrison in "Registro Público Sección Segunda Hipotecas 1912," Feb. 16, 1912, ARPPC Doc Priv 1902, 1910, 1912; Seigmund Robinow y Sohn and Hidalgo Plantation Company, March 7, 1913, ARPPC Doc Priv 1913;

"La Zacualpa-Hidalgo Settlement Delayed by Death of Mortgagee," *San Francisco Chronicle*, Dec. 17, 1916; Hidalgo Plantation Company and William Fisher, April 18, 1917, ARPPC Doc Priv 1917; "Testimonio de la escritura de préstamo de dinero garantizada con hipoteca celebrado por los Señores Guillermo S. Fisher y F Glur y Compañía," 1922, APP. For more on the rubber investment boom that swept the United States, see Henderson, "Modernization and Change in Mexico"; Schell, "American Investment in Tropical Mexico."

92. Revuelto and Banco Nacional de México, Oct. 11, 1910, ARPPC Doc Priv 1910: Sección 2a Hipotecas.

93. Chiapas, *Anuario estadístico del estado de Chiapas de 1909*.

CONCLUSION

1. Mexico, Ministerio de Hacienda y Crédito Público, *Boletin de estadística fiscal. July 1910–June 1911 (no. 366)*, 86–89.

2. Kuntz Ficker, *El comercio exterior de México en la era del capitalismo liberal, 1870–1929*, 76.

3. For example, Austin, *Labour, Land, and Capital in Ghana*; see also Ventura, "American Empire, Agrarian Reform," Ch. 3; Beckert, *Empire of Cotton*, Ch. 4; Seikaly, *Men of Capital*.

4. Womack Jr., "The Mexican Economy during the Revolution 1910–1920," 83.

5. The author went so far as to declare that per capita exports from the Soconusco were the highest in the Republic at MX$140 per person, and its exports much more impressive than that of the country's most important agricultural state, Yucatán, in both diversity and productivity per capita. "Chiapas no se mueve," *El Tiempo*, Feb. 15, 1911, 5.

6. The literature on the Mexican Revolution is vast. Setting an end date for the Revolution is as problematic as establishing its causal elements, given the variety of actors, modes of dissent, and motivations for action that the fighting would come to contain. For classics and a recent summary of the literature, see Womack, *Zapata and the Mexican Revolution*; Knight, *The Mexican Revolution*; Tutino, *From Insurrection to Revolution in Mexico*; Katz, *The Life and Times of Pancho Villa*; Barrón, *Historias de la Revolución mexicana*.

7. Waibel, *La Sierra Madre de Chiapas*, 199.

8. Maurer, *The Power and the Money*, Ch. 7; Santiago, *The Ecology of Oil*; Kuntz Ficker, *El comercio exterior de México en la era del capitalismo liberal, 1870–1929*; Kuntz Ficker, *Las exportaciones mexicanas durante la primera globalización 1870–1929*; Garner, *British Lions and Mexican Eagles*; Suarez-Potts, *The Making of Law*, Chs. 5 and 6.

9. See especially Joseph, *Revolution from Without*; Tutino, *From Insurrection to Revolution in Mexico*.

10. "Memorandum," 1911, SRE 16-4-126.

11. SRE, 1915, 16-4-145.

12. Spenser, *El Partido Socialista Chiapaneco*, 86–90, 160; Osten, *The Mexican Revolution's Wake*.

13. AGA, Asunto: Dotación, Estado: Chiapas, Municipio: Mazatán, Manuel

Lazos, exp. 43, legajo 4; AGA, Asunto: Dotación, Estado: Chiapas, Municipio: Cacahoatán, exp. 408, legajo 7; AGA, Asunto: Dotación, Estado: Chiapas, Municipio: Tapachula, El Naranjo, exp. 599, legajo 4.

14. AGA, Asunto: Dotación/Restitución, State: Chiapas, Municipio: Acacoyagua, exp. 1, legajo 5; AGA, Asunto: Dotación, Estado: Chiapas, Municipio: Acacoyagua, Los Cacaos, exp. 2, legajo 625 (723.8); "Impersonal," in AHCH, Fomento, 1913, vol. 5, exp. 25; "Juicio verbal ordinario sobre devolución y reivindicacción de una parte de terreno," April 27, 1914, AJPS 1° Civil Soconusco 1912, 51–100; Henderson, "Modernization and Change in Mexico," 255–56.

15. AGA, Estado: Chiapas, Municipio: Cacahoatán, exp. 9, legajo 408; AGA, Asunto: Dotación, Estado: Chiapas, Municipio: Tapachula, El Naranjo, exp. 4, legajo 599; AGA, Asunto: Dotación, Estado: Chiapas, Municipio: Tuxtla Chico, Manuel Lazos, exp. 3, legajo 8358.

16. Castillo and Nolan-Ferrell both treat the identity politics of ejiditarios in the border region with great detail and insight. They both point out that the creation of ejidos in the Soconusco also served to keep labor populations closer to home, lessening the burden of transit and subsistence that finqueros had long complained of. Hernández Castillo and Cronshaw, "Between Civil Disobedience and Silent Rejection"; Hernández Castillo and Nigh, "Global Processes and Local Identity among Mayan Coffee Growers in Chiapas, Mexico"; Nolan-Ferrell, *Constructing Citizenship*.

17. "Revolución en el Estado de Chiapas," 1916, SRE 17-6-10; "Memorandum referente a la revolución de Chiapas," 1916, SRE 17-9-101.

18. "Chiapas Land and Stock Company—su protección," 1920, SRE 17-13-41; "Compañía Cafetera de Chiapas—su protección," 1920, SRE 17-12-153.

19. Mahnken, *Mi vida en los cafetales*, 31–36.

20. Boyer, *Political Landscapes*; Walsh, *Building the Borderlands*; Fowler-Salamini, *Working Women, Entrepreneurs, and the Mexican Revolution*.

21. For much of the twentieth century, coffee was Mexico's second or third largest export, after automobiles and oil, and made up almost half of its agricultural exports. International market controls instituted by the International Coffee Organization in 1989 heralded a collapse in both prices and production around the world. In Mexico, they brought about the collapse of the Mexican Coffee Institute (Instituto Mexicano del Café or INMECAFE). Smallholders and ejiditarios reorganized into cooperatives to survive, and finqueros formed partnerships with foreign and multinational corporations to shore up their interests. Many reoriented toward organic and other types of specialty production. Coffee is no longer such a key part of Mexico's export basket, but it remains an important crop for much of the country's south. Since 2012, production has again fallen because of new pests and a decline in global coffee prices. In 2015, the Soconusco produced some 70,000 tons of coffee. Chiapas produced more than 380,000 tons of coffee that year, down from highs of over 500,000 tons a few years before. This still represents more than 40 percent of Mexico's total coffee production. Other districts in the country and in the state produce more coffee than the Soconusco, but internal consumption in Mexico has grown and the district remains one of the largest exporters of coffee. "Cierre de la producción agrícola por cultivo," 2–5; Pérez-Grovas, Cervantes, and

Burnstein, "Case Study of the Coffee Sector in Mexico"; SIAP-SAGARPA, "Estadística de la Producción Agrícola en 2015."

22. "Cierre de la producción agrícola por cultivo," 2–5; Pérez-Grovas, Cervantes, and Burnstein, "Case Study of the Coffee Sector in Mexico."

23. Hernández Castillo and Nigh, "Global Processes and Local Identity among Mayan Coffee Growers in Chiapas, Mexico"; Hernández Castillo and Cronshaw, "Between Civil Disobedience and Silent Rejection"; Pérez-Grovas, Cervantes, and Burnstein, "Case Study of the Coffee Sector in Mexico"; Hudson and Hudson, "Justice, Sustainability, and the Fair Trade Movement"; Milford, "Coffee, Co-Operatives and Competition"; Renard and Breña, "The Mexican Coffee Crisis."

24. "Cierre de la producción agrícola por cultivo."

Bibliography

ARCHIVES CONSULTED

Chiapas
AHCH   Archivo Histórico de Chiapas (Tuxtla Gutiérrez)
AMT   Archivo Municipal de Tapachula (Tapachula)
APP   Archivo Perú-París (Tapachula)
APJS   Archivo del Poder Judicial del Soconusco (Tapachula)
ARPPC Archivo del Registro Público de la Propiedad y el Comercio (Tapachula)

Mexico City
AGA   Archivo General Agrario
AGN   Archivo General de la Nación
AHMR Archivo Histórico de Matías Romero, Banco de México
CGPD Colección del General Porfirio Díaz, Universidad Iberoamericana
MMOB Mapoteca Manuel Orozco y Berra
SRE   Archivo Histórico de la Secretaría de Relaciones Exteriores

United States
MCP   Mexico Colonization Papers, Latin American Library manuscripts, Tulane University, New Orleans, Louisiana

NEWSPAPERS

Mexico City
La Bandera Nacional
Boletín de la Sociedad Agrícola Mexicana
El Combate
El Cultivador
La Defensa Católica
El Foro
La Iberia
El México Gráfico
El Monitor Repúblicano
The Pan-American Magazine
La Patria
Semana Mercantil
El Siglo Diez y Nueve

El Telégrafo
El Tiempo
La Tierra
Le Trait de Union
La Voz de México

Chiapas
La Brújula
Periódico Oficial del Estado de Chiapas
El Sur de México

Tabasco
El Eco de Tabasco
Guatemala
La Estrella de Occidente

United States
Chicago Tribune
Los Angeles Times
San Francisco Chronicle
New York Times
Washington Post

PUBLISHED PRIMARY SOURCES

Bynum, Mary L. *The World's Exports of Coffee*. U.S. Department of Commerce, Bureau of Foreign and Domestic Commerce. Trade Promotion series, No. 110. Washington, D.C.: U.S. Government Printing Office, 1930.

Chiapas. *Anuario estadístico del estado de Chiapas de 1909*, n.d.

———. *Documentos relativos al congreso agrícola de Chiapas*. Tuxtla Gutierrez, Imprenta del Gobierno del Estado, dirigida por Félix Santaella, 1896.

Chiapas, and Antonio A. Moguel. *Nueva colección de leyes de hacienda vigentes en el estado de Chiapas*. Imprenta del Gobierno del Estado, 1899.

Colburn, Fredrick Henry Wait. *An Interesting and Authentic Description of a Mule-Back Ride Through the Quaint, Little-Known Department of Soconusco, Mexico*. [San Francisco?]: John W. Butler, 1901.

Comisión Guatemalteca de Límites con México. *Memoria sobre la cuestión de límites entre Guatemala y México*. Guatemala: Tipografía Nacional, 1900.

Cruz, Fernando. *La verdad histórica acerca del tratado de limites entre Guatemala y México: documentos publicados 1888*. Tipografía "La Union," 1888.

Dardón, Andrés. *La cuestión de límites entre México y Guatemala*. Guatemala, 1875.

Eisen, Gustav. "The Earthquake and Volcanic Eruption in Guatemala in 1902." *Bulletin of the American Geographical Society* 35, no. 4 (January 1, 1903): 325–52.

Escobar, Sebastián. *Informe de los recursos agrícolas del Departamento de Soco-*

nusco, en el Estado de Chiapas, y del estado que actualmente guardan. México: Gobierno en Palacio, 1871.
Escriche, Joaquín, José Vicente y Caravantes, León Galindo y de Vera, and Juan María. Biec. *Diccionario razonado de legislación y jurisprudencia*. Madrid: Imprenta de Cuesta, 1874.
Forsyth, William J. *Journal of W. J. Forsyth*. Boston: Christopher Publishing House, 1940.
García Cubas, Antonio. "Carta general de La República Mexicana." Mexico: Imprenta de Jose Mariano Fernández de Lara, 1858.
Gris, Carlos. *Sebastián Escobar y el departamento de Soconusco, Estado de Chiapas, apuntes para la historia*. Mexico: Tipografía La Luz, 1885.
Humphreys Seargeant, Helen. *San Antonio Nexapa*. New York: Vantage Press, 1952.
Islas, Emilio. *Codificación de la República Mexicana formada de orden del Sr. Secretario de Justicia e Instrucción Pública. Tomo XII Estado de Chiapas*. Mexico: Juan Flores, 1896.
Kaerger, Karl. *Agricultura y colonización en México en 1900*. 1a ed. en español. Chapingo, Mexico: Universidad Autónoma Chapingo, 1986.
Larráinzar, Manuel. *Chiapas y Soconusco: la cuestión de límites entre México y Guatemala*. Biblioteca básica del sureste. Mexico: Gobierno del Estado de Chiapas: Consejo Nacional para la Cultura y las Artes, 1996.
Litígio entre Juan Magee y Guillermo José Forsyth sobre la finca de café San Juan Las Chicharras. Quetzaltenango, Guatemala: Tipográfico la Industria, 1893.
Lozano, José María. *Estudio del derecho constitucional patrio en lo relativo a los derechos del hombre*. México: Dublán, 1876. Reprint, México: Editorial Porrúa, 1972.
Ludewig, H. Juan. *Veinte años trabajos de colonización y el cultivo del cafeto en Soconusco*. México: Imprenta y fototipia de la Secretaría de Fomento, 1909.
Mahnken, Winifred. *Mi vida en los cafetales: Tapachula 1882–1992*. Tuxtla Gutiérrez, México: Gobierno del Estado de Chiapas, 1993.
Mallen, Bernardo. *Mexico Yesterday and To-Day, 1876–1904*. Mexico: Printed by Müller Hnos., 1904.
Memoria que presenta el Ciudadano Manuel Carrascosa, como Gobernador Constitucional del Estado Libre y Soberano de Chiapas a la H. Legislatura. Correspondiente al primer bienio de su administración. Tuxtla Gutiérrez, Chiapas: Imprenta del Gobierno del Estado, 1889.
Mexico. *Censo general de la República Mexicana verificado el 28 de octubre de 1900*. México: Oficina Tipografica de la Secretaría de Fomento, 1901.
———. *Censo general de la República Mexicana, verificado el 20 de octubre de 1895*. México: Oficina Tipografica de la Secretaría de Fomento, 1897.
———. "Cierre de la producción agrícola por cultivo." Secretaría de Agricultura, Ganadería, Desarrollo Rural, Pesca y Alimentación, 2012. http://www.siap.gob.mx/cierre-de-la-produccion-agricola-por-cultivo/.
———. *Código civil del Distrito Federal y territorios de Tepic y Baja California: promulgado en 31 de marzo de 1884*. Mexico: Vda de C. Bouret, 1902.
———. *Código civil del Distrito Federal y territorio de la Baja-California*. Código civil (1870). México: Imprenta dirigida por José Batiza, 1870.

———. *Código de comercio de los Estados Unidos Mexicanos: expedido en virtud de la autorización concedida al ejecutivo por decreto de 15 de diciembre de 1883*. Mexico: Tipografía de G.A. Esteva, 1884.

———. *Código de comercio de México*. Mexico: J. M. Lara, 1854.

———. *Legislación mexicana: ó, Colección completa de las disposiciones legislativas expedidas desde la independencia de la República*. Mexico: Dublán y Lozano, 1887.

———. *Legislación de terrenos baldíos: o sea completa colección de leyes, decretos, ordenes, circulares, reglamentos, contratos y demás disposiciones supremas, relativas a terrenos baldíos de la República, publicadas hasta el mes de setiembre de 1885*. Mexico: Imprenta y librería de D. Miramontes, 1885.

———. *Ley del timbre: para documentos y libros, renta interior, contribución federal y estampillas especiales de aduanas: expedida en 31 de marzo de 1887*. Mexico: Imprenta del Gobierno, en el ex-arzobispado, 1887.

———. *Ley del timbre reformada*. Mexico: Imprenta de J.R. Barbedillo y ca., 1876.

———. *La nueva ley de la renta federal del timbre: expedida por el ejecutivo de la Unión en Abril 25 de 1893*. Mexico: A. Cougne, 1893.

———. *Proyecto de código mercantil*. Imprenta del Gobierno, 1869.

———. *Tercer censo de población de los Estados Unidos Mexicanos*. Mexico: INEGI, 1910.

Mexico, Secretaría de Fomento, Colonización e Industria. *Anuario estadístico de la República Mexicana (1893–1907)* Mexico: Dirección General de Estadística, 1894–1908.

———. *Importación y exportación de la república mexicana*. México, 1899.

———. . *Memoria 1897 a 1900*. Mexico: Secretaría de Fomento, 1908.

———. *Memoria 1892–1896*. Mexico: Secretaría de Fomento, 1897.

———. *Memoria 1883–1885*. Mexico: Secretaría de Fomento, 1887.

Mexico, Secretaría de Hacienda y Crédito Público. *Boletín de estadística fiscal. Años 1900–1911*. Mexico: Tipografía de la Oficina impresora del timbre [etc.], n.d.

———. *Boletín de estadística fiscal. Jul. 1910–Jun. 1911 (no. 366)*. Mexico: Tipografía de la Oficina impresora del timbre [etc.], 1912.

———. *Comercio exterior: Año fiscal de 1896–1897, 1897–1898, 1899–1900, 1901*.

———. *Exportaciones de los años fiscales de 1890–1895*. Tipografía de la Oficina Impresora de Estampillas, 1891–1896.

———. *Expediente de la Secretaría de Hacienda, respecto de las medidas propuestas y acordadas para impulsar el desarrollo de los elementos de riqueza agrícola del Departamento de Soconusco en el Estado de Chiapas*. México: Imprenta del Gobierno, 1871.

———. *Noticia de la exportación de mercancías (1875–1889)*. México: Imprenta del Gobierno, 1872–1890.

Mexico, Secretaría de Relaciones Exteriores. *Correspondencia diplomática cambiada entre el gobierno de los Estados Unidos Mexicanos y los de varias potencias extranjeras*. Mexico: Tipografía de G. A. Esteva, 1882.

Montúfar, Lorenzo. *Reseña histórica de Centro América*. Guatemala: Tipografía de "El Progreso," 1878.

Olsson-Seffer, Pehr. *Report on Hidalgo Plantations and Impressions of La Zacualpa Rubber Plantation.* [San Francisco]: John W. Butler, 1905.

———. *Rubber Planting in Mexico and Central America.* Kelly & Walsh, Limited, Printers, 1907.

Pineda, Emeterio. *Descripción geográfica del Departamento de Chiapas y Soconusco.* Chiapas: Imprenta de Ignacio Cumplido, 1845. Reprint, Tuxtla Gutiérrez, Chiapas: Consejo Estatal para la Cultura y las Artes de Chiapas, 1999.

Pollard, Hugh. *A Busy Time in Mexico: An Unconventional Record of Mexican Incident.* London: Constable and Co., 1913.

A Report of Secretary of State, with Accompanying Papers, in Response to Senate Resolution of January 31, 1882, Touching the Relations of the United States with Guatemala and Mexico, &c. Washington, D.C.: U.S. Government Printing Office, 1882.

Romero, Matías. *Bosquejo histórico de la agregación á México de Chiapas y Soconusco y de las negociaciones sobre limites entaladas por México con Centro-America y Guatemala.* Vol. I, 1821–1831. Mexico: Imprenta del Gobierno, en palacio, a cargo de F. Mata, 1877.

———. *Cultivo del café en la costa meridional de Chiapas.* México: Imprenta del Gobierno, 1875.

———. *Refutación de las inculpaciones hechas al c. Matías Romero por el gobierno de Guatemala.* Mexico: Imprenta poliglota de C. Ramiro y Ponce de Léon, 1876.

Sánchez, Santos. *Colección de Pragmáticas . . . de Carlos IV.* Spain: J. Del Collado, 1805.

SIAP-SAGARPA. "Estadística de la Producción Agrícola en 2015," https://datos.gob.mx/busca/dataset/estadistica-de-la-produccion-agricola. 2016.

"Soconusco." In *Annual Series of Trade Reports, Serial no. 3739 to 3916,* pp. 39–41. UK: House of Commons Parliamentary Papers, 1907.

Tratado sobre límites entre México y Guatemala, celebrado en 1882, Mexico-Guatemala, Sept. 27, 1882.

Turner, John Kenneth. *Barbarous Mexico.* Chicago: C. H. Kerr & Company, 1911.

Vallés y Pujals, Juan. *El contrato de cuenta corriente.* Barcelona: 1906.

Waibel, Leo. *La Sierra Madre de Chiapas.* México: Sociedad Mexicana de Geografía y Estadística, 1946.

La zona comprendida entre los Ríos Chixoy y Santa Isabel es de Guatemala y no de Méjico. Guatemala: Tipografía "La Unión," 1889.

BOOKS AND ARTICLES

Aboites, Luis, and Luis Jáuregui. *Penuria sin fin: historia de los impuestos en México siglos XVIII–XX.* 1. ed. Historia económica (Mexico City, Mexico). México D.F.: Instituto Mora, 2005.

Acemoglu, Daron. *Why Nations Fail: The Origins of Power, Prosperity and Poverty.* London: Profile, 2012.

Acemoglu, Daron, and Alexander Wolitzky. "The Economics of Labor Coercion." *Econometrica* 79, no. 2 (2011): 555–600.

Adelman, Jeremy. "Agricultural Credit in the Province of Buenos Aires, Argentina, 1890–1914." *Journal of Latin American Studies* 22, no. 1 (1990): 69–87.

———. *Frontier Development: Land, Labour, and Capital on the Wheatlands of Argentina and Canada, 1890–1914*. Oxford Historical Monographs. New York: Clarendon Press, 1994.

———. "Institutions, Property, and Economic Development in Latin America." In *The Other Mirror: Grand Theory through the Lens of Latin America*, edited by Miguel Angel Centeno and Fernando Lopez-Alves, 27–54. Princeton, N.J.: Princeton University Press, 2001.

———. "Liberalism and Constitutionalism in Latin America in the 19th Century." *History Compass* 12, no. 6 (2014): 508–16.

———. *Republic of Capital: Buenos Aires and the Legal Transformation of the Atlantic World*. Stanford, Calif.: Stanford University Press, 1999.

Adelman, Jeremy, and Stephen Aron. "From Borderlands to Borders: Empires, Nation-States, and the Peoples in between in North American History." *American Historical Review* 104, no. 3 (1999): 814–41.

Aguilar Rivera, José Antonio. *Las elecciones y el gobierno representativo en México (1810–1910)*. Biblioteca mexicana (Consejo Nacional para la Cultura y las Artes (Mexico)). Serie Historia y antropología. Mexico, D.F.: Fondo de Cultura Económica, 2010.

Akaki, Pablo Pérez. "Los siglos XIX y XX en la cafeticultura nacional: de la bonanza a la crisis del grano de oro mexicano." *Revista de Historia* no. 67 (2013): 159–99.

Anna, Timothy E. *Forging Mexico: 1821–1835*. Lincoln: University of Nebraska Press, 1998.

Appelbaum, Nancy P. *Mapping the Country of Regions: The Chorographic Commission of Nineteenth-Century Colombia*. Reprint edition. Chapel Hill: University of North Carolina Press, 2016.

Augustine-Adams, Kif. "Constructing Mexico: Marriage, Law and Women's Dependent Citizenship in the Late-Nineteenth and Early-Twentieth Centuries." *Gender & History* 18, no. 1 (2006): 20–34.

Austin, Gareth. *Labour, Land, and Capital in Ghana: From Slavery to Free Labour in Asante, 1807–1956*. Rochester, N.Y.: University of Rochester Press, 2005.

Barrón, Luis. *Historias de la Revolución mexicana*. 1. ed. Herramientas para la historia. México, D.F.: Fondo de Cultura Económica: Centro de Investigación y Docencia Económicas, 2004.

Baud, Michiel, and Alma Parra. "Respuestas, resistencias y acomodos a los procesos modernizadores en América Latina. Viejos problemas, nuevas perspectivas. Conclusiones generales." In *Pueblos, comunidades y municipios frente a los proyectos modernizadores en América Latina, siglo XIX*, edited by Antonio Escobar Ohmstede, Romana Falcón, and Raymond Buve, 246–51. San Luis Potosí, México: El Colegio de San Luis; Amsterdam: El Colegio de San Luis, 2002.

Baud, Michiel, and Willem Van Schendel. "Toward a Comparative History of Borderlands." *Journal of World History* 8, no. 2 (1997): 211–42.

Bauer, Arnold J. "Rural Workers in Spanish America: Problems of Peonage and Oppression." *Hispanic American Historical Review* 59, no. 1 (1979): 34–63.

Baumann, Friederike. "Terratenientes, campesinos y la expansión de la agricultura capitalista en Chiapas, 1896–1916." *Mesoamérica* 4 (1983).

Bazant, Jan. "Peones, arrendatarios y aparceros: 1868–1904." *Historia Mexicana* 24, no. 1 (1974): 94–121.
Beatty, Edward. *Institutions and Investment: The Political Basis of Industrialization in Mexico Before 1911*. Stanford, Calif.: Stanford University Press, 2001.
———. *Technology and the Search for Progress in Modern Mexico*. The Fletcher Jones Foundation Humanities Imprint. Oakland, Calif.: University of California Press, 2015.
Bechis, Martha. "La 'organización nacional' y las tribus pampeanas en Argentina durante el siglo XIX." In *Pueblos, comunidades y municipios frente a los proyectos modernizadores en América Latina, siglo XIX*, edited by Antonio Escobar Ohmstede, Romana Falcón, and Raymond Buve, 83–105. San Luis Potosí, México: El Colegio de San Luis; Amsterdam: El Colegio de San Luis, 2002.
Beck, Thorsten. "Legal Institutions and Economic Development." In *The Oxford Handbook of Capitalism*, edited by Dennis C. Mueller. New York: Oxford University Press, 2012.
Beckert, Sven. *Empire of Cotton: A Global History*. 1st ed. New York: Knopf, 2014.
Benjamin, Thomas. *A Rich Land, a Poor People: Politics and Society in Modern Chiapas*. 1st ed. Albuquerque: University of New Mexico Press, 1989.
Bergquist, Charles W. *Coffee and Conflict in Colombia, 1886–1910*. Durham, N.C: Duke University Press, 1978.
Bernstein, Harry. *Matías Romero, 1837–1898*. Sección de obras de historia. México: Fondo de Cultura Económica, 1973.
Bess, Michael Kirkland. "Revolutionary Paths." *Mexican Studies/Estudios Mexicanos* 32, no. 1 (2016): 56–82.
Bieber, Judy. *Power, Patronage, and Political Violence: State Building on a Brazilian Frontier, 1822–1889*. Lincoln: University of Nebraska Press, 1999.
Blake, Michael, and Hector Neff. "Evidence for the Diversity of Late Archaic and Early Formative Plant Use in the Soconusco Region of Mexico and Guatemala." In *Early Mesoamerican Social Transformations: Archaic and Formative Lifeways in the Soconusco Region*, edited by Richard G. Lesure, 47–66. Berkeley: University of California Press, 2011.
Borrás, Leopoldo. "Soconusco." *Artes de México*, no. 192 (1976): 115–16.
Bortz, Jeffrey, and Stephen H. Haber. *The Mexican Economy, 1870–1930: Essays on the Economic History of Institutions, Revolution, and Growth*. Stanford, Calif.: Stanford University Press, 2002.
Boyer, Christopher R. *Political Landscapes: Forests, Conservation, and Community in Mexico*. Durham, N.C.: Duke University Press, 2015.
Brading, D. A. *Caudillo and Peasant in the Mexican Revolution*. New York: Cambridge University Press, 1980.
———. *Haciendas and Ranchos in the Mexican Bajío, León, 1700–1860*. New York: Cambridge University Press, 1978.
———. "Liberal Patriotism and the Mexican Reforma." *Journal of Latin American Studies* 20, no. 1 (1988): 27–48.
Brass, Tom, and Marcel van der Linden. *Free and Unfree Labour: The Debate Continues*. International and Comparative Social History 5. Bern: Peter Lang, 1997.
Bravo Regidor, Carlos. "Elecciones de gobernadores durante el Porfiriato." In *Las*

elecciones y el gobierno representativo en México (1810–1910), edited by José Antonio Aguilar Rivera, 257–81. Mexico City: Fondo de Cultura, 2010.

Brubaker, Rogers. "Migration, Membership, and the Modern Nation-State: Internal and External Dimensions of the Politics of Belonging." *Journal of Interdisciplinary History* 41, no. 1 (2010): 61–78.

Bucheli, Marcelo. *Bananas and Business: The United Fruit Company in Colombia, 1899–2000*. New York: New York University Press, 2005.

Buchenau, Jürgen. *In the Shadow of the Giant: The Making of Mexico's Central America Policy, 1876–1930*. Tuscaloosa: University of Alabama Press, 1996.

———. "Small Numbers, Great Impact: Mexico and Its Immigrants, 1821–1973." *Journal of American Ethnic History* 20, no. 3 (2001): 23–49.

Bunker, Steven B. *Creating Mexican Consumer Culture in the Age of Porfirio Díaz*. Albuquerque: University of New Mexico Press, 2012.

Burnett, D. Graham. *Masters of All They Surveyed: Exploration, Geography, and a British El Dorado*. Chicago: University of Chicago Press, 2000.

Cahill, David Patrick, Blanca Tovías, and Janine Gasco, eds. "Beyond the Indian/Ladino Dichotomy: Shifting Identities in Colonial and Contemporary Chiapas, Mexico." In *New World, First Nations: Native Peoples of Mesoamerica and the Andes under Colonial Rule*, 115–28. Brighton, U.K.: Sussex Academic Press, 2006.

Cambranes, J. C. *Coffee and Peasants: The Origins of the Modern Plantation Economy in Guatemala, 1853–1897*. Stockholm, Sweden: Institute of Latin American Studies, 1985.

Candiani, Vera S. *Dreaming of Dry Land: Environmental Transformation in Colonial Mexico City*. Stanford, Calif.: Stanford University Press, 2014.

Caplan, Karen Deborah. *Indigenous Citizens: Local Liberalism in Early National Oaxaca and Yucatán*. Stanford, Calif.: Stanford University Press, 2010.

Cardoso, Ciro Flamarion Santana. *Historia económica de América Latina*. Crítica/Historia. Barcelona: Crítica, 1979.

Cardoso, Fernando Henrique, and Enzo Faletto. *Dependency and Development in Latin America*. Berkeley: University of California Press, 1979.

Carmagnani, Marcello. *Estado y mercado: la economía pública del liberalismo mexicano, 1850–1911*. 1a ed. Fideicomiso Historia de las Américas/Serie Hacienda. México, D.F.: El Colegio de México, 1994.

———. "El Federalismo liberal mexicano." In *Federalismos latinoamericanos: México, Brasil, Argentina*, edited by Marcello Carmagnani and Germán José Bidart Campos, 135–79. Sección de obras de historia. México, D.F.: El Colegio de México, 1993.

———. "Vectors of Liberal Economic Culture in Mexico." In *The Divine Charter: Constitutionalism and Liberalism in Nineteenth-Century Mexico*, edited by Jaime E. Rodríguez O., 285–304. Latin American Silhouettes. Lanham, Md.: Rowman & Littlefield, 2005.

Castillo, Manuel Angel, Mónica Toussaint Ribot, and Mario Vázquez Olivera. *Espacios diversos, historia en común: México, Guatemala y Belice: La construcción de una frontera*. México, D.F.: Secretaría de Relaciones Exteriores, 2006.

Centeno, Miguel Angel, and Agustin E. Ferraro. "Republics of the Possible: State Building in Latin America and Spain." In *State and Nation Making in Latin*

America and Spain: Republics of the Possible, 3–24. Cambridge: Cambridge University Press, 2013.

———, eds. *State and Nation Making in Latin America and Spain: Republics of the Possible*. Cambridge: Cambridge University Press, 2013.

Centeno, Miguel Angel, and Fernando Lopez-Alves. "Introduction." In *The Other Mirror: Grand Theory through the Lens of Latin America*, edited by Miguel Angel Centeno and Fernando López-Alvez, 3–23. Princeton, N.J.: Princeton University Press, 2001.

Charlip, Julie A. *Cultivating Coffee: The Farmers of Carazo, Nicaragua, 1880–1930*. Athens: Ohio University Press, 2003.

———. " 'So That Land Takes on Value': Coffee and Land in Carazo, Nicaragua." *Latin American Perspectives* 26, no. 1 (January 1, 1999): 92–105.

Chassen de Lopez, Francie R. *From Liberal to Revolutionary Oaxaca: The View from the South; Mexico, 1867–1911*. University Park: Pennsylvania State University Press, 2004.

Chinchilla Aguilar, Ernesto, and Janine Gasco. "La Provincia de Soconusco desde la Conquista hasta 1700." In *Historia general de Guatemala*, edited by Jorge Luján Muñoz, 673–81. Guatemala: Asociación de Amigos del País, 1993.

Chowning, Margaret. "Reassessing the Prospects for Profit in Nineteenth-Century Mexican Agriculture from a Regional Perspective: Michoacán, 1810–60." In *How Latin America Fell Behind*, edited by Stephen Haber, 179–215. Stanford, Calif.: Stanford University Press, 1997.

———. *Wealth and Power in Provincial Mexico: Michoacán from the Late Colony to the Revolution*. Stanford, Calif.: Stanford University Press, 1999.

Clarence-Smith, William Gervase, and Steven Topik. *The Global Coffee Economy in Africa, Asia and Latin America, 1500–1989*. Cambridge: Cambridge University Press, 2003.

Coatsworth, John H. "Desigualdad, instituciones y crecimiento económico en América Latina." *Economía* 35, no. 69 (2012): 204–30.

———. *Growth against Development: The Economic Impact of Railroads in Porfirian, Mexico*. DeKalb: Northern Illinois University Press, 1981.

———. "Obstacles to Economic Growth in Nineteenth-Century Mexico." *The American Historical Review* 83, no. 1 (1978): 80–100.

———. *Los orígenes del atraso: nueve ensayos de historia económica de México en los siglos XVIII y XIX*. 1. ed. México, D.F.: Alianza Editorial Mexicana, 1990.

Coe, Michael D., and Kent V. Flannery. *Early Cultures and Human Ecology in South Coastal Guatemala*. Washington, D.C.: Smithsonian Press; U.S. Government Printing Office, 1967.

Coerver, Don M. *The Porfirian Interregnum: The Presidency of Manuel González of Mexico, 1880–1884*. Fort Worth: Texas Christian University Press, 1979.

Colegio de México. *Estadísticas económicas del Porfiriato: comercio exterior de México, 1877–1911*. México, D.F.: Colegio de México. 1960.

Connolly, Priscilla. *El contratista de Don Porfirio: obras públicas, deuda y desarrollo desigual*. 1. ed. México, D.F.: El Colegio de Michoacán, 1997.

———. "Introducción a obras públicas." In *Ferrocarriles y obras públicas*, edited by Sandra Kuntz Ficker and Priscilla Connolly, 1a ed., 141–64. México, D.F.:

Instituto Mora, El Colegio de Michoacán, El Colegio de México, Instituto de Investigaciones Históricas-UNAM, 1999.
Cook, Karen S. *Cooperation without Trust*. New York: Russell Sage Foundation, 2005.
Corbett, Barbara Marie. "Republican Hacienda and Federalist Politics: The Making of 'Liberal' Oligarchy in San Luis Potosi, 1767–1853." PhD diss., Princeton University, 1997.
Córdova Santamaría, Susana. *Café y sociedad en Huatusco, Veracruz: formación de la cultura cafetalera (1870–1930)*. 1. ed. México, D.F: Conaculta, 2005.
Corr, John. "The Enlightenment Surfaces in Nineteenth-Century Mexico: Scientific Thinking Attempts to Deliver Order and Progress." *History of Science* 52, no. 1 (March 2014): 98–123, 125.
Cosío Villegas, Daniel. "La aventura de Matías." *Historia Mexicana* 8, no. 1 (July 1, 1958): 35–59.
———. *Historia moderna de Mexico. Vol. VI, El Porfiriato: la vida política exterior, primera parte*. México: Editorial Hermes, 1960.
———. *Historia moderna de Mexico. Vol. VII, El Porfiriato: la vida económica*. México: Editorial Hermes, 1965.
———. *Historia moderna de Mexico. Vol. IX, El Porfiriato: la vida politica interior*. México: Editorial Hermes, 1972.
Craib, Raymond B. *Cartographic Mexico: A History of State Fixations and Fugitive Landscapes*. Durham, N.C.: Duke University Press, 2004.
Cribelli, Teresa. *Industrial Forests and Mechanical Marvels: Modernization in Nineteenth-Century Brazil*. New York: Cambridge University Press, 2016.
Curtin, Philip D. *The Rise and Fall of the Plantation Complex: Essays in Atlantic History*. 2nd ed. Studies in Comparative World History. Cambridge: Cambridge University Press, 1998.
Cushman, Gregory T. *Guano and the Opening of the Pacific World: A Global Ecological History*. Studies in Environment and History. New York: Cambridge University Press, 2013.
De la Fuente, Ariel. *Children of Facundo: Caudillo and Gaucho Insurgency during the Argentine State-Formation Process (La Rioja, 1853–1870)*. Durham, N.C.: Duke University Press, 2000.
Dore, Elizabeth. "Patriarchy from Above, Patriarchy from Below: Debt Peonage on Nicaraguan Coffee Estates, 1870–1930." In *The Global Coffee Economy in Africa, Asia and Latin America, 1500–1989*, edited by W. G Clarence-Smith and Steven Topik, 209–35. Cambridge: Cambridge University Press, 2003.
Dym, Jordana. "Citizen of Which Republic?: Foreigners and the Construction of National Citizenship in Central America, 1823–1845." *The Americas* 64, no. 4 (2008): 477–511.
———. "Taking a Walk on the Wild Side: Experiencing the Spaces of Colonial Latin America." *Colonial Latin American Review* 21, no. 1 (April 1, 2012): 3–16.
Dym, Jordana, and Karl Offen, eds. *Mapping Latin America: A Cartographic Reader*. Chicago: University of Chicago Press, 2011.
Engerman, Stanley L., and Kenneth Lee Sokoloff. *Economic Development in the*

Americas since 1500: Endowments and Institutions. NBER Series on Long-Term Factors in Economic Development. New York: Cambridge University Press, 2012.

Escobar Ohmstede, Antonio, and Matthew Butler. "Introduction: Transitions and Closures in Nineteenth- and Twentieth-Century Mexican Agrarian History." In *Mexico in Transition: New Perspectives on Mexican Agrarian History, Nineteenth and Twentieth Centuries*. Mexico City: CIESAS, 2013.

———, eds. *Mexico in Transition: New Perspectives on Mexican Agrarian History, Nineteenth and Twentieth Centuries*. Mexico City: CIESAS, 2013.

Escobar Ohmstede, Antonio, Romana Falcón, and Raymond Buve. *Pueblos, comunidades y municipios frente a los proyectos modernizadores en América Latina, siglo XIX*. San Luis Potosí, México: El Colegio de San Luis; Amsterdam: El Colegio de San Luis, 2002.

Escobar Ohmstede, Antonio, and Teresa Rojas Rabiela. *Estructuras y formas agrarias en México: del pasado y del presente*. México, D.F.: Registro Agrario Nacional, Secretaría de la reforma Agraria: Archivo General Agrario: Centro de Investigaciones y Estudios Superiores en Antropología Social, 2001.

Escobar Ohmstede, Antonio, and Frans J. Schryer. "Las sociedades agrarias en el norte de Hidalgo, 1856–1900." *Mexican Studies/Estudios Mexicanos* 8, no. 1 (1992): 1–21.

Falcón, Romana. "Esplendor y ocaso de los caciques militares. San Luis Potosí en la Revolución Mexicana." *Mexican Studies/Estudios Mexicanos* 4, no. 2 (1988): 265–93.

———. "El estado liberal ante las rebeliones populares. México, 1867–1876." *Historia Mexicana* 54, no. 4 (2005): 973–1048.

———. *El jefe político: un dominio negociado en el mundo rural del Estado de México, 1856–1911*. Primera edición. México, D.F.: El Colegio de México, Centro de Estudios Históricos, 2015.

———. *Revolución y caciquismo: San Luis Potosí, 1910–1938*. 1a ed. México, D.F.: Centro de Estudios Históricos, Colegio de México, 1984.

Falcón, Romana, and Raymond Buve. *Don Porfirio presidente—, nunca omnipotente: hallazgos, reflexiones y debates, 1876–1911*. 1a ed. El pasado del presente. México: Universidad Iberoamericana, Departamento de Historia, 1998.

Fenner, Justus. "Los deslindes de terrenos baldíos en Chiapas, México, en el contexto internacional y nacional, 1881–1917." PhD diss., Colegio de Michoacán, 2009.

Findling, John E. *Close Neighbors, Distant Friends: United States–Central American Relations*. New York: Greenwood, 1987.

Follett, Richard J. *Plantation Kingdom: The American South and Its Global Commodities*. Marcus Cunliffe Lecture Series. Baltimore: Johns Hopkins University Press, 2016.

Font, Mauricio A. *Coffee and Transformation in São Paulo, Brazil*. New ed. Lanham, Md.: Lexington Books, 2010.

Fowler, Will. *Celebrating Insurrection: The Commemoration and Representation of the Nineteenth-Century Mexican Pronunciamiento*. Lincoln: University of Nebraska Press, 2013.

———. *Forceful Negotiations: The Origins of the Pronunciamiento in Nineteenth-*

Century Mexico. Mexican Experience. Lincoln: University of Nebraska Press, 2010.

Fowler-Salamini, Heather. *Working Women, Entrepreneurs, and the Mexican Revolution: The Coffee Culture of Córdoba, Veracruz.* Lincoln: University of Nebraska Press, 2013.

Francois, Marie Eileen. *A Culture of Everyday Credit: Housekeeping, Pawnbroking, and Governance in Mexico City, 1750–1920.* Engendering Latin America. Lincoln: University of Nebraska Press, 2006.

Frazer, Chris. *Bandit Nation: A History of Outlaws and Cultural Struggle in Mexico, 1810–1920.* Lincoln: University of Nebraska Press, 2006.

Gallini, Stefania. "Coffee Grounds." In *Mapping Latin America: A Cartographic Reader*, edited by Jordana Dym and Karl Offen, 168–71. Chicago: University of Chicago Press, 2011.

———. *Una historia ambiental del café en Guatemala: la Costa Cuca entre 1830 y 1902.* Ciudad de Guatemala: Asociación para el Avance de las Ciencias Sociales en Guatemala, 2009.

García Cantú, Gastón. *El socialismo en México, siglo XIX.* Hombre y su tiempo. Mexico: Ediciones Era, 1969.

Garner, Paul H. *British Lions and Mexican Eagles: Business, Politics, and Empire in the Career of Weetman Pearson in Mexico, 1889–1919.* Stanford, Calif.: Stanford University Press, 2011.

———. "The Politics of National Development in Late Porfirian Mexico: The Reconstruction of the Tehuantepec National Railway 1896–1907." *Bulletin of Latin American Research* 14, no. 3 (1995): 339–56.

———. *Porfirio Díaz.* Profiles in Power. Harlow, England: Longman, 2001.

Gasco, Janine. "Cacao and Commerce in the Late Postclassic Xoconochco." In *Rethinking the Aztec Economy*, edited by Deborah Nichols, Frances Berdan, and Michael E. Smith. Tucson: University of Arizona Press, 2016.

———. "Cacao and Economic Inequality in Colonial Soconusco, Chiapas, Mexico." *Journal of Anthropological Research* 52, no. 4 (1996): 385–409.

———. "Consolidation of the Colonial Regime: Native Society in Western Central America." *Historical Archaeology* 31, no. 1 (1997): 55–63.

———. "Indian Survival and Ladinoization in Colonial Soconusco." In *The Spanish Borderlands in Pan-American Perspective*, Vol. 3 of *Columbian Consequences* edited by David Hurst Thomas, 301–18. Washington, D.C.: Smithsonian Institution Press, 1991.

———. "Linguistic Patterns, Material Culture, and Identity in Late Postclassic to Postcolonial Soconusco." In *Archaeology and Identity on the Pacific Coast and Southern Highlands of Mesoamerica*, edited by Claudia Garcia-DesLauriers and Michael W. Love. Salt Lake City: University of Utah Press, 2016.

———. "Soconusco Cacao Farmers Past and Present." In *Chocolate in Mesoamerica: A Cultural History of Cacao*, edited by Cameron L. McNeil, 322–37. Maya Studies. Gainesville: University Press of Florida, 2006.

Gibbings, Julie. "'The Shadow of Slavery': Historical Time, Labor, and Citizenship in Nineteenth-Century Alta Verapaz, Guatemala." *Hispanic American Historical Review* 96, no. 1 (2016): 73–107.

Gibson, Charles. *The Aztecs under Spanish Rule: A History of the Indians of the Valley of Mexico, 1519–1810*. Stanford, Calif.: Stanford University Press, 1964.
Glade, William. "Economy, 1870–1914." In *Latin America: Economy and Society, 1870–1930*, edited by Leslie Bethell, 1–56. Cambridge: Cambridge University Press, 1989.
Gomez, Josue, Douglas J. Kennett, Hector Neff, Michael D. Glascock, and Barbara Voorhies. "Early Formative Pottery Production, Mobility, and Exchange on the Pacific Coast of Southern Mexico." *Journal of Island and Coastal Archaeology* 6, no. 3 (2011): 333–350.
Gómez Galvarriato, Aurora. *Industry and Revolution: Social and Economic Change in the Orizaba Valley, Mexico*. Cambridge, Mass.: Harvard University Press, 2013.
Gómez Serrano, Jesús. *Haciendas y ranchos de Aguascalientes: estudio regional sobre la tenencia de la tierra y el desarrollo agrícola en el siglo XIX*. 1. ed. Aguascalientes: Universidad Autónoma de Aguascalientes, Fomento Cultural Banamex, 2000.
Gonzales, Michael J. "Capitalist Agriculture and Labour Contracting in Northern Peru, 1880–1905." *Journal of Latin American Studies* 12, no. 2 (1980): 291–315.
González Navarro, Moisés. "Kaerger: Peonaje, esclavitud y cuasiesclavitud en México." *Historia Mexicana* 36, no. 3 (1987): 527–51.
Gootenberg, Paul. *Between Silver and Guano: Commercial Policy and the State in Postindependence Peru*. Princeton, N.J.: Princeton University Press, 1989.
———. *Imagining Development: Economic Ideas in Peru's "Fictitious Prosperity" of Guano, 1840–1880*. Berkeley: University of California Press, 1993.
Graham, Richard. *Patronage and Politics in Nineteenth-Century Brazil*. Stanford, Calif.: Stanford University Press, 1990.
Grandin, Greg. *Fordlandia: The Rise and Fall of Henry Ford's Forgotten Jungle City*. New York: Metropolitan Books, 2009.
Green, Stan, Guy P. C. Thomson, and David G. Lafrance. "Patriotism, Politics, and Popular Liberalism in Nineteenth-Century Mexico: Juan Francisco Lucas and the Puebla Sierra." *American Historical Review* 105, no. 4 (2000): 1355.
Greenow, Linda L. *Credit and Socioeconomic Change in Colonial Mexico: Loans and Mortgages in Guadalajara, 1720–1820*. Latin American Studies, no. 12. Boulder, Colo.: Westview, 1983.
Guardino, Peter F. *The Time of Liberty: Popular Political Culture in Oaxaca, 1750–1850*. Latin America Otherwise. Durham, N.C.: Duke University Press, 2005.
Gudiño, María Rosa. "Finqueros extranjeros en el Soconusco, legislación y colonización, 1875–1910." In *Estudios campesinos en el Archivo General Agrario*, vol. 2, edited by Lourdes Romero Navarrete: 15–86. México, D.F: Registro Agrario Nacional, Archivo General Agrario, CIESAS, 1999.
Gudmundson, Lowell. *Central America, 1821–1871: Liberalism before Liberal Reform*. Tuscaloosa: University of Alabama Press, 1995.
———. "Peasant, Farmer, Proletarian: Class Formation in a Smallholder Coffee Economy, 1850–1950." *The Hispanic American Historical Review* 69, no. 2 (1989): 221–57.
Guerra, François-Xavier. *México: del Antiguo Régimen a la Revolución*. Sección de obras de historia. México, D.F: Fondo de Cultura Económica, 1988.

Guldi, Jo. *Roads to Power: Britain Invents the Infrastructure State.* Cambridge, Mass.: Harvard University Press, 2012.
Gunder Frank, Andre. *Capitalism and Underdevelopment in Latin America: Historical Studies of Chile and Brazil.* Revised ed. Harmondsworth, U.K.: Penguin, 1971.
Haber, Stephen H. "Assessing the Obstacles to Industrialisation: The Mexican Economy, 1830–1940." *Journal of Latin American Studies* 24, no. 1 (February 1992): 1–32.
———. *Crony Capitalism and Economic Growth in Latin America: Theory and Evidence.* Stanford, Calif.: Hoover Institution Press, Stanford University, 2002.
———, ed. *How Latin America Fell Behind: Essays on the Economic Histories of Brazil and Mexico, 1800–1914.* Stanford, Calif.: Stanford University Press, 1997.
———. "Industrial Concentration and the Capital Markets: A Comparative Study of Brazil, Mexico, and the United States, 1830–1930." *The Journal of Economic History* 51, no. 3 (1991): 559–80.
———. *The Politics of Property Rights: Political Instability, Credible Commitments, and Economic Growth in Mexico, 1876–1929.* Political Economy of Institutions and Decisions. Cambridge: Cambridge University Press, 2003.
Hagan, Jim, and Andrew Wells. "Brassed-Off: The Question of Labour Unfreedom Revisited." *International Review of Social History* 45, no. 3 (2000): 475–85.
Hale, Charles A. *Emilio Rabasa and the Survival of Porfirian Liberalism: The Man, His Career, and His Ideas, 1856–1930.* Stanford, Calif.: Stanford University Press, 2008.
———. "Political and Social Ideas in Latin America, 1870–1930." In *Cambridge History of Latin America,* edited by Leslie Bethell, 367–441. Cambridge: Cambridge University Press, 1986.
———. *The Transformation of Liberalism in Late Nineteenth-Century Mexico.* Princeton, N.J: Princeton University Press, 1989.
Halperín Donghi, Tulio. *The Contemporary History of Latin America.* Durham, N.C.: Duke University Press, 1993.
Hamnett, Brian R. "Liberalism Divided: Regional Politics and the National Project during the Mexican Restored Republic, 1867–1876." *The Hispanic American Historical Review* 76, no. 4 (1996): 659–89.
Hanley, Anne G. "Is It Who You Know? Entrepreneurs and Bankers in São Paulo, Brazil, at the Turn of the Twentieth Century." *Enterprise and Society* 5, no. 2 (June 2004): 187–225.
———. *Native Capital: Financial Institutions and Economic Development in São Paulo, Brazil, 1850–1920.* Stanford, Calif.: Stanford University Press, 2005.
Hanley, Anne G., and Luciana Suarez Lopes. "Municipal Plenty, Municipal Poverty, and Brazilian Economic Development, 1836–1850." *Latin American Research Review* 52, no. 3 (2017): 361–77.
Harris, Steven M. "The Global Construction of International Law in the Nineteenth Century: The Case of Arbitration." *Journal of World History* 27, no. 2 (2016): 303–25.
Hart, Laurie Kain. "Culture, Civilization, and Demarcation at the Northwest Borders of Greece." *American Ethnologist* 26, no. 1 (1999): 196–220.
Hart, Paul. *Bitter Harvest: The Social Transformation of Morelos, Mexico, and the*

Origins of the Zapatista Revolution, 1840–1910. Albuquerque: University of New Mexico Press, 2005.

Helbig, Karl. *El Soconusco y su zona cafetalera en Chiapas.* Tuxtla Gutiérrez, Chiapas: Instituto de Ciencias y Artes de Chiapas, 1964.

Henderson, Peter V. N. "Modernization and Change in Mexico: La Zacualpa Rubber Plantation, 1890–1920." *The Hispanic American Historical Review* 73, no. 2 (1993): 235–60.

Hernández, José Angel. "From Conquest to Colonization: Indios and Colonization Policies after Mexican Independence." *Mexican Studies/Estudios Mexicanos* 26, no. 2 (2010): 291–322.

———. *Mexican American Colonization during the Nineteenth Century: A History of the U.S.-Mexico Borderlands.* New York: Cambridge University Press, 2012.

Hernández Castillo, Rosalva Aída, and Francine Cronshaw. "Between Civil Disobedience and Silent Rejection: Differing Responses by Mam Peasants to the Zapatista Rebellion." *Latin American Perspectives* 28, no. 2 (2001): 98–119.

Hernández Castillo, Rosalva Aída, and Ronald Nigh. "Global Processes and Local Identity among Mayan Coffee Growers in Chiapas, Mexico." *American Anthropologist* 100, no. 1 (1998): 136–47.

Herzog, Tamar. *Defining Nations: Immigrants and Citizens in Early Modern Spain and Spanish America.* New Haven, Conn.: Yale University Press, 2003.

Hobsbawm, E. J. *Nations and Nationalism since 1780: Programme, Myth, Reality.* Wiles Lectures. New York: Cambridge University Press, 1990.

Holden, Robert H. *Armies without Nations: Public Violence and State Formation in Central America, 1821–1960.* New York: Oxford University Press, 2004.

———. *Mexico and the Survey of Public Lands: The Management of Modernization, 1876–1911.* DeKalb: Northern Illinois University Press, 1994.

Holloway, Thomas H. *Immigrants on the Land: Coffee and Society in São Paulo, 1886–1934.* Chapel Hill: University of North Carolina Press, 1980.

Howe, K. R. "Tourists, Sailors and Labourers: A Survey of Early Labour Recruiting in Southern Melanesia." *Journal of Pacific History* 13, no. 1 (1978): 22–35.

Hu-DeHart, Evelyn. *Yaqui Resistance and Survival: The Struggle for Land and Autonomy, 1821–1910.* Madison: University of Wisconsin Press, 1984.

Hudson, Mark, and Ian Hudson. "Justice, Sustainability, and the Fair Trade Movement: A Case Study of Coffee Production in Chiapas." *Social Justice* 31, no. 3 (97) (January 1, 2004): 130–46.

Jaksic, Iván, and Eduardo Posada-Carbó. *Liberalismo y poder: Latinoamérica en el siglo XIX.* 1. ed. Sección de obras de historia. Santiago, Chile: Fondo de Cultura Económica, 2011.

Johnson, Walter. "The Pedestal and the Veil: Rethinking the Capitalism/Slavery Question." *Journal of the Early Republic* 24, no. 2 (2004): 299–308.

Joseph, G. M. *Revolution from Without: Yucatán, Mexico, and the United States, 1880–1924.* 42. Cambridge: Cambridge University Press, 1982.

Karnes, Thomas L. *The Failure of Union: Central America, 1824–1960.* Chapel Hill: University of North Carolina Press, 1961.

Katz, Friedrich. "Labor Conditions on Haciendas in Porfirian Mexico: Some Trends and Tendencies." *The Hispanic American Historical Review* 54, no. 1 (1974): 1–47.

———. *The Life and Times of Pancho Villa*. Stanford, Calif.: Stanford University Press, 1998.

———. "Mexico: Restored Republic and Porfiriato, 1867–1910." In Vol. 5 of *Cambridge History of Latin America*, edited by Leslie Bethell, 3–81. Cambridge: Cambridge University Press, 1986.

———. *Riot, Rebellion, and Revolution: Rural Social Conflict in Mexico*. Princeton Legacy Library. Princeton, N.J.: Princeton University Press, 2014.

Knight, Alan. "Debt Bondage in Latin America." In *Slavery and Other Forms of Unfree Labour*, edited by Léonie J. Archer, 102–17. London: Routledge, 1988.

———. "Mexican Peonage: What Was It and Why Was It?" *Journal of Latin American Studies* 18, no. 1 (1986): 41–74.

———. *The Mexican Revolution*. Cambridge: Cambridge University Press, 1986.

———. "Review of How Latin America Fell Behind: Essays on the Economic History of Brazil and Mexico, 1800–1914." *The Economic History Review*, New Series, 51, no. 3 (1998): 637–38.

Knight, Alan, and W. G. Pansters. *Caciquismo in Twentieth-Century Mexico*. London: Institute for the Study of the Americas, 2005.

Kourí, Emilio H. "La invención del ejido." *Nexos* 37, no. 445 (2015): 54–62.

———. *A Pueblo Divided: Business, Property, and Community in Papantla, Mexico*. Stanford, Calif.: Stanford University Press, 2004.

Kraay, Hendrik, and Thomas Whigham. *I Die with My Country: Perspectives on the Paraguayan War, 1864–1870*. Studies in War, Society, and the Military. Lincoln: University of Nebraska Press, 2004.

Kuntz Ficker, Sandra. *El comercio exterior de México en la era del capitalismo liberal, 1870–1929*. México, D.F: El Colegio de México, Centro de Estudios Históricos, 2007.

———. *Las exportaciones mexicanas durante la primera globalización 1870–1929*. México, D.F.: El Colegio de México, 2009.

———. "Los ferrocarriles y la formación del espacio económico en México, 1880–1910." In *Ferrocarriles y obras públicas*, edited by Sandra Kuntz Ficker and Priscilla Connolly, 105–37. Mexico: Instituto Mora, 1999.

Kuntz Ficker, Sandra, and Paolo Riguzzi, eds. *Ferrocarriles y vida económica en México, 1850–1950: del surgimiento tardío al decaimiento precoz*. 1a ed. México: El Colegio Mexiquense, 1996.

Larson, Brooke. *Trials of Nation Making*. Illustrated edition. Cambridge: Cambridge University Press, 2007.

Lauria-Santiago, Aldo. *An Agrarian Republic: Commercial Agriculture and the Politics of Peasant Communities in El Salvador, 1823–1914*. Pitt Latin American Series. Pittsburgh: University of Pittsburgh Press, 1999.

Lesure, Richard G. "Early Social Transformations in the Soconusco." In *Early Mesoamerican Social Transformations: Archaic and Formative Lifeways in the Soconusco Region*, edited by Richard G. Lesure, 1–24. Berkeley: University of California Press, 2011.

Levy, Juliette. *The Making of a Market: Credit, Henequen, and Notaries in Yucatán, 1850–1900.* University Park: Pennsylvania State University Press, 2012.
Lindley, Richard B. *Haciendas and Economic Development: Guadalajara, Mexico, at Independence.* 1st ed. Latin American Monographs, no. 58. Austin: University of Texas Press, 1983.
Lockhart, James. *The Nahuas after the Conquest: A Social and Cultural History of the Indians of Central Mexico, Sixteenth through Eighteenth Centuries.* Stanford, Calif.: Stanford University Press, 1992.
Lopes, Maria-Aparecida. "Historias de la cartografía de Iberoamérica. Nuevos caminos, viejos problemas." *Investigaciones geográficas*, no. 71, 2010.
Love, Joseph LeRoy, and Nils Jacobsen, eds. *Guiding the Invisible Hand: Economic Liberalism and the State in Latin American History.* New York: Praeger, 1988.
Loveman, Brian. "Critique of Arnold J. Bauer's 'Rural Workers in Spanish America: Problems of Peonage and Oppression.'" *Hispanic American Historical Review* 59, no. 3 (1979): 478–85.
Lowe, Gareth W. *Izapa: An Introduction to the Ruins and Monuments.* Papers of the New World Archaeological Foundation, no. 31. Provo, Utah: New World Archaeological Foundation, Brigham Young University, 1982.
Lurtz, Casey. "Developing the Mexican Countryside: The Department of Fomento's Social Project of Modernization." *Business History Review* 90, no. 3 (2016): 1–25.
Lynch, John. *Caudillos in Spanish America, 1800–1850.* Oxford: Clarendon Press, 1992.
MacGregor, Josefina. "Introducción." In *Textos escogidos*, 13–26. México, D.F.: Consejo Nacional para la Cultura y las Artes, 1992.
MacLeod, Murdo J. *Spanish Central America: A Socioeconomic History, 1520–1720.* 1st University of Texas Press ed. LLILAS Special Publications. Austin: University of Texas Press, Teresa Lozano Long Institute of Latin American Studies, 2008.
Mallon, Florencia E. *Peasant and Nation: The Making of Postcolonial Mexico and Peru.* Berkeley: University of California Press, 1995.
Marichal, Carlos. "Obstacles to the Development of Capital Markets in Nineteenth-Century Mexico." In *How Latin America Fell Behind*, edited by Stephen Haber, 118–45. Stanford, Calif.: Stanford University Press, 1997.
Márquez Colín, Graciela. "La administración hacendaria de Matías Romero." Centro de Estudios Económicos, El Colegio de México, 1999.
Maurer, Noel. "Banks and Entrepreneurs in Porfirian Mexico: Inside Exploitation or Sound Business Strategy?" *Journal of Latin American Studies* 31, no. 2 (1999): 331–61.
———. *The Power and the Money: The Mexican Financial System, 1876–1932.* Social Science History. Stanford, Calif.: Stanford University Press, 2002.
McCreery, David. "Coffee and Indigenous Labor in Guatemala, 1871–1980." In *The Global Coffee Economy in Africa, Asia and Latin America, 1500–1989*, edited by W. G. Clarence-Smith and Steven Topik, 191–208. Cambridge: Cambridge University Press, 2003.
———. *Rural Guatemala, 1760–1940.* Stanford, Calif.: Stanford University Press, 1994.

McCreery, David, and Doug Munro. "The Cargo of the Montserrat: Gilbertese Labor in Guatemalan Coffee, 1890–1908." *The Americas* 49, no. 3 (1993): 271–95.

Melillo, Edward D. "The First Green Revolution: Debt Peonage and the Making of the Nitrogen Fertilizer Trade, 1840–1930." *American Historical Review* 117, no. 4 (2012): 1028–60.

Méndez, Cecilia. *The Plebeian Republic: The Huanta Rebellion and the Making of the Peruvian State, 1820–1850*. Durham, N.C.: Duke University Press, 2005.

Mendoza García, Edgar. *Los bienes de comunidad y la defensa de las tierras en la Mixteca oaxaqueña: cohesión y autonomía del municipio de Santo Domingo Tepenene, 1856–1912*. Mexico: Senado de la República, 2004.

Michaels, George H., and Barbara Voorhies. "Late Archaic Period Coastal Collectors in Southern Mesoamerica: The Chantuto People Revisited." In *Pacific Latin America in Prehistory: The Evolution of Archaic and Formative Cultures*, edited by Michael Blake, 39–54. Pullman, Wash.: WSU Press, 1999.

Milford, Anna. "Coffee, Co-Operatives and Competition: The Impact of Fair Trade." *CMI Report* R 2004: 6 (2004).

Miller, Shawn William. *An Environmental History of Latin America*. New York: Cambridge University Press, 2007.

Mirow, Matthew C. *Latin American Law: A History of Private Law and Institutions in Spanish America*. 1st ed. Austin: University of Texas Press, 2004.

Misawa Saito, Katsuhito. "La colonia Enomoto de Chiapas: Estrategia expansionista y proyectos migratorios japoneses a fines del siglo XIX el caso de Mexico." Master's thesis, UNAM, 1982.

Molina Pérez, Valente. *Por los rieles de Chiapas: construcción del ferrocarril panamericano*. México: Gobierno de Chiapas, 2006.

Moya, José C. "A Continent of Immigrants: Postcolonial Shifts in the Western Hemisphere." *Hispanic American Historical Review* 86, no. 1 (2006): 1–28.

Mundy, Barbara E. "The Images of Eighteenth-Century Urban Reform in Mexico City and the Plan of José Antonio Alzate." *Colonial Latin American Review* 21, no. 1 (2012): 45–75.

Neufeld, Stephen B. *The Blood Contingent: The Military and the Making of Modern Mexico, 1876–1911*. Albuquerque: University of New Mexico Press.

Nolan-Ferrell, Catherine. *Constructing Citizenship: Transnational Workers and Revolution on the Mexico-Guatemala Border, 1880–1950*. Tucson: University of Arizona Press, 2012.

———. "El desarrollo de una región sin una identidad nacional: La zona del Soconusco, Chiapas, 1880–1920." In *Chiapas: de la independencia a la revolución*, edited by Mercedes Olivera Bustamante and María Dolores Palomo Infante, 1. ed., 301–12. Historias. México, D.F.: CIESAS, 2005.

North, Douglass C. "Institutions." *Journal of Economic Perspectives* 5, no. 1 (1991): 97–112.

———. *Institutions, Institutional Change, and Economic Performance*. Political Economy of Institutions and Decisions. Cambridge: Cambridge University Press, 1990.

Northrup, David. "Free and Unfree Labor Migration, 1600–1900: An Introduction." *Journal of World History* 14, no. 2 (2003): 125–30.

Nugent, Walter T. K. "New World Frontiers: Comparisons and Agendas." In *Where*

Cultures Meet: Frontiers in Latin American History, edited by David J. Weber and Jane M. Rausch, 72–85. Jaguar Books on Latin America, no. 6. Wilmington, Del.: SR Books, 1994.
O'Gorman, Edmundo. *Historia de las divisiones territoriales de México*. 4. ed. rev. México: Editorial Porrúa, 1968.
Oñate, Abdiel. *Banqueros y hacendados: la quimera de la modernización*. México, D.F.: Universidad Autónoma Metropolitana, Unidad Xochimilco, 1991.
Orellana, Sandra L. *Ethnohistory of the Pacific Coast*. Lancaster, Calif.: Labyrinthos, 1995.
Ortiz Hernández, María de los Angeles. "Formación histórico-política de la región del Soconusco, Chiapas. La oligarquía de Tapachula, 1842–1890." In *Concentración del poder y tenencia de la tierra: el caso del Soconusco*. México, D.F.: SEP, Cultura, 1985.
Osten, Sarah. *The Mexican Revolution's Wake: The Making of a Political System, 1920–1929*. Cambridge: Cambridge University Press, 2018.
Overmyer-Velázquez, Mark. *Visions of the Emerald City: Modernity, Tradition, and the Formation of Porfirian Oaxaca, Mexico*. Durham, N.C.: Duke University Press, 2006.
Palacios, Marco. *Coffee in Colombia, 1850–1970: An Economic, Social, and Political History*. Cambridge: Cambridge University Press, 1980.
Palmer, Steven. "Central American Union or Guatemalan Republic? The National Question in Liberal Guatemala, 1871–1885." *The Americas* 49, no. 4 (April 1, 1993): 513–530.
Passananti, Thomas P. "Dynamizing the Economy in a Façon Irréguliére: A New Look at Financial Politics in Porfirian Mexico." *Mexican Studies/Estudios Mexicanos* 24, no. 1 (2008): 1–29.
———. "Managing Finance and Financiers: The State and the Politics of Debt, Banking, and Money in Porfirian Mexico." PhD diss., University of Chicago, 2001.
Patch, Robert W. "Imperial Politics and Local Economy in Colonial Central America: 1670–1770." *Past & Present* 143, no. 1 (1994): 77-107.
Pawson, Eric. *Transport and Economy: The Turnpike Roads of Eighteenth Century Britain*. London: Academic Press, 1977.
Peloso, Vincent C. *Peasants on Plantations: Subaltern Strategies of Labor and Resistance in the Pisco Valley, Peru*. Latin America Otherwise. Durham, N.C.: Duke University Press, 1999.
Pérez-Grovas, Victor, Edith Cervantes, and John Burnstein. "Case Study of the Coffee Sector in Mexico." Case Study. Cornell University, July 2001.
Pérez Meléndez, Jose. "The Business of Peopling: Colonization and Politics in Imperial Brazil, 1822–1860." PhD diss., University of Chicago, 2016.
Perry, Laurens Ballard. *Juárez and Díaz: Machine Politics in Mexico*. The Origins of Modern Mexico. DeKalb: Northern Illinois University Press, 1978.
Pichardo Hernández, Hugo, and José Omar Moncada Maya. "La labor geográfica de Antonio García Cubas en el Ministerio de Hacienda, 1868–1876." *Estudios de historia moderna y contemporánea de México*, no. 31 (2006): 83–107.
Pineda, Yovanna. *Industrial Development in a Frontier Economy: The Industrializa-*

tion of Argentina, 1890–1930. Social Science History. Stanford, Calif.: Stanford University Press, 2009.

Posada-Carbó, Eduardo, and Iván Jaksic. "Shipwrecks and Survivals: Liberalism in Nineteenth-Century Latin America." *Intellectual History Review* 23, no. 4 (2013): 479–98.

Powis, Terry G., Ann Cyphers, Nilesh W. Gaikwad, Louis Grivetti, and Kong Cheong. "Cacao Use and the San Lorenzo Olmec." *Proceedings of the National Academy of Sciences* 108, no. 21 (2011): 8595–600.

Pozas, Ricardo. "El trabajo en las plantaciones de café y el cambio sociocultural del indio." *Revista mexicana de estudios antropológicos* 12 (1952): 31–48.

Premo, Bianca. *The Enlightenment on Trial: Ordinary Litigants and Colonialism in the Spanish Empire*. Oxford: Oxford University Press, 2017.

Purnell, Jennie. "With All Due Respect: Popular Resistance to the Privatization of Communal Lands in Nineteenth-Century Michoacán." *Latin American Research Review* 34, no. 1 (1999): 85–121.

Quiroz, Alfonso. *Banqueros en conflicto: estructura financiera y economía peruana, 1884–1930*. 1. ed. Lima, Perú: Centro de Investigación, Universidad del Pacífico.

Raat, W. Dirk. *El positivismo durante el Porfiriato, 1876–1910*. 1. ed. México: Secretaría de Educación Pública, Dirección General de Divulgación, 1975.

Rebert, Paula. *La Gran Línea: Mapping the United States-Mexico Boundary, 1849–1857*. Austin: University of Texas Press, 2001.

Renard, María Cristina. *El Soconusco: una economía cafetalera*. 1. ed. en español. México: Universidad Autónoma Chapingo, Dirección de Difusión Cultural, 1993.

Renard, Marie-Christine, and Mariana Ortega Breña. "The Mexican Coffee Crisis." *Latin American Perspectives* 37, no. 2 (2010): 21–33.

Rendón Garcini, Ricardo. *El prosperato: el juego de equilibrios de un gobierno estatal (Tlaxcala de 1885 a 1911)*. México: Siglo Veintiuno, Universidad Iberoamericana, 1993.

Ridings, Eugene W. "Class Sector Unity in an Export Economy: The Case of Nineteenth-Century Brazil." *The Hispanic American Historical Review* 58, no. 3 (1978): 432–50.

Riguzzi, Paolo. "The Legal System, Institutional Change, and Financial Regulation in Mexico, 1870–1910: Mortgage Contracts and Long-Term Credit." In *The Mexican Economy, 1870–1930?: Essays on the Economic History of Institutions, Revolution, and Growth*, edited by Jeffrey Bortz and Stephen H. Haber, 120–59. Stanford, Calif.: Stanford University Press, 2002.

———. "Sistema financiero, banca privada y crédito agrícola en México, 1897–1913: ¿Un desencuentro anunciado?" *Mexican Studies/Estudios Mexicanos* 21, no. 2 (2005): 333–67.

Rodríguez O., Jaime E., ed. *The Divine Charter: Constitutionalism and Liberalism in Nineteenth-Century Mexico*. Latin American Silhouettes. Lanham, Md.: Rowman & Littlefield, 2005.

Roseberry, William. "La Falta de Brazos: Land and Labor in the Coffee Economies of Nineteenth-Century Latin America." *Theory and Society* 20, no. 3 (1991): 351–81.

Roseberry, William, Lowell Gudmundson, and Mario Samper K., eds. *Coffee, Society, and Power in Latin America*. Baltimore: Johns Hopkins University Press, 1995.

Rosenzweig, Fernando. *El desarrollo económico de México, 1800–1910*. Toluca, México: El Colegio Mexiquense, 1989.

Rugeley, Terry. *The River People in Flood Time: The Civil Wars in Tabasco, Spoiler of Empires*. Stanford, Calif.: Stanford University Press, 2014.

Rus, Jan. "Coffee and the Recolonization of Highland Chiapas, Mexico: Indian Communities and Plantation Labor, 1892–1912." In *The Global Coffee Economy in Africa, Asia, and Latin America, 1500–1989*. Cambridge: Cambridge University Press, 2003.

———. "Revoluciones contenidas: los indígenas y la lucha por Los Altos de Chiapas, 1910–1925." *Mesoamérica* 25, no. 46 (2004): 57–85.

———. "Whose Caste War? Indians, Ladinos, and the 'Caste War' of 1869." In *Spaniards and Indians in Southeastern Mesoamerica: Essays on the History of Ethnic Relations*, edited by Murdo J. MacLeod and Robert Wasserstrom. Lincoln: University of Nebraska Press, 1983.

Sábato, Hilda. *Agrarian Capitalism and the World Market: Buenos Aires in the Pastoral Age, 1840–1890*. 1st ed. Albuquerque: University of New Mexico Press, 1990.

———. "On Political Citizenship in Nineteenth-Century Latin America." *American Historical Review* 106, no. 4 (2001): 1290–315.

Sahlins, Peter. *Boundaries: The Making of France and Spain in the Pyrenees*. Berkeley: University of California Press, 1989.

Salvucci, Richard J. *Politics, Markets, and Mexico's "London Debt," 1823–1887*. Cambridge Latin American Studies 93. New York: Cambridge University Press, 2009.

Samper K., Mario. "Los paisajes sociales del café. Reflexiones comparadas." In *Tierra, café y sociedad: ensayos sobre la historia agraria centroamericana*, edited by Hector Perez Brignoli and Mario Samper K., 9–24. San José, Costa Rica: Programa Costa Rica, FLACSO, 1994.

Samper K., Mario, Radin Fernando, Steven Topik, and W. G. Clarence-Smith. "Appendix: Historical Statistics of Coffee Production and Trade from 1700 to 1960." In *The Global Coffee Economy in Africa, Asia and Latin America, 1500–1989*, 411–62. Cambridge: Cambridge University Press, 2003.

Sánchez-Albornoz, Nicolás. "Population." In *Latin America: Economy and Society, 1870–1930*, edited by Leslie Bethell, 83–114. Cambridge: Cambridge University Press, 1998.

Sanders, James E. *Contentious Republicans: Popular Politics, Race, and Class in Nineteenth-Century Colombia*. Durham, N.C.: Duke University Press, 2004.

Santiago, Myrna I. *The Ecology of Oil: Environment, Labor, and the Mexican Revolution, 1900–1938*. Studies in Environment and History. New York: Cambridge University Press, 2006.

Schaefer, Timo H. *Liberalism as Utopia: The Rise and Fall of Legal Rule in Post-Colonial Mexico, 1820–1900*. Cambridge: Cambridge University Press, 2017.

Schell, William. "American Investment in Tropical Mexico: Rubber Plantations, Fraud, and Dollar Diplomacy, 1897–1913." *Business History Review* 64, no. 2 (1990): 217–54.

Schryer, Frans J. "Peasants and the Law: A History of Land Tenure and Conflict in the Huasteca." *Journal of Latin American Studies* 18, no. 2 (1986): 283–311.

Scott, James C. *Seeing like a State: How Certain Schemes to Improve the Human Condition Have Failed.* New Haven, Conn.: Yale University Press, 1998.

Seikaly, Sherene. *Men of Capital: Scarcity and Economy in Mandate Palestine.* Stanford, Calif.: Stanford University Press, 2016.

Shelton, Laura. *For Tranquility and Order: Family and Community on Mexico's Northern Frontier, 1800–1850.* Tucson: University of Arizona Press, 2010.

Sikkink, Kathryn. *Ideas and Institutions: Developmentalism in Brazil and Argentina.* Ithaca, N.Y.: Cornell University Press, 1991.

Sklansky, Jeffrey. "The Elusive Sovereign: New Intellectual and Social Histories of Capitalism." *Modern Intellectual History* 9, no. 1 (2012): 233–48.

Skuban, William E. *Lines in the Sand: Nationalism and Identity on the Peruvian-Chilean Frontier.* Albuquerque: University of New Mexico Press, 2007.

Slotkin, Richard. *Regeneration through Violence: The Mythology of the American Frontier, 1600–1860.* 1st Harper Perennial ed. New York: HarperPerennial, 1996.

Smith, Benjamin. "Rewriting the Moral Economy: Agricultural Societies and Economic Change in Oaxaca's Mixteca Baja, 1830–1910." In *Mexico in Transition: New Perspectives on Mexican Agrarian History, Nineteenth and Twentieth*, edited by Antonio Escobar Ohmstede and Matthew Butler, 81–107. Mexico City: CIESAS, 2013.

Solórzano F., Juan Carlos. "Haciendas, ladinos y explotación colonial: Guatemala, El Salvador y Chiapas en el siglo XVII." *Anuario de Estudios Centroamericanos* 10 (1984): 95–123.

Solow, Barbara L., and Stanley L. Engerman. *British Capitalism and Caribbean Slavery: The Legacy of Eric Williams.* Studies in Interdisciplinary History. Cambridge: Cambridge University Press, 1987.

Soluri, John. "Bananas Before Plantations. Smallholders, Shippers, and Colonial Policy in Jamaica, 1870–1910." *Iberoamericana* 6, no. 23 (2006): 143–59.

Spalding, Karen. *Huarochirí, an Andean Society under Inca and Spanish Rule.* Stanford, Calif.: Stanford University Press, 1984.

Spenser, Daniela. *El Partido Socialista Chiapaneco: rescate y reconstrucción de su historia.* México, D.F.: CIESAS, 1988.

———. "Soconusco: The Formation of a Coffee Economy in Chiapas." In *Other Mexicos: Essays on Regional Mexican History, 1876–1911*, edited by Thomas Benjamin and William McNellie, 1st ed. Albuquerque: University of New Mexico Press, 1984.

Stein, Stanley J. *Vassouras: A Brazilian Coffee County, 1850–1900.* Studies in American Negro Life. New York: Atheneum, 1974.

Striffler, Steve, and Mark Moberg. *Banana Wars: Power, Production, and History in the Americas.* Durham, N.C.: Duke University Press, 2003.

Suarez-Potts, William J. *The Making of Law: The Supreme Court and Labor Legislation in Mexico, 1875–1931.* Stanford, Calif.: Stanford University Press, 2012.

Sumner, Jaclyn Ann. "National Autocracy, Regional Governance: Tlaxcala, Mexico, 1885–1909." PhD diss., University of Chicago, 2014.

Sweigart, Joseph Earl. *Coffee Factorage and the Emergence of a Brazilian Capital Market, 1850–1888*. New York: Garland, 1987.
Tenenbaum, Barbara A. "Agiotista." *Encyclopedia of Latin American History and Culture*. Detroit: Gale/Cengage, 2008.
Tenorio-Trillo, Mauricio. *I Speak of the City: Mexico City at the Turn of the Twentieth Century*. Chicago: University of Chicago Press, 2012.
———. *Mexico at the World's Fairs: Crafting a Modern Nation*. Berkeley: University of California Press, 1996.
Thomson, Guy P. C. "Popular Aspects of Liberalism in Mexico, 1848–1888." *Bulletin of Latin American Research* 10, no. 3 (1991): 265–92.
———. "Porfirio Díaz y el ocaso del partido de La Montaña (1879–1892). ¿Fin al liberalismo popular en la sierra de Puebla?" In *Don Porfirio presidente—, nunca omnipotente: hallazgos, reflexiones y debates, 1876–1911*, edited by Romana Falcón and Raymond Buve, 1a. ed., 361–82. El pasado del presente. México: Universidad Iberoamericana, Departamento de Historia, 1998.
Thurner, Mark. "'Republicanos' and 'La Comunidad de Peruanos': Unimagined Political Communities in Postcolonial Andean Peru." *Journal of Latin American Studies* 27, no. 2 (1995): 291–318.
Topik, Steven. "Coffee Anyone? Recent Research on Latin American Coffee Societies." *Hispanic American Historical Review* 80, no. 2 (2000): 225–66.
Topik, Steven, and Allen Wells, eds. *Global Markets Transformed: 1870–1945*. Cambridge, Mass.: Belknap Press of Harvard University Press, 2014.
———. *The Second Conquest of Latin America: Coffee, Henequen, and Oil During the Export Boom, 1850–1930*. 1st ed. Austin: University of Texas Press, Institute of Latin American Studies, 1998.
Toussaint Ribot, Mónica Magdalena, and Mario Vázquez Olivera. *Territorio, nación y soberanía: Matías Romero ante el conflicto de límites entre México y Guatemala*. México, D.F: Secretaría de Relaciones Exteriores, Consultoría Jurídica, Dirección General del Acervo Histórico Diplomático, 2012.
Triner, Gail D. "Banks, Regions, and Nation in Brazil, 1889–1930." *Latin American Perspectives* 26, no. 1 (1999): 129–50.
Tutino, John. *From Insurrection to Revolution in Mexico: Social Bases of Agrarian Violence, 1750–1940*. Princeton, N.J: Princeton University Press, 1986.
———. *Making a New World: Founding Capitalism in the Bajío and Spanish North America*. Durham, N.C.: Duke University Press, 2011.
Valerio-Jiménez, Omar S. "Neglected Citizens and Willing Traders: The Villas del Norte (Tamaulipas) in Mexico's Northern Borderlands, 1749–1846." *Mexican Studies/Estudios Mexicanos* 18, no. 2 (2002): 251–96.
Van Hoy, Teresa M. "La Marcha Violenta? Railroads and Land in 19th-Century Mexico." *Bulletin of Latin American Research* 19, no. 1 (2000): 33–61.
Vanderwood, Paul J. *Disorder and Progress: Bandits, Police, and Mexican Development*. Lincoln: University of Nebraska Press, 1981.
———. "Mexico's Rurales: Reputation versus Reality." *The Americas* 34, no. 1 (1977): 102–112.
Vázquez Olivera, Mario. *El Imperio Mexicano y el Reino de Guatemala: proyecto político y campaña militar 1821–1823*. México, D.F.: Fondo de Cultura

Económica, Universidad Nacional Autónoma de México, Centro de Investigación sobre América Latina y el Caribe, 2009.

———. "¿Repúblicas hermanas?" In *En busca de una nación soberana: relaciones internacionales de México, siglos XIX y XX*, edited by Jorge A Schiavon, Daniela Spenser, and Mario Vazquez Olivera, 72–90. Mexico, D.F.: Centro de Investigación y Docencia Económicas, 2006.

Ventura, Theresa Marie. "American Empire, Agrarian Reform and the Problem of Tropical Nature in the Philippines, 1898–1916." PhD diss., Columbia University, 2009.

Villafuerte Solís, Daniel, and Darío Betancourt Aduen, eds. *El café en la frontera sur: la producción y los productores del Soconusco, Chiapas*. 1. ed. Ocozocoautla de Espinosa, Chiapas, México: Instituto Chiapaneco de Cultura, Departamento de Patrimonio Cultural e Investigación, 1993.

Viqueira Albán, Juan Pedro. "Indios y ladinos, arraigados y migrantes en Chiapas. Un esbozo de historia demográfica de larga duración." In *Caras y mascaras del Mexico etnico: La participación indígena en las formaciones del Estado mexicano*, edited by Andrew Roth Seneff, 221–70. Colección Debates. Zamora, Michoacán: El Colegio de Michoacán, 2010.

Voorhies, Barbara. *Postclassic Soconusco Society: The Late Prehistory of the Coast of Chiapas, Mexico*. IMS Monograph 14. Albany, N.Y.: Institute for Mesoamerican Studies, University at Albany. Distributed by University of Texas Press, 2004.

———. "Whither the King's Traders? Reevaluating Fifteenth-Century Xoconochco as a Port of Trade." In *Ancient Trade and Tribute: Economies of the Soconusco Region of Mesoamerica*, 21–47. Salt Lake City: University of Utah Press, 1988.

Voorhies, Barbara, and Janine Gasco. "The Ultimate Tribute: The Role of the Soconusco as an Aztec Tributary." In *Ancient Trade and Tribute: Economies of the Soconusco Region of Mesoamerica*, 48–94. Salt Lake City: University of Utah Press, 1988.

Wade, Lizzie. "How a Mormon Lawyer Transformed Archaeology in Mexico—and Ended up Losing His Faith." *Science*, January 16, 2018. http://www.sciencemag.org/news/2018/01/how-mormon-lawyer-transformed-archaeology-mexico-and-ended-losing-his-faith.

Walsh, Casey. *Building the Borderlands: A Transnational History of Irrigated Cotton Along the Mexico-Texas Border*. 1st ed. Environmental History Series, no. 22. College Station: Texas A&M University Press, 2008.

Washbrook, Sarah. "'Una Esclavitud Simulada': Debt Peonage in the State of Chiapas, Mexico, 1876–1911." *Journal of Peasant Studies* 33, no. 3 (2006): 367–412.

———. "Exports, Ethnicity and Labour Markets." PhD diss., University of Oxford, 2005.

———. *Producing Modernity in Mexico: Labour, Race, and the State in Chiapas, 1876–1914*. Oxford: Oxford University Press for the British Academy, 2012.

Wasserman, Mark. *Capitalists, Caciques, and Revolution: The Native Elite and Foreign Enterprise in Chihuahua, Mexico, 1854–1911*. Chapel Hill: University of North Carolina Press, 1984.

———. *Pesos and Politics: Business, Elites, Foreigners, and Government in Mexico, 1854–1940*. Stanford, Calif.: Stanford University Press, 2015.

Weinstein, Barbara. *The Amazon Rubber Boom, 1850–1920.* Stanford, Calif.: Stanford University Press, 1983.
Wells, Allen. "Family Elites in a Boom-and-Bust Economy: The Molinas and Peóns of Porfirian Yucatán." *Hispanic American Historical Review* 62, no. 2 (May 1982): 224–53.
———. "From Hacienda to Plantation: The Transformation of Santo Domingo Xcuyum." In *Land, Labor and Capital in Modern Yucatán: Essays in Regional History and Political Economy,* edited by Jeffery Brannon and G. M Joseph, 112–42. Tuscaloosa: University of Alabama Press, 1991.
———. *Yucatán's Gilded Age: Haciendas, Henequen, and International Harvester, 1860–1915.* 1st ed. Albuquerque: University of New Mexico Press, 1985.
Wiemers, Eugene L. "Agriculture and Credit in Nineteenth-Century Mexico: Orizaba and Córdoba, 1822–71." *Hispanic American Historical Review* 65, no. 3 (1985): 519–46.
Williams, Eric Eustace. *Capitalism and Slavery.* Chapel Hill: University of North Carolina Press, 1994.
Wilson, Thomas M., and Hastings Donnan. *Border Identities: Nation and State at International Frontiers.* Cambridge: Cambridge University Press, 1998.
Wolf, Eric R. "Closed Corporate Peasant Communities in Mesoamerica and Central Java." *Southwestern Journal of Anthropology* 13, no. 1 (1957): 1–18.
———. "The Vicissitudes of the Closed Corporate Peasant Community." *American Ethnologist* 13, no. 2 (1986): 325–29.
Wolf, Eric R., and Sidney Wilfred Mintz. "Haciendas and Plantation in Middle America and the Antilles." *Social and Economic Studies* 6, no. 3 (1957): 380–412.
Womack, John, Jr. "The Mexican Economy during the Revolution 1910–1920: Historiography and Analysis." *Marxist Perspectives* 1, no. 4 (1978): 80–123.
———. "Mexican Political Historiography." In *Investigaciones contemporaneas sobre historia de Mexico: memorias de la tercera reunion de historiadores Mexicanos y Norteamericanos, Oaxtepec, Morelos, 4–7 de noviembre de 1969,* 478–92. Austin: University of Texas Press, 1971.
———. *Zapata and the Mexican Revolution.* New York: Vintage Books, 1970.
Yarrington, Doug. *A Coffee Frontier: Land, Society, and Politics in Duaca, Venezuela, 1830–1936.* Pitt Latin American Series. Pittsburgh, Pa.: University of Pittsburgh Press, 1997.
Zucker, Lynne G. "Production of Trust: Institutional Sources of Economic Structure, 1840–1920." *Research in Organizational Behavior* 8 (January 1, 1986): 53–111.
Zuleta Miranda, María Cecilia. *De cultivos y contribuciones: agricultura y Hacienda estatal en México en la "época de la prosperidad": Morelos y Yucatán 1870–1910.* 1a. ed. Biblioteca de signos, 39. México, D.F.: Universidad Autónoma Metropolitana, Unidad Iztapalapa, Departamento de Filosofia, 2006.
———. "Hacienda pública y exportación henequenera en Yucatán, 1880–1910." *Historia Mexicana* 54, no. 1 (2004): 179–247.

Index

NOTE: page numbers followed by *m*, *f*, and *t* refer to maps, figures and tables respectively. Those followed by n refer to notes, with note number.

Acacoyagua: *ejidos* privatization in, 219n87; population, by year, 177t
Agricultural Congress of 1896, 132–35, 136, 139, 226n60
agriculture in the Soconusco: under Spanish rule, 21–22; traditional practices, and undisturbed forest, 20–21. *See also* coffee cultivation; plantation economy in the Soconusco
Ahuitzotl (Mexica emperor), 20
Amores, Aurora Caravantes de, 114
Amores, Nicolás, 114
Arthur, Chester A., 55

Bado, Antonio, 141, 145
Bado, Richard, 81
Bado, widow. *See* Rosales de Bado, Herlinda
Bado family business, 141; debts owed by, 141; debts owed to, 141, 146; and diverse array of commercial institutions in the Soconusco, 142, 143; and futures contracts on coffee, 152, 153, 154–55, 156; as link between local and global commerce, 141, 145, 147; liquidation of debts, 145–47, 157, 160, 164; mortgage-backed loans issued by, 157; and protections of incorporation, 145, 150, 161; public registration of debts, 148
Barrios, and Romero: complaints about incursion into Mexico by, 30, 48; negotiations over Mexican-Guatemalan border, 49–50, 51, 57; negotiations over property sale, 29, 49; souring of relations between, 50
Barrios, Justo Rufino: death of, 57; and Guatemalan claims on the Soconusco, 29–30, 49, 51, 52, 55, 56; Mexico's early support for, 48; plantation owned by, 57, 195n115
Bejarano, Nicolás, 133, 134–35

Blaine, James, 52, 55
borderland, the Soconusco as, 46–51, 56–58, 195–96n2. *See also* Guatemala, lack of clear border with
Bravo, Camilo, 128
Brewer, Louis, 80
Brickwood, Albert, 218–19n85
businesses. *See* merchants in the Soconusco

Cacahoatán, 2*m*; cooperation of planters and smallholders in, 95; history of, 94; influx of migrants to, 95; and Mexican Revolution land reform, 114–15; planters in, 72; planters in government of, 95; population, by year, 177t; refounding of, and *ejidos*, 36; registering of fincas titles in, 96, 97; size of, 214n25
Cacahoatán, *ejidos* privatization in, 94–99, 106, 107, 218n78, 220–21n100; aggressive planter's land grab and, 97–98; effort to exclude foreign-born *vecinos*, 106; resold properties, 107; slow compliance with, 91
cacao production in the Soconusco: coexistence with undisturbed forest, 20–21, 186n12; history of, 8, 18, 20, 42; influence on region, 18; under Spanish rule, 21–22
caciques: Díaz administration's alliance with, as necessary compromise, 64–65, 68–69, 70–71, 72; Díaz's replacement with loyalists, 75–77, 206n85; and establishment of local institutions, 85; government of Chiapas, effort to overthrow, 67; power of, as independent of government structure, 76; scholarship on, 201n19; support for Díaz, 30, 31, 67. *See also* Escobar, as *cacique*
Caja de Préstamos para Obras de Irrigación y Fomento de la Agricultura, 163, 237n90

Cándano, Mauro, 207n100–101
Candiani, Lauro, 76, 207n100
Canel, Camilo, 215n46
Cárdenas, Lucio, 79
Carrascosa, Manuel, 215n50
Casa Viuda de Bado, 145, 160
Catholic Church, as source of credit, Mexican seizure of assets and, 40–41, 151
cattle ranches in the Soconusco: after independence, 22, 23, 24–25; binding of laborers in debt peonage, 36–37, 120; and insecurity of property rights, 36, 100; investment in coffee export, 24–25, 39–40, 42, 121; later conversion to rubber plantations, 112; small labor pool required for, 36; under Spanish rule, 22
census of 1895, 60
census of 1910, 183n35, 228n90
Chamula, 130
Chiapas: competing claims for, after independence, 22–23, 50–51, 55; disputes between entrenched and emerging elites in, 77; efforts to tax residents of the Soconusco, 49, 82; fears of Guatemalan annexation, 199n63; lack of funds for infrastructure development, 83, 84, 210–11n132; land grants to Guatemalan groups, 59; move of capital, 130; as part of Mexico, Mexican Constitution of 1857 on, 51, 52, 54–55; political and economic elite of, 119–20; and privatization of *ejidos*, 96, 214n30; privatization programs for public lands, 48, 90. *See also* Escobar, as governor of Chiapas; Guatemalan-Mexican border, negotiation of
Chinese migrants: as merchants, 8, 147; as potential workers, 38, 121
citizenship of residents of the Soconusco: establishment of Guatemalan-Mexican border and, 58–61, 200n77; vs. *vecindad*, 59
coffee cultivation in Guatemala, as model for the Soconusco, 24
coffee cultivation in Latin America, scholarship on, 12
coffee cultivation in the Soconusco, 38–40, 41; early efforts at, 22, 187n21; types grown, 179n5. *See also* coffee plantations (*finca*) in the Soconusco; plantation economy in the Soconusco
coffee exports from Mexico: predominance of small producers in southeast, 172–73; rank among Mexican imports, 239n21; by year, 175t–76t

coffee exports from the Soconusco, growth of, 3–4, 4f, 13, 75, 91, 129, 167, 169–70, 172; and increases in tax revenue, 82; and need for credit, 144; and need for laborers, 138; primary markets, 79, 154; recent declines in, 239n21; smallholder production and, 4, 179n7; by year, 175t–76t
coffee plantations (fincas) in the Soconusco: acreage planted or prepared, in 1874, 41–42; and coffee price drop of late 1890s, recovery from, 161, 164; and consistence of laws across national borders, 79–80; debt owed by workers as portion of value, 128; economic promise of, 41–42; finca stores, 129; increased value after cultivation, 112; and influx of workers, 10–11, 183–84n35; and land concessions granted by Mexico, 2; large, small number of, 113; long-term investment required for, 39; long-term security required for, 33, 36; modern owners of, 16; naming of, 111–12; nationalities of managers of, 223n21; necessity of clearing forest land, 36; percentage of acreage planted in coffee, 15, 127–28, 179n7; registering of titles for, 96, 97; Romero's securing of loans to establish, 41; sales of, by origin of purchaser, 111, 111t; Sebastián Escobar's attacks on export infrastructure and, 67–68; size of, 8, 112, 115, 182n22, 213n21, 214n27, 218–19n85; types of coffee grown, 179n5; value of, 125, 224n29; wealthy elite willing to risk experimentation with, 24–25, 39–40. *See also* coffee exports from the Soconusco, growth of; coffee price crash of late 1890s; credit in the Soconusco, for planters and merchants; Humphreys coffee plantation; infrastructure needed for export economy; investment in coffee cultivation; plantation economy in the Soconusco; planters (*finqueros*) in the Soconusco; public lands, legal title to; San Juan las Chicharras finca
coffee plants, size of, 179n5
coffee price crash of 1989, causes of, 239n21
coffee price crash of late 1890s: growth of production despite, 138; planters' overfinancing and, 158; restructuring of lending practices following, 160, 161–65, 234n55; and wave of loan defaults, business failures, and plantation sales,

Index 269

133–34, 145–46, 151, 152, 160–61, 236nn76–77
commercial and civil codes of Mexico: distinction between, 229n2; early-twentieth-century restructuring of loan practices and, 161; growth in use of, 165; and monetizing of debt, 147, 230–31nn24–25; protections of incorporation under, 144, 145, 150, 161, 164, 229n5; provision of penalties for nonpayment of debt, 148; provisions for public registration of debts, 144, 147–51; regulations and protections for loan market in, 144, 145, 146–47, 147–51
commercial houses, foreign. *See* foreign commercial houses
Comte, Auguste, 66
contract law: lack of, as obstacle to creation of plantation economy, 33, 39, 41; legal requirements for registering contracts, 93, 144, 148, 231n29; and public registration of debts, 144, 147–51, 153, 159, 231–32n32, 232–33nn37–39
contract law, establishment of: and credit markets, 157, 165; Guatemalan-Mexican border treaty and, 57; public's support for, 148–49; through planters' use, 78–80
court contract registers: legal requirements for registering contracts, 93, 144, 148, 231n29; recording of labor contracts in, 222n9; registering of loans, 144, 147–51, 153, 159, 231–32n32, 232–33nn37–39
Coutiño, Apolinar, 150
credit: lack of, as problem throughout Latin America, 40–41; multiple forms of, 143
credit in the Soconusco: as blend of foreign and local forms, 15, 157; community growth beyond trust-based system, 147–48; costs and damages clauses in loan contracts, 149, 153, 156; dependence of economy on, 141, 142, 144–46, 165; early lack of, as obstacle to developing plantation system, 32, 38–42; and economy growth, 165; lack of laws regulating repayment and, 147
credit in the Soconusco, and Mexican commercial and civil codes: early-twentieth-century restructuring of loan practices and, 161; growth in use of, 165; monetizing of debt in, 147, 230–31nn24–25; protections of incorporation under, 144, 145, 150, 161, 164, 229n5; provision of penalties for nonpayment, 148; provisions for public registration of debts, 144, 147–51; regulations and protections for loan market in, 144, 145, 146–47, 147–51
credit in the Soconusco, everyday forms of, 143–51, 159; amounts and terms of loans, 149
credit in the Soconusco, for planters and merchants, 151–65; after coffee crisis of late 1890s, 161; amount of loans, 155, 155*t*, 158, 158*t*, 164; arrival of banks and, 151, 163–64; early informal network for, 151–52; elite's embrace of regulation of, 152; foreign commercial houses and, 8, 152, 154–56, 158, 159, 162; futures contracts, 152–53, 153–56, 234n59, 234n61; growth in number and size of loans, 159; land as collateral for, 89–90, 91, 110, 151; late-nineteenth-century proliferation of mortgages, 158, 158*t*; longer-term loans, introduction of, 156–59; loose credit of 1890s, effects of, 15; Mexicans as debtors, 159; mid-sized loans, merchants and planters as source for, 156, 159, 163; as necessity for establishing coffee plantation, 151; plantation land as collateral for, 153, 155, 157–59; planters' tendency to over-borrow, 151, 152, 155, 156; restructuring of lending practices after crisis of late 1890s, 160, 161–65, 234n55; Romero's securing of loans to begin coffee production, 41, 194–95n109; tragic consequences of, 163–64; volume of, in early twentieth century, 164–65; and wave of defaults in coffee crisis of 1890s, 133–34, 145–46, 151, 152, 160–61, 236nn76–77
crony capitalism, under Díaz, 81, 85
currency shortages: and need for everyday credit, 144; and payment of plantation laborers, 38

debt peonage: on cattle ranches in the Soconusco, 36–37, 120; in highlands, efforts to change system, 130–35, 136–37; in Latin America, 118; in Sierra Madre highlands, 120
de León, Timoteo, 153
Department of Fomento: and Chiapas customs officials, 70; and cost of land, 213n20; and economic promise of export agriculture, 25, 150–51, 154; and infrastructure development, 210n126; and land claims, 102; land grants to Guatema-

lan groups, 59; modernization projects of, 25, 30; and securing title to property, 35
Department of Fomento of Chiapas, 83
Díaz, Felix, 171
Díaz, José María, 96
Díaz, Porfirio: ambitions for Mexico's international role, 50; American press on, 131; *caciques*' support for, 30, 31, 67; and campaign promise not to seek reelection, 65, 67, 199n59; and Chiapas highland elites, effort to undermine, 130; and control of elections, 206n85; election as president, 31; emphasis on bureaucracy over politics, 64; and land privatization, 90, 216n52; and La Noria Rebellion, 65–66, 67; and reelection, Constitutional reforms allowing, 75; support for Mexican identity of Chiapas, 50–51; support for regional self-rule, 65, 67, 68; support of federalism, 31; and Tuxtepec Rebellion, 67
Díaz, Porfirio, and consolidation of national bureaucracy: alliance with caciques as necessary compromise, 64–65, 68–69, 70–71, 72; and *caciques*, replacement of, 75–77, 206n85; and increased foreign investment, 68; as lengthy process, 68; local actors' role in, 64; need for reliable allies, 71; and reach of army or rural police, 71, 75

economic reform in Mexico, and broadening of official commercial life, 142
economic restructuring of Latin America, smallholders and, 5
ejido (communally held village lands): challenges to village ownership of, 87; expansions of, in post-independence period, 23–24, 36, 94; as predominant system in Sierra Madre de Chiapas foothills, 34; as primary producers of coffee in the Soconusco, 16; restoration of, in Mexican Revolution, 108, 114–15, 170–71, 220–21n100; Soconusco court cases on, 79; as type of land claim, 35
ejido privatization, 94–99, 104–9; accumulation of *ejido* lands by some smallholders, 106; benefits of, 95; cost-free parcels for poorer *vecinos*, 107; cost of land titles, 96; cost of parcels in, 106; cost of resold land, 107; delayed payments for, 105–6; factors accelerating, 104, 105; as gradual process, 92, 94, 95–96, 96–97, 98–99, 104, 108, 114; issues created by, 87; management by individual villages, 92, 94–99, 104–5, 106, 217n68; and Mexican Revolution land reform, 108, 114–15, 170–71, 220–21n100; national and state laws requiring, 35, 79, 89, 90, 99, 214n30; as part of government's liberal reform program, 90; problems with, 106, 114, 219n87; and property taxes, 95; size of parcels in, 106; state guidelines for, 214n30; state's inability to enforce laws on, 89, 94, 97; surveying for, 105, 217n68; *vecinos* as purchasers of, 106, 107, 108–9
elites, definition of, 7
elites of Latin America, role in economic globalization, 7
elites of Sierra Madre highlands: control of labor by, 119–20, 130, 136, 139; planters' efforts to break labor control of, 130–35, 136–37; power of, 132, 135
elites of the Soconusco: early experimentation with export crops, 24–25, 39–40, 42; frequent conflict among, 9; land ownership by, 8; mix of locals and newcomers in, 8; relative modesty of wealth, 9; revival of commercial connections to Europe, 39–40. *See also* planters (*finqueros*) in the Soconusco
Elorza, Manuel Salvador, 208n110
Escobar, Sebastián: assassination of, 76–77, 101, 129; and efforts to privatize public lands, 101, 216n52; on Guatemalan expansionism, 30; investment in coffee cultivation, 24–25, 39, 121; as *jefe político* of the Soconusco, 24, 32, 188–89n38; on labor shortages, 37; as municipal president of Tapachula, 70, 72, 76; opposition to coffee export industry, 67–68, 71, 72, 85; power of, as independent of official position, 72, 76, 204n64; properties sold by, 157; on property rights in the Soconusco, 35; requests for Mexican government aid in defending the Soconusco, 47, 54; and Romero, 26, 27–28, 30–31, 34–35, 39, 49, 66–67, 69–70; support for Díaz, 67; violent defense of interests by, 28; and War of the Reform, 188n36
Escobar, as *cacique*, 24, 201n19; attacks on federal officials and supporters, 63, 67–68, 69, 72; and control of courts, 31; Díaz administration's alliance with, as necessary compromise, 64–65, 68–69,

70–71, 72; Díaz's wresting of power from, 76–77, 206n85; exposure of brutality in press, 63, 67; ignoring of legal norms by, 64, 66–67; opposition to federal government intervention in local affairs, 30, 31, 66–67

Escobar, as governor of Chiapas: attraction of federal intervention, 70; corruption and violence of, 69; exposure of brutality in press, 69–70; relinquishment of post, 68, 70; removal and replacement of existing governor, 67, 68, 69, 202n27, 203nn40

Escuintla, 2m, 177t

Espadas, Manuel Trinidad, 107

expansionist imaginary of settlers, 1; and invisibility of local people, 1–2, 3; as traditional narrative, 4

export boom in Latin America. *See* Latin American export boom

export economy in Mexico: Mexican Revolution and, 169; products in, 168; World War I and, 170. *See also* coffee exports from Mexico

export economy in the Soconusco: as product of compromises among multiple parties, 15; range of actors shaping, 167–68, 169; rapid growth of, 168; under Spanish rule, 21, 22; transformation of the Soconusco by, 167. *See also* coffee exports from the Soconusco, growth of; plantation economy in the Soconusco

expositions, international, Soconusco planters' products in, 143, 154, 233n50

Farrera, Agustín, 209n119

federal government, and infrastructure development: lack of resources for, 82–83; and subsidies and exemptions for private companies, 83

federal government involvement in the Soconusco: lack of government programs, 82–83; lack of need for, 81; residents' tendency to avoid, 31, 81–84, 85, 209n119. *See also* land privatization; taxes

federalism vs. centralism debate: in Latin America, 31; and opposition to federal intervention in the Soconusco, 31

Figueroa, Manual, 207n100

Figueroa, Teófilo, 208n110

Figueroa, Virgilio, 217n68

finca. *See* coffee plantations (*finca*) in the Soconusco

finqueros. *See* planters (*finqueros*) in the Soconusco

foreign commercial houses, as source of credit for the Soconusco, 8, 152, 154–56, 158, 159, 162

foreign settlers in the Soconusco: economic failure of most, 8; origins of, 8–9

forest in the Soconusco: necessity of clearing to cultivate coffee, 36; as undisturbed by traditional agriculture, 20–21

Forsyth, William, 117–18, 123–27, 223n21, 223n23, 224n31

Frelinghuysen, Frederick T., 55

Frontera Díaz [Frontera Hidalgo], 2m; *ejido*s privatization in, 107; population, by year, 177t

fundo legal: exemption from privatization requirements, 94; towns' privatization of land in, 105

futures contracts: foreign commercial houses and, 154–56; introduction to the Soconusco, 152–53, 234n59, 234n61

García Cubas, Antonio, 30, 47

Garfield, James, 55

German immigrants to the Soconusco, 4, 8, 9, 73, 111, 170, 223n21, 228n95

Gilbert Islands, workers from, 221n3; as effort to reduce labor costs, 123–24, 126; recruiting of, 123; smallpox epidemic and, 118, 123, 124

globalization, economic: and circulation of workers, 118; development of, 6–12, 180n14; and integration of spaces of production and consumption, 6; and Latin American economic growth, 5, 6–7, 181n16; as product of individual choices, 7; range of exported commodities, 6, 191nn15–16; and spread of liberal economic institutions, 6

global markets, the Soconusco's connections to: early resistance to, 18–19; and economic growth, 141; and imported goods, 142–43, 165; and international investment, advertising for, 143, 153–54; as not inevitable, 19, 32; as product of myriad individual choices, 5–6, 11, 12; smallholders' shaping of, 11. *See also* plantation economy in the Soconusco

Gomez, Plácido, 102, 207n100

González, Manuel, 56

Grant, Ulysses S., 193n100, 210n127

Gris, Carlos, 63, 66, 69, 72, 98, 154

Gris, Manuel, 63–64
Guatemala, lack of clear border with: as blow to Mexican national pride, 46, 47, 48–49, 50; early inability to address, 30, 46; and incursions by Guatemalan tax collectors, 47–48; and lack of functioning legal system, 28, 29; as obstacle to economic development, 12, 13, 28, 29–30, 42; and planters' access to Guatemalan workers, 46; and property rights, ambiguity of, 45, 46; relative unimportance with small population, 46; and settlement in the Soconusco by Guatemalan smallholders, 46–47; and violent attacks, 28, 29–30, 42, 45–46, 47
Guatemalan laborers on plantations: incentives offered to attract, 117, 121–22, 124, 136, 137–38; large number of, 138; in the modern Soconusco, 172; number of, 138. *See also* laborers for plantations (*mozos*)
Guatemalan-Mexican border, negotiation of, 51–56; development into national Mexican issue, 51–52; Díaz's commitment to retaining Chiapas, 50–51; earlier Barrios-Romero negotiations, 49–50, 51; and expansionism of Barrios regime, 29–30, 51; Guatemala's effort to involve US in, 52, 55–56; Guatemala's views on raids in the Soconusco, 54; and Mexican national pride, 49, 52, 54–55; Mexican troops sent to border region, 54; Mexico's use of complaints from the Soconusco in, 55, 61; souring of relations and, 50, 52–54
Guatemalan-Mexican border treaty of 1882: allowances for easy border passage, 46, 56, 58–61, 60; benefits of established border, 57, 60; and citizenship of Soconusco residents, 58–61, 200n77; delays in finalizing border, 57; as diplomatic success for Mexico, 56, 60; Guatemalan dissatisfaction with, 56–57; land received by each party in, 56; and property rights in the Soconusco, 57–58, 60
Guatemalan villagers in the Soconusco, 46–47, 54, 59–60; and *ejido* restoration in Mexican Revolution, 171; influx into Sierra Madre foothills, 10; migration to Mexico in political turmoil of 1890s, 59. *See also* Guatemalan laborers on plantations
guild laws in Mexico, 142

hacienda, vs. *rancho*, 182n22
Harrison, Oliver Herbert, 102, 113, 163–64, 220n97

Hornedo, Julian, 207n100
Huehuetán, 2m; *ejidos* privatization in, 107; population, by year, 177t; size of, 214n25
Huixtla, 2m, 177t
Huller, Louis, 216n52
Humphreys, Helen, 1–2, 3, 102, 111, 172
Humphreys coffee plantation: early crops, 3; laborers on, as non-local, 3; recruitment of workers by, 222n14; staking of land claim for, 2–3; time required to clear and plant, 3; uncertain property rights of, 2, 3, 101
Humphreys family, arrival in the Soconusco, 1–2

Ibarra, José Encarnación, 95, 96, 100, 104, 208n110
ICOM. *See* International Company of Mexico
Indigenous Colony, 113, 130, 138
indigenous villagers from Guatemala: and the border, 46, 57; as laborers, 117, 124, 137–39, 172, 182n27; as land claimants, 49, 58, 95, 138; as potential workforce, 49, 121
indigenous villagers from the highlands of Chiapas: and highland elites, 119–20, 130, 132, 135–36, 139; as potential laborers, 38, 119, 130, 131, 137; and seasonal migration, 117, 137–39
infrastructure needed for export economy: Escobar regime's opposition to, 67–68, 71–75, 85; lack of, as obstacle to coffee cultivation, 24, 25, 38–41; lack of outside aid for, 83–84, 111n132; planters' development of, 83, 167; Romero's efforts to provide, 40, 48, 83. *See also* transportation infrastructure
INMECAFE (Instituto Mexicano del Café), 239n21
institutions: definition of, 64; necessary predictability provided by, 64; stabilization of, under Díaz, 64
institutions, in the Soconusco, post-independence: complaints about corruption of, 73, 205n74; control by Escobar's allies, 72, 73, 205n73
institutions, modern, in the Soconusco: benefits for stable property rights, 91; establishment of, 73–75, 78–80, 142, 165; and establishment of rule of law, 63–64, 84–85; lack of, until late nineteenth century, 38, 64; shaping of, by local actors,

64. *See also* contract law; credit in the Soconusco; infrastructure needed for export economy; legal system, modern, in the Soconusco; property rights in the Soconusco
Instituto Mexicano del Café (INMECAFE), 239n21
International Coffee Organization, 239n21
International Company of Mexico (ICOM), 101, 216n52
international investment, Mexico's difficulty in attracting, 40
interstate duties (*alcabalas*), 83
investment in coffee cultivation: growth of interest in, 42; lack of, as obstacle to creation of plantation economy, 41–42; long-term commitment required for, 39; by Romero, failure of, 41, 195n111; by wealthy cattle ranchers, 24–25, 39–40, 42. *See also* credit in the Soconusco, for planters and merchants
Ixtal Colón finca, 122

Japanese colony in the Soconusco, 8, 219n87
jefe político (district political chief), role of, 188–89n38
jefe políticos of the Soconusco District: Díaz administration seizure of control of, 76–77, 207n100–101; Díaz-appointed, lack of local traction, 77; Sebastián Escobar as, 24, 32, 188–89n38
Juárez, Benito: and border with Guatemala, 48; death of, 30; and development of state infrastructure, 66; Díaz revolt against, 65–66; federalism of, 30, 65; modernization efforts under, 50; and privatization of public lands, 90; return to power (1867), 25, 30; and War of the Reform, 188n36

Kaerger, Karl, 127, 179n7, 183n35, 234n59
Kahle, Guillermo, 227n81
Keller, Santiago, 97–98

labor contracts: provisions in, 222n9; recording of, in court contract registers, 222n9
laborers for plantations (*mozos*): debts owed by, as noncoercive, 128–29; flight of dissatisfied workers, 38, 118, 122, 128, 138, 227n83; high cost of, 122–25, 127, 128–29, 138–39, 223n17; incentivized contract labor system, planters efforts to change, 118, 119, 122–25; influx into the Soconusco, 10–11, 183–84n35; lack of currency for payment of, 38; large number needed, 121; law requiring weekly cash payment of wages, 139–40; laws restricting indebtedness of, 136–37, 138–39, 139–40; Mexican Revolution and, 170; migratory, impact on home villages, 222–25; necessity of recruiting from broad area, 119, 124; need for, growth of coffee industry and, 138; number needed for harvest, 127; number of, by 1910, 138; from tierra fría, 124, 125, 127, 136, 137–38; turnover of, 128; unpaid debts owed to planters, 124–25, 126–29, 133, 134, 223n16, 227n87, 228n93; wages paid in kind, 129; women as, 127; work of, described, 117
laborers for plantations, shortage of: and cost of recruiting workers, 124–25, 137, 138–39; efforts to import workers, failure of, 118, 123–24, 126, 130; government efforts to resolve, 130–35, 138, 139; as intractable problem, 129–30; land sales as enticement for, 113, 220n93; as obstacle to development of plantation system, 14, 15, 32, 36–38, 126, 127–28; and planters' constant efforts to find workers, 118, 121; and planters' efforts to change incentivized contract labor system, 18, 118, 119, 122–25; slow process of redirecting laborers from other pursuits, 119, 122, 136, 123, 137, 139; smallholders' lack of interest in plantation wage work and, 3, 4–5, 36, 115, 118, 119, 172; and workers' power to negotiate wages and incentives (incentivized contract labor system), 14, 37, 38, 118, 119, 121–22, 122–25, 126–29, 136, 137–38, 139–40, 170
laborers from the Gilbert Islands, 221n3; as effort to reduce labor costs, 123–24, 126; smallpox epidemic and, 118, 123, 124
laborers from Guatemala: incentives offered to attract, 117, 121–22, 124, 136, 137–38; large number of, 138; in the modern Soconusco, 172; number of, 138
laborers from highlands of Sierra Madre, 117, 122; efforts to break highland elites control over, 130–35, 136–37; highland elites' control over, 119–20, 130, 136, 139; slow increases in, 138
laborers in global economy: circulation of, 118; degrees of coercion applied to, 118

laborers on cattle ranches, debt peonage of, 36–37
labor law of 1896, 136–37, 138–39
labor law of 1914, 139–40
land ownership in the Soconusco: and contemporary maps, deceptiveness of, 88, 89, 89*m*; difficulty of surveying volcanic landscape and, 88; and naming of properties, 96, 111–12; need for rationalization of, 88; by planters, increases in holdings, 93; rancher oligarchy and, 24; restrictions on foreign ownership, 59, 199n71, 230n14. *See also* property rights in the Soconusco; public lands, legal title to
land ownership in the Soconusco by smallholders: as constraint on plantation locations, 109, 110, 114, 115, 167–68; increases in holdings, 43, 88, 93, 113–14, 215n46; purchase of leftover parcels of public land, 113, 172; retention of holdings, 43, 88, 106, 108–9, 108*t*, 113, 115; and rising value of land, 115. *See also ejido* privatization
land privatization: benefits of, 89–90, 91, 99, 115; cost per hectare, 92–93, 93*f*; export economy as driver of, 89, 91, 92, 101, 102, 104, 105; and exposure of land to seizure for debt, 115; majority of purchases by local residents, 108, 108*t*; population growth as driver of, 104, 105; separation of processes for planters and smallholders, 92, 93, 114; and smallholders retention and increase of holdings, 88, 93; state's inability to enforce laws on, 89, 94, 97; towns' privatization of *fundo legal* lands, 105; two-pronged approach to, 90. *See also ejido* privatization; public land privatization
La Noria Rebellion, 67
Latin America: debt peonage in, 118; "falling behind," causes of, 181n16; federalism vs. centralism debate in, 31; geography of, as obstacle to enforcement of central authority, 28; globalism and economic growth in, 5, 6–7, 181n16; lack of credit as problem in, 40–41; large tracts of public land in nineteenth century, 34; scholarship on coffee cultivation in, 12; spread of liberal institutions in, 5; spread of political liberalism in, 5, 181n18, 186n6; vagueness of property boundaries in nineteenth century, 34
Latin America, smallholders in: importance to export boom, 4–5, 7, 10, 179n7; loss and retention of land by, 7, 10, 14, 37, 43, 181n17; use of economic and legal tools of global economy, 9–10
Latin American export boom, 3; fortunes made in, 8; historians' precursorism and, 11–12; plantation as totemic institution of, 169; and political stability, 7–8; products in, 168; traditional narrative of, 4–5, 179–80n8
Latin American independence: and competing claims for the Soconusco, 22–23; political turmoil following, 22
legal system, modern, in the Soconusco: benefits of, 80; consistency with laws of Atlantic nations, 80; and diminished violence, 63–64, 84–85, 112–13; and economic growth, 165; establishment of, 63–64; foundation for, in Guatemalan-Mexican border treaty, 57, 58, 60; lack of, as obstacle to creation of plantation economy, 28, 33, 35; reluctance to involve state or federal courts in, 81; and Sebastián Escobar's rule as *jefe político*, 64; through planters' use, 78–80. *See also* contract law
legal system in the Soconusco, post-independence: control by local elite, 31, 38; and new planters, local elites' unwillingness to support, 38
legal traditions, local, and integration into global markets, 9–10
León, Francisco, 130–32, 135, 207n101, 226n56
Lerdo de Tejada, Sebastián, 48, 50, 66, 67
Lesher, Charles, 126–29, 139
Ley Lerdo of 1856, 34, 90, 94
liberalism, economic: spread in Latin America, 5; spread through economic globalization, 6
liberalism, political: Latin American reshaping of, 181n18, 186n6; residents of the Soconusco's engagement with at local level, 85; smallholders' embrace of, 23; spread in Latin America, 5
liberalism in the Soconusco, economic and institutional features of: early efforts toward, 12–13, 18, 25–27; investors' calls for, 42–43; lack of, as obstacle to creation of plantation economy, 12; Mexican governments' efforts to facilitate, 32–33; and opposition to local loss of control, 18, 26, 30–31, 42–43; rapid spread of, 168;

shaping of by local forces, 168, 169. *See also* credit in the Soconusco; institutions, modern, in the Soconusco
libros de conocimiento, 148–49, 164, 222n9, 231–32n32
local governments, income sources for, 83
local rule: Escobar's struggle to maintain in the Soconusco, 30, 31, 63, 66–67, 67–68, 69, 72; by local political bosses, 28, 30–32, 42, 63, 84; Mexican debate on, 31, 65–68
Lozano, José Maria, 131

Magee, John, 123–26, 139, 157, 223n23, 224n31
Mallen, Bernardo, 74, 133–34
map of registered land in the Soconusco, by MLCC, 109, 109*m*
maps of Mexico: accurate, effort to create, 47; and geographical knowledge as mark of modern state, 46, 47, 48, 60; in Guatemalan-Mexican border dispute, 52, 53*m*; historiography of, 211–12n5
Mariscal, Ignacio, 52–53, 54–55, 56
Maximilian I (emperor of Mexico), 25, 65, 188n36
Maya laborers. *See* indigenous villagers
Mazatán: and Mexican Revolution land reform, 115; population, by year, 177*t*; size of, 214n25
merchants in the Soconusco: and everyday credit, 144–46; merchandise carried by stores, 144; and protections of incorporation, 144, 145, 150, 161, 164, 229n5; as source of credit, 8, 156, 159, 163
Metapa, 177*t*
Mexican-American War, and fixing of Mexico's northern border, 29, 47
Mexican Coffee Institute (INMECAFE), 239n21
Mexican Constitution of 1857: and Chiapas as part of Mexico, 51, 52, 54–55; individual rights in, 131
Mexican Constitution of 1917, 170
Mexican Land and Colonization Company (MLCC): colonization clause in contract of, 220n93; government factions working to undermine, 110, 218n83; inaccuracy of surveying by, 110, 112–13, 219–20n92, 219n90; increased sales in late nineteenth century, 155; management of land privatization by, 91–92, 99–100, 101–4, 108–9, 109*m*, 110; map of registered land parcels in the Soconusco, 109, 109*m*, 114; patchwork of properties created by, 110, 113; payment of, 110, 216n55; planter opposition to, 104; refusal to recognize existing quasi-legal land titles, 102–4
Mexican Revolution: ambiguity of end date for, 238n6; and *ejido* restoration, 108, 114–15, 220–21n100; and extortion and violence in the Soconusco, 171; and foreign residents of the Soconusco, anxiety of, 170, 171; historians' precursorism and, 11; land reform in, 108, 114–15, 170–71, 220–21n100; and Mexican export economy, 169; as revolution from without, 170; the Soconusco's lack of involvement in, 15–16, 169–72
Mexican Society of Geography and Statistics, 30
Mexico: and geographical knowledge as mark of modern state, 46, 47, 48, 60; geography of, as obstacle to central authority, 28; internal migration in late nineteenth century, 60; international migration to, 60–61; national debt, effort to renegotiate, 40, 50; northern border, fixing of, 29, 47; political struggles of late nineteenth century, 12; as unstable concept in 1870s, 30, 47; urbanization in, 60. *See also* federal government
MLCC. *See* Mexican Land and Colonization Company
Molina, Manuel, 96
Montúfar, Lorenzo, 51, 55
Mora, José, 215n50
Motozintla, 2*m*, 117, 122, 170
Moya de Ramírez, Genoveva, 79
mozos. See laborers for plantations
Muñoz, Eulogio, 87–88
Muñoz, José María, 87–88
Muñoz, Pedro, 87–88

notaries: land transactions requiring, 93; number in the Soconusco, 80, 208n110, 231n31, 232n32; and public registration of debts, 148, 231n31

Orantes, Teóefilo, 191n75
Ortega, Rafael, 79, 157

Panama Railroad Company, 40
Pan American Railway Company, 84
Paniagua, Enoch, 208n110
Partido Socialista Chiapaneco, 170

Pérez, Ángel María, 209n116
Pérez, Esteban, 45, 52–53, 54, 58
Pérez, Juan, 45, 52–53, 54, 58
Pérez, Julio, 45, 52–53, 54, 58
Pérez, Tomás, 45, 52–53, 54, 58
plantation, as totemic institution of export boom, 169
plantation complex, history of, 185n43
plantation economy, obstacles to creation of, 12–14; competing interests of stakeholders as, 27; for early speculators, 13, 17–18, 25, 26; ill-defined border with Guatemala as, 12, 13, 28, 29–30, 42; insecurity of property rights as, 32, 34–36, 45, 46, 58, 91, 100; lack of administrative stability as, 12–13; lack of contract norms as, 33, 39, 41; lack of credit as, 32, 38–42; lack of export infrastructure as, 24, 25, 38–41; lack of modern legal system as, 28, 33, 35; Mexican political conflict as, 12; potential violent attacks from Guatemala as, 28; shortage of labor as, 14, 15, 32, 36–38, 126, 127–28; smallholders production as, 5, 12; violent rule of local political bosses as, 28, 30–32, 42
plantation economy in the Soconusco: diverse group of producers influencing, 169; as driver of land privatization, 89, 91, 92, 101, 102, 104, 105; as driver of real estate market, 92, 92f, 93f, 107, 115; establishment of Guatemalan-Mexican border and, 57; establishment of rule of law and, 63–64, 84–85; establishment of shipping connections and, 40; long-term credit as necessity for, 151, 165; long-term investment required for, 39; modern challenges and experiments with solutions, 173; reliability of institutions needed for, 64. *See also* coffee plantations (*finca*) in the Soconusco; infrastructure needed for export economy
plantations (*fincas*) in the Soconusco: modern, crops grown by, 173; modern owners of, 16; naming of, 111–12; on northern coastal plains, 112. *See also* coffee plantations (*fincas*) in the Soconusco
planters (*finqueros*) in the Soconusco: avoidance of Tapachula and Escobar, 72, 95, 97, 204–5n71; citizenship of, 59; community of, 111, 162; and development of institutions, 71–75, 85; early, obstacles to success of, 17–18; futures contracts with other planters, 156; and incentivized contract labor system, efforts to undermine, 18, 118, 119, 122–25; involvement in local politics, 23, 59, 72, 77, 81, 95, 130, 133; isolation from state politics, 77; land ownership by, 8, 182n22; number of, in 1876, 72; range of nationalities of, 111; residence on plantations, 111; and restrictions on landownership by noncitizens, 59; sale of crops, 8; taxes paid by, 82, 209n123; tax incentives to attract, 82, 154, 209n122

Porfiriato, as historical term, 11, 64, 68
positivism: and expansion of Mexican bureaucracy, 66; Mexican liberalism and, 7, 135, 186n6
press: attacks on highlands debt peonage system, 131, 132, 134, 136, 137; coverage of the Soconusco's economic promise, 154
property boundaries, vagueness of, in nineteenth-century Latin America, 34
property rights in the Soconusco: cattle ranching and, 36, 100; on coastal plains, elites' ability to document, 34; establishment of Guatemalan-Mexican border and, 57–58, 60; informal methods of securing, 31, 35; insecurity of, as obstacle to developing plantation system, 32, 34–36, 45, 46, 58, 91, 100; limited need for in the sparsely-populated early Soconusco, 33; and property tax payments as proof of ownership, 82, 100; in Sierra Madre de Chiapas foothills, difficulty of establishing, 34; and stable institutions, benefits of, 91. *See also* land ownership in the Soconusco; public lands, legal title to
public land (*terrenos baldíos/tierras baldías*), large tracts of, in Latin America of nineteenth century, 34
public land privatization: benefits of, 89–90, 91, 99; concessions to encourage land development, 100–101, 215n50; government programs for, 34, 48, 89–90; as incentive for European and North American settlers, 90; as part of government's liberal reform program, 90; private companies contracted to manage, 90–91, 99–100
public lands, legal title to: and attraction of investors, 153–54; cost of securing, 102–3; difficulties of surveying, 102, 103m; difficulty of establishing through

official federal channels, 34–35, 100, 104, 191n75; and diminished violence, 112–13; establishment through Mexican Land and Colonization Company, 91–92, 100–101, 101–4, 108–9, 109m, 110; and inaccuracy of MLCC surveying, 110, 112–13, 219–20n92, 219n90; necessity of repurchasing already-possessed plantation lands from MLCC, 102–4; patchwork of properties created by, 110, 113; quasi-legal titles created by local surveys, 100, 104; smallholders' purchase of leftover parcels, 113; value as loan collateral, 89–90, 91, 110, 151
public records office in the Soconusco: and diminished violence, 112–13; establishment of (1894), 80; need for, 80

Rabasa, Emilio: and Chiapas highland elites, effort to undermine, 130–31, 132; and *ejido* privatization, 107, 218n75; on Escobar's corruption, 216n52; on Escobar's power as *cacique*, 206n85; as governor of Chiapas, 76, 77
raiders: burning of Romero's plantations, 17, 26, 31, 50; destruction of Soconusco plantations, 26; from Guatemala, 28, 29–30; as mask for attacks on local rivals, 13, 31, 46
railroad line to the Soconusco: construction of, 4f, 84, 211nn136–37; plans for, 215n50; Romero's efforts to provide, 1, 40, 83, 193n100, 210n127
railroads: Mexico's efforts to build, 40, 50, 83, 210n126, 210n131; as tool of federal government control, 71, 75
rancho vs. *hacienda*, definition of, 182n22
real estate market: cost of land per hectare, 92–93, 93f; export industry as driver of, 92, 92f, 93f, 107, 115; rising value of plantation land and, 112, 115; rising value of smallholder land and, 115
repartimiento system, in Sierra Madre highlands, 120, 221–22n7
Revuelto, José, 163–64
road construction: to facilitate laborers' travel to plantations, 83–84, 138; Mexican efforts toward, 210–11n132; Soconusco residents' desire for, 83, 84
Robledo, Camilo, 79
Rock, Miles, 57
Rodas y Martínas, Joaquín, 207n101
Romero, Matías: career of, 25, 189n39; and Chiapas, support for Mexican identity of, 50, 52; and Escobar, 26, 27–28, 30–31, 34–35, 39, 49, 66–67, 69–70; manual for coffee planters, 37; and negotiations over Guatemalan-Mexican border, 49, 51, 55–56; and privatization of public lands, 90, 91; search for investment opportunities, 185n2; and Soconusco lands, villagers squatting on, 49, 58–59
Romero, and Barrios: complaints about incursion into Mexico by, 30, 48; negotiations over Mexican-Guatemalan border, 49–50, 51, 57; negotiations over property sale, 29, 49; souring of relations between, 50
Romero, and the Soconusco: bureaucrats accompanying Romero to, 30–31; burning of his plantations in, 17, 26, 31, 50; collapse of plans for coffee fortune from, 17, 26; correspondence with elite of, 13, 25, 26, 27–28, 32, 35, 39; corruption in, 71; difficulty acquiring title to land in, 34–35, 191n75; efforts to impose liberal economic policies on, 18, 25–27; efforts to increase labor pool in, 121; efforts to link to transportation networks, 40, 48, 83, 193n100, 210n127; investment in, 26; labor shortages in, 37–38; land purchases in, 49; loss of some property in establishment of Guatemalan-Mexican border, 57–58; move to, 17, 26, 30–31; obstacles to plantation development in, 13, 17–18; phases of intervention in, 25–26; plantation investments in, 41, 42–43; recruitment of investors for, 63; securing of loans to begin coffee production, 41, 153, 194–95n109; shift to alliance with recently-arrived planters, 27
Rosales de Bado, Herlinda, 141, 145–47, 150, 157, 158, 160, 162
rubber production: on coastal plains of the Soconusco, 34, 64, 112, 167; large producers in the Soconusco, 113, 164; in late-nineteenth century, 6; long-term investment required for, 39; and population growth, 112; size of properties producing, 115, 168; villagers' and, 9
rule of law. *See* legal system, modern, in the Soconusco
rural production, scholarship on, 12

Saenz, León, 95
Salas, Isaac de Jesús, 207n100

Salas, Sara, 157
San Antonio Nexapa, Humphreys family arrival in, 3
San Benito, 2*m*; in 1888, 1–2; development as port, 40, 193–94nn101–102; Escobar attack on (1876), 67; establishment of regular shipping service to, 40; as only exit point for exports before railroad construction, 73, 79
San Carlos *finca*, laborers on, 127
San Cristóbal de Las Casas: as center of Chiapas elite, 119–20, 130; move of state capital from, 130
Sandoval, Toribio, 215n46
San Juan las Chicharras *finca*: cost of recruiting laborers, 124–25; and delays prior to first harvest, 125; incentives paid to workers, 126–29; increase in value of, 139; labor costs of, 122–25, 127, 139; legal title to, 104; number of laborers during harvest time, 117, 127; percentage of land planted in coffee, 117, 127–28, 221n2; in receivership, 125, 126; size of, 117; as supposed model of scientific management, 123; violent confrontation between owners of, 123, 224n31; wages paid in kind, 129; workers' accumulation of unpaid debts, 124–25, 126–29; workers brought from Gilbert Islands, 118, 123–24, 126, 221n3
Santa Anna, Antonio López de, 23, 46, 51
Santa María volcano eruption (1902), 161, 176*t*
Scholz, Gustavo, 112, 133
shipping: first shipping connection to global markets, 40; need for sufficient production to attract, 33. *See also* infrastructure needed for export economy; railroad line to the Soconusco; San Benito; transportation infrastructure
Sierra Madre de Chiapas, and Soconusco climate, 19–20
Sierra Madre de Chiapas foothills: division into properties, 14; influx of settlers to, 10, 24; as mostly unclaimed land before late nineteenth century, 10, 22, 91; property rights in, difficulty of establishing, 34; as site of Humphreys family land claim, 2. *See also* public land privatization
Sierra Madre de Chiapas highlands: efforts to break highland elites' control over labor, 130–35, 136–37; elite control of labor in, 119–20, 130, 136, 139; indigenous avoidance of population collapse in, 120; power of elite in, 132, 135
El Siglo Diez y Nueve, 54
smallholders, in Latin America: and economic and legal tools of global economy, use of, 9–10; importance to export boom, 4–5, 7, 10, 179n7; loss and retention of land by, 7, 10, 14, 37, 43, 181n17
smallholders in the Soconusco: crops grown by, 2–3, 11, 39; and economic and legal tools of global economy, use of, 9–10, 11; growth of coffee market and, 11; lack of interest in plantation wage work, 3, 4–5, 36, 118, 119, 172; market crops grown by, 2–3, 9, 11, 39; migrants from Guatemala, 45; mix of locals and newcomers in, 10; modern cooperatives formed by, 173; number of, 11, 184n36; as obstacle to creation of plantation economies, 5; participation in global markets, 9, 11; predominance in modern region, 172–73; sale of coffee crops, 3–4, 11, 39, 106, 179n7; shaping of emerging institutions, 11; size of landholdings, 184n36; traditional lending network among, 39, 144; and *vecindad*, 54, 59; and wealth from coffee exports, 106. *See also ejido* privatization; land ownership in the Soconusco by smallholders
Socialist Party of Chiapas, 170
Sociedad Mexicana de Geografía y Estadística, 30
Soconusco District, 2*m*; capital circulation, in early twentieth century, 164–65; climate of, 19–20; colonization, characteristics of, 212n14; de facto independence in mid-nineteenth century, 23–24, 28; fertile soils of, 19; foreign investment in, in early twentieth century, 164; land sales in, by origin of purchaser, 108, 108*t*; and Mexican Revolution, lack of involvement with, 15–16, 169–72; under Mexica rule, 21; Nueva Alemania (New Germany) region of, 4, 8, 111; in post-independence period, government and politics of, 23–24; in present, as largest Mexican exporter of coffee, 16; public opinion, 183nn34–35; residents' focus on local government, 81–84, 85; under Spanish rule, 21–22; transformation by export economy, 167; as typical of frontier regions, 12; and Zapatista upris-

ing, 173. *See also* cattle ranches in the Soconusco
Soconusco District, geography of: and climate, 19, 20*m*; and isolation, 33; and natural disasters, 33
Soconusco District, *jefe políticos* of: Díaz administration seizure of control of, 76–77, 207n100–101; Díaz-appointed, lack of local traction, 77; Sebastián Escobar as, 24, 32, 188–89n38
Soconusco District, population of, 177*t*; in 1870s, 36; in 1880s, 91, 205n71; crash under Spanish rule, 21–22; growth of, 10, 24, 167; growth of, as driver of land privatization, 104, 105; preconquest, 20
Soconusco economy: dependence on credit, 141, 142, 144–46, 165; diverse array of commercial institutions in, 142; employment in, 10–11. *See also* global markets, the Soconusco's connections to
Spanish rule in the Soconusco, 21–22
Sres. A. Bado y Cía, 145
state bureaucracy, efforts to extend, and ongoing battle for local rule, 65–68
state legislature, Soconusco residents in, 81, 209n116
subsistence agriculture: and availability of land, 38; forest in the Soconusco as undisturbed by, 20–21; growth of export crops in combination with, 2–3, 7, 9–10, 130, 165, 168; in highlands, elite's undermining of, 120; as norm for smallholders in the Soconusco, 119; by plantation workers attracted to the Soconusco, 10–11, 46, 117, 124, 126, 127–28, 156. *See also* ejido (communally held village lands); smallholders
Suchiate, 177*t*

Taboada, Benito, 79
Tapachula, 2*m*; arrival of Humphreys family in, 2; and coffee crisis of late 1890s, 160; cost of land in, 112; courts in, late-nineteenth-century growth in use of, 78; *ejido*s expansion in, 36; *ejido*s privatization in, 104–5; land sales in, 108*t*, 109*t*; loan market in, 156; merchants in, 144, 147, 162–63; and Mexican Revolution, 170, 171; modern, described, 172; planters avoidance of, 72, 95, 97, 204–5n71; population, by year, 177*t*; post-Escobar opening of politics in, 81; registration of loans in, 147; smallholder land purchases in, 114; taxes on residents in, 82

taxes: incentives to attract new planters, 82, 154, 209n122; limited state income from, 83; local governments and, 83; Soconusco residents' payment of, 82
taxes, property: *ejido* privatization and, 95; payment of as proof of property ownership, 82, 100
technocrats (*científicos*), and expansion of Mexican bureaucracy, 66
terrenos baldíos/tierras baldías. See public land
Texas, secession of, and property ownership, 199n71
Tonintaná las Chicharras finca, 157–58
transportation infrastructure: development of San Benito as port, 40, 193–94nn101–102; initial lack of goods to transport, 40; lack of, as obstacle to creation of plantation economy, 38, 39–40, 41; Romero's development of, 40. *See also* railroad line to the Soconusco
Trejo, Alejandro, 209n116
Tuxtepec Rebellion, 50, 67, 78
Tuxtla Chico, 2*m*; land sales in, 108, 108*t*, 111*t*; population, by year, 177*t*
Tuxtla Gutiérrez, move of state capital to, 130
Tuzantán, 2*m*; *ejido*s privatization in, 106; population, by year, 177*t*

Union Juárez, 2*m*; *ejido*s privatization in, 107, 218n75; and land privatization, slow compliance with, 91; planters in, 72; population, by year, 177*t*; and property ownership, challenges to, 87–88
United States: and Guatemalan-Mexican border negotiations, 52, 54, 55–56; involvement in Mexican-Guatemalan border dispute, 45

vecindad/vecino: definition of, 23; of Guatemalans living in Mexican Soconusco, 54; vs. Mexican citizenship, 59
villagers. *See* smallholders
violence: assassination of *cacique* Sebastián Escobar, 76–77, 101, 129; establishment of Guatemalan-Mexican border and, 57; establishment of rule of law and, 63–64, 84–85, 112–13; and flight of local workers, 38; lack of clear border with Guatemala and, 28 29–30, 42, 45–46, 47; lack

of rule of law and, 98; as obstacle to establishing plantation economy, 27–28, 30–32, 42; and ongoing battle for local rule, 65–68; against overly-aggressive planter, 98; rule by local political bosses and, 28, 30–32, 42, 63, 84. *See also* raiders

War of the Reform, 65, 188n36
whitening, and Mexican concessions to encourage land development, 215n50

women: and commerce, 230n15; as laborers for plantations (*mozos*), 127. *See also* Rosales de Bado, Herlinda
World War I, and demand for Mexican exports, 170

Zapata, Emiliano, 90
Zapatista uprising, the Soconusco and, 173
Zepeda, Juan Felix, 208n110

The authorized representative in the EU for product safety and compliance is:
Mare Nostrum Group
B.V Doelen 72
4831 GR Breda
The Netherlands

www.ingramcontent.com/pod-product-compliance
Lightning Source LLC
Chambersburg PA
CBHW022000220426
43663CB00007B/891